P9-CFI-365
3 2109 00099 1381

GUIDE TO STATE INFORMATION AND REFERENCE SOURCES, NUMBER 7

MARYLAND

A GUIDE TO INFORMATION AND REFERENCE SOURCES

by

MICHAEL M. REYNOLDS

RESEARCH AND REFERENCE
PUBLICATIONS, INC.

RESEARCH AND REFERENCE PUBLICATIONS, INC.
P.O. Box 901
Adelphi, Maryland 20783

Reynolds, Michael M.
Maryland: A Guide to Information and Reference Sources.
(Guide to State Information and Reference Sources, No. 7)

1. Maryland - Bibliography. I. Title. II. Series.

Z1293.R 015.752

ISBN 0-917698-00-2

CONTENTS*

*Only a few subdivisions are indicated in some sections. Specific subjects can be located in the index.

INTRODUCTION

This volume attempts to provide a comprehensive subject guide to the most significant information and reference materials on Maryland. It is intended to meet the casual or research needs of high school and college students, interested amateurs, researchers, and librarians for information about the places, people, events, characteristics, and phenomena associated with Maryland. It can also be used as a selection aid for juveniles and adults who want to read on Maryland subjects and for teachers who want to direct their students to the best printed materials about Maryland. While it will be useful as a buying guide for public, secondary school, and academic libraries, it is not intended to be exhaustive on any topic. The items selected were drawn from items listed in card catalogs, bibliographies, and citations listed in books and articles. Altogether over 4,000 items were examined directly.

A first priority was given to identifying the more standard types of reference sources on Maryland, such as bibliographies and directories. However, this _Guide_ is more than merely a guide to reference materials, as it includes works on Maryland which are in themselves valuable descriptions of places and events and analyses of significant subjects or issues.

The _Guide_ is generally limited to published monographs and series, including official publications. In fact, special care was taken to include the official publications of Maryland, since the state government is assuming an increasingly greater role as a publisher and information resource in its concern for meeting its service obligations and as a means of keeping the public informed. Special care was also taken to include bibliographic and glossary notes in the annotations. With this feature the user will have marked out an exhaustive bibliography on Maryland and a dictionary of words and phrases peculiar to Maryland. Though out-of-print and ephemeral items are included, these were considered, nonetheless, to be valuable; they often represent the only or the best source of information. Also included are some general works which treat of Maryland in a separate section.

Because it was feared that an excess of listings would tend to diminish the _Guide_'s effectiveness as a reference tool, theses, dissertations, and journal articles are only occasionally included--usually among the secondary works augmenting a subject. (Users of the _Guide_ will find these are adequately covered by the items included in the _Guide_.) Also, unless a work was considered to be of special interest, only the important general sources were included for biography, religion, the counties, and the regions of Maryland.

Arrangement

The classified arrangement offers the user the opportunity of examining the best materials on the total broad subject, of going from the general to the specific as his own focus becomes more defined, of seeing relationships between the different items and determining how they might complement each other, and of appraising the extent to which information is available within the range of a subject. The entries are numbered consecutively. Very frequently, however, additional items are included under a single number. These represent works of a supplementary or of a more specialized nature and provide an opportunity for further extending the scope of an investigation.

Indexes

The "Index of Authors, Editors, Compilers and Illustrators" lists all individuals and corporate bodies who were directly involved in preparing items, or whose creative efforts are represented in the work. The "Subject Index" includes and supplements the headings which appear in the "Contents" and in the volume itself. In order to add a dimension not possible in a classified arrangement, items were grouped under place and general topics whenever feasible. In addition, though the subjects indicated in the annotations are only representative of the content of the work, these have often been analyzed for inclusion in the index.

LIST OF ABBREVIATIONS

dept.	department	n.p.	no place of publication
div.	division	no., nos.	number, numbers
e.g.	for example	p.	page, pages
ed.	edition	ports.	portraits
enl.	enlarged	pt.	part
i.e.	that is	rev.	revised
illus.	illustrations	ser.	series
introd.	introduction	vol.	volume
n.d.	no date		

BIBLIOGRAPHIES

1. BAER, Elizabeth. Seventeenth Century Maryland: A Bibliography. Baltimore: John Work Garrett Library, 1949. 219 p. [248 p.]

   Supersedes John W. Garrett, "Seventeenth Century Books Relating to Maryland" in Maryland Historical Magazine 34 (1939): 1-39.

   A chronological list of 209 books, pamphlets, broadsides, and maps accompanied by a descriptive text, which were printed between 1612 and 1700 and which deal with Maryland.

2. ENOCH PRATT FREE LIBRARY, Baltimore. Books on Maryland Added in [1934-1964] Baltimore: 1935-1965. Annual.

   Lists materials added to the collection regardless of when published. Arranged under form (e.g. fiction, biography, maps) or fields (e.g. history and description, government and law, economics and planning).

Government Publications

3. MARYLAND. Hall of Records. Maryland State Publications Received at the Hall of Records [July 1, 1969/June 30, 1971-] Annapolis: 1969/1971- . Monthly, with biennial cumulation.

   The Maryland Hall of Records is a legal depository for state publications. Arranged by key word in the department name, with agencies under their department. "Maryland State Publications Received at the Hall of Records" appeared in each number of the Maryland Manual between 1947 and 1969.

   Two useful selected listings:

   MARYLAND. Dept. of Education. Maryland Instructional Materials List. Baltimore: 1954- . Irregular. A selection aid for libraries and individuals of state and local agencies' materials which have instructional value. Includes materials on history, geology, health, geography.

   "MARYLAND State Documents." The Crab [1971-] (Maryland Library Association).

Government Publications - Baltimore County

4. PARSONS, Richard. Baltimore County Publications. 3d ed. Towson, Md.: Baltimore County Public Library, 1976. 56 p.

   An annotated list of current county agency publications, as well as selected non-county materials which might be useful to the citizen. Arranged by agency, with a separate section on maps. Subject index.

Imprints and Publishing

5. WROTH, Lawrence C. A History of Printing in Colonial Maryland, 1686-1776. Baltimore: Typothetae of Baltimore, 1922. 275 p. illus.

   Bibliographical footnotes.

   A historical and biographical account, with separate chapters on individual printers and publishers and on Baltimore, which lists, locates, describes, and comments on nearly 400 items.

   Continued by

6. WHEELER, Joseph T. The Maryland Press, 1777-1790. Baltimore: Maryland Historical Society, 1938. 226 p.

   Chapters on individual printers and a chapter on printing in Baltimore, Easton, Hagerstown, and Georgetown. "Bibliography of Maryland Imprints, 1770-1790" (p. 77-206) lists 550 items and gives full collation and the location of copies.

   Continued by

7. MINICK, Amanda R. A History of Printing in Maryland, 1791-1800, with a Bibliography of Works Printed in the State During the Period. Baltimore: Enoch Pratt Free Library, 1949. 603 p. illus., ports.

   Provides a chronicle of printing in the towns of Maryland, biographies of the printers, and commentary on the materials produced. The "Imprint Bibliography" (p. 225-480) lists 637 items alphabetically under year. Index.

   Continued by

8. BRISTOL, Roger P. Maryland Imprints, 1801-1810. Charlottesville, Va.: University of Virginia Press for the Bibliographical Society of the University of Virginia, 1953. 310 p.

   A chronological record of 942 books and periodicals, giving location. Lists "Printers and Booksellers of Maryland Imprints, 1801-1810": p. 279-285.

   More specialized works:

GILMER, Gertrude. "Maryland Magazines--Ante Bellum, 1793-1861." Maryland Historical Magazine 29 (1934): 120-131.

KEIDEL, George C. "Early Maryland Newspapers: A List of Titles." Maryland Historical Magazine 28 (1933): 119-137, 244-257, 328-344; 29 (1934): 25-34, 132-144, 223-236, 310-321; 30 (1935): 149-156. This covers the period 1727-1860.

REICHMAN, Felix. "German Printing in Maryland: A Check List, 1768-1950." In Society for the History of Germans in Maryland. Report 27 (1950): 9-70. A Chronological list of 812 items, giving location of copies, and a summary of German newspapers and magazines. Introductory essay gives background on men involved.

SILVER, Rollo G. The Baltimore Book Trade, 1800-1825. New York: New York Public Library, 1953. 56 p. Reprinted from New York Public Library Bulletin 57 (Mr./Jl. 1953). Includes an introductory chapter on the literary and publishing life of Baltimore and a directory of individuals and firms associated with printing, publishing, or bookselling.

The following unpublished checklists of Maryland imprints were prepared at the Catholic University of America as theses:

1811-14: Webb, Erna M. (1954. 136 p.)
1815-18: Alagia, Damian P. (1951. 159 p.)
1819-22: Franklin, Aurelia W. (1951. 297 p.)
1823-26: Dunegan, Florence M. (1952. 151 p.)
1831-34: Murphy, Robert B. (1952. 199 p.)
1839: Titus, Thomas R. (1963. 86 p.)
1840: Nelson, Cecil P. (1958. 154 p.)
1841-42: Luney, Alice W. (1959. 144 p.)
1843-46: Donnelly, Frederic D. (1953. 241 p.)
1847-49: King, Sarah B. (1954. 201 p.)
1850-52: Spencer, Helen I. (1953. 215 p.)
1853-54: Rodriguez, Adelaide V. (1953. 175 p.)
1855-57: Davis, Vashti A. (1953. 209 p.)
1859: Gildea, Matthew E. (1965. 116 p.)
1860: O'Neill, Maureen (1963. 135 p.)
1861: Neavill, Helen A. (1962. 106 p.)
1862: Lambert, Robert A. (1963. 84 p.)
1863: Rosenthal, Elaine P. (1962. 88 p.)
1864-66: Chin, Elisabeth M. (1963. 253 p.)
1867-69: Thompson, John H. (1953. 265 p.)
1870-71: Bennett, Emily (1953. 230 p.)
1872-73: Raymond, Anne (1954. 111 p.)
1874-76: Quigg, Dorothy (1951. 260 p.)

Periodical Index

9. BALTIMORE COUNTY, Md. Public Library. Index to "Baltimore" Magazine [1964-1969] Prepared by the staff of the Towson Area Branch, Baltimore County Public Library. Towson, Md.: 1971. 32 p.

Baltimore Magazine is published monthly by the Chamber of Commerce of Metropolitan Baltimore, Inc.

Union Lists

10. AMERICAN LIBRARY ASSOCIATION. Reference Services Division. Maryland Chapter. Union List of Serials in Maryland. Bound Brook, N.J.: Literature Services Associates, 1962. 1 vol. (various pagings)

    Records the holdings of 120 Maryland libraries for 72,000 serial publications.

11. INTERLIBRARY USERS ASSOCIATION. Journal Holdings in the Washington-Baltimore Area [1976-] Rockville, Md.: Sigma Data Computing Corp., 1976- . Annual.

    Shows the holdings in 65 libraries, mostly technical, of approximately 7,500 titles. Directory of information on the participating libraries includes each library's loan and copying policies.

12. PARSONS, Richard, ed. Guide to Specialized Subject Collections in Maryland Libraries. 2d ed., rev. and enl. Baltimore: Baltimore County Public Library, 1974. 342 p.

    Pt. 1 is a directory of libraries, giving subject emphasis, special collections, and interlibrary loan and copying services. Pt. 2 is a union list of abstracts, reports, bibliographies, and indexes which appear serially. Pt. 3 is a subject index.

LIBRARIES

Directories

13. CHURCH AND SYNAGOGUE LIBRARY ASSOCIATION. Directory of Church and Synagogue Libraries in Maryland. Bryn Mawr, Pa.: 1973. 11 p.

    A geographical directory of approximately 125 libraries. Gives size of collection and hours when opened.

14. MARYLAND. Council for Higher Education. Subject Area Strengths and Special Collections in Maryland. Prelim. unedited ed. Baltimore: Maryland Council for Higher Education, Maryland Dept. of Education, and Special Libraries Association--Baltimore Chapter, 1971. 258 p.

    A directory to the services, facilities, and special collections of public, special, academic, and governmental libraries in Maryland.

History

15. KALISCH, Philip A. The Enoch Pratt Free Library: A Social History. Metuchen, N.J.: Scarecrow Press, 1969. 264 p. port.

    Bibliography: p. 237-357.

ASSOCIATIONS

Knights of Columbus

16. BAUERNSCHUB, John P. Columbianism in Maryland, 1879-1965. Baltimore: Knights of Columbus, Maryland State Council, 1965. 275 p. ports.

    A brief history of the Knights of Columbus in Maryland and each of its component Councils.

Masons

17. FREEMASONS. Maryland. Royal Arch Masons. Grand Chapter. Grand Chapter of Royal Arch Masons of Maryland: Centennial Anniversary, June 24th...1897. Baltimore: C. H. Curley, 1897. 335 p. illus., ports.

    Includes historical sections and biographical sketches of Grand High Priests, 1797-1897.

18. SCHULTZ, Edward T. History of Freemasonry in Maryland of All the Rites Introduced into Maryland, from the Earliest Time to the Present. Baltimore: J. H. Medairy & Co., 1884-1888. 4 vols.

    Continued by

19. EVERSTINE, Carl N. History of the Grand Lodge of Ancient, Free and Accepted Masons of Maryland, 1888-1950. Baltimore: 1951. 2 vols.

Women's Clubs

20. MARYLAND FEDERATION OF WOMEN'S CLUBS, Inc. Directory. Baltimore. Annual.

    Arranged by District with clubs listed under city. Gives for each the date of organization, number of members, annual meeting date, and the names and addresses of its officers.

BIOGRAPHIES

21. AGNUS, Felix. The Book of Maryland; "Men and Institutions," A Work for Press Reference... Baltimore: Maryland Biographical Association, 1920. 350 p. ports.

    Designed to meet the demands of newspapers for a reference source on representative men.

22. BALTIMORE AMERICAN. Distinguished Men of Baltimore and of Maryland. Baltimore: 1914. 154 p. ports.

    Half tone photographs and some brief biography of men prominent in the commercial, professional, political, and social activity of the state. Also photographs of some of Baltimore's buildings.

23. THE BIOGRAPHICAL Cyclopedia of Representative Men of Maryland and the District of Columbia. Baltimore: National Biographical Publishing Co., 1879. 716 p. ports.

    Relatively complete.

    This can be supplemented by the following:

    SPENCER, Richard H., ed. Genealogical and Memorial Encyclopedia of the State of Maryland. New York: American Historical Society, 1919. 2 vols. ports.

    WARFIELD, Joshua D. The Founders of Anne Arundel and Howard Counties, Maryland; A Genealogical and Biographical Review from Wills, Deeds, and Church Records. Baltimore: Regional Publishing Co., 1967. 543 p. Reprint of 1905 edition.

24. LUCKETT, Margie, ed. Maryland Women, Baltimore, Maryland. Baltimore: King Bros., Inc., Press, 1931-1942. 3 vols. ports.

25. ROLLO, Vera A. F. Maryland Personality Parade. With 1970 photographs by Joseph H. Cromwell. Poems by Thomas Seymour. 2d ed. Lanham, Md.: Maryland Historical Press, 1970- . illus.

    Bibliography: vol. 1, p. 129-130; glossary: vol. 1, p. 131-134.

    A history for juveniles, through the lives of representative Marylanders.

26. TERCENTENARY History of Maryland, by Matthew P. Andrews. Chicago: S. J. Clarke Publishing Co., 1925. 4 vols. illus., ports., maps.

    Vol. 1, by Matthew P. Andrews, is a general and thorough history of Maryland to 1925, with the largest portion covering the period to the War of 1812. Vol. 4 has the title "Tercentenary History of Maryland, Embodying Biographical Records of Colonists, Pioneers, Judges, Governors, Military Officers, etc.," compiled principally by Henry F. Powell. Vols. 2 and 3 are biographical and like vol. 4 contain portraits for many of the subjects.

27. WHO'S Who in the East [1 (1942/1943-] Chicago: Marquis Who's Who, 1943- . Annual.

    An alphabetical listing which includes Marylanders.

CALENDARS OF EVENTS

28. MARYLAND. Dept. of Natural Resources. The DNR Calendar of Special Events, Meetings, Hearings and Other Activities of Public Interest. Annapolis. Flyer. Monthly.

    Includes state and local activities, covering governmental, social, and community affairs.

29. MARYLAND. Div. of Tourist Development. Four Seasons in Maryland. Annapolis. Flyer. Annual.

    Chronological list of events, with a brief descriptive note and an address and phone number for further information.

    Much the same information is in

    MARYLAND. Div. of Tourist Development. Calendar of Events in Maryland. Annapolis. Flyer. Quarterly.

DESCRIPTIONS AND GUIDE BOOKS

Descriptions

30. BODINE, A. Aubrey. The Face of Maryland. 2d ed. Baltimore: Bodine and Associates, 1967. 160 p. illus., ports., map.

    Sensitive and perceptive photographs of Marylanders at work and at play, buildings, homes, and a wide range of other Maryland subjects.

    An earlier work also consists of photographs of Maryland with a special interest in Baltimore:

    BODINE, A. Aubrey. My Maryland; America in Miniature. Introd. by Neil H. Swanson. Baltimore: Camera Magazine, 1952. 174 p. illus., map.

31. MARYLAND. Div. of Tourist Development. Maryland. Annapolis. Irregular.

    A small pamphlet that provides general information on Maryland history, education, climate, geography, population, taxes, etc.

    An earlier work:

    MARYLAND. Dept. of Education. Maryland Picture Portfolio Series. Baltimore: 1954-1956. 24 vols. illus., maps. For every county and Baltimore City, presents 24 illustrations, each with a separate page of descriptive text presenting six "Living in...County" topics: geographical, historical, occupational, industrial, social, scenic, and unique. Some of the material is out-of-date, but it is still useful at the elementary school level.

    Also available:

    MARYLAND. Geological Survey. "County Maps." On a scale of one mile to one inch, these show elevations, streams, highways, and populated areas.

32. SCHAUN, George and Virginia Schaun. The Greenberry Series on Maryland. Annapolis: Greenberry Publications, 1962-1968. 6 vols. illus., maps.

    Brief articles on Maryland topics, ranging from the Great Seal, iron making in Maryland, early money, ethnic groups, to biographical sketches of distinguished individuals associated with Maryland. For use in classroom discussion of Maryland social studies and history. The authors' Biographical Sketches of Maryland (1969) contains the biographical sketches in the Greenberry Series, as well as those of Samuel Chase, Sir Francis Nicholson, and Gilbert H. Grosvenor.

________ ________. Index to Volumes 1-6 (1969).

This can be supplemented with the following:

BAILEY, Bernadine. Picture Book of Maryland. Pictures by Kurt Wiese. Chicago: Albert Whitman and Co., 1955. 1 vol. (unpaged) illus. A small book written and illustrated for children.

TITUS, Charles. The Old Line State; Her Heritage. Illustrated by Thomas E. Jones. Cambridge, Md.: Tidewater Publishers, 1971. 85 p. illus. Descriptions and short bibliographies of significant Maryland places and homes. Arranged by region and Baltimore.

Descriptions - Chesapeake Bay

33. BODINE, A. Aubrey. Chesapeake Bay and Tidewater. 3d ed. Baltimore: Bodine & Associates, 1967. 160 p. illus.

    A photographic study.

34. BURGESS, Robert H. Chesapeake Circle. Cambridge, Md.: Cornell Maritime Press, 1965. 211 p. illus., maps.

    The Chesapeake Bay scene and pictures, with an emphasis on the commercial activity.

    Another valuable record of the significance and diversity of the Chesapeake Bay:

    BREWINGTON, Marion V. Chesapeake Bay: A Pictorial Maritime History. 2d ed. Cambridge, Md.: Cornell Maritime Press, 1956. illus., maps.

35. de GAST, Robert. Western Wind, Eastern Shore. Baltimore: Johns Hopkins University Press, 1975. 192 p. illus., maps.

    "Suggested Reading": p. 176.

    A pictorial record and daily log of a 24 day sail around the Delmarva Peninsula using the Eastern Shore backwaters.

    Companion volumes:

    de GAST, Robert. The Lighthouses of the Chesapeake. Baltimore: Johns Hopkins University Press, 1973. 173 p. illus. Bibliography: p. 172. A narrative and pictorial tour guide of the Chesapeake Bay's 32 standing lighthouses offering histories, photographs, Coast and Geodetic charts of location. In addition, the location and a description of 42 lighthouses which have been destroyed are given.

de GAST, Robert. The Oystermen of the Chesapeake. Camden, Me.: International Marine Publishing Co., 1970. 1 vol. (unpaged) illus. Mostly photographs, but good ones.

LANG, Varley. Follow the Water. Winston Salem, N.C.: John F. Blair, Publisher, 1961. 222 p. An informal account of the watermen of Chesapeake Bay.

Guide Books

36. MARYLAND. Civil War Centennial Commission. Maryland Remembers; A Guide to Historic Places and People of the Civil War in Maryland. Hagerstown, Md.: 1961. 64 p. map.

    The events of the Civil War in Maryland arranged by county, then places (many are identified with markers) within each county.

37. MARYLAND. Div. of Tourist Development. Driving Tours of Maryland. Annapolis. illus., maps.

    Nine tours which offer an opportunity to explore the variety and richness of Maryland. Gives background information, descriptions of places of interest, and driving distances.

    Also available is the

    MARYLAND Official Highway Map. Baltimore: Maryland State Roads Commission. Annual. Folded map.

38. MARYLAND. Div. of Tourist Development. Maryland, 1976; A Group Tour Guide to "America in Miniature." Annapolis: 1976. 104 p. illus., maps.

    Designed for group tour companies.

    Includes calendars of events, historic sites, entertainment, boat cruises, driving tours, and sources of additional information. Portions of this have been included in the Maryland Bicentennial Commission. Official Maryland Guide to Landmarks of the Revolutionary Era in Maryland (Annapolis: 1975), which is arranged in separate parts for the Southern, Central, Western Maryland, and Eastern Shore Regions.

39. MARYLAND; A New Guide to the Old Line State. Compiled and edited by Edward C. Papenfuse and others. Baltimore: Johns Hopkins University Press, 1976. 528 p. illus., maps.

    Revision of W.P.A. Writers' Program edition (1940).

    Does not include, unfortunately, the introductory information on Maryland's historical, social, economic, and industrial background found in the W.P.A. edition. Offers a series of excursions for systematically visiting those places which are significant for their association with distinguished individuals and notable events, or which represent a valuable experience in themselves.

40. MARYLAND HISTORICAL TRUST. Historic Sites Inventory. Annapolis: 1973- . 9 vols. to be published, covering all regions of the state. illus., maps.

Already published: vol. 1: "Lower Southern Maryland" (Charles, St. Mary's, and Calvert Counties); vol. 2: "Lower Eastern Shore" (Wicomico, Somerset, and Worcester Counties).

To include more than 10,000 significant national and state landmarks, arranged by county within the region. For each landmark there is a descriptive note, location, significant dates, whether public or private, and accessibility to the public.

41. SHOSTECK, Robert. Weekender's Guide; Places of Historic, Scenic and Recreational Interest within 200 Miles of the Washington-Baltimore Area. Washington: Potomac Books, 1975. 448 p. maps.

A useful handbook arranged by region, that gives camping, skiing, special interests, and the bicentennial trail. Includes what to read for each area, where to stay, and where to eat.

Guide Books - Annapolis

42. SCHAUN, George. Annapolis, Guide Book and Tours of the Naval Academy. Drawings by John Moll. Annapolis: Greenberry Press, 1971. 52 p. illus.

A walking tour.

More about the Naval Academy can be found in

BANNING, Kendall. Annapolis Today. Revised by A. Stuart Pitt. 6th ed. Annapolis: United States Naval Institute, 1963. 329 p. illus. An introduction to life at the U.S. Naval Academy and a brief history of the Academy.

Guide Books - Antietam

43. TILBERG, Frederick. Antietam National Battlefield Site, Maryland. Rev. ed. Washington: 1961. 60 p. illus., maps. (U.S. National Park Service. Historical Handbook Series, no. 31)

Story of the battle.

Guide Books - Baltimore

44. WAESCHE, James F. Baltimore Today...A Guide to Its Pleasures, Treasures and Past... Photographs by A. Aubrey Bodine. Baltimore: Bodine and Associates, 1969. 96 p. illus., maps.

    History and details of landmarks, walking and driving tours. Includes Annapolis and surrounding counties.

Guide Books - Fort McHenry

45. LESSEM, Harold I. and George C. MacKenzie. Fort McHenry National Monument and Historic Shrine, Maryland. Washington: National Park Service, 1950. 38 p. illus., ports., maps. (U.S. National Park Service. Historical Handbook Series, no. 5)

    A history of the Fort from the Revolutionary War through World War II, with the emphasis on the War of 1812, Battle of Baltimore, and the writing of the "Star Spangled Banner."

PLACES AND PLACE NAMES

Places

46. MARYLAND. State Planning Dept. Gazetteer of Maryland. Prepared jointly by Maryland State Planning Dept. and Dept. of Geology, Mines and Water Resources. Baltimore: Johns Hopkins Press, 1941. 242 p. map. (Its Publication no. 33; Maryland. Geological Survey. General Reports, vol. 14)

    Supersedes Henry Gannett, ...A Gazetteer of Maryland (1904).

    Places in Maryland are identified with specific descriptive terms, distance to nearest place, longitude and latitude.

    Older gazetteers such as Richard S. Fisher, Gazetteer of the State of Maryland... (1852) sometimes include places not found in later works.

47. MARYLAND. State Planning Dept. Maryland Manual of Coordinates. 3d ed. Annapolis: 1969. 170 p. map. (Its Publication no. 155)

    An alphabetical listing of about 11,000 cities, towns and known place names, public open space and recreational areas, historical architectural structures, historical landmarks, housing subdivisions and developments, and railroad stations. Uses the Maryland Coordinate System to locate each place.

Place Names

48. JESSOP, Jennie E. The Origin of Names in Baltimore County. Cockeysville, Md.: Baltimore County Historical Society, Publications Committee, 1974. 20 p.

    References: p. 18.

49. KENNY, Hamill T. The Origin and Meaning of the Indian Place Names of Maryland. Baltimore: Waverly Press, 1961. 186 p.

    Bibliography: p. 161-175.

    A scholarly work that includes an introductory essay on the ethnology of the names and Algonquin linguistics.

Each place in the dictionary is located and previous opinions, commentary, and conclusions on the name are provided with their sources. The appendix lists extinct, misplaced, and scantily documented names, apparently Indian.

AGRICULTURE

50. MARYLAND. University. Agriculture '76. College Park, Md.: 1970. 6 vols. illus., maps.

    Bibliographical footnotes.

    Contents: 1. The setting and the people; 2. Production, processing, and marketing; 3. Resources and services in production; 4. Impact on economy; 5. Contributions to people and environment; 6. Recommendations for future University of Maryland agricultural programs.

    An in-depth study of Maryland agriculture, with projections for 1976 and 1986.

    An older work:

    BALTIMORE ASSOCIATION OF COMMERCE. Maryland Development Bureau. The Agricultural Industry of Maryland, by W. S. Hamill. Baltimore: 1934. 332 p. illus., maps. Describes conditions and trends in Maryland agriculture. Contains background chapters on topographic features, climate, soils.

Calendar of Events

51. MARYLAND. State Fair Board. Maryland Agricultural Fair and Show Schedule [1958-] Timonium, Md.: 1958- . Flyer. Annual.

    A chronological listing of state and local events, including fairs, meetings, shows, educational courses, etc., sponsored by governmental agencies, associations, and private groups.

History

52. CRANDALL, Gilbert A. Breadbasket of the Revolution--Maryland Agriculture 1776-1976. Annapolis: Maryland Agriculture Week Committee, 1976. 28 p. illus.

53. CRAVEN, Avery. Soil Exhaustion as a Factor in the Agricultural History of Virginia and Maryland, 1606-1860. Gloucester, Mass.: P. Smith, 1965. 179 p. (University of Illinois Studies in Social Sciences, vol. 13, no. 1)

Reprint of 1926 edition.

Bibliography: p. 165-172.

Though there is an emphasis on Virginia, the early chapters and the inferences suggested are of value for an understanding of the relationship between agriculture and the development of colonial Maryland and Maryland's subsequent history.

54. JENKINS, Mary M. I. and Eben C. Jenkins. The First Hundred Years: Maryland State Grange 1874-1974. N.p.: Maryland State Grange, 1974. 281 p. illus.

Bibliography: p. 271; glossary of Grange terms: p. 268-270.

Gives biographies of Masters and rosters of officers.

Statistics

55. MARYLAND. Dept. of Agriculture. Div. of Marketing. Maryland Agricultural Statistics; Annual Summary for [1962-] Annapolis: 1953- . Annual.

Covers products, labor, farms.

56. MARYLAND. University. Extension Service. Maryland Agricultural Statistics: Historical Series, 1919-1952. College Park, Md.: n.d. 134 p. (Its Extension Bulletin no. X-7)

Prepared by the Maryland Crop Reporting Service.

Statistics for grains, hay, and other field crops; fruits and vegetables; livestock and livestock products; prices; and farm economic data. Statistical information for the period 1866 to 1918 is found in its Extension Bulletin no. 3 (1944).

57. U.S. Bureau of the Census. 1969 Census of Agriculture: Maryland. Washington: U.S. Govt. Print. Off., 1972. 1 vol. (various pagings)

Gives state and county data on farms, farm characteristics and farm products for 1969 and earlier years. Includes such information as land use, size of farm, income and sales, production and expense, livestock and poultry, machinery and equipment.

ECONOMICS AND COMMERCE

Atlas

58. MARYLAND. Dept. of Economic and Community Development. An Economic and Social Atlas of Maryland. Rev. ed. by Derek Thompson, Joseph W. Wiedel and others. Annapolis: 1974. 2 vols. illus., maps.

    Prepared in cooperation with the University of Maryland Dept. of Geography and also issued as Maryland. University. Dept. of Geography. Occasional Papers in Geography, no. 3.

    "Bibliographic Guide to Sources": vol. 1, p. 99-126 and vol. 2, p. 250-306.

    A general study of the social and economic attributes of Maryland and its constituent counties and local governmental units, organized around the theme of people as producers and consumers. Vol. 1 in four parts: population, production and employment, labor force and consumers, and government services. Vol. 2 is a statistical summary.

Bibliography

59. U.S. National Capital Planning Commission. Research Office. Bibliography of Studies and Reports on the District of Columbia and the Washington Metropolitan Area; Population, Economic Activities, Housing, Land Use, Visitors and Tourism. Washington: 1967. 45 p.

    Lists published studies and reports and unpublished papers and research material completed since 1950 under socio-economic topics. Indicates geographic coverage, thereby indicating which parts of Maryland are included.

Directories

60. BLACK Business Directory [1970-] Baltimore: Black Economic Research Team, 1970- . Annual.

    Arranged by business and profession.

61. DIRECTORY of Maryland Exporters-Importers [1970-] Annapolis: Maryland Dept. of Economic and Community Development, 1970- . Triennial.

Supersedes Baltimore Association of Commerce. Export and Import Bureau. Exporters and Importers of Maryland, U.S.A.

Firms engaged in international trade, listed by products and services and also alphabetically.

62. DIRECTORY of Maryland Manufacturers [1926-] Annapolis: Maryland Dept. of Economic and Community Development, 1926- . Biennial. Title varies.

Lists firms alphabetically; manufacturers by cities, giving officers, number of employees, and products; and manufacturers by industry. Index of products.

63. MARYLAND. Port Administration. Port of Baltimore Handbook [1973/1974-] Baltimore: 1973- . Biennial. illus.

Continues Maryland Port Authority, Port of Baltimore Handbook.

Gives the history of the port, cargo facilities available, fees and charges, other ports available in Maryland, and a directory of services.

Some additional directory information:

PORT of Baltimore Directory [1957/1958-] Baltimore: Maryland Port Administration, 1957- . Biennial. Title varies. Information on port services and the personnel of the businesses, public agencies, and other organizations associated with the Baltimore maritime community.

64. MARYLAND NATURAL FOOD ASSOCIATES. Maryland Natural Food Directory, 1973. Natural Food Associates. 12 p.

Lists food stores and locations where natural food products are sold.

History

65. BLANDI, Joseph G. Maryland Business Corporations, 1783-1852. Baltimore: Johns Hopkins Press, 1934. 116 p. (Johns Hopkins Studies in Historical and Political Science, ser. 52, no. 3)

A study of the factors affecting the nature and growth of business corporations. Appendix lists "Business Charters Granted by Maryland, 1783-1852" (p. 93-111).

Other more specialized works dealing with business history are the following:

KELLEY, William J. Brewing in Maryland; From Colonial

Times to the Present. Baltimore: 1965. 735 p. A chronicle of brewers and breweries.

HARVEY, Katherine A. The Best-Dressed Miners; Life and Labor in the Maryland Coal Region, 1835-1910. Ithaca, N.Y.: Cornell University Press, 1969. 488 p. map. The social history of the miners of Allegany County, who as miners were not typical.

The histories of mill towns are found in

FILBY, Vera R. Savage, Maryland. Savage, Md.: Savage Civic Association, 1965. 39 p.

HOLLAND, Celia M. Ellicott City, Maryland, Mill Town U.S.A. Chicago: Adams Press, 1970. 273 p.

66. GOULD, Clarence P. The Land System in Maryland, 1720-1765. Baltimore: Johns Hopkins Press, 1915. 106 p. (Johns Hopkins Studies in Historical and Political Science, ser. 31, no. 1)

    An analysis of the granting of land, the charges on it and its management, and manors as a land system.

67. GOULD, Clarence P. Money and Transportation in Maryland, 1720-1765. Baltimore: Johns Hopkins Press, 1915. 76 p. (Johns Hopkins Studies in Historical and Political Science, ser. 33, no. 1)

    Bibliographic footnotes.

    Deals primarily with the process and practices of exchange for goods and services, with chapters on coinage, bills of exchange, tobacco and paper currency, and barter. Covers transportation and communication briefly.

History - Baltimore

68. GOULD, Clarence P. "The Economic Causes of the Rise of Baltimore." In Essays in Colonial History Presented to Charles McLean Andrews by His Students, p. 225-251. New Haven, Conn.: Yale University Press, 1931.

    The consequences of a developing grain trade and a diminishing tobacco culture.

State and Local Finances

69. MARYLAND. Comptroller of the Treasury. Annual Report [1851?-] Annapolis: 1853?- . Annual. Title varies.

    A financial statement of Maryland, showing sources of income and the disbursements of funds.

70. MARYLAND. Dept. of Assessment and Taxation. Biennial Report [1 (1914/1915)-] Maryland: 1916- .

Gives assessed property values; state and county tax rates; state and county taxable basis; and public service, railroad, and bank receipts subject to tax.

The Maryland Dept. of Assessments and Taxation Tax Map Books (Baltimore. Irregular) for each county (cities and towns excluded) show property lines, names of owners, deed references, and acreages.

71. MARYLAND. Dept. of Budget and Fiscal Planning. Fiscal Digest of the State of Maryland for the...Year [1938-] Annapolis: 1937- . Annual.

Gives estimated revenue and details of appropriations for operating purposes.

72. MARYLAND. Div. of Fiscal Services. Local Government Finances in Maryland; Report [1 (1947/1948)-] Baltimore. Annual.

Summary of financial information of counties, Baltimore City, incorporated municipalities, and special districts, covering revenue, expenditures, public debt, and debt service payments.

73. MARYLAND. Governor. The Maryland State Budget for the Fiscal Year Ending [1918/1919-1919/1920-] Submitted to the General Assembly of Maryland. Annapolis: 1918- . Annual.

Summary data of funds requested for the legislative, executive, and judicial branches and for capital improvements. For each state agency shows the request for major categories of expenditures by budget unit or activity.

This information can also be found in

MARYLAND. Dept. of Budget and Fiscal Planning. Maryland State Budget. Annapolis. Annual.

Statistics

74. MARYLAND. Dept. of Economic and Community Development. Maryland Development Digest [vol. 1, no. 1 (Aug. 1971)-] Annapolis: 1971- . Monthly. Title varies.

Supersedes Maryland Economic Indicators.

Provides news notes and data on the Maryland economy which may demonstrate trends, industrial and financial, and employment statistics.

Useful for earlier data:

FEDERAL RESERVE BANK OF RICHMOND. Research Dept. Business and Financial Indicators [Feb. 1956-April 1973] Richmond. Monthly. Covers Maryland, District of Columbia, Virginia, West Virginia, North Carolina, and South

Carolina. Data is given by state on banking, manufacturing, prices, construction, payroll, etc., and is compared to previous months and the past year.

75. MARYLAND. Dept. of Economic and Community Development. The Maryland Economy [no. 1 (1960)-] Annapolis: 1960- . Irregular.

Offers narrative summaries and extensive tables of statewide economic activity and both national and state perspectives.

76. MARYLAND. Dept. of State Planning. The Economy of Maryland, Projections of Employment to 1980. Baltimore: 1968. 126 p. (Its Publication no. 143)

Designed to provide projections of economic activity for the nation, Maryland, and regions in Maryland. Provides employment data by industry and by region for 1950-1980, at ten year intervals.

77. MARYLAND. Dept. of State Planning. Maryland County Economic Data Book [1950-] Baltimore: 1950- . Irregular. (Its Publication no. 66)

Provides social and economic data for the state and each county on population, employment, manufacturing, agriculture, business, family income, assessed real estate, retail sales, sales taxes, and estimated effective buying income. For each county also carries a brief descriptive note and the points of interest.

78. MARYLAND. Dept. of State Planning. Maryland Family Income Characteristics: 1970 Census. Baltimore: 1972. 103 p. maps. (Its Publication no. 178)

Provides statistical data and income trends by election districts within counties for 1960 and 1970, based on the U.S. 1970 Census.

79. MARYLAND. Dept. of State Planning. Maryland 1970 Social Indicator Series. Baltimore: 1973-1974. 4 vols. illus., maps. (Its Publication nos. 200, 201, 202, 203)

Vol. 1: Educational characteristics; vol. 2: Age and mobility characteristics; vol. 3: Income characteristics; vol. 4: Labor force and employment characteristics.

Presents socio-economic data for election districts and places with populations of 2,500 persons or more. Data is derived from the U.S. 1970 Census.

80. MARYLAND. Div. of Business and Industrial Development. Community Economic Inventory. Annapolis: 1962- .

Baltimore City is treated as a county; some counties are covered by more than one edition.

Contains brief information on geographic and economic characteristics, climate, population, labor, existing industry, industrial parks and schools, market area, communications, utilities, government and taxes, education, recreation, and natural resources.

81. MARYLAND Statistical Abstract [1967-] Annapolis: Maryland Dept. of Economic Development. Biennial.

Complements Item 75.

The most complete statistical record--not an analysis--of the composition, changes and trends in population, income, business, agriculture, natural resources, social services, and other aspects of Maryland, at the state and county levels. Each of the sections has a narrative background statement. The appendix of the 1975 volume contains a number of historical time series of significant economic indicators.

82. U.S. Bureau of the Census. County Business Patterns, Maryland [1946-] Washington: U.S. Govt. Print. Off., 1946- . Annual.

Presents first quarter employment and payroll statistics by state, county, Baltimore City and standard metropolitan statistical area, and by industry.

Additional data on business activity:

U.S. Bureau of the Census. 1972 Census of Retail Trade: Area Statistics, Maryland. Washington: U.S. Govt. Print. Off., 1974. 1 vol. (various pagings) Information by state, counties, standard metropolitan statistical areas, and cities with more than 500 establishments, on firms that sell goods or services for personal or household consumption.

U.S. Bureau of the Census. 1972 Census of Retail Trade: Major Retail Centers in Standard Metropolitan Statistical Areas: Maryland. Washington: U.S. Govt. Print. Off., 1975. 1 vol. (various pagings) maps. Information arranged by kinds of businesses.

U.S. Bureau of the Census. 1972 Census of Retail Trade: Wholesale Trade, Area Statistics, Maryland. Washington: U.S. Govt. Print. Off., 1974. 1 vol. (various pagings) For state, county, standard metropolitan statistical areas, and cities of 5,000 or more, gives information by type of operation and kind of business.

U.S. Bureau of the Census. 1972 Census of Selected Service Industries: Area Statistics, Maryland. Washington: U.S. Govt. Print. Off., 1974. 1 vol. (various pagings) Presents data on a variety of personal and business services for state, standard metropolitan statistical areas, and cities with 300 selected establishments or more.

Includes by detailed kinds of business such things as number of establishments, receipts, payroll, and employment.

83. U.S. Bureau of the Census. 1970 Census of Housing, Detailed Housing Characteristics, Maryland. Washington: U.S. Govt. Print. Off., 1971. 1 vol. (various pagings)

Includes data gathered from the 15 and 5 percent samples on counties and those areas and places of more than 2,500. Covers such things as structural and plumbing characteristics, equipment and finance characteristics, fuels and appliances, and occupancy, financial, and appliances characteristics. Its General Housing Characteristics, Maryland (Washington: U.S. Govt. Print. Off., 1971) gives the complete data count.

84. U.S. Bureau of the Census. 1972 Census of Manufacturers, Maryland. Washington: U.S. Govt. Print. Off., 1975. 27 p.

For industry and industry group shows data and comparable data for earlier years, on such things as value of shipments, value added by manufacturing, employment, payrolls, and man-hours. Similar totals for all manufacturing industries are given for counties, standard metropolitan statistical areas, and cities with significant activity.

EDUCATION

85. "HANDBOOK [for Maryland Teachers]" The Maryland Teacher. Annual. Title varies.

    Issued as a number of The Maryland Teacher.

    Includes a variety of information on the Maryland State Teachers Association, such as directory of officers, by-laws, General Council members, Treasurer's report, committees of MSTA. Also includes such things as teachers' salary schedule, county and Baltimore City leave provisions, and information on the state retirement system.

86. MARYLAND. Council for Higher Education. Admissions and Financial Aid Information for Maryland's Public and Private Postsecondary Educational Institutions [1970-] Annapolis. Annual. Title varies.

    Provides information on state and federal financial aid, student transfer, profile of expenses, admissions, and financial aid for institutions.

Directories

87. MARYLAND. Dept. of Education. Directory of Public Education [1971/1972-] Baltimore. Annual. Title varies.

    Continues its Directory of School Officials in the State of Maryland.

    Gives state education agency personnel, members of local boards of education, local superintendents of schools, administrative and supervisory staffs, principals, and state-aided public libraries and trustees.

88. MARYLAND. Dept. of Education. Maryland Nonpublic Schools Approved by the State Superintendent of Schools [1950-] Baltimore: 1951- . Annual. Title varies.

    An official listing of nursery schools, kindergartens, elementary and secondary schools, educational institutions for the handicapped, and tutoring schools.

89. MARYLAND. Dept. of Education. Maryland Nonpublic Specialized Schools Approved [1948-] Baltimore: 1948- . Annual. Title varies.

Lists schools which meet the minimum state standards for schools of each type. Arranged by specialization, such as art, mechanics, business, electronics, modeling, piano, real estate, etc.

90. MARYLAND. Dept. of Education. State Accredited Maryland Colleges and Universities [1959-] Baltimore: 1959- . Annual. Title varies.

Separate lists of degree-granting institutions, specialized collegiate institutions (non-degree granting), and approved teacher education programs. For each indicates major programs, costs, enrollment, etc.

Directories - Baltimore

91. BALTIMORE. Dept. of Education. Baltimore City Public Schools Directory [1858-] Baltimore: 1858- . Annual. Title varies.

Gives the addresses and telephone numbers of personnel in central administration, schools, offices, and warehouses; and the schedule of staff meetings.

History

92. DUNLAP, William C. Quaker Education in Baltimore and Virginia Yearly Meeting...With an Account of Certain Meetings of Delaware and the Eastern Shore Affiliated with Philadelphia. Philadelphia: 1936. 574 p. illus.

Bibliography: p. 541-548.

Traces the origin and development of Quaker education through extensive use of official Quaker records. Chapters on the education of Indians and of Blacks cover the period to 1870.

93. McCORMICK, Leo J. Church-State Relationships in Education in Maryland. Washington: The Catholic University of America, 1942. 294 p. (Ph.D., Catholic University of America, 1941)

Bibliography: p. 277-287.

A useful source for the history of education in colonial Maryland and historical information on individual private denominational schools in Maryland from 1694 to 1940.

94. STEINER, Bernard C., ed. History of Education in Maryland. Washington: U.S. Govt. Print. Off., 1894. 331 p. (U.S. Office

of Education. Contributions to American Educational History, no. 19)

Introduction to the history of education in Maryland with histories of individual educational institutions, including those that no longer exist.

The following are also of historical value:

FLEXNER, Abraham and Frank P. Bachman. Public Education in Maryland: A Report to the Maryland Survey Commission. 4th ed. New York: General Education Board, 1919. 230 p.

VAVRINA, Vernon S. History of Public Education in the City of Baltimore, 1829-1956. 2 vols. (Ph.D., Catholic University of America, 1958) Has an extensive bibliography which includes much of the state, as well as Baltimore.

Laws, Statutes, Etc.

95. MARYLAND. Dept. of Education. Requirements for Certificates for Administrators, Supervisors, and Teachers. Baltimore: Maryland Dept. of Education, Div. of Certification and Accreditation, 1975. 46 p. Irregular.

Also appears as a number of the Maryland School Bulletin and as a publication of the Maryland State Teachers Association.

Kept up to date by the Maryland Dept. of Education Div. of Certification and Accreditation Certification Newsletter, which in addition provides information relevant to preparation for certification.

96. MARYLAND. Laws, statutes, etc. The Public School Laws of Maryland, Including the Code of Bylaws of the Maryland State Board of Education. Charlottesville, Va.: The Michie Co., 1975. 596 p. Irregular.

Reprinted from the Annotated Code of Maryland, 1957 and 1975 Cumulative Supplement; also issued by the Maryland Dept. of Education as Maryland School Bulletin 51, no. 1 (June 1975).

Provides annotations and interpretations, court cases, and indexes to the laws which apply to education in Maryland.

Statistics

97. MARYLAND. Council for Higher Education. Higher Education Data Book [1972/1973-] Annapolis: 1973- . Annual.

Survey and data on number of students, faculty, facilities, finance, and academic programs of all accredited higher education schools in Maryland.

98. MARYLAND. Dept. of Education. Annual Report; A Statistical Review for the Year Ending [1865-] Baltimore. Annual. Title varies.

Covers such things as enrollment in public, parochial, and private schools, special education, staff, adult education, finances. Some of the data covers the past ten years.

99. MARYLAND. Dept. of Education. Facts about Maryland Schools; A Statistical Handbook [1967/1968-] Baltimore: 1968- . Annual. Title varies.

A summary of data and information about public education, such as enrollment, staff, adult education, and Maryland's ranking relative to the other states.

Individual Institutions
(arranged by institution)

100. LEONHART, James C. One Hundred Years of the Baltimore City College. Baltimore: Roebuck, 1939. 307 p. illus., ports.

101. KNIPP, Anna H. and Thaddeus P. Thomas. The History of Goucher College. Baltimore: Goucher College, 1938. 659 p.

102. FRENCH, John C. A History of the University Founded by Johns Hopkins. Baltimore: Johns Hopkins Press, 1946. 492 p. illus., ports.

Continued by

103. HAWKINS, Hugh. Pioneer: A History of the Johns Hopkins University, 1874-1889. Ithaca, N.Y.: Cornell University Press, 1960. 368 p.

104. RYAN, John J. Historical Sketch of Loyola College, Baltimore, 1852-1902. N.p.: 1903. 247 p.

105. CALCOTT, George H. A History of the University of Maryland. Baltimore: Maryland Historical Society, 1966. 422 p. illus.

106. FOX, William L. Montgomery's First Community College. Rockville, Md.: Montgomery College, 1970. 115 p.

107. CAMERON, Mary D. College of Notre Dame of Baltimore, 1895-1945. New York: D. X. McMullen Co., 1947. 219 p. illus., ports.

108. RYAN, Edmund G., S.J. An Academic History of Woodstock College in Maryland (1869-1944): The First Jesuit Seminary in North America. 269 p. (Ph.D., Catholic University of America, 1964)

FINE ARTS

109. PRIME, Alfred C. The Arts and Crafts in Philadelphia, Maryland, and South Carolina [1721-1800]; Gleanings from Newspapers. Topsfield, Mass.: Walpole Society, 1929-1932. 2 vols. illus., ports.

    A classified record, by crafts, of notices and advertisements of the work of artists and artisans appearing in 18th century newspapers, including the Maryland Journal (Baltimore), 1773-1795, and Maryland Gazette (Annapolis), 1729-1796.

Baltimore

110. RUSK, William S. Art in Baltimore: Monuments and Memorials. Rev. ed. Baltimore: Norman, Remington, 1929. 147 p. illus.

    A handbook of Baltimore's public monuments and memorials, giving for each its history and description, the career of the subject, the inscription, the sculptor, and criticism of the monument as a work of art.

Architecture

111. BEIRNE, Rosamond R. and John H. Scarff. William Buckland, 1734-1774: Architect of Virginia and Maryland. Baltimore: Maryland Historical Society, 1958. 175 p. illus., port., map. (Maryland Historical Society. Studies in Maryland History, no. 4)

    Chapter 6 deals with his work in Annapolis.

112. COFFIN, Lewis A. and Arthur C. Holden. Brick Architecture of the Colonial Period in Maryland and Virginia. New York: Architectural Book Publishing Co., 1919. 118 plates. illus.

    Photographs and drawings with measurements.

    A complementary work:

    RIDGELY, Helen W. The Old Brick Churches of Maryland. Illustrated by Sophie De Butts Stewart. New York: A.D.F. Randolph and Co., 1894. 129 p. illus. Also contains many anecdotes about Maryland history.

113. FORMAN, Henry C. Early Manor and Plantation Houses of Maryland; An Architectural and Historical Compendium, 1634-1800. Easton, Md.: 1934. 271 p. illus.

Views, descriptions, and plans of about 300 manors and houses and a chronological table of dates of houses. (Omits 40 or so of the great mansions because of coverage in other works.) Arranged by county, each with an architectural analysis as an introduction.

Complementary to this:

FORMAN, Henry C. Maryland Architecture; A Short History, from 1634 through the Civil War. Cambridge, Md.: Tidewater Publishers, 1968. 102 p. illus. A historical overview by architectural style.

FORMAN, Henry C. Tidewater Maryland Architecture and Gardens. New York: Architectural Book Publishing Co., 1956. 208 p. illus. Arranged regionally: Lower Eastern Shore, Upper Eastern Shore, Southern Maryland, Upper Bay and Baltimore. Provides details on construction.

114. FORMAN, Henry C. Old Buildings, Gardens and Furniture in Tidewater Maryland. Cambridge, Md.: Tidewater Publishers, 1967. 305 p. illus.

Primarily a history of the architecture of colonial plantation homes, with some plans of their gardens and outhouses, and descriptions of household equipment and furniture. Pt. 1 deals with early Maryland and pts. 2-5 are organized by region.

Much valuable information for architectural consideration is in

REPS, John W. Tidewater Towns: City Planning in Colonial Virginia and Maryland. Williamsburg, Va.: Colonial Williamsburg Foundation, 1972. 345 p. illus., maps. Chapters on 17th and 18th century town planning in Maryland, with a chapter on Annapolis.

115. HAMMOND, John M. Colonial Mansions of Maryland and Delaware. Philadelphia: J. B. Lippincott Co., 1914. 304 p. illus.

Chapters on 29 Maryland homes commenting on their architectural details and those who were involved with them.

Two useful illustrated works on colonial houses:

SWANN, Don. Colonial and Historic Houses of Maryland. One hundred original etchings with a descriptive text by Don Swann, Jr. Baltimore: Johns Hopkins University Press, 1975. 224 p. Reprint of 1939 edition.

WILSON, Everett B. Maryland's Colonial Mansions and Other Early Houses. New York: A. S. Barnes and Co., 1965. 249 p. Photographs of 202 early houses, some inside detail, furniture.

Architecture - Annapolis

116. DAVIS, Deering. Annapolis Houses, 1700-1775. New York: Book Bonanza, 1963. 124 p. illus., ports., map.

Reprint of 1947 edition.

Bibliography: p. 121.

Covers the early history of Annapolis, the architecture of Annapolis, the work of William Buckland, and individual houses and their histories.

Also of interest:

BEIRNE, Rosamond R. and Edith R. Bevan. The Hammond-Harwood House and Its Owners. Rev. ed. Annapolis: 1954. 63 p. illus., ports. A brief informal account of one outstanding home.

HISTORIC ANNAPOLIS, Inc. A Guide to Domestic and Commercial Architectural Styles in Annapolis. Annapolis: 1975. 23 p. illus., map. An introduction to the significant characteristics of 15 architectural styles, indicating where these styles may be found in Annapolis houses.

117. RADOFF, Morris L. Buildings of the State of Maryland at Annapolis. Annapolis: Maryland Hall of Records, 1954. 140 p. illus. (Maryland. Hall of Records. Publication no. 9)

A documentary history with useful architectural and urban history.

118. RADOFF, Morris L. The State House at Annapolis. Annapolis: Maryland Hall of Records, 1972. 128 p. illus., maps. (Maryland. Hall of Records Publication no. 17)

Supersedes the material in his Buildings of the State of Maryland at Annapolis (1954).

Bibliographical footnotes.

Records the process of construction of America's oldest state capitol, the changes made in it, and the men who worked on it. Contains verbatim copies of the plaques and inscriptions in the Capitol.

Architecture - Baltimore

119. ALEXANDER, Robert L. The Architecture of Maximilian Godefroy. Baltimore: Johns Hopkins University Press, 1974. 246 p. illus., port.

During his stay in Baltimore from 1805 to 1819, Godefroy was involved with every public building in the City. This careful study on the architectural history of the city offers information on such structures as St. Mary's Chapel, the Unitarian Church, and the Battle Monument, and is a valuable guide to his work that still stands.

120. DORSEY, John R. and James D. Dilts. A Guide to Baltimore Architecture. Foreword by John Dos Passos. Cambridge, Md.: Tidewater Publishers in cooperation with the Peale Museum, 1973. 246 p. illus., maps.

A guidebook for 13 architectural excursions through old and new Baltimore. Each part has a historical, architectural, and cultural introduction, and for each structure included there is a note on its construction and architectural details.

121. HOWLAND, Richard H. and Eleanor P. Spencer. The Architecture of Baltimore, A Pictorial History. Baltimore: Johns Hopkins Press, 1953. 149 p. illus., maps.

The standard work, covering the period to the early 20th century.

Several shorter works which deal with particular structures:

DEHLER, Katherine B. The Thomas-Jencks-Gladding House; One West Mt. Vernon Place. Contemporary photos by A. Aubrey Bodine. Baltimore: Bodine, 1968. 84 p. illus.

HUNTER, Wilbur H. The Story of America's Oldest Museum Building. Baltimore: The Peale Museum, 1964. 36 p. illus., ports.

MILLER, J. Jefferson, II. The Washington Monument in Baltimore. Baltimore: Peale Museum, 1966. 15 p.

Architecture - Montgomery County

122. FARQUHAR, Roger B. Old Homes and History of Montgomery County, Maryland. 2d ed. Silver Spring, Md.: 1962. 366 p. illus.

Bibliography: p. 356.

Gives a brief history of the County, with separate chapters on such topics as education, agriculture, government. The largest part of the work consists of photographs and commentary on the homes. (There is a brief section on historic Georgetown houses.)

Clothing

123. MARYLAND HISTORICAL SOCIETY. Parade of Maryland Fashion. Baltimore: 1970. 35 p. illus.

Primarily women's dress.

Cooking

124. ANDREWS, Wilson H. (Nelson) and Frances H. Kelley. Maryland's Way; As Told by a Collection of Traditional Receipts, Selected from Three Centuries of Maryland Cooking. 8th ed. Annapolis: Hammond-Harwood House Association, 1975 (c1966). 372 p. illus.

    Bicentennial edition.

    The recipes are based on those found in early Maryland notebooks. The source, date, and the place associated with it are indicated for each.

125. MARYLAND Seafood Cookbook. Annapolis: Maryland Seafood Marketing Authority, 1973. 48 p. illus.

    Over 60 recipes for crab, clam, fish, lobster, and oyster.

126. STIEFF, Frederick P. Eat, Drink & Be Merry in Maryland: An Anthology from a Great Tradition. Illus. by Edwin Tunis. New York: G. P. Putnam's Sons, 1932. 326 p. illus., maps.

    Over 500 recipes "obtained at the source": old manor houses, inns, taverns, etc. No recipe was taken from a printed page unless that source was over 100 years old.

    Useful for anecdotal materials:

    LATROBE, Ferdinand C. Chesapeake Bay Cook Book: Bayfood Edition. Baltimore: 1956. 54 p.

    LATROBE, Ferdinand C. The Diamondback Terrapin. Baltimore: Twentieth Century Press, 1939. 29 p. illus.

127. TAWES, Helen A. My Favorite Maryland Recipes. New York: Random House, 1964. 179 p. illus.

    The wife of the former Maryland Governor and the daughter of a famous cook provides Maryland recipes from the past and the present, as well as more than 30 complete menus served at the Executive Mansion.

Furniture

128. BALTIMORE. Museum of Art. Maryland Queen Anne and Chippendale Furniture of the Eighteenth Century. New York: Published by October House for the Baltimore Museum of Art, 1968. 128 p. illus., map.

    Records and establishes Maryland cabinetmaking in the decorative arts with 178 photographs of the pieces exhibited at the Baltimore Museum of Arts in 1968. Also has lists of Maryland cabinetmakers and clockmakers.

    Additional information on furniture makers:

BERKLEY, Henry J. "A Register of the Cabinet Makers and Allied Trades in Maryland, As Shown by the Newspapers and Directories, 1746 to 1820." Maryland Historical Magazine 25 (1940): 1-27.

Furniture - Baltimore

129. BALTIMORE. Museum of Art. Baltimore Furniture; The Work of Baltimore and Annapolis Cabinetmakers from 1760 to 1810. Baltimore: 1947. 195 p. illus.

Deals with the furniture of the Hepplewhite-Sheraton period with a separate section on the Chippendale period. There are photographs of the 125 pieces with descriptions and provenance. Includes a register of Annapolis and Baltimore cabinetmakers of 1760-1810.

130. ELDER, William V. Baltimore Painted Furniture, 1800-1840. Introd. and commentary by William V. Elder, III. Baltimore: Baltimore Museum of Art, 1972. 132 p. illus.

An overview of the work of Baltimore cabinetmakers and decorative artists. Lists "Cabinetmakers and Allied Tradesmen Working in Baltimore, 1800-1840," p. 93-129.

Glass

131. FORD, Everett and Janice Ford. Pre-Prohibition Beer Bottles and Breweries of Baltimore. [Baltimore] 1974. 46 p. illus.

Gives breweries with historical information, illustrations and descriptions of the bottles of Baltimore breweries, breweries distributing in Baltimore, Baltimore beer bottlers, and bottle manufacturers.

132. MARYLAND HISTORICAL SOCIETY. Amelung Glass: An Exhibition of Wares from New Bremen, Maryland. Baltimore: 1952. 20 p. illus.

Foreword by James W. Foster.

Bibliography: p. 20.

Movies

133. HEADLEY, Robert K., Jr. Exit: A History of Movies in Baltimore. University Park, Md.: 1974. 162 p. illus.

Provides a listing and description of the movie houses in the Baltimore area.

Music - Baltimore

134. CLARK, Kenneth S. Baltimore, Cradle of Municipal Music (Anniversary Edition) Baltimore: Republished by the City of Baltimore, 1941. 64 p. illus.

    An informal history of the public support for music in Baltimore and of the Baltimore Symphony Orchestra from 1914 to 1941. Lists compositions played by the Orchestra for 1916-1941, soloists, and guest conductors.

135. KEEFER, Lubov B. Baltimore's Music; The Haven of the American Composer. Baltimore: 1962. 343 p.

    Bibliography: p. 298-312.

    A historical survey of serious music with valuable material on Asger Hamerik, Hans Bülow, George Peabody and the Peabody Institute, and the German contribution.

Painting and Illustration

136. BALTIMORE. Museum of Art. Two Hundred and Fifty Years of Painting in Maryland. Baltimore: 1945. 78 p. illus.

    Includes "A Survey of Painting in Maryland," by J. Hall Pleasants.

    Discusses 200 pictures, a large number of which are shown, by the more important 18th and 19th century Maryland painters. The detailed notes on both the artists and their subjects make it a valuable source for the history of painting in Maryland.

137. McCAULEY, Lois B. Maryland Historical Prints, 1752 to 1889; A Selection from the Robert G. Merrick Collection, Maryland Historical Society and Other Maryland Collections. Baltimore: Maryland Historical Society, 1975. 259 p. illus.

    Bibliography: p. 243-249.

    Contains 338 engravings and lithographs, representing a pictorial record of Maryland and Baltimore. Each print is described as to location and historical significance, and is analyzed. Includes biographical sketches of each printmaker represented.

Pottery

138. HOLLAND, Eugenia C. Edwin Bennett and the Products of His Baltimore Pottery. Baltimore: Maryland Historical Society, 1973. 44 p. illus.

    Bibliography: p. 20-24.

Offers a biographical sketch, an account of his work, formulas and pottery marks, and a description of 132 items.

A check list of Baltimore potters is given in

PEARCE, John N. The Early Baltimore Potters and Their Wares, 1763-1850. 150 p. (M.A., University of Delaware, 1959)

Silver

139. BALTIMORE. Museum of Art. Eighteenth and Nineteenth Century Maryland Silver in the Collection of the Baltimore Museum of Art ... Text by Jennifer F. Gouldsborough; edited by Ann B. Harper. Baltimore: 1975. 204 p. illus.

"Selected Bibliography": p. 201-204.

An illustrated catalog of pieces with descriptive notes and, for many items, hallmarks. Separate sections on Maryland silver, Maryland silversmiths with their marks, and marks on Maryland silver.

140. HILL, Harry W. Maryland's Colonial Charm Portrayed in Silver. Baltimore: Waverly Press, 1938. 269 p. illus.

A shorter edition was published in 1963.

Bibliography: p. 267-269.

A description of the scenes on the silver service presented by the Citizens of Maryland to the cruiser Maryland.

141. PLEASANTS, Jacob H. and Howard Sill. Maryland Silversmiths, 1715-1830, with Illustrations of Their Silver and Their Marks and with a Facsimile of the Design Book of William Faris. Harrison, N.Y.: Robert Alan Green, Publisher, 1972. 324 p. illus., ports.

Reprint of 1930 edition.

Encyclopedia of silversmiths and clock and watchmakers, covering the activities of silversmiths throughout Maryland with biographical information and their marks. Chapters on the Baltimore Assay Office and silversmith marks, lists of apprentices, indentured silversmiths, Maryland watch and clock makers not known to have worked as silversmiths, and a table of initials of Maryland silversmiths, watch and clock makers, and allied craftsmen.

FOLKLORE

142. CAREY, George G. The Faraway Time and Place; Lore of the Eastern Shore. Washington: Robert B. Luce, 1971. 256 p. illus.

    The folk culture of the maritime Eastern Shore, with an emphasis on the white waterman in the region between the Nanticoke and Pocomoke Rivers. Contains anecdotes on heroes, tall tales and windies, stories and jests, legends, belief tales and popular belief, folk speech and naming, and folk verse and riddles.

143. CAREY, George G. Maryland Folk Legends and Folk Songs. Cambridge, Md.: Tidewater Publishers, 1971. 120 p. illus.

    An enlarged version of his "An Introductory Guide to Maryland Folklore and Folklife." In Maryland Study Commission on Maryland Folklore. Final Report, pt. 1 (1970).

    Bibliography: p. 92-93.

    Stresses the Eastern Shore and Western Maryland. Chapters on haunted places and remarkable events, local folk heroes and characters, urban and modern legends, and Mrs. Alice Ridgeway Tucker.

144. WHITNEY, Annie W. and Caroline C. Bullock. Folk-Lore from Maryland. New York: Kraus, 1969. 239 p. (American Folklore Society. Memoirs, vol. 28)

    Reprint of 1925 edition.

    A classified listing of sayings, including such categories as omens, rural life, charms, ghosts, devil, conjuring, and Christmas. Rhymes, games and songs, riddles, and tales are treated separately.

GENEALOGY

Bibliography

145. PASSANO, Eleanor P. An Index of the Source Records of Maryland, Genealogical, Biographical, Historical. Baltimore: Waverly Press, 1967. 478 p.

    Reprint of 1940 edition.

    Bibliography: p. 363-466; "Bibliography of Other States Containing References to Maryland Families": p. 467-478.

    A primary source book (though there are errors, omissions, and some items no longer available) that lists and indicates the location of Maryland reference materials and records of families or individuals who have lived in Maryland. The first part is an index containing approximately 20,000 surnames.

Guides

146. MEYER, Mary K. Genealogical Research in Maryland: A Guide. Rev. and enl. ed. Baltimore: Maryland Historical Society, 1976. 109 p.

    Bibliography: p. 61-108.

    A well organized introduction to the significant genealogical collections in Maryland; sources for available records, including church, tax, census, military, etc.; general and county bibliographical material. In addition there are directories of county historical societies and genealogical publishers in Maryland. Important current genealogical accessions to the Maryland Historical Society are listed in the Maryland Historical Magazine 66 (1971)- .

    Other helpful guides:

    BROWN, Mary R. An Illustrated Genealogy of the Counties of Maryland and the District of Columbia as a Guide for Locating Records. Baltimore: Maryland Historical Society, 1967. 64 p. maps. Useful for indicating the county boundary changes which have taken place in Maryland.

    McCAY, Betty L. Sources for Genealogical Searching in Maryland. Indianapolis: 1972. 21 p. Lists items under records, such as census, land, and court. Also provides information on genealogical magazines, maps and atlases, libraries and historical societies, and guides and references.

Heraldry

147. NEWMAN, Harry W. Heraldic Marylandiana; A Compilation of Maryland Armorial Families Which Used Coats of Arms in the Colonial and Early Post-Revolutionary Periods... Washington: 1968. 188 p. illus.

    A dictionary of Maryland seals and shields, giving brief description, historical note, and the source of the reference.

Records - General

148. BRUMBAUGH, Gaius M. Maryland Records, Colonial, Revolutionary, County and Church, from Original Sources. Baltimore: Williams and Wilkins, 1915-1928. 2 vols. map.

    Includes the 1776 census records for Prince George's Frederick, Charles, Anne Arundel, Caroline, Dorchester, Harford, Queen Anne's, and Talbot Counties; marriage licenses for Prince George's, Frederick, St. Mary's, Anne Arundel, Charles, Montgomery, and Washington Counties; tombstone inscriptions and poll tax records for Frederick County; muster rolls for Prince George's County; oaths of fidelity for Harford and Prince George's Counties; land tax and naturalization records; and some Revolutionary War pension records.

149. HARTSTOCK, Elisabeth and Gust Skordas. Land Office and Prerogative Court Records of Colonial Maryland. Annapolis: Maryland Hall of Records, 1946. 124 p. (Maryland. Hall of Records. Publication no. 4)

    An inventory of those records located at the Maryland Hall of Records which provide county land inventories, estate accounts, and wills to 1777.

Records - Census

150. U.S. Bureau of the Census. Heads of Families at the First Census of the United States Taken in the Year 1790: Maryland. Baltimore: Genealogical Publishing Co., 1965. 189 p.

    Reprint of 1907 edition.

    Arranged by county, it shows the number of free white males 16 and upward, under 16, free white females, all other free persons, and slaves. Index of names.

Records - Land Patents

151. SKORDAS, Gust. The Early Settlers of Maryland; An Index to Names of Immigrants Compiled from Records of Land Patents, 1633-1680, in the Hall of Records, Annapolis, Maryland. Genealogical Publishing Co., 1968. 525 p.

Based on J. M. Brewer and others, List of Early Maryland Settlers, 1634-1682, completed by Arthur Trader.

An alphabetical listing indicating in what record book the name was found; adds remarks which act as further identification.

Records - Marriage

152. BARNES, Robert W. Marriages and Deaths from the Maryland Gazette, 1727-1839. Baltimore: Genealogical Publishing Co., 1973. 233 p.

Bibliography: p. 226-227.

Lists, alphabetically, approximately 3,000 abstracts published in Maryland's oldest newspaper. The appendix contains abstracts on clergy mentioned in the marriage notices. Index of brides and others named.

Also useful:

RIDGELY, Helen W. Historic Graves of Maryland and the District of Columbia... Baltimore: Genealogical Publishing Co., 1967. 296 p. illus. Reprint of 1908 edition. A narrative account covering the colonial and revolutionary period, arranged by county, which is replete with local history. Includes many private burial places.

153. BARNES, Robert W. Maryland Marriages, 1634-1777. Baltimore: Genealogical Publishing Co., 1975. 233 p.

An alphabetical listing of names located in church records and other documents at the Maryland Historical Society and the Maryland Hall of Records.

See also

MEYER, Mary K. Divorces and Names Changed in Maryland by Act of the Legislature, 1634-1854. Pasadena, Md.: 1970. 143 p. An alphabetical listing of names located in the published Laws of Maryland up to 1854.

Records - Wills

154. COTTON, Jane B. The Maryland Calendar of Wills. Baltimore: Genealogical Publishing Co., 1968. 8 vols.

Reprint of 1904-1928 edition.

Vols. 4-7 compiled by Jane B. Cotton and Roberta B. Henry.

A chronological listing of abstracts for the period 1635 to 1743, representing 23 original will volumes in the Maryland Hall of Records. Abstract indicates occupation, place of residence, persons mentioned, executors, and location in original volume. Index of persons and places.

155. HUME, Joan. American Index Library. Maryland. Baltimore: Magna Carta Book Co., 1970. 4 vols.

Vol. 1: Allegany County, 1784-1960; vol. 2: St. Mary's County, 1622-1960; Somerset County, 1664-1955; vol. 3: Garrett County, 1872-1960; Harford County, 1774-1960; vol. 4: Howard County, 1774-1960; Kent County, 1674-1960.

Index of wills located at county court houses.

156. MAGRUDER, James M. Index to Maryland Colonial Wills, 1634-1777, in the Hall of Records, Annapolis, Md. With a new introd. and additions by Louise E. Magruder. Baltimore: Genealogical Publishing Co., 1967. 3 vols. in 1.

Reprint of 1933 edition.

Alphabetical listing of testators in the 41 volumes of the Maryland Hall of Records' Land Office records, giving year of probate, county, and the reference to where found.

157. MAGRUDER, James M. Magruder's Maryland Colonial Abstracts: Wills, Accounts and Inventories, 1772-1777. Baltimore: Genealogical Publishing Co., 1968. 5 vols. in 1.

Reprint of 1934-1939 edition.

Based on Maryland Land Office records. General and testators' indexes.

Registers and Rosters - Revolutionary War

158. BRUMBAUGH, Gaius M. and Margaret R. Hodges. Revolutionary Records of Maryland. Washington: Rufus H. Darby Printing Co., 1924. 56 p.

Records of the oaths of fidelity for Calvert, Montgomery, Prince George's, and Washington Counties.

159. MARYLAND HISTORICAL SOCIETY. Muster Rolls and Other Records of Service of Maryland Troops in the American Revolution, 1775-1783. Baltimore: Genealogical Publishing Co., 1972. 736 p. (Archives of Maryland, vol. 18)

Reprint of 1900 edition.

The various lists are printed as found. General index of names.

160. STEUART, Rieman. A History of the Maryland Line in the Revolutionary War, 1775-1783. Towson, Md.: Society of the Cincinnati, 1969. 169 p.

A record of the roster of companies; includes biographical sketches of officers from Maryland.

Registers and Rosters - War of 1812

161. HICKMAN, Nathaniel, ed. The Citizen Soldiers at North Point and Fort McHenry, September 12 & 13, 1814. Baltimore: C. C. Saffell, 1889. 137 p.

Rosters of Maryland units.

Registers and Rosters - Civil War

162. MARYLAND. Commission on the Publication of the Histories of the Maryland Volunteers During the Civil War. History and Roster of Maryland Volunteers, War of 1861-5. Baltimore: Guggenheimer, Weil & Co., 1898-1899. 2 vols.

Vol. 1 includes the history and roster of Maryland units; vol. 2 includes sailors, marines, and colored troops. For each, gives rank, enlistment and discharge dates, and remarks on status.

Registers and Rosters - Spanish American War

163. RILEY, Hugh R. and Charles S. Carrington. Roster of the Soldiers and Sailors Who Served in Organizations from Maryland During the Spanish-American War. Compiled under the authority of the House of Delegates of Maryland. Baltimore: J. C. Dulaney Co., 1901. 51 p.

Registers and Rosters - World War I

164. MARYLAND. War Records Commission. Maryland in the World War, 1917-1919; Military and Naval Service Records. Baltimore: Maryland War Records Commission, 1933. 2 vols. maps.

Vol. 1: Introduction. Service Records A to J. Vol. 2: Service Records J to Z.

Registers and Rosters - World War II

165. MARYLAND HISTORICAL SOCIETY. War Records Division. Maryland in World War II; Register of Service Personnel. Prepared for the State of Maryland. Baltimore: 1965. 5 vols.

Lists name, rank, branch of service, serial number, and the community of those Marylanders who served from September 1, 1940, to December 31, 1946. Indicates those who died while in service.

GEOGRAPHY

166. DANDO, William A. and Thomas D. Rabenhorst. Introduction to Maryland. Fenton, Mich.: American Geographic, 1970. 59 p. illus., maps.

    Introduction to Maryland geography for schools.

    Also for school use:

    ROLLO, Vera A. F. Ask Me! (About Maryland); A Geography of Maryland. Lanham, Md.: Maryland Historical Press, 1975. 68 p. illus.

167. MARYLAND. Geological Survey. County Reports. Baltimore: 1900- . Irregular.

    Each volume deals with the geography, natural resources, and industries of a county. This includes Allegany (1900), Anne Arundel (1916), Baltimore (1929), Calvert (1907), Carroll and Frederick (1946), Cecil (1902), Charles (1948), Garrett (1902), Harford (1969), Howard and Montgomery (1964), Kent (1926), Prince George's (1911), Queen Anne's (1926), St. Mary's (1907), Talbot (1927), and Washington (1951).

    Also available for Calvert County:

    DANDO, William A. and Thomas D. Rabenhorst. Atlas of Calvert County. College Park, Md.: University of Maryland Dept. of Geography, 1969. 36 p. maps. Separate chapters on modern economics, geography, etc.

168. VOKES, Harold E. Geography and Geology of Maryland. Rev. ed. Baltimore: Maryland Geological Survey, 1968. 243 p. maps. (Maryland. Geological Survey. Bulletin no. 19)

    Offers an encyclopedic non-technical compendium of the physical features, natural resources, climate, and economic geography of Maryland, as well as a technical presentation of the geology of Maryland.

    Older works which are, nevertheless, still valuable:

    ABBE, Cleveland, Jr. "A General Report on the Physiography of Maryland." In Maryland. Weather Service. [Reports] 1899. Vol. 1, pt. 2, p. 41-216. illus., maps. A general discussion of the more important physiographic features of Maryland.

CLARK, Bullock, Edward B. Mathews, and others. "The Physical Features of Maryland." In Maryland. Geological Survey. Reports, vol. 6, pt. 1, p. 27-261. Baltimore: Johns Hopkins Press, 1906. illus. Includes detailed descriptions of the early investigations of the State's physical features: physiography, geology, mineral resources, agricultural soils, climate, hydrography, forestry, and characteristic fossils of Maryland formations.

Less extensive is the following:

CLARK, William B. "The Geography of Maryland." In Maryland. Geological Survey. Report, vol. 10, pt. 1, p. 39-168. Baltimore: Johns Hopkins Press, 1918. illus. Popular summary of physical features of Maryland. After general introductory essay on Maryland, it covers geology; physiography; climate; flora and fauna; natural resources, including mineral resources, soils and crops, forests, water products; manufacturers; cities and towns; suggestions for physiographic and geologic excursions.

Boundaries

169. BAYLIFF, William H. The Maryland-Pennsylvania and Maryland-Delaware Boundaries. 2d ed. Annapolis: Maryland Board of Natural Resources, 1959. 120 p. illus., maps. (Maryland. Board of Natural Resources. Bulletin no. 4)

References: p. 49-50.

Deals with the history of the boundary controversy, the Mason and Dixon surveys, resurveys, and the 1950 boundary inspections, with photographs of the boundary markers.

Other sources of information on markers:

MATHEWS, Edward B. and Wilbur A. Nelson. Report on the Marking of the Boundary Line Along the Potomac River in Accordance with the Award of 1877. Baltimore: Waverly Press, 1930. 33 p. maps.

U.S. Coast and Geodetic Survey. Tidal Bench Marks, Maryland. T-20. [Washington] 1939. 61 p.; and its Supplement A. T-20A. [Washington] 1942. 13 p. Gives the location and elevations of the mean low and high water level as established by the U.S. Coast and Geodetic Survey and other federal, state, and municipal organizations.

170. MARYLAND. Geological Survey. Report on the Resurvey of the Maryland-Pennsylvania Boundary, Part of the Mason and Dixon Line. Baltimore: 1908. 412 p. illus., maps. (Its Report, vol. 7)

Reprinted 1909.

Devoted to the resurvey of the official boundary between Maryland and Pennsylvania. Pt. 3 (p. 103-203): Edward B. Mathews, "History of the Boundary Dispute Between the

Baltimores and the Penns Resulting in the Original Mason and Dixon Line." Pt. 4 (p. 205-403): Edward L. Burchard and Edward B. Mathews, "Manuscripts and Publications Relating to the Mason and Dixon Line and Other Lines in Pennsylvania, Maryland and the Virginias involving the Charter Rights of Lord Baltimore and the Penns."

Mathews' work is a narrative account of the tensions, legal actions, efforts of the various surveys, and arrangements to 1892; Burchard and Mathews' work is a comprehensive bibliography which includes manuscript and published sources (even parts of books) with notes or abstracts and publication information.

Maps and Map-Making

171. MATHEWS, Edward B. "Bibliography and Cartography of Maryland, Including Publications Relating to the Physiography, Geology, and Mineral Resources." In Maryland. Geological Survey. Report, vol. 1, pt. 4, p. 229-332. Baltimore: Johns Hopkins Press, 1897.

    A chronological listing, covering 1612 to 1896, of monographs, reports, journal articles, and even parts of works which discuss Maryland. A brief descriptive note is provided for many of the items.

172. MATHEWS, Edward B. Maps and Map-Makers of Maryland, Including a History of Cartographic Progress in Maryland. Baltimore: Johns Hopkins Press, 1898. 337-488 p. maps.

    Reprint of Maryland. Geological Survey. Special Publication, vol. 2, pt. 3b, p. 337-488 (1898).

    Bibliographical footnotes.

    A chronological resumé of the cartography of Maryland from the early European maps to the geologic, magnetic, and climatological maps of the 1897 geological survey. Depicts the conditions under which the earliest maps were drawn, produced, and published. Includes information on the maps of the boundary controversies, county atlases, the early work of the U.S. Coast and Geodetic Survey in Maryland, and the Maryland Geological Survey.

HEALTH AND WELFARE

Directories

173. BALTIMORE. Health Dept. Directory of Mental Health and Mental Retardation Services with Related and Allied Resources, 1969. Baltimore: 1969. 337 p.

 Pt. 1: Alphabetized listing of public and private agencies whose primary purpose is or which have organizational units dedicated to serving the emotionally or mentally ill; pt. 2: Allied or related services which may be utilized in habilitation or rehabilitation; pt. 3: Comprehensive services for special populations. Analytical index.

174. DIRECTORY of Community Services in Maryland. 15th ed. Baltimore: Health and Welfare Council of Central Maryland, 1975. 476 p.

 Lists approximately 1,800 agencies and organizations with a major concern for the sponsorship or operation of a continuing program of service to Maryland citizens in employment, court, corrections, police, and planning. Arranged alphabetically, giving the address, telephone number, name of executive or president, short statement on function, and source of funding. Subject and geographic indexes.

175. DIRECTORY of Services for Handicapped Children. A Listing of Services in Maryland for Children, Adolescents, and Young Adults with Physical, Mental and Emotional Handicaps, Other Special Health Conditions and Learning Problems. Compiled by the Kennedy Council of the John F. Kennedy Institute for Habilitation of the Mentally and Physically Handicapped Child in collaboration with the United Order of True Sisters. Baltimore: 1973. 602 p.

 Public and private agencies, arranged by county, giving persons who are served, staff, admissions procedures, and description. County, handicapping condition, and service indexes.

176. MARYLAND. Dept. of Health and Mental Hygiene. Directory of Maryland Mental Health Facilities and Alcoholic Treatment Centers. 1975 ed. Baltimore: 1975. Irregular. Title varies.

Public and private programs, arranged by county and Baltimore City. Includes the Regional Health Director for each county, telephone numbers, and for larger facilities hours of service. Since 1972 this agency has also issued a Directory of Facilities (Baltimore: 1972-) indicating what services are available in the Department itself.

177. MARYLAND. Dept. of Social Services. Directory of Special Child Care Resources in Maryland--Voluntary Agencies and Institutions. Baltimore: 1967. 1 vol. (looseleaf)

Kept up to date with supplementary materials.

In two sections, institutions and agencies. Under each resource listed, it provides description of purpose and auspices, staffing, population served, the facility, daily living experience, professional services, referral procedure and admission criteria, and continuing services and discharge planning.

178. MARYLAND. Drug Abuse Administration. Comprehensive Guide of Organizations Offering Services for Drug Related Problems. Rev. 5th ed. Baltimore: 1974. 58 p.

Public and private agencies arranged by geographical areas. Information includes services offered, eligibility, and telephone number.

HISTORY

Archival and Manuscript Sources

179. ARCHIVES of Maryland...[vol. 1-   ] Published by authority of the State under the direction of the Maryland Historical Society. Baltimore: Maryland Historical Society, 1883-   .

    A valuable primary source for colonial and early state history. Sub-series includes Proceedings and Acts of the General Assembly, 1637-1774 (32 vols.); Proceedings of the Council, 1777-1784 (8 vols.); Proceedings of the Provincial Court, 1637-1679 (9 vols.); as well as records of the Council of Safety, County Courts, correspondence of Governor Horatio Sharpe, 1757-1761, and muster rolls and other records of Revolutionary War service.

180. MARYLAND. Hall of Records. Calendar of Maryland State Papers, Nos. 1-5. Annapolis: 1943-1958. 5 vols. in 7 vols. (Its Publications, nos. 1, 6, 7, 8, 10)

    The Rainbow Series: No. 1, Black Books; No. 2, Bank Stock Papers (Blue Books); No. 3, Brown Books; No. 4, Red Books (3 parts); No. 5, Executive Miscellanea.

    Abstracts of communications and documents in the Maryland Hall of Records, primarily in the colonial period and early 19th century, with publication information. Indexes of names and places.

181. MARYLAND. Hall of Records. Catalogue of Archival Material, Hall of Records, State of Maryland. Annapolis: 1942. 161 p. (Its Publications, no. 2)

    A record of its holdings of state and local public records, church records, private papers, and newspapers. Each section has an introductory sketch.

182. MARYLAND. Hall of Records. The County Courthouses and Records of Maryland. Annapolis: 1960-1963. 2 vols. illus. (Its Publications, nos. 12-13)

    Bibliographical footnotes.

    Vol. 1 provides a brief history of the courts of each county and Baltimore City and of the courthouses; vol.

2 is an inventory of county records, wherever found. The introductory sections in vol. 2 provide a sketch of Maryland county governments and the records they produce, as well as a glossary of terms.

This can be supplemented by

HISTORICAL RECORDS SURVEY. Maryland. Inventory of the County and Town Archives of Maryland. Baltimore: 1937-1941. 8 vols. No. 1: Allegany; no. 2: Anne Arundel; no. 6: Carroll; no. 11: Garrett; no. 13: Howard; no. 15: Montgomery; no. 21: Washington; no. 22: Wicomico.

183. PEDLEY, Avril J. The Manuscript Collections of the Maryland Historical Society. Baltimore: Maryland Historical Society, 1968. 390 p.

Lists 1,724 manuscript collections containing over one million items acquired from 1844 to 1968. Represents primary research materials on Maryland and the nation for social, economic, military, political, and religious history. Especially valuable for the colonial and antebellum period.

Kept current by

"ACCESSIONS of the Manuscript Division Since the Publication of Manuscript Collections of Maryland Historical Society in August 1968." Maryland Historical Magazine 68 (1973)- . Irregular.

Archival and Manuscript Sources - Montgomery County

184. MALLOY, Mary G. and Jane Sween. A Selective Guide to the Historic Records of Montgomery County, Maryland. Rockville, Md.: Montgomery County Dept. of Public Libraries, 1974. 36 p.

A directory of agencies and organizations, indicating resources available and services provided.

Atlas

185. RAYMOND, PARISH, PINE & PLAVNIK. The State of Maryland Historical Atlas; A Review of Events and Forces. Annapolis: Maryland Dept. of Economic and Community Development, 1973. 62 p. illus., maps.

Through the use of such themes as people who have lived in Maryland, traditions of home building and town planning, institutions for religion and education, transportation, and Black history, this reviews significant events and forces, identifies the sites on which they occurred, and illustrates the relationship between the sites and the events.

Bibliographic Guide

186. MANAKEE, Harold R. A Student's Guide to Localized History. New York: Columbia University, Teachers College, 1969. 35 p. map.

An introductory guide to Maryland history with chapters on "Exploration and Settlement," "Colonial Development," "The Revolutionary War," "Growing with the New Nation," "A State Divided," "The State Matures," and "Modern Maryland." Each chapter has a short history of the period, an annotated bibliography of scholarly and juvenile works, and "Objectives for Fieldtrips."

Bibliographies

187. LAWTON, Elizabeth and Raymond S. Sweeney. Maryland History: A Selective Bibliography Showing the Holdings of Some of the Major Libraries in the Baltimore-Washington Metropolitan Area. Rockville, Md.: The Montgomery County Historical Society, 1975. 210 p.

An extensive but unannotated bibliography of books, pamphlets, theses, and dissertations. Arranged by historical period or by such topics as arts and letters, education, medicine, religion.

Other useful bibliographies:

BROWN, Dorothy M. and Richard R. Duncan. "A Selected Bibliography of Articles on Maryland History in Other Journals." Maryland Historical Magazine 69 (1974): 300-316. A retrospective list of approximately 350 items arranged by historical period.

COX, Richard J. "A Bibliography of Articles and Books on Maryland [1974-]" Maryland Historical Magazine 70 (1975)- . Annual. Arranged under topics.

DUNCAN, Richard R. and Dorothy M. Brown. Master's Theses and Doctoral Dissertations on Maryland History. Baltimore: Maryland Historical Society, 1970. 41 p. Lists approximately 650 theses and dissertations accepted by American universities in history, education, economics, political science, and library science.

GIDDENS, Paul H. "Bibliography of Maryland During the Time of Governor Horatio Sharpe, 1753-1769." Maryland Historical Magazine 31 (1936): 6-16.

"MARYLAND Bibliography [1951-1954]" Maryland Historical Magazine 47 (1952)-50 (1955) March issue. Printed references to all phases of Maryland history, and works by Maryland historians, even if not on Maryland, arranged under form of publication, i.e. books, pamphlets and leaflets and journal articles. Does not include articles in the Maryland Historical Magazine.

188. STEINER, Bernard C. Descriptions of Maryland. Baltimore: Johns

Hopkins University, 1904. 94 p. (Johns Hopkins University Studies in Historical and Political Science, ser. 22, nos. 11-12)

A bibliographic essay and chronological bibliography, covering the period from 1526 to 1895, of travelers' accounts and reminiscences of Maryland. Includes parts of books and journal articles, as well as regimental histories and fiction.

This is supplemented by

THOMPSON, Lawrence S. "Foreign Travelers in Maryland, 1900-1950." Maryland Historical Magazine 48 (1953): 337-343. A bibliography and commentary on travel accounts with portions on Maryland, though most deal primarily with Baltimore.

Handbooks

189. HEYL, Edgar G. I Didn't Know That! An Exhibition of First Happenings in Maryland. Baltimore: Maryland Historical Society, 1973. 61 p. illus.

A chronological inventory, from 1634 to 1973, of 176 firsts, ranging from law, religion, ethnic groups to aviation and technology. The source of information for each item is given.

Also containing firsts in Maryland:

GRAHAM, Stirling. You Will Find It in Maryland. Baltimore: Record and Goldsborough, 1945. 91 p. illus.

190. JACKSON, Elmer M., Jr. Maryland Symbols: The Stories Behind Their Selection as Emblems by the Free State's General Assembly, with a Touch of History, Folklore, and an Intimate Glimpse of Fascinating Wildlife, Whims and Habits. Annapolis: Capital-Gazette Press, 1964. 200 p. illus., ports.

Stories for all ages of the history and folklore of the official symbols, e.g. bird, dog, flower, tree, song, flag, seal, sport (jousting), and the unofficial symbols, e.g. terrapin, oyster, blue crab, striped bass.

Also of use:

CULVER, Francis B. The Maryland State Flag and Colonial County Colors. Baltimore: Printed by Waverly Press, 1934. 29 p. illus. Brief history of the State Flag.

HALL, Clayton C. The Great Seal of Maryland; A Paper Read before the Maryland Historical Society, December 14, 1885. Baltimore: 1886. 52 p. (Maryland Historical Society. Fund Publication no. 23) Traces the history in manuscript sources of the Seal and the circumstances of the changes made in it.

191. SCHAUN, George and Virginia Schaun. Holidays and Special Days of Maryland, Their Meaning and Observances. Annapolis: Greenberry

Publications, 1965. 116 p. illus., maps.

List of Useful Publications": p. 113.

Notes on present-day observances, some national, observances of the past, and how Marylanders formerly celebrated.

General Works

192. ANDREWS, Matthew P. History of Maryland: Province and State. Hatboro, Pa.: Tradition Press, 1965. 721 p.

Reprint of 1929 edition.

A history, largely political, which is useful for describing opposing positions on issues. Although it extends to 1929, the 17th and 18th centuries are emphasized. There is also a great deal on the rise of Baltimore.

193. MANAKEE, Beta E., Harold R. Manakee, and Joseph L. Wheeler. My Maryland; Her Story for Boys and Girls. Rev. and enl. under the editorship of John M. Gambrill. Baltimore: Maryland Historical Society, 1971. 446 p. illus., ports., maps.

An outstanding school text for intermediate grades. Appendices list proprietors, governors, Marylanders in national government, Maryland holidays, etc. Unfortunately, the first edition's (1934) "Readings for Teachers of Maryland History" (p. 405-411) is omitted.

Another useful elementary school text, which does have a bibliography, is

ROLLO, Vera A. F. Your Maryland. With a preface by Verne E. Chatelain. 2d rev. ed. Lanham, Md.: Maryland Historical Press, 1971. 414 p. ports., maps.

194. RADOFF, Morris L., ed. The Old Line State, A History of Maryland. Annapolis: Historical Records Association, 1956. 3 vols. illus., ports.

Vol. 1 also published as Maryland Hall of Records Publication no. 16 (1971).

Vol. 1 consists of essays on Maryland state and regional history, politics and government, Baltimore, Annapolis, and such subjects as shipbuilding, commerce and industry, architecture, and military. Vols. 2 and 3 are devoted to biographies of Marylanders.

195. SCHARF, John T. History of Maryland from the Earliest Period to the Present Day. Hatboro, Pa.: Tradition Press, 1967. 3 vols. illus., ports., maps.

Reprint of 1879 edition.

A valuable history written with considerable detail and an extensive use of a variety of contemporary sources. (The reprint edition has a new index.)

Another mid-nineteenth century history, still useful for its history of Maryland in the Revolutionary War, is

McSHERRY, James. History of Maryland. Edited and continued by Bartlett B. James. Spartanburg, S.C.: Reprint Co., 1968. 437 p. A reprint of the 1904 edition.

Also of interest:

SHEFF, Mildred K. The Position of Women in Maryland in the Nineteenth Century. 90 p. (M.A., University of Maryland, 1946) Describes the economic, educational, and legal aspects, and the contributions of individual women.

196. WALSH, Richard and Richard L. Fox, eds. Maryland: A History, 1632-1974. Baltimore: Maryland Historical Society, 1974. 955 p. illus., ports.

Each chapter is followed by a valuable bibliographical essay.

A set of informative monographs that treat broadly of Maryland's social, cultural, political, economic, and industrial background. Especially useful for the post Civil War period.

Colonial Period

197. ANDREWS, Matthew P. The Founding of Maryland. Baltimore: Williams and Wilkins; New York: D. Appleton Century, 1933. 376 p. ports., maps.

References: p. 338-350.

A popularly written yet detailed account of the political, social, and economic history of the Palatinate period. 1634-1689.

198. HALL, Clayton C., ed. Narratives of Early Maryland, 1633-1684. New York: Scribner's Sons, 1910. 460 p. map.

Reprints of documents and accounts of Early Maryland, each with a brief introduction. Includes "Instructions to the Colonists," by Lord Baltimore; "A Brief Relation of the Voyage unto Maryland," by Father Andrew White; "A Character of the Province of Maryland," by George Alsop; "Journal of the Dutch Embassy to Maryland," by Augustine Herrman; and "Letter of Governor Leonard Calvert to Lord Baltimore."

Another valuable contemporary account of Maryland and Annapolis:

EDDIS, William. Letters from America. Edited by Aubrey C. Land. Cambridge, Mass.: Belknap Press of Harvard University Press, 1969. 237 p.

199. IVES, Joseph M. The Ark and the Dove; The Beginnings of Civil and Religious Liberties in America. New York: Longmans, Green and Co., 1936. 435 p.

Bibliography: p. 419-423.

The contributions of George and Cecil Calvert, Father Andrew White, Thomas Cornwaleys, Charles Carroll of Carrollton, Bishop John Carroll, and Daniel Carroll to religious toleration and the American system of government.

200. MERENESS, Newton D. Maryland as a Proprietary Province. New York: Macmillan Co., 1901. 530 p.

Bibliography: p. 521-524.

A carefully documented institutional history of proprietorship in Maryland, its evolution, development, and complexity. Covers the land system, territorial revenue, the Assembly, industrial and social development, government and military affairs, local government, finance, religion, the Church and the clergy, and relations with England.

Other works which contribute to the study of the social life of the colonial period:

BROWNE, William H. Maryland: The History of a Palatinate. Boston: Houghton, Mifflin, 1904. 381 p. A readable and yet scholarly classroom text dealing largely with the colonial period.

HALL, Clayton C. The Lords Baltimore and the Maryland Palatinate. 2d ed. Baltimore: Nunn & Co., 1904. 217 p. Six lectures on the proprietors, religious toleration, social life and customs, and the economics of colonial Maryland.

JOHNSON, John H. Old Maryland Manors. Baltimore: Johns Hopkins University, 1883. 38 p. (Johns Hopkins Studies in Historical and Political Science, ser. 1, no. 7) Descriptions of the social life on the manor, with considerable information on the court leet.

McCORMAC, Eugene. White Servitude in Maryland, 1634-1820. Baltimore: Johns Hopkins Press, 1904. 112 p. (Johns Hopkins University Studies in Historical and Political Science, ser. 22, nos. 3-4) Offers a look at practices associated with indentured servants and convict laborers.

NEILL, Edward D. The Founders of Maryland as Portrayed in Manuscripts, Provincial Records and Early Documents. Albany: J. Munsell, 1876. 193 p. Provides an account of settlement, religion, history, Henry Fleet, Leonard Calvert, Thomas Cornwallis, William Claiborne, Jerome Hawley.

NEWMAN, Harry W. Seigniory in Early Maryland, with a List of Manors and Manor Lords. Washington: Descendants of Lords of the Maryland Manors, 1949. 69 p. illus.

RICHARDSON, Hester D. Sidelights on Maryland History, with Sketches of Early Maryland Families. Baltimore: Genealogical Publishing Co., 1967. 2 vols. ports. Reprint of 1913 edition. Also reprinted by Tidewater Publishers (1967). Originally published in the Baltimore Sunday Sun and not intended as a sustained integrated history. Vol. 1 consists of brief accounts, based on the information found in manuscripts and the original Calvert papers, of such topics as the theatre, libraries, education, witchcraft, and the colonial business woman. Vol. 2 contains genealogical sketches on over 100 Maryland families.

STEINER, Bernard C. Beginnings of Maryland, 1631-1639. Baltimore: Johns Hopkins, 1903. 112 p. (Johns Hopkins University Studies in Historical and Political Science, ser. 21, nos. 8-10) Primarily concerned with the conflict between William Claiborne and the Calvert interests.

THOMAS, James W. Chronicles of Maryland. Cumberland, Md.: Eddy Press, 1913. 389 p. illus. Useful for chapters on land tenure, early churches, the judicial system, St. Mary's County, the Great Seal, and the State Flag.

201. SEMMES, Raphael. Captains and Mariners of Early Maryland. Baltimore: Johns Hopkins Press, 1937. 856 p.

Bibliography: p. 819-825.

The nautical history of 17th century Maryland, with detailed descriptions of explorers and colonial life and an extensive portion on the Indians. Fifteen appendices provide more details on topics covered in the text. Person, Indian, and topical indexes.

A much briefer popular summary:

BYRON, Gilbert. Early Explorations of the Chesapeake Bay. Baltimore: Maryland Historical Society, 1960. 23 p. illus., maps.

202. SEMMES, Raphael. Crime and Punishment in Early Maryland. Baltimore: Johns Hopkins Press, 1938. 334 p.

"Bibliographical Chapter Notes": p. 259-317.

Provides a thorough description of colonial life as he weaves accounts of the legal system and the rigor of life. Chapters on trial, punishment, and imprisonment; houses, clothing, and theft; livestock and hog stealing; drunkenness, profanity, and witchcraft; adultery, fornication, and bastardy; defamation.

Another examination of witchcraft, describing cases brought to trial in Maryland:

PARKE, Francis N. Witchcraft in Maryland. Baltimore: 1937. 50 p. Published in part in the Maryland Historical Magazine 31 (1936): 271-298.

Colonial Period - Juvenile Works

203. FINLAYSON, Ann. Colonial Maryland. New York: Thomas Nelson, 1974. 160 p. illus., ports., maps.

Bibliography: p. 151-153.

Covers the time to the end of the Revolution.

204. MASON, Francis van Wyck. The Maryland Colony. New York: Crowell-Collier Press, 1969. 134 p. illus., ports., maps.

Bibliography: p. 125.

205. SCHAUN, George and Virginia Schaun. Everyday Life in Colonial Maryland. 13th ed. Annapolis: Greenberry Publications, 1973. 130 p. illus., maps.

"Lists of Useful Publications": p. 128.

Covers a wide range of topics, including entertainment and sport, medicine, transportation, heating, and lighting.

Revolutionary Period

206. BARKER, Charles A. The Background of the Revolution in Maryland. New Haven, Conn.: Yale University Press, 1940. 419 p.

Bibliographical note: p. 385-399.

A thorough and readable study of the social, economic, and political climate in the 50 years preceding the Revolution.

Three additional works:

DOLE, Esther. Maryland During the American Revolution. [Baltimore] Printed by Waverly Press, 1941. 294 p. A good school text.

LARRABEE, Harold A. A Decision at the Chesapeake. New York: C. N. Porter, 1964. 317 p. maps. Provides an account of naval and land operations and engagements, concentrating on the Battle of Chesapeake Bay (1781), between the French and British fleets, which ultimately resulted in the seige at Yorktown.

TRUITT, Charles J. Breadbasket of the Revolution; Delmarva in the War for Independence. Salisbury, Md.: Historical Books, 1975. 240 p. A general history of the role of the Delmarva Peninsula in the Revolutionary War, with special attention to its contributions in materials and food.

207. MARYLAND in the Revolution. Annapolis: Maryland Magazine, 1976. 48 p. illus., ports.

A colorful collection of articles taken from the Maryland Magazine on the burning of the Peggy Stewart; Robert Eden, the last Provincial Governor; Lambert Wicks; Maryland militia at the Battle of Long Island; and material on William Paca and Charles Carroll.

War of 1812

208. CRANWELL, John P. and William B. Crane. Men of Marque; A History of Private Armed Vessels Out of Baltimore During the War of 1812.

Bibliography: p. 415-418.

Lively account of men, ships, and battles.

209. FILBY, P. William and Edward C. Howard. Star Spangled Books: Books, Sheet Music, Newspapers and Persons Associated with "The Star-Spangled Banner." Baltimore: Maryland Historical Society, 1972. 175 p. illus.

Narrative accounts, by contributors, of the writing, legends, publication, and individuals associated with the music and poem; followed by a catalog describing 170 items.

210. MANAKEE, Harold R. and Beta K. Manakee. The Star Spangled Banner: The Story of Its Writing by Francis Scott Key. Baltimore: Maryland Historical Society, 1954. 26 p. illus., map.

A brief and well written account for juveniles.

211. MARINE, William M. The British Invasion of Maryland, 1812-1815. Edited, with an appendix containing 11,000 names, by Louis H. Dielman. Hatboro, Pa.: Tradition Press, 1965. 519 p. map.

Reprint of 1913 edition.

The standard work covering the causes of the War; attitude of Marylanders toward it; the riot and burning of the Baltimore Federal Republic; the Baltimore privateers, Joshua Barney and Thomas Boyle; British incursions in the Chesapeake Bay region; Battles of Bladensburg and Baltimore and the engagement at Caulk's Field. Soldiers who served are listed in "Maryland Roster, War of 1812" (p. 195-495).

Additional works:

Byron, Gilbert. The War of 1812 on the Chesapeake Bay. Baltimore: Maryland Historical Society, 1964. 94 p. illus., ports., maps. A good school level account of the war.

LORD, Walter. The Dawn's Early Light. New York: Norton, 1972. 384 p. illus. A popular account of the War of 1812.

MULLER, Charles G. The Darkest Day: 1814; The Washington-Baltimore Campaign. Philadelphia: J. B. Lippincott Co., 1963. 232 p. map. Bibliography: p. 217-224. Includes a good account of the Battle of Bladensburg.

Mexican-American War

212. KENLY, John R. Memoirs of a Maryland Volunteer. War with Mexico in the Years 1846, -7, -8. Philadelphia: J. B. Lippincott & Co., 1873. 521 p.

A personal narrative. The appendix lists Maryland and Washington volunteer officers.

Civil War Period

213. BROWN, George W. Baltimore and the 19th of April, 1861. Baltimore: N. Murray, Publication Agent, Johns Hopkins University, 1887. 176 p.

A first hand description by Baltimore's Mayor in 1861 of the events leading up to the fight between the 6th Regiment of Massachusetts Volunteers and the mob of citizens, the fight itself, and the subsequent seizure of Federal Hill, suspension of the writ of habeas corpus, and imprisonment of citizens.

214. GOLDSBOROUGH, W. W. The Maryland Line in the Confederate Army. Baltimore: Kelly, Piet & Co., 1900. 371 p. ports.

Account of the Maryland units and men who fought on the side of the Confederacy.

Indexed in

MARYLAND. Hall of Records. Index to The Maryland Line in the Confederate Army, 1861-1865, by Mrs. Charles L. Lewys. Annapolis: 1944. 74 p. (Its Publication no. 3)

215. MANAKEE, Harold R. Maryland in the Civil War. Baltimore: Maryland Historical Society, 1961. 173 p. illus., maps.

Bibliography: p. 158-162.

Written for schools, this offers an introduction to the period and deals with the importance Maryland held for both sides. Covers such aspects as John Brown's raid, the "Baltimore Plot," prison camps, and Lincoln's assassination.

Valuable also:

EVITTS, William J. A Matter of Allegiances; Maryland from 1850-1861. Baltimore: Johns Hopkins University Press, 1974. 212 p. maps. (Johns Hopkins University Studies in Historical and Political Science, ser. 92, no. 1) "Bibliographic Essay": p. 197-205. A study of

Maryland as a microcosm of a nation undergoing a process of social and political change, adjustment, and economic growth, brought about by immigration, urbanization, political realignment, constitutional reform, and questions about slavery.

216. MURFIN, James V. The Gleam of Bayonets; The Battle of Antietam and the Maryland Campaign of 1862. Maps by James D. Bowlby. Introd. by James I. Robertson, Jr. New York: Thomas Yoseloff, 1965. 451 p. illus., ports., maps.

Bibliography: p. 429-436.

Antietam, the battle and the events leading up to it, and its economic and political consequences.

Another valuable source for the Civil War in Maryland:

KLEIN, Frederick S., ed. Just South of Gettysburg: Carroll County, Maryland, in the Civil War. Personal Accounts and Descriptions of a Maryland Border County, 1861-1865. Westminster, Md.: Newman Press, 1963. 247 p. illus., maps.

Reconstruction Period

217. MYERS, William S. The Self-Reconstruction of Maryland, 1864-1867. Baltimore: Johns Hopkins Press, 1909. 131 p. (Johns Hopkins University Studies in Historical and Political Science, ser. 27, nos. 1-2)

The standard work.

Modern Period

218. MARYLAND HISTORICAL SOCIETY. War Records Division. Maryland in World War II. Prepared for the State of Maryland. Baltimore: 1956-1958. 4 vols. illus., ports., maps.

Bibliography: vol. 1, p. 363-366.

Vol. 1: Military Participation; vol. 2: Industry and Agriculture; vol. 3: Home Front Volunteer Services; vol. 4: Gold Star Honor Roll.

219. MARYLAND. State Planning Dept. The Counties of Maryland and Baltimore City: Their Origin, Growth and Development, 1634-1967. Baltimore: 1968. 106 p. map.

Supersedes 1963 edition.

Bibliography: p. 105-106.

Brief summary accounts which give for each county its history, economic and financial information, interesting sights, and the activities of major governmental agencies.

Material on the establishment of the counties can be found in

MATHEWS, Edward B. The Counties of Maryland, Their Origin, Boundaries, and Election Districts. Cleveland, Ohio: Bell & Howell, 1967. 154 p. maps. Reprint of Maryland. Geological Survey. Report, vol. 6, pt. 5, p. 419-572 (1906).

Regional - Potomac Valley

220. GUTHEIM, Frederick. The Potomac. Illus. by Mitchell Jamieson. New York: Rinehart, 1949. 436 p. illus., maps.

"Bibliographical Notes": p. 399-413.

The Potomac in the life of the nation, with material on the tidewater frontier, tobacco culture, the routes to the West, and the Civil War.

A juvenile fictionalized narrative of the exploration of the Potomac from 1606 to 1746, using contemporary sources, is

HOBBS, Horace P. Pioneers of the Potowmack: Beinge a Briefe Historie of Ye Discoverie & Exploration of Ye River Patawomeke... 2d ed. Ann Arbor, Mich.: 1964. 155 p. illus., maps. Bibliography: p. 150-155.

221. WILSTACH, Paul. Potomac Landings. Photographs by Roger B. Whitman and others. Indianapolis: Bobbs-Merrill, 1932. 378 p. ports., maps.

An informal history largely devoted to the social life

and customs of the colonial period in Maryland and Virginia. Includes material on architecture, education, religious life, and travel.

Regional - Potomac Valley - Bibliographic Guide

222. SANDERLIN, Walter S. The Potomac Valley: Students' Guide to Localized History. New York: Teachers College Press, 1969. 44 p.

Includes bibliographical references.

Sections on the physical setting and pre-history, the Indians and colonial period, Potomac route to the West, economic and social growth, the Civil War, and the retreat from industrialization. Each section includes a general introduction, suggested readings, and field trips.

Regional - Tidewater and Eastern Shore

223. CLARK, Charles B., ed. The Eastern Shore of Maryland and Virginia. New York: Lewis Historical Publishing Co., 1950. 3 vols. illus., ports.

Offers a great amount of information, with bibliographic notes. Vol. 1 is largely a chronological history, dealing with the period up to the Civil War; vol. 2 covers such topics as government, religion, architecture, sports, literature, the institutions of the Eastern Shore, and sketches of the individual counties. Much of the material in vols. 1 and 2 is written by contributors. Vol. 3 is devoted to biographies and family histories.

224. EARLE, Swepson. The Chesapeake Bay Country. 4th ed., rev. Baltimore: Thomsen, 1934. 522 p. illus., ports., maps.

"Books...consulted": p. 16.

History and description of past times on the Eastern Shore and Southern Maryland, with stories of the old homes, counties, and notables.

This can be supplemented with

BURGESS, Robert H. This Was Chesapeake Bay. Cambridge, Md.: Cornell Maritime Press, 1963. 210 p. illus. Tales of Chesapeake and photographs of the Chesapeake Bay.

225. EARLE, Swepson and Percy G. Skirven, eds. Maryland's Colonial Eastern Shore; Historical Sketches of Counties and of Some Notable Structures. Baltimore: Munder-Thomsen Press, 1916. 203 p. illus., map.

Kent County, by P. G. Skirven; Talbot County, by J. H. K. Shannahan; Somerset County, by H. F. Lankford; Dorchester County, by W. L. Henry; Cecil County, by H. L.

Constable; Queen Anne's County, by D. W. Thom; Worcester County, by S. K. Dennis; Caroline County, by E. T. Tubbs; Wicomico County, by L. I. Pollitt; Washington College, by J. W. Cain.

A valuable source for early maps:

The 1877 Atlases and Other Early Maps of the Eastern Shore of Maryland. Salisbury, Md.: Wicomico Bicentennial Commission, 1976. 144 p. maps. The maps are listed by county. Includes the John Smith map (1629), part of the Augustine Herrman map (1673), and city and town maps.

226. MIDDLETON, Arthur P. Tobacco Court, A Maritime History of Chesapeake Bay in the Colonial Era. Newport News, Va.: Mariners' Museum, 1953. 482 p. illus., maps.

Bibliography: p. 431-452.

The maritime and mercantile history of the colonial Maryland and Virginia region of the Chesapeake Bay and its tributaries. Emphasizes the period 1660-1763 and the effects of the waterways on large-scale tobacco production, transportation, and defense of the Bay; the pattern of settlement; and the practice of privateering.

227. WILSTACH, Paul. Tidewater Maryland. New York: Tudor Publications, 1945. 383 p. illus., ports., map.

Reprint of 1931 edition.

Informal historical and descriptive accounts, including the old manors, Labadists, Acadians, and place names.

Other informal works:

FOOTNER, Hulbert. Rivers of the Eastern Shore; Seventeen Maryland Rivers. Illus. by Aaron Sopher. New York: Farrar & Rinehart, 1944. 375 p. illus. "Sources": p. 362-368. History and folklore of the area along the bayside rivers of the Eastern Shore.

SHANNAHAN, John H. K. Tales of Old Maryland; History and Romance on the Eastern Shore of Maryland. Baltimore: Meyer & Thalneimer, 1907. 80 p. Tales and little stories about the places and people, including Patty Cannon, Frederick Douglass, the Wye House, Myrtle Grove, and the Old Quaker Meeting House in Talbot County.

Regional - Western Maryland

228. SCHARF, John T. History of Western Maryland; Being a History of Frederick, Montgomery, Carroll, Washington, Allegany and Garrett Counties...Including Sketches of Their Representative Men. Baltimore: Regional Publishing Co., 1968. 2 vols. illus., ports., maps.

Reprint of 1882 edition.

The first part deals with a general history of Western Maryland to the Civil War. The counties are treated separately and such areas as educational institutions, industries, economic life, and town histories are covered. Vol. 1, p. 145-161, lists Revolutionary War soldiers who were assigned tracts.

Counties and Cities

Allegany County

229. THOMAS, James W. and Thomas J. C. Williams. History of Allegany County, Maryland...To This is Added a Biographical and Genealogical Record of Representative Families... Baltimore: Regional Publishing Co., 1969. 2 vols. illus., ports.

Reprint of 1923 edition.

Vol. 1 is history, vol. 2 biography.

Annapolis

230. NORRIS, Walter B. Annapolis: Its Colonial and Naval Story. New York: Thomas Y. Crowell Co., 1925. 323 p. illus., ports.

An excellent account of life in colonial and revolutionary Annapolis and of the decline of Annapolis.

Also useful:

BALTZ, Shirley V. The Quays of the City, an Account of the Bustling Eighteenth Century Port of Annapolis. Annapolis: Liberty Tree, 1975. 63 p. maps. Footnotes: p. 58-63. Looks at the activity and the social and economic life on the docks and along the main streets.

RILEY, Elihu S. The Ancient City. A History of Annapolis in Maryland. Annapolis: Printing Office, 1887. 395 p.

STEVENS, William O. Annapolis: Anne Arundel's Town. New York: Dodd, Mead Co., 1937. 339 p.

Baltimore (County and City)

231. SCHARF, John T. History of Baltimore City and County. Baltimore: Regional Publishing Co., 1971. 2 vols. illus., ports., maps.

Reprint of 1881 edition.

The standard history covering the period up to 1880. Comprehensive with separate chapters on such topics as geology, aborigines, amusements, and events. These are interspersed with biographical sketches, often with portraits of outstanding men. Especially good for its use of documents and reliance on newspapers. Scharf's earlier Chronicles of Baltimore (1874) is not as well organized and much of it is incorporated in this later work.

Baltimore City

232. BEIRNE, Francis F. The Amiable Baltimoreans. Hatboro, Pa.: Tradition Press, 1968. 400 p.

Reprint of 1951 edition.

Bibliography: p. 380-382.

Popular treatment of events, people, places, and activities.

See also

BEIRNE, Francis F. Baltimore: A Picture History, 1858-1968. Compiled under the auspices of the Maryland Historical Society. Baltimore: Bodine, 1968. 185 p. illus., ports., maps. An earlier volume covered 1858-1958. Contains good drawings of early Baltimore.

BODINE, A. Aubrey. Bodine's Baltimore: 46 Years in the Life of a City. Photographs by A. Aubrey Bodine. Commentary by William H. Hunter. Baltimore: Bodine Associates, 1973. 150 p. illus. Photographs taken between 1924 and 1970.

233. HALL, Clayton C., ed. Baltimore: Its History and Its People. New York: Lewis Historical Publishing Co., 1912. 3 vols. ports., maps.

Vol. 1 is a chronicle consisting of essays covering the social, cultural, and political history of Baltimore and is especially useful for economic history. Vols. 2 and 3 consist of personal histories of the makers of the city and the genealogies of their families.

Other useful companion works:

BALTIMORE MUNICIPAL JOURNAL. Baltimore 200th Anniversary, 1729-1929. Baltimore: Fleet-McGinley, 1929. 297 p. illus., ports. A good long history of the city with chapters on the various ethnic groups.

HIRSCHFELD, Charles. Baltimore, 1870-1900; Studies in Social History. Baltimore: Johns Hopkins Press, 1941. 176 p. (Johns Hopkins Studies in Historical and Political Science, ser. 59, no. 2) Bibliography: p. 161-167. Covers the growth of population and industry, public education, and organized charity.

HOWARD, George W. The Monumental City--Its Past History and Present Resources. Baltimore: J. D. Ehlers, 1889. 1,164 p. A detailed history of Baltimore and its institutions.

SEMMES, Raphael. Baltimore as Seen by Visitors. Baltimore: Maryland Historical Society, 1953. 208 p. illus.

(Maryland Historical Society. Studies in Maryland History, no. 2) Bibliography: p. 181-194. Descriptions of the city and its people between the end of the revolution and the outbreak of the Civil War. Taken from diaries, memoirs, and reminiscences.

VEXLER, Robert I., ed. Baltimore: A Chronological and Documentary History, 1632-1970. Dobbs Ferry, N.Y.: Oceana Publications, 1975. 156 p.

WILLIAMS, Harold A. Baltimore Afire; Being an Account of One of America's Great Conflagrations. Baltimore: Schneiderich & Sons, 1954. 92 p. illus. A well illustrated record of the 1904 fire.

234. OWENS, Hamilton. Baltimore on the Chesapeake. Garden City, N.Y.: Doubleday, Doran & Co., 1941. 342 p. illus., maps.

A good popular introductory history up to World War I.

Calvert County

235. STEIN, Charles F. A History of Calvert County, Maryland. Baltimore: 1960. 404 p. illus., maps.

Bibliography: p. 382-384.

History of the county into the 20th century. Includes sections on genealogy, tax assessment list for 1782, various lists of taxables of 1733.

Caroline County

236. HISTORY of Caroline County, Maryland, from Its Beginning; Materials Largely Contributed by the Teachers and Children of the County. Revised and supplemented by Laura C. Cochrane and others. With an added index by Emory Dobson. Baltimore: Regional Publishing Co., 1971. 359 p. illus., map.

Reprint of 1920 edition.

Contains biographical sketches and the history of towns.

Cecil County

237. JOHNSTON, George. History of Cecil County, Maryland, and the Early Settlements Around the Head of the Chesapeake Bay and on the Delaware River with Sketches of Some of the Old Families of Cecil County. Baltimore: Regional Publishing Co., 1972. 548 p. map.

Reprint of 1881 edition.

Also reprinted in Cecil County: A Reference Book on History, Business and General Information (Baltimore:

County Directories of Maryland, 1956, 298 p., illus., maps), which also includes later sketches of churches, places, and institutions.

Contains considerable material on social history with good coverage of Augustine Herrman's Bohemia Manor and the Labadists, the Chesapeake and Delaware and Susquehanna Canals, and the railroads.

More recent Cecil County histories which also have bibliographic information:

GIFFORD, George E. Cecil County, Maryland, 1608-1850... Rising Sun, Md.: George E. Gifford Memorial Committee, Calvert School, 1974. 241 p. illus.

MILLER, Alice E. Cecil County, Maryland; Study in Local History. Elkton, Md.: C. & L. Printing and Speciality Co., 1949. 173 p. illus., ports., maps. Bibliography: p. 165-168.

Charles County

238. KLAPTHOR, Margaret B. and Paul D. Brown. The History of Charles County, Maryland, Written in Its Tercentenary Year of 1958. La Plata, Md.: Charles County Tercentenary, Inc., 1958. 204 p. illus., ports.

Bibliography: p. 172-178.

Covers history into the 20th century with material on the Lincoln Conspiracy, agriculture, prominent Charles Countians, and the Census of 1790.

Dorchester County

239. JONES, Elias. New Revised History of Dorchester County, Maryland. Cambridge, Md.: Tidewater Publishers, 1966. 603 p. illus., ports.

The 1925 edition, corrected and with material added.

A miscellany of brief sketches can be found in

HUELLE, Walter E. Footnotes to Dorchester History. Cambridge, Md.: Tidewater Publishers, 1969. 85 p.

Frederick County

240. WILLIAMS, Thomas J. C. and Folger McKinsey. History of Frederick County, Maryland. With a Biographical Record of Representative Families. Baltimore: Regional Publishing Co., 1967. 2 vols. illus., ports.

Reprint of 1910 edition.

Vol. 1: local history. Vol. 2: biography and family.

Harford County

241. MASON, Samuel. Historical Sketches of Harford County, Maryland. 2d ed. Darlington, Md.: Little Pines Farm, 1955. 177 p. illus.

  The history of exploration and early settlements, frontier forts, iron furnaces and forges, grist mills and other mills, as well as miscellaneous sketches.

242. PRESTON, Walter W. History of Harford County, Maryland from 1608 (The Year of Smith's Expedition) to the Close of the War of 1812. Baltimore: Regional Publishing Co., 1972. 360 p. illus.

  Includes biographical sketches of outstanding men, Revolutionary War muster rolls and pay lists, and many other lists of names.

243. WRIGHT, C. Milton. Our Harford Heritage; A History of Harford County, Maryland. [N.p.: 1967] 460 p. illus.

  Useful for legends and superstitions, the origin of Harford County names, Harford County officials.

  Additional biographical information on men associated with Bel Air and Harford County in

  COBOURN, Frederick L. A Short Biography of Those Whose Portraits Adorn the Walls of the Court House, Bel Air, Maryland. Bel Air, Md.: 1942. 59 p.

Howard County

244. STEIN, Charles F. Origins and History of Howard County, Maryland. Baltimore: 1972. 383 p. illus.

  A history of Howard County from the establishment of Anne Arundel County. Includes a separate section of genealogical histories and illustrations of coats of arms.

Kent County

245. HANSON, George A. Old Kent: The Eastern Shore of Maryland. Chestertown, Md.: R. H. Collins & Sons, 1936. 248, 45 p.

  A reprint of the 1875 and 1876 installments in the Chestertown Transcript.

  Includes sketches of many families, an extensive name index, and histories of parishes.

246. USILTON, Frederick G. History of Kent County, 1630-1916. [N.p.: 1916?] 251 p. illus.

  Local history with some biography.

Montgomery County

247. BOYD, Thomas H. S. A History of Montgomery County, Maryland, from Its Earliest Settlement in 1650 to 1870. Baltimore: Regional Publishing Co., 1968. 187 p.

    A reprint of the 1879 edition. Includes chapters on land grants, eminent men, and a directory of towns with residents arranged by occupation. (The reprint includes a name index not found in the original edition.)

Prince George's County

248. HIENTON, Louise J. Prince George's Heritage: Sidelights on the Early History of Prince George's County from 1696 to 1800. Baltimore: Maryland Historical Society, 1972. 223 p. illus., ports., maps.

    Bibliographical footnotes.

    Offers material on a variety of topics, such as the establishment of the county, the county seats, the Anglican and Presbyterian Churches, the free school, the hundreds, and the county residents in the colonial and Revolutionary wars.

Queen Anne's County

249. EMORY, Frederic. Queen Anne's County, Maryland, Its Early History and Development. Baltimore: Maryland Historical Society, 1950. 629 p.

    Originally published in the Centreville Observer, 1886-1887.

    Wide-ranging history, covering up to 1881, with a minimum of genealogical concern.

St. Mary's County

250. KNIGHT, George M. Intimate Glimpses of Old Saint Mary's. 2d ed. Washington: American Good Government Society, 1942. 127 p. illus.

    Brief sketches of landmarks and the legends of the county.

    Possible additional sources of information:

    CROKER, Maria B. Tales and Traditions of Old Saint Mary's. Reisterstown, Md.: Whitmore Publishing Co., 1934. 78 p. illus. Sketches of persons, places, and events.

    FORMAN, Henry C. Jamestown and St. Mary's: Burial

Cities of Romance. Baltimore: Johns Hopkins Press, 1938. 355 p. illus., maps. Bibliographical footnotes. An analysis of the founding and decline of these two colonial cities based on excavations of the sites, with drawings of plans and elevations of probable structures.

Somerset County

251. TORRENCE, Clayton. Old Somerset on the Eastern Shore of Maryland; A Study in Foundations and Founders. Baltimore: Regional Publishing Co., 1966. 583 p.

Reprint of 1935 edition.

"References and Index...": p. 481-555.

Covers only the 17th century and is based on archival materials. Useful appendices give such information as marriages, names of settlers, and land patentees.

Talbot County

252. TILGHMAN, Oswald. History of Talbot County, Maryland, 1661-1861. Baltimore: Regional Publishing Co., 1967. 2 vols. ports.

Reprint of 1915 edition.

Vol. 1: biography; vol. 2: history.

An interesting volume:

MULLIKIN, James C. Ghost Towns of Talbot County. Easton, Md.: Easton Publishing Co., 1961. 51 p. illus., map. The stories of the former river port towns of York, Doncaster (or Wyetown), Dover, and Kingston.

Washington County

253. WILLIAMS, Thomas J. C. A History of Washington County, Maryland ...Including a History of Hagerstown... Baltimore: Regional Publishing Co., 1968. 2 vols. illus., ports.

Reprint of 1906 edition.

Vol. 1: history; vol. 2: biography and family histories.

INDIANS AND PREHISTORIC GROUPS

254. BRINTON, Daniel G. The Lenâpé and Their Legends; With the Complete Text and Symbols of the Walam Olum. New York: AMS Press, 1969. 262 p. illus. (Library of Aboriginal American Literature, no. 5)

    Reprint of 1884 edition.

    An investigation into the history, literature, and language of the Algonkin and Iroquois, which includes those tribes in the area of Maryland.

255. FERGUSON, Alice L. L. and Henry G. Ferguson. The Piscataway Indians of Southern Maryland. Accokeek, Md.: Alice Ferguson Foundation, 1960. 46 p. illus., maps.

    An expansion of Alice L. L. Ferguson, Moyaone and the Piscataway Indians (1937).

    Sources: p. 44-46.

    Covers the history of the Piscataway Indians from their earliest appearance through the 18th century.

    Another useful record of the Indians in the region:

    DeLaBARRE, Reamer R. Chesapeake Bay Indian Population. 66 p. (M.A., Johns Hopkins University, 1958) An ethnological study on the number and density of the various groups of Indians living in the Chesapeake Bay area in the period 1600-1700.

256. MANAKEE, Harold R. Indians of Early Maryland; A Book on Maryland Life. Baltimore: Maryland Historical Society, 1959. 47 p. illus., map.

    Written at the elementary school level, it generalizes on the everyday life and the customs of the Indians who inhabited the region.

Archaeology

257. GRAHAM, William J. Indians of Port Tobacco River, Maryland, and Their Burial Places. Washington: 1935. 35 p. illus., map.

    Bibliographical footnotes.

Presents the findings of the archaeological investigations of several sites, as well as general background information.

258. MacCORD, Howard A., Karl Schmitt, and Richard G. Slattery. The Shepard Site Study (18mo3) Montgomery Co. Md. 1957. Baltimore: Archeological Society of Baltimore, 1959. 32 p. illus., maps. (Archeological Society of Maryland. Bulletin no. 1)

"Literature Cited": p. 31-32.

Includes descriptions of the geographical setting, site, cultural remains, as well as the history of the site and a comparison with other archaeological sites in Maryland and Virginia.

259. STEARNS, Richard E. The Hughes Site: An Aboriginal Village Site on the Potomac River in Montgomery County, Maryland. Baltimore: Natural History Society of Maryland, 1940. 15 p. illus., map. (Natural History Society of Maryland. Proceedings, no. 6)

An account of an archaeological dig.

260. STEARNS, Richard E. Some Indian Village Sites of the Lower Patapsco River. Baltimore: Natural History Society of Maryland, 1949. 6 p. illus., map. (Natural History Society of Maryland. Proceedings, no. 10)

Primarily consists of pictures of shards and artifacts.

261. STEARNS, Richard E. Some Indian Village Sites of Tidewater Maryland. Baltimore: Natural History Society of Maryland, 1943. 30 p. illus., maps. (Natural History Society of Maryland. Proceedings, no. 9)

Bibliography: p. 30.

Archaeological descriptions of various sites and artifacts.

262. STEPHENSON, Robert L., Alice L. L. Ferguson, and Henry G. Ferguson. The Accokeek Creek Site, A Middle Atlantic Seaboard Culture Sequence. Ann Arbor, Mich.: University of Michigan, 1963. 215 p. illus., maps. (Michigan. University. Museum of Anthropology. Anthropological Papers, no. 20)

A complete revision of Robert L. Stephenson, The Prehistoric People of Accokeek Creek (1959).

"References Cited": p. 206-215.

Offers an analysis of the artifacts from before 500 B.C. to 1700 A.D. Covers the historical setting, topography, excavations and field work, and includes a cultural reconstruction and chronology.

Another such study:

HOLMES, William H. Stone Implements of the Potomac-

Chesapeake Tidewater Province. Washington: 1897. 152 p. illus. (U.S. Bureau of American Ethnology. Annual Report 15 (1893/1894))

263. WRIGHT, Henry T. An Archaeological Sequence in the Middle Chesapeake Region, Maryland. Annapolis: Maryland Geological Survey, 1973. 41 p. (Maryland. Geological Survey. Archaeological Studies, no. 1)

A study of sites in the Severn River drainage area near Annapolis.

JOURNALISM

264. CHRISTIAN, Charles M., ed. Two Hundred Years with the Maryland Gazette, 1727-1927. Annapolis: Capital-Gazette Press, 1927. 180 p.

    The history of the state's oldest newspaper.

265. THE SUNPAPERS of Baltimore, Henry Mencken, general editor. New York: Albert A. Knopf, 1937. 430 p. illus., ports.

    A chronological (from 1837 to 1937) popular treatment of Maryland's most influential newspaper. The chapters are written by Gerald W. Johnson, Frank R. Kent, Henry L. Mencken, and Hamilton Owens.

266. WINCHESTER, Paul and Frank W. Webb. Newspapers and Newspaper Men of Maryland, Past and Present. Baltimore: Frank L. Sibley & Co., 1905. 178 p. ports.

    Brief sketches.

    An essay on 18th century newspapers:

    KEIDEL, George C. Earliest German Newspapers in Baltimore. Washington: 1927. 12 p.

LAW

Biography

267. SAMS, Conway W. and Elihu S. Riley. Bench and Bar of Maryland, A History 1634 to 1901. Chicago: Lewis Publishing Co., 1901. 2 vols.

    Primarily consists of biographical sketches of lawyers.

Encyclopedia

268. WEST'S Maryland Law Encyclopedia, Based on Maryland Statutes; Case Law, State and Federal; Attorney General Opinions and Law Reviews. Brooklyn: American Law Book Co., 1960- . 25 vols.

    Kept up-to-date by pocket parts and replacement volumes.

    Sets forth the law of Maryland in narrative form with footnote references to the cases, statutes, rules, and court decisions which make the law, frequently with parenthetical notes. Index.

    ________. Forms. Washington: Washington Law Book Co., 1961-

    Probate, procedures, and uniform commercial code forms, as well as rules and practice with commentary.

Constitution

269. MARYLAND. Constitution. Constitution of Maryland with Amendments to January 1, 1973, and Constitution of the United States of America. Annapolis: Maryland Secretary of State, 1973. 148 p.

    Citations to amendments are provided in the footnotes.

270. MARYLAND. Constitutional Convention Commission. Constitutional Revision Study Documents of the Constitutional Convention Commission of Maryland. Annapolis: 1968. 1,188 p.

    Contains much useful legal and historical background information.

271. ROLLO, Vera A. F. Maryland's Constitution and Government. Lanham,

Md.: Maryland Historical Press, 1968. 160 p. illus.

________ ________. Supplement. 1975. 20 p.

Glossary: p. 156-159.

Alongside each section of the Maryland Constitution an easy to read commentary is provided.

Constitution - Bibliography

272. BROWNE, Cynthia E. Maryland; A Bibliography. [Westport, Conn.] Greenwood Press, 1972. 4 p.

Lists the proceedings, debates, reports, and other records of Maryland Constitutional Conventions from 1776. Intended to accompany a microfiche collection of the material available from Greenwood Press.

History - Colonial Period

273. WILHELM, Lewis W. Local Institutions of Maryland. Baltimore: N. Murray, Publication Agent, Johns Hopkins University, 1885. 129 p. (Johns Hopkins University Studies in Historical and Political Science, ser. 3, nos. 5-7)

The legal and organizational processes involved in the colonial land system, hundred, county, and town.

Laws, Statutes, Etc.

274. MARYLAND. Laws, statutes, etc. The Annotated Code of the Public General Laws of Maryland. 1957. Charlottesville, Va.: Michie Co. 19 vols. Title varies.

Kept up to date by replacement volumes and pocket supplements.

The authorized code of Maryland laws. Includes historical citation at the end of each section, indicating the number of that section in earlier codes, citation to acts from which law was derived and by which it has been amended, and the effects of amendments. Vol. 9B is "Rules of Procedure and Appendix of Forms."

Will be superseded by

275. MARYLAND. Laws, statutes, etc. The Annotated Code of the Public General Laws of Maryland. Charlottesville, Va.: Michie Co., 1974- . (In process)

Kept up to date with supplements.

Volumes have been published for Agriculture (1974); Commercial Law (1975); Corporations and Associations (1975); Real Property (1974); Courts and Judicial Proceedings

(1974); Estates and Trusts (1974); Natural Resources (1974).

Narrative presentation of the law in effect with citations to sources. Arranged by titles, with tables of comparable sections of the 1957 Annotated Code... collation. Each volume has a separate index.

276. MARYLAND. Laws, statutes, etc. Laws...Made and Passed at the Session of the General Assembly... Annapolis: Maryland Dept. of Legislative Reference. Issued for each regular and special session.

Copies of the laws passed, joint resolutions, executive orders, and bills vetoed by the Governor. Text indicates the effect on the Maryland Annotated Code. Separate volumes for local laws, giving amendments to municipal charters and county laws.

277. MARYLAND. Dept. of Legislative Reference. Synopsis of Laws Enacted by the State of Maryland...Legislative Session. Annapolis: 1916- . Annual.

Prepared for the use of the public pending the publication of the laws themselves, this gives a brief description of each act passed by the General Assembly and approved by the Governor. Synopsis includes bill number and legislator who introduced it. Also contains a list of bills vetoed by the Governor and tables giving the sections of the Maryland Annotated Code and of the public general and public local laws enacted, amended, or repealed by the particular session. Guide to the Acts.

278. MARYLAND. Div. of State Documents. Maryland Register [1, no. 1 (Oct. 1974)-] Annapolis. Bi-weekly, with additional issues in January, April, July, and October.

The official record of legislative, judicial, and administrative laws and regulations, both proposed and final. The certified documents are filed with the Division of State Documents and are available for inspection.

279. SHRIVER, J. Nicholas, Jr., and Shale D. Stiller. How to Live--and Die--With Maryland Probate. Houston, Tex.: Gulf Publishing Co., 1972. 184 p.

Published under the auspices of the Section of Estate and Trust Law of the Maryland State Bar Association.

A popular treatment.

Laws, Statutes, Etc. - Indexes

280. SHEPARD'S CITATIONS, Inc. Shepard's Maryland Citations. 3d ed. Colorado Springs, Colo.: 1959- . 3 vols.

There are separate volumes for "Case" (1959) and for "Statute" (1959); "Case" and "Statute" supplement, 1959-1972; and supplements to bound volumes.

An index to citations of decisions by Maryland and federal courts on Maryland cases and to the Maryland Constitution, codes, laws, home rule charters, ordinances, and court rules, as well as by Maryland Courts to the U.S. Constitution and federal statutes.

Reports

281. MARYLAND. Court of Appeals. Maryland Reports; Cases Adjudged in the Court of Appeals of Maryland [vol. 1 (1850)-] Charlottesville, Va.: Mitchie Co. Title varies.

Opinions of the Court of Appeals in cases brought to it for consideration.

LITERATURE

282. BALL, Donald L. Eastern Shore of Maryland Literature; A Critical Essay with Bibliography. N.p.: Lewis Historical Publishing Co., 1950. 38 p. illus.

    Reprinted from Charles B. Clark, ed., The Eastern Shore of Maryland (1950), vol. 2, p. 787-819.

    Brief biographies of the writers and poets associated with the Eastern Shore with summaries of their work. Covers historical fiction, romantic fiction, realistic fiction, non-fictional prose, and poetry.

283. JOHNSTON, George. The Poets and Poetry of Cecil County, Maryland. Elkton, Md.: 1887. 302 p.

    Contains an introductory biography for each poet.

284. JOPP, Harold D. and Robert H. Ingersoll. Shoremen: An Anthology of Eastern Shore Verse and Prose. Cambridge, Md.: Tidewater Publishers, 1974. 316 p.

    By people of the Eastern Shore or about the Eastern Shore.

285. LEMAY, Joseph A. L. Men of Letters in Colonial Maryland. Knoxville, Tenn.: University of Tennessee Press, 1972. 407 p. illus.

    "Bibliographical Notes": p. 349-387.

    A biographical study of ten men of letters associated with Maryland from the "Wilderness," writings of Andrew White, George Alsop, and John Hammond; through "The Planter," works of Ebenezer Cook and Richard Lewis; to "The Club," efforts of Jonas Green, Alexander Hamilton, James Sterling, Thomas Bacon, and William Parks.

286. MARYLAND Poets. Foreword by Maria B. Carter. New York: 1932. 160 p.

    An anthology of 48 poets.

287. NOBLE, Edwin M. and Edward T. Tubbs. Maryland in Prose and Poetry; Recitations and Readings Pertaining to the State. Baltimore:

Lehmen Printing Co., 1909. 248 p.

Extracts of a variety of historical material with notes and biographical sketches. Intended to be used for Maryland Day observances in schools.

288. RALEY, Loker. <u>300 Years: The Poets and Poetry of Maryland</u>. New York: H. Harrison, 1937. 171 p.

A representative collection with introductory biographical and critical information.

Earlier volumes of this type:

PERINE, George C. <u>Poets and Verse--Writers of Maryland; With Selections from Their Works</u>. Cincinnati: The Editor Publishing Co., 1898. 318 p.

SHEPHERD, Henry E., ed. <u>The Representative Authors of Maryland, from the Earliest Time to the Present Day, with Biographical Notes and Comments upon Their Works</u>. New York: Whitehall Publishing Co., 1911. 234 p. ports. A biographical handbook, arranged by broad period. Has a chapter on women writers of the late 19th and early 20th centuries.

MEDICINE

289. CORDELL, Eugene F. The Medical Annals of Maryland, 1799-1899. Prepared for the Centennial of the Medical and Chirurgical Faculty. Baltimore: Williams and Wilkins, 1903. 889 p.

    A chronological history of the Medical and Chirurgical Faculty of the State of Maryland (the State Medical Association), biographical sketches of members, and a chronology of medicine in Maryland.

290. MEDICAL AND CHIRURGICAL FACULTY OF THE STATE OF MARYLAND. Celebration of the Sesquicentennial of the Medical and Chirurgical Faculty of the State of Maryland, 1799-1949. Baltimore: 1949. 67 p. ports.

    In two parts, "A Brief History of the Medical and Chirurgical Society of Maryland," by John C. French (p. 1-58), and "Presidents of the Society, 1799-1909" (p. 59-65).

291. QUINAN, John R. Medical Annals of Baltimore from 1608 to 1880 Including Events, Men, and Literature. Baltimore: I. Friedenwald, 1884. 274 p. ports.

    Contains chronology (p. 9-52); biographical sketches with bibliography of their works (p. 53-185); and military service of Baltimore physicians, 1730-1880.

    More specialized works:

    ABRAHAM, Harold J. The Extinct Medical Schools of Baltimore, Maryland. Baltimore: Maryland Historical Society, 1969. 332 p. illus. The histories of the Washington Medical College-University School of Medicine; Woman's Medical College of Baltimore; Maryland Medical College of Baltimore; Baltimore University School of Medicine; Southern Homeopathic-Atlantic Medical College. Lists professors, graduates and matriculates, courses, textbooks, buildings, and equipment.

    CHESNEY, Alan M. The Johns Hopkins Hospital and the Johns Hopkins University School of Medicine; A Chronicle. Baltimore: Johns Hopkins Press, 1943-1963. 3 vols. Covers 1867-1914.

    Continued by

TURNER, Thomas B. Heritage of Excellence: The Johns Hopkins Medical Institutions, 1914-1947. Baltimore: Johns Hopkins University Press, 1974. 648 p. illus.

CORDELL, Eugene F. Historical Sketch of the University of Maryland, School of Medicine (1807-1890)... Baltimore: I. Friedenwald, 1891. 218 p. ports.

Pharmacy

292. SWAIN, Robert L. Drugs and Druggists of Early Maryland. Baltimore: Maryland Pharmaceutical Association, 1941. 83 p. illus.

References: p. 16-17, 32-33.

Pt. 1 (1608-1699) deals with drugs; pt. 2 (1700-1776) with druggists.

NATURAL RESOURCES

293. MARYLAND. Dept. of State Planning and the Smithsonian Institution Center for Natural Areas. Compendium of Natural Features Information. Baltimore: 1975. 2 vols. maps.

    Supersedes Roy G. Metzger, Catalog of Natural Areas in Maryland (1968).

    Bibliography: vol. 1, section 1, p. 27-29; section 2, p. 141-148.

    Vol. 1, section 1, "Catalog of Natural Features in Maryland; An Update," lists by county 679 areas where natural processes predominate and which are not significantly influenced deliberately or accidentally by man. This includes archaeological sites, caves, rock outcrops, lakes or ponds, springs, natural areas, wildlife habitat, wetlands, stream valleys, wilderness areas, nesting sites, altogether representing over 800,000 acres. For each site the location, size, description, significant features, ownership, etc., are given. Vol. 1, section 2 reproduces Dale W. Jenkins' "Natural Areas of the Chesapeake Bay Region: Ecological Priorities" (Smithsonian Institution Center for Natural Areas). Vol. 2 contains maps of the locations. Valuable supplementary studies appear as appendices in vol. 1: Stephen L. Keiley, "Description of the Chesapeake Bay Region"; Gary S. Waggoner, "Biotic Communities of the Chesapeake Bay Region"; Anne LaBastille, "Rare, Endangered and Threatened Vertebrate Species of the Chesapeake Bay Region"; Russell L. Kalogiski and others, "Rare, Endangered, and Endemic Plants of the Chesapeake Bay Region"; David W. Kunhardt, "Presently Protected Areas of Chesapeake Bay."

    A much earlier but still useful general description:

    MARYLAND. Board of World's Fair Managers. Maryland, Its Resources, Industries and Institutions. Prepared for the Board of World's Fair Managers of Maryland by the members of Johns Hopkins University faculty and others. Baltimore: Sun Job Printing Office, 1893. 504 p. illus., map.

294. U.S. Dept. of the Interior. Office of Information. Natural Resources in Maryland. Washington: U.S. Govt. Print. Off., 1969. 54 p. illus.

Gives introductory information on Maryland's history, physical characteristics, Indian heritage, water and mineral resources, fish and wildlife, parks and recreation. Also gives the programs of the federal natural resources agencies in Maryland.

Less comprehensive works:

FULLER, Kent B. From Pine Creek to Cranesville Swamp; A Review of the Natural Resources of Western Maryland. College Park, Md.: 1973. 20 p. illus. (Maryland. University. Natural Resources Institute. Educational Series, no. 97) A school level introduction to the natural resources of the four counties of Western Maryland (Allegany, Frederick, Garrett, Washington).

MARYLAND. University. Natural Resources Institute. Assateague Ecological Studies. Final Report. College Park, Md.: 1970. 3 pts. illus., maps. (Its Contributions, no. 446) Pt. 1: "Environmental Information." Pt. 2: "Environmental Threats." Pt. 3: "Suggestions for Land Use and Park Management." Bibliographies and a "Bibliography of Natural, Political, and Historical Aspects of Assateague Island, Maryland-Virginia and Vicinity," by J. Mark Odel, p. 1, p. 390-426. Pt. 1 includes the origin and geological history, commercial fisheries history, and data on such aspects of Assateague as submerged vegetation, finfish, crustaceans.

TRUITT, Reginald V. Assateague...the "Place Across": A Saga of Assateague Island. College Park, Md.: Maryland University Natural Resources Institute, 1971. 48 p. illus. (Maryland. University. Natural Resources Institute. Educational Series, no. 90) Bibliography: p. 48. A popular history of this barrier reef.

Bibliographies

295. MANSUETI, Romeo. Maryland Natural Resources Bibliography; Guide to Key Works Dealing with Zoology, Botany, Geology and Related Subjects. Solomons, Md.: Maryland Dept. of Research and Education, Chesapeake Biological Laboratory, 1955. 27 p. (Maryland. Dept. of Research and Education. Resource Study Report no. 7)

A comprehensive classified bibliography of over 1,000 items on the specific natural resources in Maryland, including animals, plants, minerals, weather, Indians. Includes work for the contiguous states and the District of Columbia.

296. MARYLAND. University. Natural Resources Institute. Publications of the Natural Resources Institute, University of Maryland. College Park, Md.: 1961- . Irregular.

Also covers the work of Chesapeake Biological Laboratory from 1927 to 1941 and the Maryland Dept. of Research and Education from 1941 to 1961.

Directory

297. ENVIRONMENTAL Resources in the Baltimore Region. Compiled and published by Baltimore Environmental Center and the Citizens Health Coucil, Regional Planning Council. Baltimore: 1972. 1 vol. (unpaged)

    Lists organizations in Baltimore City and Anne Arundel, Baltimore, Carroll, Harford, and Howard Counties under areas of concern.

Chesapeake Bay

298. BLAIR, Carvel H. and Willits D. Ansel. Chesapeake Bay: Notes & Sketches. Cambridge, Md.: Tidewater Publishers, 1970. 163 p. illus.

    Deals with history and natural history of the Bay, as well as the problem of pollution.

299. KLINGEL, Gilbert C. The Bay. Illus. by Natalie H. Davis. New foreword by the author. Hatboro, Pa.: Tradition Press, 1967. 278 p. illus.

    Reprint of 1951 edition.

    A naturalist's popular account of the life on, below, and above the Bay.

300. LIPPSON, Alice J. The Chesapeake Bay in Maryland; An Atlas of Natural Resources. Edited and illustrated...for the Natural Resources Institute of the University of Maryland. Baltimore: Johns Hopkins University Press, 1973. 55 p. illus., maps.

    Non-technical catalog and summary of the aquatic resources, fish, plants, geese, marshes, etc., with maps showing the distribution and life patterns of each species.

301. MARYLAND. Dept. of State Planning. Integrity of the Chesapeake Bay. Condensed by the Maryland Dept. of State Planning with the assistance of Urban Research and Development Corporation from Wallace, McHarg, Roberts and Todd, Inc., Maryland Chesapeake Bay Study. Baltimore: 1972. 52 p. illus., maps. (Its Publication no. 184)

    A summary of the major findings of the first comprehensive inventory of natural resources and economic development problems, including a description of the general characteristics of the Bay's physical and commercial value, economic viability, and population. Eight major problems which have ramifications for the Bay's natural and human ecology are also discussed.

    Works which deal with the utilization of the Bay's resources:

CHRISTY, Francis T. The Exploitation of a Common Property Natural Resource: The Maryland Oyster Industry. 222 p. (Ph.D., University of Michigan, 1964) Bibliography: p. 218-222; glossary of terms, p. 216-217. Woven through the text is a sensitive look at the oysterman's way of life.

SHERWOOD, Arthur W. Understanding the Chesapeake; A Layman's Guide. Cambridge, Md.: Tidewater Publishers, 1973. 114 p. illus. Bibliography: p. 110-111. Presents a variety of approaches, including those of the sailor, businessman, geologist, and amateur naturalist, to the ecosystems of the Bay and to the importance of the Bay to Maryland.

WALSH, Harry M. The Outlaw Gunner. Cambridge, Md.: Tidewater Publishers, 1971. 178 p. illus. An informal account of market gunning and trapping in the Chesapeake Bay.

WARNER, William W. Beautiful Swimmers: Waterman, Crabs, and the Chesapeake Bay. Drawings by Consuelo Hanks. Boston: Little, Brown, 1976. 304 p. illus. Bibliography: p. 293-295. The life and work of the crabbers of the Chesapeake Bay.

Chesapeake Bay - Directory

302. WILSON, William G. Organizations Concerned with the Chesapeake Bay: A Directory... Annapolis: Chesapeake Bay Foundation, Anne Arundel County Chapter, 1973. 53 p.

Describes the activities of public and private groups having an interest in the water, giving the chief official and organizational publications.

Fish and Fisheries - Bibliographies

303. SCHWARTZ, Frank J. Bibliography of Maryland Fisheries, Including Published and Unpublished Papers on the Fisheries and Related Fields of Tidewater Maryland. Solomons, Md.: Chesapeake Biological Laboratory, 1960. 35 p. (Maryland. Dept. of Research and Education. Contributions, no. 144)

A listing of 1,218 research items which bear on aquatic tidewater or oceanic situations in Maryland. Subject index.

Less comprehensive but complementary:

MANSUETI, Romeo. A Brief Bibliographic Review of the History of Fish and Fisheries of the Lower Susquehanna River Region in Maryland and Pennsylvania. Solomons, Md.: Maryland Dept. of Research and Education, 1958. 14 p. (Maryland. Dept. of Research and Education. Chesapeake Biological Laboratory, ref. 58-40) Lists 163 items. These include technical reports, documents, journal articles, and newspaper articles. Some items have a brief descriptive note.

Forests and Forestry - Bibliography

304. MARYLAND. Dept. of State Planning and Maryland [Dept. of Natural Resources] Forest Service. A Bibliography of Literature Related to Maryland's Forest Base. N.p.: 1976. [7]-16 p.

An alphabetical listing of approximately 125 items relating directly or indirectly to forests and forestry in Maryland. Includes ecology, taxonomy, utilization, and wildlife. Subject index.

Rocks and Minerals

305. MARYLAND. Dept. of Education. Maryland's Rocks and Minerals. Baltimore: 1962. 77 p. illus., maps. (Its Conservation Series, book 4)

Designed for school use, it presents material on Maryland's rocks, geology, and minerals, including identification and distribution information.

306. OSTRANDER, Charles W. and Walter E. Price, Jr. Minerals of Maryland. Baltimore: Natural History Society of Maryland, 1940. 92 p. illus.

"Bibliography and References": p. 83-88.

A comprehensive summary of Maryland mineral localities, giving their location, rock formations, and the minerals collected or reported. Also includes a checklist of all known minerals found in Maryland and their principal location, meteoritic falls and finds in Maryland, a list of fluorescent and luminous minerals in Maryland, and a history of mineralogy in Maryland. Index to mineral localities.

Soils

307. MARYLAND. State Planning Dept. Natural Soil Groups Technical Report. Baltimore: 1973. 153 p. illus., maps. (Its Publication no. 199)

To be used with 23 county maps (1: 63,360), excluding Baltimore City.

An interpretive guide to the county soil maps. Provides background on over 300 soil types aggregated into 30 groups. For each soil group gives its unique value, and cropland, urban, recreation, wildlife, and woodland utilization characteristics. Appendix lists natural soil group alphabetically by county.

308. MILLER, Fred P. Maryland Soils. College Park, Md.: Maryland University Cooperative Extension Service, 1967. 42 p. illus., map. (Maryland. University. Cooperative Extension Service. Extension Bulletin no. 212)

References: p. 42.

An introduction to the conditions which contributed to the formation and characteristics of Maryland soils, with chapters on the properties of soils, soil classification, soil surveys and their use, and soil associations.

309. U.S. Dept. of Agriculture. Soil Conservation Service. Soil Survey. Washington: U.S. Govt. Print. Off., 1900- . Irregular. illus., maps.

Prepared in cooperation with the Maryland Agricultural Experiment Station.

Starting in 1900 soil surveys were done for Maryland counties. These have been revised irregularly. The latest are as follows: Allegany (1921); Anne Arundel (1973); Baltimore (1917); Calvert (1971); Caroline (1964); Carroll (1969); Cecil (1973); Charles (1974); Dorchester (1963); Frederick (1960); Garrett (1974); Harford (1975); Howard (1968); Kent (1930); Montgomery (1961); Prince George's (1967); Queen Anne's (1966); Somerset (1966); St. Mary's (1923); Talbot (1970); Washington (1962); Wicomico (1970); and Worcester (1973).

For each county contains general background information on the nature of the county, such as relief, geology, drainage, climate, farming, water supplies, description of each soil, and management of the soil.

Water

310. MARYLAND. Geological Survey. "Bulletin Series." Baltimore: 1944- .

Descriptions of such aspects of water as the water-bearing properties of the geologic units and surface and ground water resources and quality are provided in the "Bulletin Series" as follows: no. 4: Baltimore area (1952); nos. 5 and 26: Anne Arundel (1949); no. 8: Calvert (1951); no. 10: Prince George's (1952); no. 11: St. Mary's (1953); no. 13: Garrett (1954); no. 14: Howard and Montgomery (1954); no. 15: Southern Maryland Coastal Plain (1955); no. 16: Somerset, Wicomico, and Worcester (1955); no. 17: Baltimore and Harford (1956); no. 18: Caroline, Dorchester, and Talbot (1956); no. 21: Cecil, Kent, and Queen Anne's (1958); no. 22: Carroll and Frederick (1958); no. 24: Allegany and Washington (1961); no. 29: Prince George's (1966); no. 30: Charles (1968).

311. WALKER, Patrick N. Flow Characteristics of Maryland Streams. Baltimore: Maryland Geological Survey, 1971. 160 p. (Maryland. Geological Survey. Report of Investigations, no. 16)

Information on mean annual discharge, magnitude and frequency of high and low flows, and flow-duration data for 112 gauging stations.

312. WALKER, Patrick N. Water in Maryland: A Review of the Free State's Liquid Assets. Baltimore: Maryland Geological Survey, 1970. 52 p. illus., maps. (Maryland Geological Survey. Educational Series, no. 2)

An easily understood presentation on Maryland's water, covering such aspects as where it is, where it comes from, how good it is, and how it is used.

Water - Bibliographies

313. BRAUN, Duane. The Potomac River Basin; A Bibliography of Reference Sources. Compiled for the Interstate Commission on the Potomac River Basin. Bethesda, Md.: Interstate Commission on the Potomac River Basin, 1974. 43 p.

An annotated chronological listing of technical, scientific, and planning material produced between 1907 and 1973 on such topics as pollution, drainage, erosion, flood control, water supply and utilization. Subject and geographical indexes.

314. STAUBLE, Jane F. and Douglas H. Wood. The Chesapeake Bay Bibliography: Maryland Waters. Gloucester Point, Va.: Virginia Institute of Marine Science, 1975. 1 vol. (various pagings) (Virginia Institute of Marine Science, Gloucester, Va. Special Scientific Report no. 73)

Vol. 3 in Virginia Institute of Marine Science, "Chesapeake Bay Bibliography" series.

A comprehensive subject listing of books, periodical articles, government, institutional, and academic reports, and theses and dissertations on the Bay from the fall line of the Susquehanna River to the Maryland-Virginia state line. Covers all aspects of the Bay, including natural resources management, utilization, pollution.

315. U.S. Dept. of the Interior. Water Resources Scientific Information Center. Legal Aspects of Water Pollution in Delaware, Maryland and Virginia; A Bibliography. Washington: 1972. 127 p. (Its WRSIC 72-206)

Abstracts of statutes, cases, and studies and reports. Significant descriptor index and comprehensive index.

POLITICS AND GOVERNMENT

316. BARD, Harry. Maryland State and Government: Its New Dynamics. Cambridge, Md.: Tidewater Publishers, 1974. 386 p. illus.

 Revised edition of his Maryland Today.

 A text offering a brief survey of the legislative, judicial, and administrative processes of the state and local government. Arranged under the topics "Structure and Processes of Government"; "Services to the People: The Social Problem Areas"; "Services to the People: Environmental and Economic Areas"; "Services to Government: By Government."

Bibliography

317. FRIEDMAN, Robert S. A Selected Bibliography of Maryland State and Local Government. College Park, Md.: University of Maryland Bureau of Governmental Research, 1956. 120 p.

 An extensive classified listing of monographs, reports, journal articles, and official publications. Subdivided under state government, local government, and intergovernmental affairs. Index of authors and issuing agencies.

Biographies

318. COYLE, Wilbur F. The Mayors of Baltimore. Baltimore: Baltimore Municipal Journal, 1919. 190 p. ports.

 Brief biographies and for each an account of their major contributions to Baltimore. The portraits are taken from those in City Hall.

319. ESSARY, Jesse F. Maryland in National Politics, from Charles Carroll to Albert C. Richie. 2d ed. Baltimore: John Murphy Co., 1932. 352 p. ports.

 A popular and favorable presentation of the careers of 15 Maryland notables.

Directories of Services

320. MARYLAND. Community Development Administration. Maryland State Programs for Local Government. Annapolis: 1974- . (looseleaf)

    A directory of selected state programs which provide financial and/or technical assistance and services to communities, public bodies, families, and individuals for their general improvement or welfare. For each program the information includes the program objective, specific use, restrictions, type of assistance, eligibility requirements, geographic coverage, program accomplishments, legal authorization, and related programs.

321. MARYLAND. Dept. of State Planning. Catalog of State Assistance Programs. Baltimore: 1974. 1 vol. (various pagings) (Its Publication no. 196)

    Provides information on state assistance programs, e.g. grants, loans, information, and services available to state and local agencies and the general public. Gives type of assistance available, state agency administering, eligibility requirements, application procedures, and sources for additional information. Arranged by major types of services, such as natural resources, personnel, transportation. Index of assistance services.

Church and State

322. HANLEY, Thomas O. Their Rights and Liberties; The Beginnings of Religious and Political Freedom in Maryland. Westminster, Md.: Newman Press, 1959. 142 p. illus.

    Bibliography: p. 131-137.

    Concentrates on the period from 1634 to the Toleration Act (1649), the traditions of English Catholicism in Maryland, and the role of Cecil Calvert.

323. PETRIE, George. Church and State in Early Maryland. Baltimore: Johns Hopkins Press, 1892. 50 p. (Johns Hopkins University Studies in Historical and Political Science, ser. 10, no. 4)

    An analysis of religious toleration in Maryland and the relation of State to Church up to the time of the establishment of the Church of England in 1692.

    A later study:

    WERLINE, Albert W. Problems of Church and State in Maryland During the Seventeenth and Eighteenth Century. South Lancaster, Mass.: College Press, 1948. 236 p. (Ph.D., Columbia University, 1947)

Election Statistics

324. WENTWORTH, Evelyn L. Election Statistics in Maryland, 1934-1958. College Park, Md.: University of Maryland Bureau of Governmental Research, 1959. 80 p.

Tabulations and graphs, by counties and Baltimore City and by Congressional district for Congressional elections, of registrations, general election turnout, and returns for the offices of President, Governor, and Congressmen.

General Assembly

325. BELL, George A. and Jean E. Spencer. The Legislative Process in Maryland: A Study of the General Assembly. 2d ed. College Park, Md.: University of Maryland Bureau of Governmental Research, 1963. 97 p.

Bibliographical footnotes.

For the general reader, a guide to the legislative process and to the work of the legislature.

326. MARYLAND. Dept. of Fiscal Services. Maryland Legislator's Handbook [1970-] Annapolis: 1970- . Irregular. maps.

A concise introductory guide for members of the General Assembly on the organization, practices, and procedures of the General Assembly, with rosters of legislators. Includes information on the other branches of government, bill drafting, and how a bill becomes a law.

A chronicle of the work of the General Assembly:

RILEY, Elihu S. A History of the General Assembly of Maryland, 1635-1904. Baltimore: 1905. 423 p.

327. MARYLAND. General Assembly. [Collected] Documents [1829-1920] Annual.

A collection of official documents, which frequently includes the annual reports of state agencies, reports of legislative and special committees and commissions, the Governor's annual and other messages to the General Assemblies, and his inaugural address.

See also

MARYLAND. General Assembly. House. Journal of Proceedings. Senate. Journal of Proceedings. Annual. The minutes of the daily activities, giving the roll call, synopsis of bills and their disposition at each reading, the roll call vote on each bill and resolution, and lists of bills passed.

328. MARYLAND Manual...A Compendium of Legal, Historical and Official Information Relating to the State of Maryland. Annapolis:

Maryland Hall of Records, 1885- . Biennial. ports.

Supplements, which are abridged versions reflecting organizational and personnel changes, issued every other year.

Includes a historical sketch of Maryland, biographical sketches of elected officials, state agency responsibilities and administrators, membership of boards and commissions, information on county government, a directory of local officials, state symbols, fiscal information, election statistics, Maryland Constitution, and other useful information.

General Assembly - Rosters

329. MARYLAND. General Assembly. Roster and List of Committees of the General Assembly of Maryland [1910-] Annapolis: 1910- . Annual.

Gives elected legislators by district with their addresses and their Senate and House Committee assignments.

330. PAPENFUSE, Edward C. and others. Directory of Maryland Legislators, 1635-1789. Annapolis: Maryland Bicentennial Commission, 1974. 56 p.

The Maryland Bicentennial Commission plans to publish three volumes on the History of Maryland Legislators. This listing is preliminary to that work.

A record of service of the roughly 4,000 individuals who served in the upper and lower houses, of governors, acting chief executives, members of conventions, councils of safety, and the Governor's council. Pt. 1 lists legislators by county and pt. 2 alphabetically.

Governor - Biographies

331. WHITE, Frank F. The Governors of Maryland, 1777-1970. Annapolis: Maryland Hall of Records Commission, 1970. 351 p. illus., ports. (Maryland. Hall of Records Commission. Publication no. 15)

Bibliographical references.

Offers a chronological, biographical, and administrative survey from Thomas Johnson to Marvin Mandel, with a separate chapter devoted to each governor. For each, the presentation is uniform with an introductory section, family background, education, career prior to becoming governor, administration, career following governorship, and commentary. There is a valuable introductory essay on the office of the Governorship (p. xiii-xxiv) by Gust Skordas.

Governor - History

332. ROHR, Charles J. The Governor of Maryland: A Constitutional Study. Baltimore: Johns Hopkins Press, 1932. 175 p. (Johns Hopkins University Studies in Historical and Political Science, ser. 50, no. 3)

    Bibliography: p. 165-172.

    Study of the historical growth of the office from the colonial period, with rigorous attention to the office as an institution and not to the men who occupied it.

History - Colonial and Revolutionary Periods

333. CARR, Lois G. and David W. Jordan. Maryland's Revolution of Government, 1689-1692. Ithaca, N.Y.: Cornell University Press, 1974. 321 p. map. (St. Mary's City Commission. Publication no. 1)

    An analysis of the social changes which led to the overthrow of the proprietary government.

334. HOFFMAN, Ronald. A Spirit of Dissension: Economics, Politics, and the Revolution in Maryland. Baltimore: Johns Hopkins University Press, 1973. 280 p.

    Includes bibliographical references.

    An analysis of the effect of diverse regional and economic interests on the state constitution and fiscal policy, the conflict between classes, and those with power and those without power in the years immediately preceding the Revolution.

335. SKAGGS, David C. Roots of Maryland Democracy, 1753-1776. Westport, Conn.: Greenwood Press, 1973. 253 p. maps. (Contributions in American History, no. 30)

    Bibliography: p. 235-238.

    Emphasizes the religious, ethnic, and economic factors which led to the Revolution.

    The strains of this work are continued in

    CROWL, Philip A. Maryland During and After the Revolution. Baltimore: Johns Hopkins Press, 1943. 185 p. (Johns Hopkins University Studies in Historical and Political Science, ser. 61, no. 1) Bibliographical note: p. 169-172. A political and economic history, focusing on the federal constitution, currency, and public and private debt.

336. SPARKS, Francis E. Causes of the Maryland Revolution of 1689. Baltimore: Johns Hopkins Press, 1896. 108 p. (Johns Hopkins University Studies in Historical and Political Science, ser. 14,

nos. 11-12)

Reprinted by Johnson Reprint Co. (1973).

Bibliography: p. 109.

A history of the Maryland Constitution of 1658 and the influence of the events in Virginia and England on the attempt to establish a palatinate form of government in Maryland.

Another valuable specialized study on this period:

OWINGS, Donnell M. His Lordship's Patronage: Offices of Profit in Colonial Maryland. Baltimore: Maryland Historical Society, 1953. 214 p. (Maryland Historical Society. Studies in Maryland History, no. 1) Bibliography: p. 187-193. Examines the influence and the place within the government structure of those positions which provided enough income to support a gentry.

History - Federalist Period

337. RENZULLI, L. Marx, Jr. Maryland: The Federalist Years. Madison, N.J.: Fairleigh Dickinson University Press, 1972. 354 p. illus.

Bibliography: p. 322-337.

A study of the political history of Maryland in the period 1787-1818, the Federalist Party in Maryland, and the War of 1812.

A collection of writings by contemporaries on the nature of constitutional government and on the responsibilities of representation can be found in

YAZAWA, Melvin, ed. Representative Government and the Revolution; The Maryland Constitutional Crisis of 1787. Baltimore: Johns Hopkins University Press, 1975. 187 p.

History - Nineteenth and Twentieth Centuries

338. BAKER, Jean H. The Politics of Continuity: Maryland Political Parties from 1858-1870. Baltimore: Johns Hopkins University Press, 1973. 239 p.

Bibliographical essay: p. 222-228.

An analysis of the effects of political and social issues, e.g. sectionalism, nativism, slavery and the Free Negro, and Reconstruction, on Maryland's political parties.

A description of the political tensions in one attempt to address the issue of Blacks is

CAMPBELL, Penelope. Maryland in Africa: The Maryland State Colonization Society, 1831-1837. Urbana, Ill.: University of Illinois Press, 1971. 264 p. illus., ports., maps.

A useful work on nativism in Maryland:

SCHMECKEBIER, Lawrence F. History of the Know-Nothing Party in Maryland. Baltimore: Johns Hopkins Press, 1899. 125 p.

339. CLARK, Charles B. Politics in Maryland During the Civil War. Chestertown, Md.: 1952. 201 p. (Ph.D., University of North Carolina, 1941)

Reprints of articles which appeared in the Maryland Historical Magazine.

340. CROOKS, James B. Politics and Progress: The Rise of Urban Progressivism in Baltimore, 1895-1911. Baton Rouge: Louisiana State University Press, 1968. 259 p. illus., ports.

"Notes on Sources": p. 237-246.

A study of society, politics, Blacks, and change in Baltimore.

Another valuable work for this period:

CALLCOTT, Margaret L. The Negro in Maryland Politics, 1870-1912. Baltimore: Johns Hopkins Press, 1969. 199 p. (Johns Hopkins University Studies in Historical and Political Science, ser. 87, no. 1) Bibliographical note: p. 190-193. An analysis of Black participation in the political process, and the influence of the Black vote on political power and on maintaining the two party system.

341. KENT, Frank R. The Story of Maryland Politics: An Outline History of the Big Political Battles of the State from 1846 to 1910, with Sketches and Incidents of the Men and Measures That Figured as Factors and the Names of Most of Those That Held Office in That Period. Hatboro, Pa.: Tradition Press, 1968. 439 p. ports.

Reprint of 1911 edition.

An informal view of Maryland politics by a newspaperman.

Judiciary

342. BYRD, Elbert M. The Judicial Process in Maryland. College Park, Md.: University of Maryland Bureau of Governmental Research, 1961. 83 p.

"Selected Bibliography": p. 81-83.

Extensive study of the structure and intergovernmental relations of the judiciary.

Local Government

343. BOWEN, Don L. and Robert S. Friedman. Local Government in Maryland. College Park, Md.: University of Maryland Bureau of

Governmental Research, 1955. 143 p. illus., map.

Bibliographical footnotes.

A survey which can act as an introductory text to the administration of counties, municipalities, Baltimore City, and other local governmental units.

344. SPENCER, Jean E. Contemporary Local Government in Maryland. College Park, Md.: University of Maryland Bureau of Governmental Research, 1965. 116 p. illus.

Bibliographical footnotes.

Analyzes the ability of local governments to function as agents of the state and yet be capable of responding uniquely to a need for area functions and services.

Both of the above works can be used in conjunction with

MARYLAND MUNICIPAL LEAGUE. Committee on the Functions of the Municipal Government. The Challenge to Municipal Government. Annapolis: 1974. 75 p. A report and recommendation on the role and responsibility of the municipal government in performing public safety, recreation, planning and zoning, public works, and sanitation services.

Local Government - Bibliography

345. MARYLAND. Morgan State University. Baltimore Urban Studies Institute. Baltimore Metropolitan Area Urban Affairs Bibliography. Baltimore: 1967. 70 p.

A listing of over 500 publications pertaining to the Baltimore metropolitan area. Arranged under such topics as commerce and industry, crime, race relations, welfare services, and government.

Local Government - Directories

346. DIRECTORY of Maryland Municipal Officials. Annapolis: Maryland Municipal League, 1952- . Annual. Loose-leaf.

Department heads arranged by governmental unit under counties and municipalities. Separate listings of regional agency and state agency units and their key personnel.

347. MARYLAND. State Planning Dept. Directory of Maryland Planning Agencies [1950-] Baltimore: 1950- . maps. Irregular. Title varies.

Lists official state, county, local, and regional planning and renewal agencies and organizations, giving commission membership and planning activities.

POPULATION

348. MARYLAND. Center for Health Statistics. Maryland Population Estimates 1974 and Projections to 1980. Baltimore: 1975. 14 p.

Supersedes earlier estimates and projections and is updated to cover ensuing five year periods.

Estimates total resident population by political subdivision, race, and broad age range group as of July 1, 1974; projections by political subdivision to July 1, 1980.

349. MARYLAND. Center for Health Statistics. Vital Statistics Report [1960-] Baltimore: 1961- . Annual.

Gives a narrative account of the highlights for each year, which acts to interpret the extensive tables on population, births, deaths, marriages, and divorces. Includes tables of selected retrospective vital statistics and comparative vital statistics for Maryland and the United States. Preliminary reports appear in the Maryland Center for Health Statistics Advance Vital Statistics. The Center's Components of Population Change, Maryland: 1960-1970 provides data on natural increase and net migration for the resident population by political subdivision.

350. MARYLAND. State Planning Dept. Dynamics of Urban Expansion in Maryland: Changes in Population Density by County Election Districts, 1900-1960. Baltimore: 1964. 1 vol. (unpaged) maps. (Its Publication no. 130)

Tables show persons per square mile by ten year periods and maps show how population density changed between 1950 and 1960.

351. MARYLAND. State Planning Dept. Division of Research Programs. Maryland Population and Housing Statistics: 1970 Census. Baltimore: 1971. 1 vol. (various pagings) (Maryland. State Planning Dept. Publication no. 174)

A planning document, this report presents an analysis of population and housing attributes for 1970, such as fertility, births, migration, changes in age, racial characteristics, and indicators of housing quality, as well as information from past censuses. Appendices provide data on population and housing by geographical area.

352. MARYLAND. State Planning Dept. Division of Research Programs. Maryland Population, 1930-1970, by Election Districts, Cities and Towns. Baltimore: 1971. 104 p. maps. (Maryland. State Planning Dept. Publication no. 171)

Provides statistical data at ten year intervals for population change, as well as 1970 population density.

353. U.S. Bureau of the Census. 1970 Census of Population. Detailed Characteristics, Maryland. Washington: U.S. Govt. Print. Off., 1972. 1 vol. (various pagings)

Presents statistical data on the social and economic characteristics for the state, standard metropolitan statistical areas, urban and rural, and city levels, based on the 5 and 15 percent U.S. Census sample. Includes such categories as race and nativity, school enrollment, years of school completed, family composition, income, place of work.

354. U.S. Bureau of the Census. 1970 Census of Population. General Population Characteristics, Maryland. Washington: U.S. Govt. Print. Off., 1971. 1 vol. (various pagings)

Presents statistics on basic demographic characteristics of the state, counties and Baltimore City, county subdivisions, and incorporated and unincorporated places, based on the U.S. Census 100 percent questionnaire. Includes such characteristics as race by sex for 1900 to 1970; age by race and sex from 1900 to 1970; household relationships by race and sex; general characteristics by places of various size; and rural population.

RELIGION

Biography

355. WEIS, Frederick L. The Colonial Clergy of Maryland, Delaware and Georgia. Lancaster, Mass.: Society of the Descendants of Colonial Clergy, 1950. 104 p.

    In "The Colonial Clergy of Maryland, 1629-1776" (p. 31-70), includes an alphabetical listing of clergy of all the denominations, giving date and place of birth and death, education, when served, and denomination. Also contains "Friends Meetings in Maryland, 1656-1776" (p. 99-100) and "Colonial Churches in Maryland, 1656-1776" (p. 94-99).

History

356. GAMBRELL, Theodore C. Church Life in Colonial Maryland. Baltimore: G. Lycett, 1885. 309 p.

    Presents a good description of church organization and the significance of the church in the colonial period.

    Also useful for a description of church life and practice in colonial Maryland is

    INGLE, Edward. Parish Institutions of Maryland, with Illustrations from Parish Records. Baltimore: Johns Hopkins University, 1883. 48 p. (Johns Hopkins University Studies in Historical and Political Science, ser. 1, no. 6)

357. THE MARYLAND Act of Religious Toleration. An interpretation by Gerald W. Johnson. Baltimore: Committee for the 300th Anniversary of the Maryland Act of Religious Toleration, 1949. 15 p. ports.

    Presents the history of the Act and a facsimile of the original copy.

358. RUSSELL, William T. Maryland: The Land of Sanctuary. A History of Religious Toleration in Maryland...to the American Revolution. 2d ed. Baltimore: J. H. Furst Co., 1908. 621 p. ports.

Bibliography: p. xix-xxxviii.

A Catholic view of the period of settlement to 1775, with extensive treatment of the Calverts, the Toleration Act of 1649, and the consequences of the 1689 Protestant Revolution.

Denominations

Baptist

359. WATTS, Joseph T. The Rise and Progress of Maryland Baptists. N.p.: Issued by the State Mission Board of the Maryland Baptist Union Association, 1953. 266 p. illus.

Bibliography: p. 260.

History from colonial times to 1952 with an emphasis on the Maryland Baptist Union Association and its executive board. There is a chapter on Negro Baptists in Maryland.

360. WEISHAMPEL, John F. History of Baptist Churches in Maryland Connected with the Maryland Baptist Union Association. Baltimore: 1885. 220 p. illus., ports.

After dealing briefly with the early history of the Baptists in Maryland, the Baltimore Baptist Association, and the Baptist Union Association, it gives the histories of the Baptist churches in Maryland from 1742 through 1885.

Catholic

361. JOERNDT, Clarence V. St. Ignatius, Hickory, and Its Missions. Baltimore: 1972. 536 p. illus., ports.

Extensive bibliographical references.

The history and influence of the oldest Roman Catholic Church in continuous use in the Archdiocese of Baltimore.

362. SPAULDING, Henry S. Catholic Colonial Maryland, A Sketch. Milwaukee: Bruce Publishing Co., 1931. 243 p. illus., ports.

"References Used in Writing This Book": p. 233-234.

This can be supplemented with

BEITZELL, Edwin W. The Jesuit Missions of St. Mary's County, Maryland. Abell, Md.: 1959. 320 p.

HISTORY of the Redemptorists at Annapolis, Md. from 1853 to 1903 with a Short Historical Sketch of the Preceding One Hundred and Fifty Years of Catholicity in the Capital of Maryland by a Redemptorist Father. Ilchester, Md.: College Press, 1904. 253 p. illus., ports.

TREACY, William P. Old Catholic Maryland and Its Early Jesuit Missionaries. Swedesboro, N.J.: St. Joseph's Rectory, 1889. 183 p.

363. STANTON, Thomas J. A Century of Growth; or, The History of the Church in Western Maryland. Baltimore: John Murphy Co., 1900. 2 vols. ports.

The history of the Catholic Church in Maryland west of the Chesapeake Bay, except Prince George's and Montgomery Counties. Gives such information as Archdiocesan offices, officials and organizations, and parishes in the Baltimore metropolitan area. Contains a necrology of Diocesan clergy and listings of Diocesan clergy and of brothers.

Catholic - Directories

364. OFFICIAL [ ] Directory for the Archdiocese of Baltimore. Baltimore: Catholic Review, 1921- . Annual. Title varies.

Lists Archdiocesan offices, officials, and organizations; parishes in and outside the Baltimore metropolitan area; seminaries, houses of study, provincial and superior residences of men; clergy alphabetically, by ordination date, and by orders; and brothers by orders.

Church of the Brethren

365. HENRY, J. Maurice. History of the Church of the Brethren in Maryland. Elgin, Ill.: Brethren Publishing House, 1936. 536 p. illus., ports.

Traces the history of the Church from colonial times to World War I.

Biographical sketches of ministers and distinguished church members: p. 411-521.

Episcopal - Bibliographies

366. HISTORICAL RECORDS SURVEY. District of Columbia. Inventory of Church Archives in the District of Columbia. Protestant Episcopal Church. Diocese of Washington. Volume I. District of Columbia, Montgomery, Prince George's, Charles, St. Mary's Counties, Maryland. Washington: 1940. 382 p.

Bibliography: p. 315-345.

Somewhat dated but still useful as an account and guide

to the history and historical papers of the Diocese and its parishes, churches, chapels, and institutions. Chronological, geographical, and alphabetical indexes.

367. HISTORICAL RECORDS SURVEY. Maryland. Inventory of the Church Archives of Maryland. Protestant Episcopal: Diocese of Maryland. Baltimore: Maryland Historical Records Survey Project, 1940. 310 p.

Covers only the Western Shore. Includes a general history, roster of bishops, Diocesan records, and historical sketches and record inventory of parishes, churches, and missions.

Episcopal - Biography

368. ALLEN, Ethan. Clergy in Maryland of the Protestant Episcopal Church Since the Independence in 1783. Baltimore: James S. Waters, 1860. 106 p.

Gives place of birth, early religious connection, when ordained and by whom, parish associations, publications, year of death, for more than 500 clergymen. Includes a listing of the parishes of the Diocese.

Episcopal - History

369. RIGHTMYER, Nelson W. Maryland's Established Church. Baltimore: The Church Historical Society for the Diocese of Maryland, 1956. 239 p.

The history of the Episcopal Church in Maryland up to the consecration of Thomas John Claggett as first Bishop of Maryland in 1798, providing the flavor of the involvement of Church and State in each other's affairs. Appendices contain a listing of the parishes with their boundaries, ministers and curates, churches, and biographical sketches of colonial clergy.

Useful for illustrations and documents of churches:

BEIRNE, Francis F. St. Paul's Parish, Baltimore, A Chronicle of a Mother Church. Baltimore: Horn-Shafer Co., 1967. 288 p. illus. A well-written account of the first place of public worship in Baltimore and the mother church for other Episcopal churches in the city.

SKIRVEN, Percy G. The First Parishes of the Province of Maryland. Baltimore: Norman, Remington Co., 1923. 181, 21 p. Has extensive information on the parishes but only covers the period to 1692.

German Reformed

370. BREADY, Guy P. History of the Maryland Classis of the Reformed Church in America; or, The History of the Reformed Church in Maryland since 1820. Taneytown, Md.: The Carroll Record Print, 1938. 230 p. illus., ports.

   "Ministers and Licentiates of Maryland Classis": p. 274-296.

Labadist

371. JAMES, Bartlett B. The Labadist Colony in Maryland. Baltimore: Johns Hopkins Press, 1899. 45 p. (Johns Hopkins University Studies in Historical and Political Science, ser. 17, no. 6)

Lutheran

372. WENTZ, Abdel R. History of the Evangelical Lutheran Synod of Maryland of the United Lutheran Church of America, 1820-1920... Together with a Brief Sketch of Each Congregation of the Synod and Biographies of the Living Sons of the Synod in the Ministry... Harrisburg, Pa.: Printed for the Synod by the Evangelical Press, 1920. 641 p. illus., ports.

   Also of interest:

   WENTZ, Abdel R. History of the Evangelical Lutheran Church of Frederick, Maryland, 1738-1938. Harrisburg, Pa.: Evangelical Press, 1938. 375 p. illus. A useful description of early Lutheranism and frontier church life in Maryland. Includes a listing of the congregation in 1763 and a bicentennial listing of members.

Methodist

373. BAKER, Gordon P., ed. Those Incredible Methodists: A History of the Baltimore Conference of the United Methodist Church. Baltimore: Baltimore Conference, Commission on Archives and History, 1972. 597 p. maps.

   Bibliography: p. 512-526.

   The combined work of 17 authors, their essays depict the origin and growth of Baltimore Conference Methodism up to 1965. Includes valuable information on missions and slavery, Black Methodism, Morgan College (now Morgan State University), and social concerns. Provides rosters of delegates to General Conferences, 1812-1970, and bishops associated with the Conferences.

   Also still extremely useful:

   ARMSTRONG, James E. History of the Old Baltimore

Conference from the Planting of Methodism in 1773 to the Division of the Conference in 1857. Baltimore: 1907. 527 p. illus., ports. Deals with the period when Maryland was the center of Methodist influence in the United States and with the history of Methodism in Maryland. "Clerical Sketches" (p. 327-491) offers an extensive register of Maryland clerics.

LEWIS, Thomas H., comp. Historical Record of the Maryland Annual Conference of the Methodist Protestant Church from the First Session, 1829, to the One Hundred and Eleventh (Concluding) Session, 1939. 5th rev. ed. Baltimore: 1939. 281 p. The chapter on "Maryland in Methodism" provides a good general history. Contains a register of all ministers admitted to membership and a record of ministerial appointments.

Presbyterian

374. McILVAIN, J. W. Early Presbyterianism in Maryland. Baltimore: Johns Hopkins Press, 1890. 33 p. (Johns Hopkins University Studies in Historical and Political Science, ser. 8, p. 313-345)

Supplementary notes to the Johns Hopkins University Studies in Historical and Political Science, 1890, no. 3.

Attempts an account of Presbyterianism and of the earliest ministers, such as Francis Doughty, Matthew Hill, Francis Makemie, from the founding of the Colony to 1706, the date of the formation of the first Presbytery.

Also useful:

BOULDEN, James E. The Presbyterians of Baltimore: Their Churches and Historic Grave-Yards. Baltimore: Wm. K. Boyle and Son, 1875. 134 p. illus.

GARDNER, John H. First Presbyterian Church of Baltimore. Baltimore: First Presbyterian Church, 1962. 203 p. Good account of a single church.

SMITH, Joseph T. Eighty Years: Embracing the History of Presbyterianism in Baltimore. Philadelphia: Westminster Press, 1899. 279 p. Useful for its biographies of pastors.

Quaker - Bibliography

375. JACOBSEN, Phebe R. Quaker Records in Maryland. Annapolis: Maryland Hall of Records, 1966. 154 p. (Maryland. Hall of Records. Publication no. 14)

"Selected Bibliography": p. 144-145; glossary of terms: p. 141-143.

Guide to Quaker records, either in the original or on

microfilm, in the custody of the Hall of Records.

Quaker - History

376. CARROLL, Kenneth L. Quakerism on the Eastern Shore. Baltimore: Maryland Historical Society, 1970. 328 p. illus.

Bibliography: p. 287-292.

A thoroughly researched history of the settlement, social life, and decline of the Quakers on the Eastern Shore from 1665 to the 20th century. Describes the relationship of the Friends to the civil authorities, the Established Church, and to the holding of slaves. The appendix records the births, marriages, and deaths of the Third Haven Monthly Meeting, the Northwest Fork Monthly Meeting, and the Cecil Monthly Meeting.

More specialized historical works:

CARROLL, Kenneth L. Joseph Nichols and the Nicholites. Easton, Md.: Easton Publishing Co., 1962. 116 p. The story of the Eastern Shore sect, "New Quakers," which originated in Maryland and flourished in the last half of the 18th century.

HARRISON, Samuel A. Wenlock Christison, and the Early Friends in Talbot County, Maryland. Baltimore: Maryland Historical Society, 1878. 76 p. Provides an intimate glimpse of Quaker life and the interaction with the affairs of state in the 17th century.

KELLY, J. Reaney. Quakers in the Founding of Anne Arundel County, Maryland. Baltimore: Maryland Historical Society, 1963. 146 p. illus., ports., maps. Describes the settlement of West River Meeting, Herring Creek Meeting, and Indian Spring Meeting and the influence of a flourishing Quaker community in the 17th century.

377. FORBUSH, Bliss A. A History of Baltimore Yearly Meeting of Friends: Three Hundred Years of Quakerism in Maryland, Virginia, the District of Columbia, and Central Pennsylvania. Sandy Spring, Md.: Baltimore Yearly Meeting of Friends, 1972. 174 p. illus., map.

Bibliography: p. 162-163.

A broad scale history which includes much of the material found in

BROWN, Levi K. An Account of the Meetings of the Society of Friends within the Limits of Baltimore Yearly Meetings. Philadelphia: T. Ellwood Zell, 1875. 64 p.

THOMAS, Anna B. The Story of the Baltimore Yearly Meeting from 1672 to 1938. Baltimore: Weant Press, 1938. 142 p.

SCIENCES

Directories

378. DIRECTORY of Science Resources for Maryland [1st (1963)-] Annapolis: Maryland Dept. of Economic Development. Irregular, usually biennial. Title varies.

    Gives the principal activities, facilities, and staffing of firms and organizations engaged in research and development or in providing engineering and technical support to private organizations and to state and federal research and development agencies. Also lists universities and other educational institutions with science oriented vocational activities, professional organizations, and information sources in the region. Geographic and principal activities indexes.

Botany

379. HERMANN, Frederick J. A Checklist of Plants in the Washington-Baltimore Area. 2d ed. Washington: Conference on District Flora, Smithsonian Institution, 1946. 134 p.

    Records approximately 2,500 species, varieties, and forms of vascular plants known to occur in Maryland west of the Chesapeake Bay.

    Also useful:

    NORTON, John B. S. and Russell G. Brown. A Catalog of the Vascular Plants of Maryland. College Park, Md.: University of Maryland Agricultural Experiment Station, 1946. 50 p. Reprint from Castania 11 (1946): 1-50. Identifies 2,334 species, forms, and varieties native to or established in the state of Maryland which grow without cultivation.

380. KRAUSS, Robert W. and others. Checklist of the Plant Species of the Chesapeake Bay Occurring within the Hightide Limits of the Bay and Its Tributaries. College Park, Md.: 1971. 1 vol. (unpaged) (Maryland. University. Dept. of Botany. Technical Bulletin, 2002)

    Lists algae, fungi, and bryophytes, giving area where collected and a reference to source documents.

381. SHREVE, Forrest and others. The Plant Life of Maryland. Baltimore: Johns Hopkins University Press, 1910. 533 p. illus., maps. (Maryland. Weather Service [Reports] vol. 3)

Includes sections on the floristic plant geography of Maryland, ecological plant geography, agricultural features, forests and their products, and an annotated list of 1,400 plants collected or observed in Maryland and notes on their distribution.

382. TATNALL, Robert R. Flora of Delaware and the Eastern Shore; An Annotated List of Ferns and Flowering Plants of the Peninsula of Delaware, Maryland and Virginia. Wilmington, Del.: Society of Natural History of Delaware, 1946. 313 p. illus., map.

Bibliography: p. 289-290.

A list, ordered taxonomically, of names, with information on frequency of occurrence, distribution, and the location of specific collections. For those species which are not native their origin is given. Includes a useful introduction to the biology of the general region. Index to common and scientific names.

A technical floristic study of an area is

HIGGINS, Elizabeth A., Robert D. Rappleye, and Russell G. Brown. The Flora and Ecology of Assateague Island. College Park, Md.: 1971. 70 p. illus., maps. (Maryland. University. Agriculture Experiment Station. Bulletin no. A-172) Bibliography: p. 66-70.

Botany - Ferns

383. REED, Clyde F. The Ferns and Fern-Allies of Maryland and Delaware, including District of Columbia. Baltimore: Reed Herbariam, 1953. 286 p. illus., maps.

Bibliography: p. 275-278; glossary: p. 268-274.

An aid to the amateur naturalist and gardening enthusiast, as well as professional botanist, to identify species and varieties. The emphasis is on providing a general understanding of the habits and habitat but includes detailed descriptions as well. Indicates general distribution and distribution in Maryland. Preliminary chapters provide background information on earlier studies in Maryland. Indexes to scientific and common names.

Botany - Phytoplankton

384. GRIFFITH, Ruth E. Phytoplankton of Chesapeake Bay; An Illustrated Guide to Genera. Solomons, Md.: Maryland Dept. of Research and Education, 1961. 79 p. illus. (Maryland. University. Natural Resources Institute. Contributions, no. 172)

"Annotated Reference List": p. 65-68.

A useful aid to identifying the more common phytoplankton genera of the Chesapeake Bay region, giving phyla description, generic key, and references.

Botany - Weeds

385. NORTON, John B. S. Maryland Weeds and Other Harmful Plants. College Park, Md.: 1911. 71 p. illus. (Maryland. University. Agricultural Experiment Station. Bulletin no. 155)

Lists the principal weeds and poisonous plants of Maryland and includes a key for distinguishing them.

Botany - Wild Flowers

386. HARNED, Joseph E. Wild Flowers of the Alleghenies. Oakland, Md.: 1936. 675 p. illus.

A semi-popular manual, giving flowering season, location, legends, historical references, diagnostic characteristics of families, and over 400 line drawings. Contains a checklist of ferns.

Botany - Woody Plants

387. BROWN, Russell G. and Melvin L. Brown. Woody Plants of Maryland. [Baltimore: Port City Press] Distributed by the Student Supply Store, University of Maryland, College Park, 1972. 347 p. illus.

Glossary: p. 321-329.

A valuable and thorough guide for naturalists, foresters, and laymen, describing and illustrating 365 species. Contents include general descriptions of vegetation, maps of vegetation zones, and forest types. The 97 families of Maryland's woody plants are classified by reproductive and vegetative parts; keys are provided for summer and winter conditions; and the principal variables in plant identification, such as leaves, buds, flower parts, and fruits, are illustrated. Index to common and scientific names.

388. MARYLAND. Dept. of Forestry. Forest Trees of Maryland; How to Know Them. 2d ed. Baltimore: 1938. 100 p. illus.

A field book of the more common trees in Maryland, with illustrations of twig, fruit, and leaf. Also includes "Largest Tree of Each Species in Maryland on Record, September 1, 1937": p. 96-98.

Another field book useful for schools:

KAYLOR, Joseph F. Trees of Maryland. Solomons, Md.: Maryland Dept. of Research and Education, 1946. 23 p. illus. (Maryland Dept. of Research and Education. Educational Series, no. 12)

389. YINGLING, Earl L. The Big Tree Champions of Maryland. Annapolis: Maryland Forest Service, 1973. 45 p. illus.

Supersedes 1956 edition.

Lists the largest of the 134 species and five varieties of trees growing in Maryland, giving their measurements and locations and indicating national champions.

An informal account of Maryland's most famous tree and the people and places associated with it:

PRESTON, Dickson J. Wye Oak. Featuring a Bodine gallery of Wye Oak photographs. Cambridge, Md.: Tidewater Publishers, 1972. 135 p. illus.

Geology

390. MARYLAND. Geological Survey. [Reports Dealing with the Systematic Geology and Paleontology of Maryland] Baltimore: Johns Hopkins Press, 1901-1923. 8 vols. in 12. illus., maps.

Contents: vol. 1: Eocene (1901); vol. 2: Miocene. Atlas (1904); vol. 3: Pliocene and Pleistocene (1906); vol. 4: Lower Cretaceous (1911); vol. 5, pt. 1: Lower Devonian (1913); vol. 5, pt. 2: Middle and Upper Devonian (1913); vol. 6: Upper Cretaceous (1916); vol. 7: Cambrian and Ordovician Deposits of Maryland (1919); vol. 8: Silurian (1923).

Includes bibliographies.

A comprehensive study of the historical geology and paleontology of Maryland, describing the geologic formations and fauna and flora fossil remains; e.g. vol. 4 (p. 173-210) contains information on dinosaurs.

Some material is updated by the following:

ANDERSON, J. L. Cretaceous and Tertiary Subsurface Geology: The Stratigraphy, Paleontology, and Sedimentology of Three Deep Test Wells on the Eastern Shore of Maryland. Baltimore: Maryland Dept. of Geology, Mines and Water Resources, 1948. 456 p. illus. (Maryland. Geological Survey. Bulletin no. 2)

KELLOGG, Remington. Fossil Marine Mammals from the Miocene Calvert Formation of Maryland and Virginia. Washington: Smithsonian Institution, 1965-1968. 8 pts., paged continuously. 201 p. illus. (U.S. National Museum. Bulletin 247) Includes bibliographies.

VOKES, Harold E. Miocene Fossils of Maryland. Rev. ed. Baltimore: Maryland Geological Survey, 1968. 85 p. illus. (Maryland. Geological Survey. Publication no. 20)

Geology - Bibliography

391. DONOHUE, Mildred D. and Norma S. Gordon. Fossil Finds in Maryland; A Retrospective Bibliography. College Park, Md.: University of Maryland Libraries, 1967. 233 p.

Lists approximately 750 items published to 1966. The bulk of the work is an index to fossils, ages, and locations.

Geology - Caves

392. FRANZ, Richard and Dennis Slifer. Caves of Maryland. Baltimore: Maryland Geological Survey, 1971. 120 p. illus. (Maryland. Geological Survey. Educational Series, no. 3)

Supersedes William E. Davis, The Caves of Maryland (1961).

References: p. 114-118.

Lists caves alphabetically by county, giving the location and elevation, general setting, items of historical and legendary interest, geologic horizon and brief interpretation of geologic relations, physical description, and a map. Introductory material on caving, geologic setting, cave biology, and the archaeology of Maryland caves and shelters.

Geology - Guidebooks

393. GUIDEBOOKS to the Geology of Maryland. Prepared for the Field Trips of the Geological Society of America. Washington Meeting, Nov. 1950. Baltimore: Johns Hopkins Press, 1950. 1 vol. in 3 pts. illus., maps. (Johns Hopkins University. Studies in Geology, no. 16)

Includes bibliographies and route logs.

Pt. 1: Ernst Cloos, "The Geology of the South Mountain Anticlinorium"; pt. 2: Ernst Cloos and J. L. Anderson, "The Geology of Bear Island, Potomac River"; pt. 3: John T. Hack, C. C. Nikiforoff, and R. M. Overbeck, "The Coastal Plain Geology of Southern Maryland."

394. MARYLAND. Geological Survey. Guidebooks [nos. 1-4] Baltimore: 1968-1971.

Includes bibliographies and road logs.

No. 1: Glaser, John D. Coastal Plain Geology of Southern Maryland (1968), 56 p.; no. 2: Crowley, William P. and others. New Interpretations of the Eastern Piedmont Geology of Maryland or Granite and Gabbro or Grayroacke and Greenstone (1968), 43 p.; no. 3: Gernant, Robert E., Thomas G. Gibson, and Frank C. Whitmore, Jr. Environmental History of Maryland Miocene (1971), 58 p.; no. 4:

Fisher, George W. The Piedmont Crystalline Rocks of Bear Island, Potomac River, Maryland (1971), 32 p.

395. STEPHENSON, Lloyd W., Charles W. Cook, and Wendell C. Mansfield. The Chesapeake Bay Region. Washington: U.S. Govt. Print. Off., 1932. 49 p. illus., map.

International Geological Congress, 16th session, United States, 1933. Guidebook 5, Excursions A-5.

Bibliography: p. 47-49; route map.

Presents a tour of representative geologic localities, which provide the larger and better exposures of the cretaceous, tertiary, quaternary, and recent formations, and include many of the principal fossil exposures. Includes information on geography, physiography, and geologic features and history.

Meteorology

396. ABBE, Cleveland, Jr., F. J. Walz, and Oliver L. Fassig. "Report of the Meteorology of Maryland." In Maryland. Weather Service [Reports] vol. 1, pt. 3, p. 219-566. Baltimore: Johns Hopkins University Press, 1899. illus., maps.

"Publications Relating to Meteorology in Maryland and Delaware": p. 363-399.

Offers a detailed historical sketch of meteorology in Maryland beginning with Captain John Smith's 1608 account, historical statistics on temperature and precipitation, and useful general information.

A more specialized and detailed record:

FASSIG, Oliver L. The Climate and Weather of Baltimore. Baltimore: Johns Hopkins University Press, 1907. 515 p. illus., maps. (Maryland. Weather Service [Reports] vol. 2) Includes the extreme meteorological elements recorded in the city.

397. ASBAUGH, Byron L. and G. N. Brancato. Maryland's Weather. 2d ed. Solomons, Md.: Maryland Dept. of Research and Education, 1958. 48 p. illus., maps. (Maryland. Dept. of Research and Education. Educational Series, no. 38)

A general school level introduction to weather, with sections devoted to the general features of Maryland weather, the history of Maryland weather records, severe or unusual Maryland weather, and, for each county, tables giving average and yearly precipitation and the chances of killing frost in spring and fall.

Also useful:

MOYER, W. J. Climate of Maryland. Washington: U.S. Govt. Print. Off., 1968. 20 p. illus., maps. (U.S. Environmental Sciences Services Administration.

Climatography of the United States, 60-18) Bibliography: p. 6. Summary of climatic data, including freeze data for each station, normals by climatological divisions, normals, means and extremes, mean annual precipitation. Introductory summary material on Maryland's geography, physiography, climatic controls, temperature, precipitation, thunderstorms, etc.

TRUITT, Reginald V. High Winds...High Tides: A Chronicle of Maryland's Coastal Hurricanes. College Park, Md.: University of Maryland Natural Resources Institute, 1967. 36 p. illus., maps. (Maryland. University. Natural Resources Institute. Educational Series, no. 77) Bibliography: p. 35. Contains a chronology of storms, notes on coastal storms and hurricanes along the Maryland shore and on the changes in Maryland's Atlantic inlets.

WEEKS, John R. Our Climate, Useful Information Regarding the Climate between the Rocky Mountains and the Atlantic Coast with Special Reference to Maryland and Delaware. Baltimore: Maryland Weather Service, 1971. 66 p. illus., maps.

398. U.S. Environmental Science Services Administration. Climatological Data: Maryland and Delaware [1896-] Washington: Environmental Science Services Administration, Environmental Data Service, 1896- . Monthly with annual summaries.

Presents basic climatological data for all operating stations with temperature and precipitation extremes. This information is summarized in Climatic Summary of the United States. Bulletin W Supplement, 1931-1952, Maryland and Delaware (U.S. Weather Bureau. Climatography of the United States, series 11-15) Washington: 1953, 33 p., and Climatic Summary of the United States. Bulletin W Supplement, 1951-1960, Maryland (U.S. Weather Bureau. Climatography of the United States, series 86-15) Washington: 1961, 62 p.

Zoology

Invertebrates - Crayfish

399. MEREDITH, William G. and Frank J. Schwartz. Maryland Crayfishes. Solomons, Md.: Maryland Dept. of Research and Education, 1960. 32 p. illus., maps. (Maryland. Dept. of Research and Education. Contributions, no. 46)

Glossary: p. 29.

A popular account of the life history, anatomy, habitat, distribution, evolution, classification, and use as a lab animal of Maryland crayfish. Distribution maps.

Invertebrates - Insects

400. HARMAN, Dan M. A Guide to Important Forest Insects in Maryland. College Park, Md.: University of Maryland Natural Resources Institute, 1973. 18 p. illus. (Maryland. University. Natural Resources Institute. Educational Series, no. 98)

    Designed to aid students and laymen in identifying some common species likely to be met in Maryland and to associate the species with the type of damage they cause. Illustrations of insects and of characteristic damage and diagnostic features of damage are given.

Invertebrates - Lepidoptera - Butterflies

401. CLARK, Austin H. The Butterflies of the District of Columbia and Vicinity. Washington: U.S. Govt. Print. Off., 1932. 337 p. illus. (Smithsonian Institution. United States National Museum. Bulletin no. 15)

    Includes the contiguous areas of Maryland. Provides extensive notes, giving occurrence, habits, caterpillar stage, and remarks.

402. [FLADUNG, Edmund B. and others] Familiar Butterflies of Maryland. Baltimore: Natural History Society of Maryland, 1936. 30 p. illus.

    Very similar to Edmund B. Fladung, Common Butterflies of Maryland (1927).

    Semi-popular treatment.

    Short non-technical descriptions are also given in

    HAYDON, Stansbury. The Papilionidae of Maryland. Baltimore: Natural History Society of Maryland, 1933. 14 p. illus.

    HAYDON, Stansbury. The Satyridae of Maryland; A Short Description of the Satyr and Wood-Nymph Butterflies of This State with Notes on the Various Stages of Their Life Histories. Baltimore: Natural History Society of Maryland, 1934. 10 p. (Natural History Society of Maryland. Proceedings, no. 4) Includes information on occurrence.

Invertebrates - Leipdoptera - Moths

403. FLADUNG, Edmund B. Familiar Moths of Maryland; Families Saturniidae and Ceretocampidae. Baltimore: Natural History Society of Maryland, 1930. 19 p. illus.

    A semi-popular treatment of 11 common moths, principally large species, found in Maryland.

Invertebrates - Oysters

404. MARYLAND. Dept. of Education. Maryland's Sunken Treasure. Baltimore: 1953. 47 p. illus. (Its Conservation Series, book 2)

A school level description of the life story, harvesting, uses, and misuses of the Chesapeake Bay oyster.

Invertebrates - Sea Nettle

405. SCHULTZ, Leonard P. and David G. Cargo. The Sea Nettle of Chesapeake Bay. College Park, Md.: University of Maryland Natural Resources Institute, 1971. 8 p. illus. (Maryland. University. Natural Resources Institute. Educational Contribution no. 93)

The biology and characteristics of the summer sea nettle.

Invertebrates - Spiders

406. MUMA, Martin H. An Annotated List of the Spiders of Maryland. College Park, Md.: 1945. 65 p. (Maryland. University. Agricultural Experiment Station. Bulletin, A381 (Tech.))

Lists over 400 species and gives the citations to the original descriptions, ecological notes, and their distribution by county.

407. MUMA, Martin H. Common Spiders of Maryland. Baltimore: Natural History Society of Maryland, 1943. 173 p. illus.

Bibliography: p. 167; glossary: p. 168-173.

Describes 100 spiders, indicating habitat and distribution in Maryland. Indexes of common and of scientific names.

Vertebrates - Amphibia, Reptiles

408. CONANT, Roger. An Annotated Check List of the Amphibians and Reptiles of the Del-Mar-Va Peninsula. Wilmington, Del.: The Society of Natural History of Delaware, 1945. 8 p.

Covers salamanders, toads and frogs, lizards, snakes, and turtles, giving common and scientific names.

409. MANSUETI, Romeo. A Descriptive Catalogue of the Amphibians and Reptiles Found in and around Baltimore City, Maryland, within a Radius of Twenty Miles. Baltimore: Natural History Society of Maryland, 1941. 53 p. illus., map. (Natural History Society of Maryland. Proceedings, no. 7)

Gives the varieties of common names, descriptions, and range.

Vertebrates - Amphibia, Reptiles - Reptiles

410. McCAULEY, Robert H. The Reptiles of Maryland and the District of Columbia. Hagerstown, Md.: 1945. 194 p. illus., maps.

Bibliography: p. 181-188.

Thorough work on 44 species of reptiles (6 species of lizards, 26 of snakes, and 12 of turtles). For each is given the common name, physical description, sexual dimorphism, range, distribution in Maryland, habitat and habits, distribution map, and a photograph. Much useful background information is included, such as an account of herpetological observations and investigations from Capt. John Smith to 1937, the relation between life zones, and distribution of species.

A more popular and less comprehensive work:

KELLY, Howard A., Audrey W. Davis, and Harry C. Robertson. Snakes of Maryland. Baltimore: Natural History Society of Maryland, 1936. 103 p. illus.

Vertebrates - Amphibia, Reptiles - Lizards

411. McCLELLAN, William H., Romeo Mansueti, and Francis Groves. The Lizards of Central and Southern Maryland. Baltimore: Natural History Society of Maryland, 1943. 42 p. illus. (Natural History Society of Maryland. Proceedings, no. 8)

Bibliography: p. 4.

Gives such information as taxonomy, chief characteristics, size, color, distribution, environment, general conduct and disposition, and food.

Vertebrates - Amphibia, Reptiles - Turtles

412. SCHWARTZ, Frank J. Maryland Turtles. Rev. ed. College Park, Md.: University of Maryland Natural Resources Institute, 1967. 38 p. illus., maps. (Maryland. University. Institute of Natural Resources. Educational Series, no. 79)

Selected bibliography: p. 31-34.

Provides such descriptive information as size, longevity, fossils, breeding season, and known enemies. Distribution maps.

Vertebrates - Birds

413. MEANLEY, Brooke. Birds and Marshes of the Chesapeake Bay Country. Cambridge, Md.: Tidewater Publishers, 1975. 157 p.

Includes bibliographical references and a bibliography: p. 147-149.

A naturalist and birdwatcher describes the natural habits of many Maryland birds.

414. STEWART, Robert E. and Chandler S. Robbins. Birds of Maryland and District of Columbia. Washington: U.S. Govt. Print. Off., 1958. 401 p. maps. (U.S. Fish and Wildlife Service. North American Fauna, no. 62)

Supersedes Frank C. Kirkwood, "A List of the Birds of Maryland." In Maryland Academy of Sciences. Transactions 2 (1895): 241-382, and Irving E. Hampe and Haven Kolb, Preliminary List of Birds of Maryland and the District of Columbia (1947).

An annotated checklist of Maryland birds, including accidental visitors. For each species and subspecies gives the geographical, biological, and seasonal distribution and shows where and when each species is likely to occur, as well as indicating some of the more significant environmental factors. In addition, gives a sketch of the history of ornithology in Maryland and the physical and faunal areas.

415. STEWART, Robert E. Waterfowl Populations in the Upper Chesapeake Region. Washington: U.S. Govt. Print. Off., 1962. 208 p. illus.

Information, with tables, on the distribution, ecology, and harvesting of waterfowl in this primary Atlantic Coast migratory area.

Vertebrates - Fish

416. DAVIS, Robert M. Key to the Freshwater Fishes of Maryland. Annapolis: Maryland Dept. of Natural Resources, 1974. 48 p. illus. (Maryland. University. Natural Resources Institute. Educational Series, no. 101)

Provides diagnostic characteristics to identify the fishes of Maryland's inland waters; provides common and scientific names.

Supersedes much of

MANSUETI, Romeo. Revised Key to Maryland Fresh Water Fishes. Solomons, Md.: Maryland Dept. of Research and Education. Chesapeake Biological Laboratory, ref. no. 57-22) Also includes types of estuarine species which enter the tidal freshwater of the Chesapeake Bay.

417. HILDEBRAND, Samuel F. and William C. Schroeder. Fishes of Chesapeake Bay. Washington: U.S. Govt. Print. Off., 1928. 366 p. illus. (U.S. Fish and Wildlife Service. Fishery Bulletin, vol. 43)

Bibliography: p. 358-366; glossary: p. 355-358.

A survey of all fishes taken in the salt water of the

Bay, as well as those taken in the mouths of streams where the water was brackish to only slightly brackish. Arranged by order and families. The descriptions, as non-technical as possible, include chief diagnostic characters; variations among individuals, e.g. age, sex; food and feeding habits; spawning, embryology, larval development; growth rate; relative and seasonal abundance and how taken; commercial importance; size attained; habitat and general distribution; previous Chesapeake Bay sources; and scientific and common names.

418. TRUITT, Reginald, Barton A. Bean, and Henry W. Fowler. The Fishes of Maryland. Solomons, Md.: Maryland Conservation Dept., 1929. 120 p. illus. (Maryland. University. Natural Resources Institute. Contribution no. 2)

Following a general discussion of fishes, lists the fishes found in Maryland, giving identifying physical characteristics, range, and localities where found in Maryland. Index of common and scientific names.

Also useful, if less extensive:

ELSER, Harold J. Common Fishes of Maryland; How to Tell Them Apart. Solomons, Md.: 1950. 45 p. illus. (Maryland. University. Natural Resources Institute. Contribution no. 88) Intended for the use of sports fishermen and students. Through use of line drawings and notes indicates differences between those fish which resemble each other to some degree. Includes Chesapeake Bay fish, but not those caught along the Atlantic Ocean. Local names are given.

Vertebrates - Mammals

419. PARADISO, John L. Mammals of Maryland. Washington: U.S. Bureau of Sport Fisheries and Wildlife, 1969. 193 p. maps. (U.S. Fish and Wildlife Service. North American Fauna, no. 66)

References: p. 184-193.

Provides detailed systematic information, giving scientific and common names, followed by distribution maps, distinguishing characteristics, measurements, habitat, and habits. Introductory information on principal biotic or natural areas in Maryland and the effects of civilization.

A supplementary work:

MANSUETI, Romeo. "Extinct and Vanishing Mammals of Maryland and the District of Columbia.: Maryland Naturalist 20, no. 12 (1950): 1-48. Bibliography: p. 43-48. A narrative account tracing records of the mammals through extensive use of references and quotations from a variety of sources.

SPECIAL GROUPS

Blacks

420. BRACKETT, Jeffrey R. The Negro in Maryland; A Study of the Institution of Slavery. Freeport, N.Y.: Books for Libraries Press, 1969. 268 p.

Reprint of 1889 edition.

Deals with the development of African slavery in Maryland, its social, legal, and economic consequences. Includes chapters on Indians and the colonists' relations with white indentured servants, manumission, the free Negro, runaway slaves, slave revolts, and the slave code involving crime and punishment.

Supplemented by

421. BRACKETT, Jeffrey R. Notes on the Progress of Colored People in Maryland since the War... Baltimore: Johns Hopkins University, 1890. 96 p. (Johns Hopkins University Studies in Historical and Political Science, ser. 8, nos. 7-9)

Covers the political, educational, social, economic, and professional opportunities of Blacks after the Civil War.

422. KOGER, Azzie B. The Maryland Negro; 501 Facts, Figures, and Fancies about the Maryland Negro. Baltimore: 1953. 47 p. ports.

A miscellany of information including firsts, movements, religious societies, education.

423. KOGER, Azzie B. The Maryland Negro in Our Wars. Baltimore: Clarke Press, 1942. 31 p. illus., ports.

Brief notes on men, units, veteran organizations, and a list of dead.

424. KOGER, Azzie B. Negro Baptists of Maryland. Baltimore: Clarke Press, 1946. 78 p. illus., ports.

First published in 1936 as History of Negro Baptists of Maryland.

Includes history, biography of ministers and lay leaders, sketches of churches, and information on Maryland State Baptist conventions.

425. KOGER, Azzie B. The Negro Lawyer in Maryland. Baltimore: 1948. 12 p.

A narrative account of cases involving Black issues and those Black lawyers who were involved. Provides some biographical footnotes on the lawyers.

426. ROLLO, Vera A. F. The Negro in Maryland. Lanham, Md.: Maryland Historical Press, 1972. 70 p. illus.

Bibliography: p. 68-69.

Based, in large part, on her Your Maryland (1971).

School level survey with material on Benjamin Banneker and Matthew Henson.

427. WAGANDT, Charles L. The Mighty Revolution; Negro Emancipation in Maryland, 1862-1864. Baltimore: Johns Hopkins Press, 1964. 299 p. illus., maps.

Bibliography: p. 269-284.

Describes how on a smaller scale the politics of freeing the slaves in Maryland reflected the national scene, as did sectional differences and the conflicts between agricultural and urban interests and the established and the new residents.

428. WRIGHT, James M. The Free Negro in Maryland, 1634-1860. New York: Octagon Books, 1971. 362 p. (Columbia University. Studies in History, Economics, and Public Law, no. 222)

Reprint of 1921 edition.

A study of the anomalous place in society and the social and legal condition of the free Negro in Maryland. Covers manumission, the colonization movement, and the politics of the Negro issue.

Blacks - Biographies

429. BRAGG, George F. Men of Maryland. Rev. ed. Baltimore: Church Advocate Press, 1925. 160 p. ports.

Biographical sketches of Maryland Black men and women. Includes chapters on Black slaves and on free Blacks in Maryland.

Germans

430. CUNZ, Dieter. The Maryland Germans; A History. Princeton, N.J.: Princeton University Press, 1948. 476 p. illus., ports.

Bibliography: p. 439-449.

The definitive study of the immigration, culture, contribution, and assimilation of this major Maryland ethnic group.

A record of the intellectual life of the Maryland Germans can be found in

HENNINGSHAUSEN, Louis P. History of the German Society of Maryland. Baltimore: 1909. 203 p.

431. NEAD, Daniel W. The Pennsylvania-German in the Settlement of Maryland. Lancaster, Pa.: Press of the New Era Printing Co., 1914. 304 p. illus., maps.

Bibliographic footnotes.

The social and cultural influence of the Pennsylvania Germans in the settlement of Western Maryland through the Revolutionary War period. Index to proper names.

Also of interest:

SCHULTZ, Edward T. First Settlements of Germans in Maryland. Frederick, Md.: David H. Smith, 1896. 60 p. illus. Emphasizes the area around Frederick.

Irish

432. WILLIAMS, Harold A. History of the Hibernian Society of Baltimore, 1803-1957. Baltimore: Hibernian Society of Baltimore, 1957. 57 p. illus., ports.

A brief glimpse of the role of the Irish in Baltimore.

Italians

433. SANDLER, Gilbert. The Neighborhood; The Story of Baltimore's Little Italy. Photos by A. Aubrey Bodine. Drawings by Jacob Glushakow. "Impressoni" by John Dorsey. Baltimore: Bodine, 1974. 93 p. illus.

An informal look at the roots, history, institutions, and festivals of an ethnic area. Includes a walker's guide and a look at the restaurants and their owners.

Jews

434. ALTFELD, Emanuel M. The Jew's Struggle for Religious and Civil Liberty in Maryland. New York: Da Capo Press, 1970. 211 p.

Reprint of 1924 edition.

A history of the Jews in early Maryland. Especially useful for detailing the efforts of Thomas Kennedy and John Van Lear McMahon to remove the disabilities of the Jews by the passage of the "Jew Bill" (1826).

435. FEIN, Isaac M. The Making of an American Jewish Community; The History of Baltimore Jewry from 1773 to 1920. Philadelphia: Jewish Publications Society of America, 1971. 348 p. illus., ports.

Bibliography: p. 319-336.

Describes the efforts of the Jews in Baltimore to be accepted and integrated into the mainstream, while at the same time maintaining a separate identity. Includes information on notable successful individuals and institutions.

Earlier and still useful works for biography:

BLUM, Isidor, ed. The Jews of Baltimore; An Historical Summary of Their Progress and Status as Citizens of Baltimore... Baltimore: Historical Review Publishing Co., 1910. 486 p. illus., ports.

GLUSHAKOW, Abraham D. A Pictorial History of Maryland Jewry. Baltimore: Jewish Voice Publishing Co., 1955. 192 p. illus., ports.

SPORTS AND RECREATION

Baseball

436. BREADY, James H. The Home Team; A Full Century of Baseball in Baltimore, 1859-1959. A Patriotic Story with Emotion, Arithmetic, Glass Plates and Band Music. Baltimore: 1958. 62 p. illus., ports.

An illustrated chronological history of major league baseball in Baltimore.

Other contributions:

BEARD, Gordon. Birds on the Wing; The Story of the Baltimore Orioles. Garden City, N.Y.: Doubleday & Co., 1967. 179 p. illus., ports. Largely the story of the 1966 season.

LIEB, Frederick G. The Baltimore Orioles; The History of a Colorful Team in Baltimore and St. Louis. New York: G. P. Putnam's Sons, 1955. 246 p. Covers the Orioles as both a major and a minor league club.

Camping

437. MARYLAND. Div. of Tourist Development. Directory of Maryland Camp Grounds. Annapolis. Pamphlet. Annual.

Arranged by region, providing information on public and private facilities.

Canoeing

438. THOMSON, John S. Potomac White Water: A Guide to Safe Canoeing above Washington, Seneca to Little Falls. N.p.: Appalachian Books, 1974. 44 p. illus.

Bibliography: p. 41-44.

Descriptions and advice.

Fishing

439. FISHING in Maryland and the Mid-Atlantic. 1976 ed. Baltimore: Fishing in Maryland, Inc., 1975. 224 p. illus., maps.

An atlas, guide, and handbook for fishing the coastline off Maryland, Virginia, Delaware, and New Jersey and the Delaware and Chesapeake Bays. Includes fishing maps, tide tables, articles on the fishing grounds of the Chesapeake Bay, and fishing laws for each state.

440. MARYLAND. Dept. of Game and Inland Fish. Guide to Maryland Fresh Water Fishing. Annapolis. Annual.

An atlas of inland fishing areas and handbook for such things as fish identification and record catches.

441. MARYLAND. Dept. of Natural Resources. Fisheries Administration. Maryland Fishing Guide. Annapolis. Annual.

A useful handbook with brief information on regulations and seasons, lakes and ponds open to the public, public boat launching ramps, fish identification, and telephone numbers for confirmation. Its Tidewater Fishing Guide (Annapolis, annual) provides much the same information.

Hiking

442. HAHN, Thomas F. and Orville W. Crowder. Towpath Guide to the Chesapeake and Ohio Canal. Glen Echo, Md.: American Canal and Transportation Center, 1971-1973. 1 vol. in 4 pts. illus., maps.

Pt. 1: Georgetown (Tidelock) to Seneca; pt. 2: Seneca to Harpers Ferry; pt. 3: Harpers Ferry to Ft. Frederick; pt. 4: Ft. Frederick to Cumberland.

A hiker-biker-canoeist's guide to the canal with history and description of the Canal and the towpath.

443. SHOSTECK, Robert. Potomac Trail Book. Introd. by William O. Douglas. Oakton, Va.: Appalachian Books, 1976. 179 p. illus., maps.

Includes bibliographies.

Guidebook to the trails of the upper Potomac River. Also includes information on organizations, bicycling around Washington, geology, and natural history.

Horse Racing

444. GITTINGS, David S. Maryland and the Thoroughbred. Baltimore: Hoffman Brothers Co., 1932. 148 p. illus., map.

The story of horse breeding in Maryland.

445. LAWRENCE, Robert G. Maryland's Racing Industry: Its Participants, Organization, and Economic Impact. College Park, Md.: University of Maryland Cooperative Extension Service, 1972. 52 p. illus. (Maryland. University. Extension Service. Miscellaneous Publication no. 298)

Includes bibliographical references; glossary: p. 49-50.

446. ROSE, Stuart. The Maryland Hunt Cup. New York: Huntington Press, 1931. 171 p. illus., ports., map.

The history of this steeplechasing event, with a chart of the course and a "Table of Statistics, 1894-1931" (p. 109-158) with the results of each race. Includes a chapter on fox hunting in Maryland.

Hunting

447. BROWINING, Meshach. Forty-Four Years of the Life of a Hunter; Being Reminiscences of Meshach Browning, a Maryland Hunter. Roughly Written Down by Himself. Revised and illustrated by E. Stabler. Winston-Salem, N.C.: Winston Printing Co., 1942. 400 p. illus.

First published 1859.

An absorbing account of life in the woods in early 19th century Western Maryland.

448. MARYLAND. Dept. of Natural Resources. A Guide to Maryland's Public Hunting Areas. Annapolis. Annual. maps.

Descriptions and maps of state owned and cooperating private hunting areas. The Department also publishes annually its handbooks, Guide to Hunting and Fishing and Guide to Hunting and Trapping.

449. RICHARDSON, R. H., ed. Chesapeake Bay Decoys; The Men Who Made and Used Them. 2d rev. and corr. ed. N.p.: Crow Haven; Distributed by Tidewater Publications, Cambridge, Md., 1973. 200 p. illus.

Anecdotes about decoy making, hunting, and hunters. "Index to Carvers": p. 195-196.

450. WALSH, Roy E. Gunning the Chesapeake; Duck and Goose Shooting on the Eastern Shore. Cambridge, Md.: Tidewater Publishers, 1960. 117 p. illus.

Bibliography.

A how-to book on where to look for, recognize, and hunt the variety of waterfowl in the Chesapeake Bay region.

Jousting

451. CROOKS, Esther J. and Ruth W. Crooks. The Ring Tournament in the United States. Richmond, Va.: Garrett and Massie, 1936. 188 p. illus.

Contains an introductory chapter on the ring tournament. "Maryland Tournaments": p. 11-33.

Sailing and Boating

452. MARYLAND. Dept. of Natural Resources. Guide to Cruising Maryland Waters [1 (1961)-] Annapolis: 1961- . Biennial. illus., maps.

9th edition 1976.

A convenient navigational handbook of Maryland's tidal waters for small craft. Charts and detailed inserts of rivers and harbors, marine facilities, fathom curves, courses and distances, compass directions, access roads, launching ramps, buoys, and state and local laws.

A useful handbook for information on weather, radio, charts, and signaling:

MARYLAND. Dept. of Natural Resources. Boating Handbook for Maryland Waters. Annapolis. 27 p. illus.

453. STONE, William T. and Fessenden S. Blanchard. A Cruising Guide to the Chesapeake. New York: Dodd, Mead, 1973. illus., maps.

Handbook for yachtsmen with information on harbors, rivers, and creeks, including docking and restaurant information.

Stamp Collecting

454. ASSOCIATED STAMP CLUBS OF THE CHESAPEAKE AREA. Postal Markings of Maryland, 1766-1855. Edited by Roger T. Powers. Towson, Md.: 1960. 100 p. illus.

Devoted exclusively to Maryland stampless covers; contains actual size illustrations of every type of Maryland townmark and supplementary marking. Also contains railroad postmarks, private post and forwarding agents, Maryland post offices, and postal rates.

Some material on early postal service in Baltimore is given in

GREEN, Ernest. A Brief History of the Baltimore Post Office from 1753-1930 with Statistics. Baltimore: 1930. 38 p.

TRANSPORTATION

Directories

455. MARYLAND Airport Directory [1972-] Baltimore: Maryland State Aviation Administration, 1972- . 1 vol. (looseleaf) map.

Earlier editions issued by the Maryland State Aviation Commission.

Gives size, improvements, and facilities for use.

Canals - Chesapeake and Delaware Canal

456. GRAY, Ralph D. The National Waterway: A History of the Chesapeake and Delaware Canal, 1769-1965. Urbana, Ill.: University of Illinois Press, 1967. 279 p. illus.

"Bibliographic Essay": p. 259-264.

A carefully researched account of the origin, building, and operation of the Canal, emphasizing the importance of the canal to the nation, its vital role in the Civil War, and the development and decline of the Chesapeake and Delaware Canal Company.

Canals - Chesapeake and Ohio Canal

457. LIFE on the Chesapeake and Ohio Canal, 1859. Edited by Ella E. Clark and Thomas F. Hahn. York, Pa.: American Canal and Transportation Center, 1975. 48 p. illus.

A memoir of an 1859 trip by a crew man on a canal boat.

458. SANDERLIN, Walter S. The Great National Project: A History of the Chesapeake and Ohio Canal. Baltimore: Johns Hopkins Press, 1946. 331 p. (Johns Hopkins University Studies in Historical and Political Science, ser. 64, no. 1)

Bibliographic note: p. 295-303.

The standard history, tracing the economic, political, and social history of the Chesapeake and Ohio Canal and its predecessors. There are separate chapters on its construction and its significance in the Civil War.

The appendix carries information on toll rates, traffic and goods transported, and company finances.

459. WOLFE, George H. I Drove Mules on the C & O Canal. [Dover, Del.: Dover Graphic Association] 1969. 171 p. illus., ports., map.

________ ________. Supplement. N.p.: n.d. 16 p. illus.

Stories about those who lived along the Canal and those who worked on it.

A good book for children:

FRADEN, Morris. Hey-EY-EY! Adventure on the C & O Canal. Cabin John, Md.: See-and-Know Press, 1974. A journey along the C & O Canal by two children who learn about the history of the canal and the people and places associated with it.

Railroads

Baltimore and Ohio Railroad - Bibliography

460. FREEMAN, Edmund A. The Baltimore and Ohio Railroad Company and Its Subdivisions; A Bibliography. Washington: U.S. Bureau of Railway Economics Library, 1927. 378 p.

A chronological listing of monographs and reports. Entry indicates location.

Baltimore and Ohio Railroad - History

461. HUNGERFORD, Edward. The Story of the Baltimore and Ohio Railroad, 1827-1927. New York: G. P. Putnam's Sons, 1928. 2 vols. illus., ports., maps.

The standard account, with considerable material on Maryland and Baltimore.

More specialized works:

SUMMERS, Festus P. The Baltimore and Ohio in the Civil War. New York: G. P. Putnam's Sons, 1939. 304 p. illus.

WINCHESTER, Paul. The Baltimore and Ohio Railroad. Baltimore: Maryland Country Press Syndicate, 1927. 337 p. Devotes a large portion to John W. Garrett and to the B & O and Arthur Pue Gorman controversy.

462. SAGLE, Lawrence W. B & O Power; Steam, Diesel and Electric Power of the Baltimore and Ohio Railroad, 1829-1964. Captions by L. Sagle and Alvin F. Staufer. Edited by Alvin F. Staufer. Carrollton, Ohio: Printed by the Standard Printing and Publishing Co., 1964. 351 p. illus.

Supersedes his Picture History of B & O Motive Power (1952).

"Bibliographical Notes...": p. 350-351.

A pictorial history, including the engines of railroads incorporated into the B & O, with detailed technical statistics.

Maryland and Pennsylvania Railroad

463. HILTON, George W. The Ma and Pa, A History of the Maryland and Pennsylvania Railroad. Berkeley, Calif.: Howell-North, 1963. 183 p. illus., map.

Also includes information on the predecessor lines, such as the Maryland Central Railroad and the Maryland Central Railway, Baltimore and Delta, and Baltimore and Lehigh railroads. Has locomotive and equipment lists.

Western Maryland Railroad

464. WILLIAMS, Harold A. The Western Maryland Railroad Story; A Chronicle of the First Century, 1852-1952. Contemporary photography by A. Aubrey Bodine. Baltimore: Western Maryland Railway, 1952. 134 p. illus.

The highlights in the history and achievements of the railroad.

Roads

465. LE VINESS, Charles T. History of Road Building in Maryland. Baltimore: Maryland State Road Commission, 1958. 246 p. illus., maps.

A chronological history. Pt. 1 describes Maryland roads in the late 18th century, the National Road, and the roads built by banks; pts. 2 and 3 cover 40 years of the State Road Commission to 1948; pt. 5 covers the 1948-1958 period, with information on the interstate system and the Baltimore Tunnel.

This can be supplemented with

DURRENBERGER, Joseph A. Turnpikes; A Study of the Toll Road Movement in the Middle Atlantic States and Maryland. 188 p. (Ph.D., Columbia University, 1931)

HULBERT, Archer B. The Cumberland Road. Cleveland: A. H. Clark Co., 1904. 208 p. illus. (Historic Highways of America, vol. 10) Gives history and construction of the first national road, including a chapter on taverns.

SEARIGHT, Thomas B. The Old Pike; An Illustrated

Narrative of the National Road. Edited...and illustrated by Joseph E. Morse and R. Duff Green. Orange, Va.: Green Tree Press, 1971. 189 p. illus. A shortened version of the 1894 edition. Offers sketches of the life along the Road and descriptions of travel, transport, and goods.

Ships - Sailing

466. BREWINGTON, Marion V. Chesapeake Bay Log Canoes and Bugeyes. Cambridge, Md.: Cornell Maritime Press, 1963. 171 p. illus.

A combined and enlarged edition of his Chesapeake Bay Log Canoes (1937) and Chesapeake Bay Bugeyes (1941).

Bibliography: p. 111-113.

Traces the history and decline of these Chesapeake Bay vessels, with descriptions, general dimensions, and construction specifications.

See also

BREWINGTON, Marion V. Chesapeake Bay Sailing Craft. Baltimore: Maryland Historical Society and Chesapeake Bay Maritime Museum, 1966. 1 vol. (unpaged) illus. A slight volume with additional descriptions and illustrations of nine common types of Chesapeake Bay sailing craft.

467. BURGESS, Robert H. Chesapeake Sailing Craft: The Fifty-Year Period 1924-1974. Cambridge: Tidewater Publishers, 1974. 256 p. illus.

Photographs and notes on Chesapeake commercial sailing craft.

The life and death of one of the last Chesapeake Bay commercial sailing vessels can be found in

BURGESS, Robert H. Sea, Sails and Shipwreck; Career of the Four-Masted Schooner Purnell T. White. Cambridge, Md.: Cornell Maritime Press, 1970. 132 p. illus., ports.

468. CHAPPELLE, Howard I. The Baltimore Clipper; Its Origin and Development. Hatboro, Pa.: Tradition Press, 1965. 192 p. illus.

Reprint of 1930 edition.

History of the development of the Baltimore Clipper from 1782 to 1812 and its use in the War of 1812 and in the slave trade. Detailed drawings and masting rules.

Ships - Steamboats

469. BROWN, Alexander C. Steam Packets on the Chesapeake. Cambridge, Md.: Cornell Maritime Press, 1961. 192 p. illus.

A revision of his Old Bay Line (1940).

Bibliography: p. 177-183.

The history of steamboats on the Chesapeake Bay, concentrating on the Baltimore Steam Packet Company (Old Bay Line) and its competitors to 1961, when the line ceased operation. Appendix lists all steamers owned and operated by the line from 1840 to 1961 with a brief note on size and careers.

470. BURGESS, Robert H. and H. Graham Wood. Steamboats Out of Baltimore. Cambridge, Md.: Tidewater Publishers, 1968. 236 p. illus.

A pictorial history of the steamboat companies which served the river tributaries of the Chesapeake Bay from 1800 to 1930, with material on the Old Bay Line and the Chesapeake Line. Details on the vessels, cargo, landings, wages, and fares.

471. HAIN, John A. Propeller Steamers of the Chesapeake Bay. Glen Burnie, Md.: Glendale Press, 1964. 1 vol. (unpaged) illus.

Brief history of steamboats in the Bay and of the companies that operated them. Includes brief descriptive details on the ships.

472. HAIN, John A. Side Wheelers of the Chesapeake Bay: 1880-1947. Rev. ed. Glen Burnie, Md.: Glendale Press, 1962. 1 vol. (unpaged) illus.

Reprint of 1951 edition.

Brief histories of companies and agencies that operated on the Chesapeake Bay, with descriptive notes on the ships.

Trolleys

473. FARRELL, Michael R. Who Made All Our Streetcars Go? The Story of Rail Transit in Baltimore. Baltimore: NRHS Publications, 1973. 306 p. illus., maps.

Bibliography: p. 305-306; glossary: p. 299-303.

An illustrated narrative history of the age of the streetcar in Baltimore and the metropolitan area, covering descriptions of the cars, folklore, and the first electric trolley.

474. HARWOOD, Herbert H. Blue Ridge Trolley: The Hagerstown & Frederick Railway. San Marino, Calif.: Golden West Books, 1970. 144 p. illus., map.

A photographic narrative history of an interurban. Rosters of equipment.

INDEX OF AUTHORS, EDITORS, COMPILERS AND ILLUSTRATORS

SUBJECT INDEX

P9-CFP-961

Pieces of Eight

Also by Sydney J. Harris

Strictly Personal
Majority of One
Last Things First
On the Contrary
Leaving the Surface
For the Time Being
The Authentic Person
Winners and Losers
The Best of Sydney J. Harris
Would You Believe?

Pieces of Eight

Sydney J. Harris

Boston
Houghton Mifflin Company
1982

Library of Congress Cataloging in Publication Data

Harris, Sydney J.
Pieces of eight.

I. Title.
AC8.H3669 081 82-3067
ISBN 0-395-32512-9 AACR2

Printed in the United States of America

P 10 9 8 7 6 5 4 3 2 1

To my daughter Lindsay,

in loving thanks
for selecting, editing, and preparing
this material for publication in book form

FISH CREEK, WISCONSIN,
OCTOBER 1981

Contents

I.
Of the Social Animal

The Atrocity of War

I HAVE NEVER BEEN ABLE to understand the indignation aroused in so many people by "atrocities" of war. In fact, I have never been able to grasp what an "atrocity" is in wartime. For what could be more atrocious than two bands of people resolving a conflict by killing one another?

Once you decide you are going to kill, why should there be any "rules," and why should such rules be observed? The object is to win; any means will do, if winning is the prime objective. War is not a game, where lives are restored when the victor has been decided. All armies are more alike than they are different, just as all flags and all uniforms and all weapons are more alike than different. Once you have resolved that there is no way to change your opponents' views except by slaughtering them, what difference does it make how or why or where you do it?

It seems to me that the greatest hypocrisy of nations is exhibited at their resentment of "atrocities" committed by the other side. Although I think of the Allies as "good guys" and the Axis as "bad guys" in World War II, both sides bombed cities with equal destructiveness when they felt it was to their advantage.

And it was the good guys who detonated the atomic bomb, not once but twice, despite the later verdict of many competent historians that it was a cruelly unnecessary act, prompted by political rather than by military motives. It was not the bad guys who loosed that evil upon the world — an evil that is going to come back to haunt us a thousandfold.

There is no such thing as an atrocity in warfare that is greater than the atrocity of warfare itself, just as no part can be larger than the whole. Killing is the ultimate act of impiety; all other acts are merely subordinate to it.

It is possible, barely possible, to have a just war, a war waged in self-defense only, as a final desperate expedient. But this is a rare exception in history: Almost all have been avoidable, and were seen to have been so after they ended. They have been wars not of survival, but of pride, power, possession, stupidity, and vengeance.

In man's thousands of years on Earth, virtually everything has changed but this. The world is a totally different place in nearly every aspect of life, so much so that an early Greek or Roman would not recognize it as the same place.

Only one important thing has remained: the way in which sovereign states settle their disputes, by force, by violence, by death. And what is most shocking of all is the fact that we now can kill a million times as many people a thousand times as fast as ever before. The more "progress" we make in warfare, the more barbarous we become. This, beyond anything else, is our terrible legacy to the future.

Perhaps the basic tragedy of the human condition is that the world is never changed by reason, only by passion — and that passion usually replaces one form of unreason with another form.

*

Murder is an indictable offense in every nation on Earth — except when the nation as a whole decides to engage in it.

Stopping Thoughtless Pain

YOU CAN'T STOP ANYONE, including yourself, from being bigoted, if the inclination is there, but you can stop yourself from making thoughtless and offensive remarks that hurt others when you don't really intend it.

The way to do this, I have found, is to think of someone you know and respect and like who belongs to some minority group — religious, racial, sexual, or whatever — and imagine yourself making such a remark to that person.

Each of us, I hope, is acquainted at least with one person who represents such a group, and who should stand as a paradigm for the whole group in our minds. Because, obviously, if one person of the group merits our affection or respect, the whole group has the potential for it — just as every group has a potential for the worst.

At first I relished some of the Polish jokes that were making the rounds; then one day I thought of a Polish gentleman I know who is an absolutely first-rate human being, and I was privately covered with shame. Humor is the "respectable" way we cover our hostility, or sense of superiority, and I certainly don't feel superior to this decent gent.

Likewise, when racial slurs (however humorously disguised) waft my way, I recall a black lady who was employed by us for many years before she died — her good nature, her generosity, her life of sacrifice, actually, for her family — and realize how it would have pained her to hear anything like this from someone she considered a friend.

Bigotry springs almost wholly from fear, and fear comes largely from ignorance. To know any group of people well — as anthropologists in the jungle will tell you — is to like them better when you understand the reasons for their "different" behavior. No one who had lived for any time with the gentle Vietnamese people could have called them "slopes."

I cannot believe that the sexual bigots today who would penalize homosexuals include a declared one in their families or circle of friends (though no doubt more than one incognito), or they would recognize that the similarities between us and them are far greater than this one difference — and even this difference is one of degree, not of quality.

Bernard Baruch once ironically defined a "kike" as "the gentleman of Hebrew persuasion who has just left the room." It hurts, even if you have left the room. The echoes keep bouncing down the corridors of history, and there seems no end to them. Perhaps as good a place as any to begin is with the Polish jokes and all their careless variants.

The Arrogance of Ignorance

MANY PEOPLE, I find, have a strange sense of what constitutes competence. They seem to imagine that having "learned" or "studied" or even attained a degree in a particular subject or discipline gives them a kind of expertise for life.

More than once have I engaged in conversation with someone who announced at the outset that he or she majored in English, or took Shakespeare, as credentials for discussing such matters with me. (I usually forbear mentioning that I "majored in" or "took" neither.)

We must have an extremely low opinion of what learning or education actually consists of in this country if we suppose, or assume, that a year or two, or even three, of brushing against a subject in college gives us any more than a shallow introduction to it. We are then not even at the threshold of knowledge, which marks the point at which we actually know how little we know.

There is a true story about this, concerning Professor Einstein, already a white-maned man, sitting next to an eighteen-year-old girl at an American dinner party.

When the conversation flagged, the young lady asked brightly, "What are you actually by profession?" Einstein quietly replied, "I devote myself to the study of physics." And the girl retorted in surprise: "You mean to say you study physics at your age? Why, I finished mine a year ago."

'She "finished" hers, while Einstein still "studied." This is the difference, of course. There is no finish to any important discipline. There is always more to learn, and sometimes to unlearn. This is true not only intellectually but also physically — tennis pros and golf champions will regularly go back to teachers to correct their strokes.

There is much to be said against the arrogance of some intellectuals — those pedants who incessantly parade their knowledge in full-dress uniform. But the arrogance of ignorance is even more ridiculous, because it craves recognition of its views before it has taken the time and trouble to grasp the complexities behind the surface simplicities.

Einstein was "studying" physics until the day he died, realizing there was far more he did not know than he knew, even though he knew more than any other man.

In knowledge, unlike economics, there is no such product as "unearned increment" — for knowledge increases only in small, painful increments, and if it is not earned it is not handed us.

The Outrageous Stir Discrimination

MY YOUNGEST DAUGHTER has begun to learn what every minority group quickly finds out — that you are judged (and condemned) by the worst elements of your group.

She was complaining at dinner the other night about the way teen-agers are treated by most adults in positions of authority. Having recently become a teen-ager herself, she resents being lumped as a group.

"I suppose quite a few kids my age behave badly," she said, "but that's no excuse for treating all of us as if we did — especially before they know anything about us as individuals. That just makes us get mad and behave worse."

She was talking about waitresses in restaurants and clerks in drug or dime stores "who either treat us as if we didn't exist, or else keep guard as if we were all shoplifters and vandals."

She and a few thirteen-year-old friends will take a table at a snack shop and wait twenty minutes for service, while others who come later get waited on much sooner. "I suppose it's because they figure we won't order much and won't leave a big tip," she says, "but they charge us the same prices as they do adults, for rotten service."

In drugstores, her bill of complaints continues, clerks wait on other customers even if youngsters were there before them — and then the clerks do everything but shake them down to detect if they have done any shoplifting.

"Sometimes kids get so mad that they steal a few things just to get even," she confided, stating in simple terms what the sociologists have long called the theory of fulfilled expectations. That is, if you treat a person a certain way, he will respond in a fashion that meets those (low or high) expectations.

All minority groups — whether by age, race, religion, or sexual preference — know that the whole group is usually judged by the most conspicuous or the most outrageous of its members, even though they may represent 10 percent or less of the entire group. The outrageous ones call the group to our attention, while the 90 percent who conduct themselves responsibly just blend into the landscape, and we never notice their minority status.

Discrimination, prejudice, and bigotry of all sorts feed off this kind of social blindness — how many times, to take a trivial but typical example, have male motorists cussed out a bad "woman driver" without ever seeing the dozens of skilled female drivers around them? We select what we want to, or expect, or are startled into recognizing, and blacken out whatever does not happen to meet our preconceptions.

My daughter is feeling as a teen-ager, and will soon feel as a woman, what minorities have always felt and suffer from — the realization that even in this most highly individualistic of societies, we are judged less as persons than as types, and less as types than as stereotypes.

The Glorification of Criminality

THE GERMANS call delinquent boys who hang around in gangs the *halbstark,* meaning the "half-strong," which is a true and accurate description of what they are and how they feel. Someone who feels really strong doesn't have to act that way.

In English, we dignify them by calling them hoodlums, or rowdies, or toughs. These are swagger words, and the lads love to see their names in print with such descriptions. For what we publicly call people helps determine what they think of themselves.

Some years ago, when there was a particularly brutal series of murders in an Illinois state park, I commented in a column on the stories and headlines in which the killer was referred to as a fiend. When they caught him, he turned out to be (as often is the case) a psychopath and a moron. But how proud he was to be known as a fiend.

It is odd how newspapers, which should be most aware of the power of words, can be so insensitive to them. Instead of seeking the precise word, they reach lazily for the stereotyped one. Like calling a certain type of criminal a desperado, when he is just a common thief. This makes him feel more important, which is what he wanted in the first place. Ferocious criminality is a bid for attention.

Perhaps the most inappropriate phrase is "sex fiend" for the type of man who attacks women. In the great majority of cases, such men are incapable of performing normal sex acts. Peeping Toms and voyeurs are, far from being "monsters" or "menaces," quite pathetic little men who can only substitute the sight for the act.

Glorifying criminality, however, seems to be one of America's oldest customs, and we can hardly blame the press for that.

If you bother to read the true-life stories of virtually all the Western "desperados," you will learn that they were stupid, coarse, ignoble, greedy, disloyal, and sickly sadistic.

What is a criminal, anyway, but a weakling who cannot or will not play by the rules? He is no different from a man who cheats in any game because he knows he has little chance when competing fairly. One of the old slang words criminals used for a gun was *equalizer* — a beautiful verbal tipoff that they didn't feel equal to other men without one.

Hoodlums are "half-strong," as the Germans know, because they need to band together even to feel semitough, whereas the ordinary man is content to walk alone. And they thrive on inspiring fear, for without it they are painfully aware that they would evoke only contempt.

The Hat Game

HOW MANY HATS can a person wear and still remain a person? Should the hat change what is under it — the heart, the mind, the motivation?

I thought of this while reading a poignant piece in the Miami *Herald* this winter, called "Moving Targets," about the thousands of elderly people being dispossessed by condominium developers in that area.

One of the less insensitive owners said, "When I sold the building, I was wearing my businessman's hat. After I had made the final commitment . . . I put on my human being hat." It was only then that he realized how he had affected people's lives through his transaction.

But seeing things as a human being should not have to depend on which hat you happen to be wearing. It has nothing to do with hats at all, but with one's priorities of value. Even Eichmann could say that when he took off his Hitler hat, he was sympathetic toward his victims.

If you have to put on a human being hat in order to act like a *mensch,* you will be careful not to put it on until you have done all the lucrative dirty work possible under another hat.

This is precisely what all gangsters and hoodlums do. When they are accused in court of heinous crimes, their defense attorneys invariably point out that they are kind to their wives, good to their children, contribute to their churches, and give much to charity.

This is like saying that a man has to be a wife-beater, a child-molester, a church-burner, and a miser in order to be judged a menace to society. But what you do under your personal, family hat has no necessary relation to what you do under your public, professional hat.

The fragmentation and specialization of modern society makes it too easy to play the hat game. It turns us into *functions* of men and women, and gradually makes the function more important than the person. It makes us cold and impersonal and abstract in our relations with others, because the others are not real persons to us.

If communism in the world today needs to develop a "human face," as many of its advocates are now beginning to realize, capitalism no less needs to expand its "human heart." No system is self-justifying; each system must justify itself by the compassion, the decency, the fairness, the basic humanity it displays. Or it cannot last long.

The profit motive is part of an economic system, as good or bad as we care to make it; it is not a way of life. It is a way of working, not a way of living. When we permit it to take precedence over human values, we are donning a hat that is going to be shot off sooner or later. Not by the old people going down but by the young people coming up. You can bet your hat on that.

There is no way of proving your point to someone whose income or position depends upon believing the contrary.

The Boredom of Specialization

MAYBE WHAT IS BEST for us collectively is worst for us individually. Maybe what makes us prosperous as a society impoverishes us as men and women. Not an attractive thought, but one worth reflecting on.

Adam Smith mentioned the possibility when he wrote *The Wealth of Nations* some two hundred years ago, but never followed it up. He pointed out, accurately, that it was *specialization* that advanced societies; as each person learned to do a particular task well, production sped up and wealth increased.

At the same time, Smith admitted, specialized and repetitious work turned the person into more of an automaton, severely limiting his horizon and rigidifying his personality. Inevitably, the function he performed began to overshadow and dominate the whole person.

One of the few places in the so-called civilized world that this has not happened is in the small towns of Switzerland. In her fascinating book — available in paperback — *The Faces of Justice,* Sybille Bedford describes something about daily life in these towns that I had not known before.

That is the Swiss sense of the community of citizens, their dislike of specialization, "and a still-living conviction that all branches of human activity are open to all men."

In one of the large industrialized and prosperous towns on the Swiss Rhine, in fact, many of the men are able to live and work by satisfying their varied desires for the practical, the physical, and the intellectual as well. In this town, she tells us:

> Their farmer is also a locksmith and a vintner and a shipwright, and in the evening mends the clocks; the artisan keeps books; the chartered accountant runs a sawmill and the county council; the woodcutter has a chair of modern history.

There are things you do in winter, the Swiss say, and things you do in summer — you can't sit at a desk all year round.

Indeed, even the Swiss judges in the highest courts need not be lawyers at all, "for in this oldest of Western democracies the law is felt to be something that can be administered by any man of good repute."

I wonder if one of the main sources of discontent in modern industrial society is not the increasing specialization that condemns men to a single function, while the other needs and hungers of their nature go largely unsatisfied. In the ancient book of Talmud, even rabbis and scholars are enjoined to learn and live by some trade in addition to their religious or intellectual vocation.

May it be that "mankind" as an idea has grown neglected because most of us have become only parts of men, functions of men, viewing the world through our own limited operations, not with the vision of what a total human being ought to be?

Free Speech for Nazis?

IF YOU BELIEVE in democracy, do you then believe that the people have a democratic right to abolish democracy if they want to? This is what the whole argument boils down to, in the case of the Village of Skokie versus the Nazi organization that wanted to march there.

The right to free speech is Article I in the Bill of Rights, the First Amendment to the Constitution. The people who oppose the Nazi march are saying, basically, that we should not allow free speech to groups that do not believe in it and would not practice it if they controlled the state.

The people on the other side, including me, say that anything in the Constitution may be repealed or amended, if enough people so desire. The Constitution was designed precisely for this purpose. If we democratically vote to give up free speech, we have a right to do so, just as we have a right to stuff a million balloons with dollar bills and release them over the Rockies.

It is not how dangerous or how silly or how wrong-headed a

doctrine is, but the manner in which it is made into law that is regulated by the U.S. Constitution. We can legally abolish our form of government if we so desire.

All this has nothing to do with Nazis or Jews or the right to cry "Fire" falsely in a crowded theater. Every argument I have heard against permitting the Nazis to march is based on the assumption that they are a threat to our democracy and our society, or would be if we allowed them to flourish.

This is perfectly true. But every radical demand for change is a threat to our society. Our society was meant to be threatened, and to meet such threats with the voice of the people. The Constitution was framed to protect the threateners as well as the threatened. Otherwise, it would be not a democratic document but simply a weapon for sustaining the status quo.

You cannot limit free speech only to those who believe in it, because then you are saying that one section of the Constitution can never be repealed or amended, and that would be contrary to its spirit. Much as we may hate the Nazis, or any other such group, they have a right to march, to pass out inflammatory pamphlets, and to agitate peacefully for whatever changes they desire in our government.

I don't like it. I wish they would disappear. We have an obligation to resist them with all our might. But only with our legal might. When we twist the Constitution to deter them, we are giving up far more than we are gaining.

Almost everyone is kinder in the concrete than in the abstract. We will behave humanely toward a single member of a group, while at the same time condemning or denigrating the group as a collectivity; this permits us to exercise compassion and conduct hostilities at the same time without perceiving the moral contradiction.

Pistolence

I AM SICK AND TIRED of hearing about "violence" these days. "Violence" is the wrong word for what is happening. It is "pistolence." People are not hitting each other more. They are not brawling more. Crowds aren't lynching or burning or throwing people into the river. No one is complaining of stones and slings, bottles and knives.

The "violence" we speak of is 90 percent limited to pistols, to handguns, to Saturday Night Specials. Not to shotguns or rifles that hunters use. Not to machine guns or howitzers or even bombs (except for rare political demonstrations).

Let us call it by its right name and not slide out so easily by attributing it to the abstraction known as violence. We are no more violent than in the past — it is simply that we now have access to more handguns more cheaply and easily than ever before in history.

Long ago Confucius warned us that disorder in the state begins with the wrong use of words. As long as we think of violence in the abstract, we will offer all kinds of psychological and philosophical and sociological "reasons" for its rise in modern American society. And indeed, there may be many contributing factors.

But the main reason is not an abstraction at all. The effective cause is the shocking prevalence of millions of handguns, which turn any dispute or quarrel into a deadly assault.

It has become too easy for anyone to kill at a distance, without injury to himself. And people do not kill so much for crime — murder is not the criminal's object — as for pride, for passion, for jealousy, for fear, for drunkenness, for lust, for rage, and for mistake.

Violence is not usually fatal, it is not irrevocable, it is not so quickly or futilely regretted, with anything but a gun. We do not commonly slug or knife or choke or poison or drown a person to death. It takes longer, it is harder, and it threatens injury to ourselves.

It is people with guns who kill. The homicide rate in every civilized nation in Europe is only a mere fraction of ours in the United States — not because people there are less violent, but because the means of this violence has been denied them.

"Pistolence" is what is plaguing our country, killing innocent people, wrecking families, spreading fear if not panic throughout both the cities and the countryside. We can never eliminate violence from the human scene. We can, if we want to, ensure that the means of fatal violence — the gun — is at least as hard to get as a driver's license.

Our Yearning for Simplicity

ONE OF THE FAVORITE PLOYS of politicians out of office, and social critics out of temper, is to use the Roman Empire example as a warning to Americans that we are declining and decaying at an alarming rate.

And the reason we are declining and decaying is that we are acting just like those Romans. However, each speaker picks out a particular element in Roman life that he considers the dominant cause — and this always happens to agree with his own diagnosis of the American weakness.

It is much on the order of the dogmatic preacher, who selects specific passages from the Bible to dramatize his theme while neglecting other, and sometimes contrary, passages.

But the fact is that the more you know about something, the less simple it seems. To the ignorant, or the rigidly partisan, there are no hard or complex questions; it is only those who bother to delve more deeply into a subject who are no longer satisfied with simple answers that really answer nothing.

The great historian of the Roman Empire, Gibbon, spent a lifetime studying the "decline and fall" of the mighty institution. At the conclusion of his lengthy investigation, he had *no* explanation for why Rome fell.

He cited at least two dozen causes that had been offered by various commentators and observers — ranging from the blunders of individual emperors and the vanity of human wishes to the corrupting nature of luxury and the expansive vitality of the barbarians pressing upon Rome.

Gibbon himself shrugged off any explanation, though he suspected one of the chief causes to have been the internal moral decay of the ruling class, which is what Tacitus, a contemporary historian, thought.

Where scholars are cautious, modest, and tentative, politicians and demagogues have no hesitancy in stridently attributing the fall of Rome to high taxes, laziness, sexual orgies, religious indifference, extravagance, pacifism, mobocracy — or whatever the speaker thinks happens to be America's besetting sin at this point in our history.

We must learn to be wary of our desperate yearning for simplicity in an age of unprecedented complexity. We ache to find a direct explanation for what has gone wrong and a strong, straight, simple formula for putting it right. We want the message that is also a massage.

When the glib orators who seem to have the easy answers tell us in a ringing sentence why Rome fell and how we can avoid a similar fate, we can do little better than pick up Gibbon, who knew how little he knew about the past, and how little we can extrapolate it to the future.

The basic problem in communication is that it is almost impossible to discuss some things without categorizing them — and the moment you categorize them, you distort them. (It is much like the scientist, whose very observation of the particle changes the way the particle seems to behave.)

Not All Sins Are Crimes

ONE OF THE MOST TICKLISH areas in public life is the relation between religion and politics or, in the customary phrase, church and state. There is probably more heat and less light exuded on this subject than on any other single national issue.

The latest controversy is engendered by the mobilization of right-wing religious groups to elect or defeat specific candidates on "moral" issues. One such group even has the arrogance to call itself the "Moral Majority," as if it were divinely decreed to judge what is and is not moral in human behavior.

Now, every group has a right to disseminate its views, to proclaim its creed, to let voters know where it stands on all issues it feels are important. Religion cannot be divorced from politics, for social justice is one of religion's proper aims, and government is the process by which this is achieved.

But no religious group has a right to cram its views down the throat of the electorate, to insist that lawmakers pass and the government enforce a specific code of morals for the American people.

One of the great theologians of all time, the sainted Thomas Aquinas, said that everything that may be considered a sin must not be considered a crime. There are grave sins in the private and personal area that are not legitimately correctable by the state; and the attempt to force such "morality" on people can lead to the most serious and dangerous abuses of government authority.

It is richly ironic that the right wing generally is against the incursion of government control; it demands more freedom for the individual; it believes the government already has taken on too many tasks that should have been left in private hands.

Yet at the same time the right-wing religious organizations want us to elect legislators, to pass laws, even to enact a constitutional amendment empowering the government to step into an area that has traditionally been free from federal jurisdiction.

Matters between man and man can be adjudicated by government; those between man and his Maker can be settled only in some higher court. To have personal belief and private conscience controlled or dictated by the state is the highest form of blasphemy, and treason to the spirit on which our nation was founded.

Churches and religious groups have a right, indeed a duty, to propound their faith — and to persuade others to follow their course. To follow it by love, not by law; by reason, not by force. Is this not precisely the message that Jesus vainly tried to deliver to the moral majority of his own time and place?

Pride and Penitence

WHEN HE WAS PRESIDENT of the University of Chicago many years ago, Robert Hutchins was fond of saying that "the university isn't a very good school — it's just the best there is."

I remember this ironic, and possibly truthful, statement because the attitude it expresses seems to me to apply to much more than a university. I would apply it to our country as a whole.

It seems terribly important to me, in this crucial period, to keep in mind two things at the same time: that this isn't a very good country, and that it's the best there is.

If we concentrate solely on the fact that it isn't a very good country, we turn into carpers and common scolds. If we concentrate solely on the fact that it is still the best country in the world (which I firmly believe), we turn into smug and self-satisfied jingoists.

What we need so desperately to do is to hold both these ideas in tension at the same time, so that both our pride and our disappointment can mutually support our efforts, in a realistic and constructive way.

It's not a very good country that endures and permits the ills, evils, and injustices we are subjected to. It is not what a country should be, as perceived and declared by our founders. We have fallen far short of their mark, and have much to be ashamed of, much to atone for and rectify.

It's the best country there is, despite these intolerable shortcomings. It offers the most promise, the most hope, the most opportunity of any place in the world. Don't believe anyone who tells you differently.

But the trouble is that most Americans tend to polarize themselves: They turn into either intemperate critics and cynics about our system, or mindless patriots, waving the flag and advising their neighbors to move somewhere else if they don't like it here.

Both attitudes are absurd, short-sighted, and dangerous. Neither can be safely or sanely held by itself. They are complementaries, needing each other for balance. And balance — intellectually or emotionally — is the hardest attitude for most people to maintain.

Hutchins was immensely proud of his university — but his pride never blinded him to the fact that the reality was nowhere close to the ideal of what a university should be and was meant to be.

We have a right to be immensely proud of what our country has stood for, and still stands for — but our pride must not blind us to the fact that we have so often neglected or betrayed the dreams it was founded on.

Pride and penitence must go hand in hand. The flag may be waved, but it must also be washed, so that it is worthy of waving. The patriot who will brook no criticism of what we have let ourselves become is as useless, and as perilous, as the subversive who sees no good left in us.

The familiar slogan "Give until it hurts" lets us off too leniently — we are not really giving until the hurt begins, but only flattering our sense of charity.

Crime and Punishment

IN WHAT HE SUPPOSES is a rebuttal to my antihandgun pieces, a reader suggests, "How about an all-out war on crime that makes the penalty so stiff that they can't afford to commit the crime?"

There is no penalty that stiff, and there never has been. Anyone who has read anything on criminal history must know that. The reason penalties have become less extreme and severe over the centuries is simply that the harsher penalties didn't work.

Not so many hundreds of years ago, in England, the death penalty was incurred for 128 separate offenses, including the theft of a lace handkerchief. Pickpockets had their hands cut off after the first offense. Then they were publicly hanged on Tyburn Hill. And while the crowds congregated on Tyburn Hill to watch the executions, pickpockets were operating furiously; it was their best take.

In fact, when penalties become too severe, they backfire: Judges and juries grow increasingly reluctant to impose sentences, and many criminals are let off who would otherwise be convicted.

Harshness has always been the solution of the ignorant, whether in rearing a child or in rebuking a lawbreaker. What they fail to realize is that discipline is effective only in inverse ratio to the gravity of the offense.

An ordinary tractable child (or citizen) will be restrained by a punishment or a fine; if you double the fine for illegal parking, for instance — and enforce it fairly — the average motorist will desist, because it no longer pays to flout the parking laws.

But doubling or trebling or quadrupling the penalties for serious offenses does not deter the professional lawbreaker — and especially in cases of violence and murder, when criminals pay no heed to the possible consequences. (Murder, in fact, is mostly an impulsive crime.)

Even from a practical viewpoint, increased severity would not work: Our prisons are already desperately overcrowded and understaffed. It costs as much to keep one man in prison as it does to send a child to college. We lack the space, the facilities, the staff, and the money to expand our prison system, in the counties, the states, and federally.

Historically, psychologically, and practically, stiffer penalties are worse than no answer. The roots of crime are in the social order: in family life, education, housing, job opportunities, and the diminishing sense of community in modern society. Criminals are a symptom, not a cause, of our malaise. Anyone can afford to commit a crime when he feels he has nothing to lose and little to gain by being straight.

Distinguishing Fame from Notoriety

ONE OF THE PUBLIC REACTIONS to news that I have never been able to understand is the imputation that newspapers are doing a disservice when they widely report such grim matters as the attempted assassination of a President, or any other shocking news. The general recrimination goes something like this: If the newspapers didn't give such front-page coverage to these scandalous events, the people who commit them now or who might in the future would be dissuaded from their heinous acts, because they do it for publicity as much as for any other purpose.

This is close to the ancient Greek custom of blaming (and sometimes executing) the messenger for the bad news in the message he conveyed. But apart from that, it also ignores an uncomfortable fact of American public life: We as a people do not distinguish between fame and notoriety.

We look up to, and sometimes worship, success, no matter which form it takes or how it has been achieved. As a pragmatic people, we believe it is results that count; and if your results are big enough, we are usually willing to condone or overlook your dubious methods. More people left the *Godfather* films admiringly than reprovingly; it is only the petty criminal we look down on and penalize in our society.

This being the case — and I think any sociologist will bear me out — the aim of our national ethos is to gain attention, to become prominent, to be pointed out. If this can't be attained by laudable means, it will be attained by scandalous ones. "I don't care what you say about me as long as you spell my name right" is our unspoken motto.

Since we reward notoriety as much as we do genuine fame, all the egomaniacs and psychopaths and weak, obscure, frustrated fantasists yearn to see their names in lights (or in headlines, which comes to the same thing).

The newspapers, in gratifying these wishes, are only reflecting — and not magnifying or distorting — our own ethical confusion and blurring of values. Newspapers in a society, like the schools and other institutions, only give back the image of the public. But by blaming them (either for not educating our children properly or for "sensationalizing the news"), we are able to reject this unflattering portrait of ourselves.

When we begin to separate fame from notoriety, means from ends, talent from showmanship, and merit from success, then the celebrated persons in our society will be only those who deserve it, while the others fall into shame or oblivion. Not a day before then will the newspapers refract the more civilized image we covet but have not earned.

Those with a tendency to love create their own objects to love; those with a tendency to fear create their own objects to fear.

*

Superior people are only those who let it be discovered by others; the need to make it evident forfeits the very virtue they aspire to.

Urban Anonymity Cultivates Anxiety

I SUSPECT IT IS the anonymity of relationships in the city that makes life harder and more frustrating and more anxiety-producing than any other factor. For much of the time we don't know whom we are dealing with.

As a common example, my car needs its twenty-four-thousand-mile checkup. The place I bought it from, across the street from my office, went out of business last year. The nearest dealer is a stranger to me, in another part of town.

The car is left there; an hour later, the phone rings. It is the service manager. This and such has to be done to the car, beyond the normal inspection servicing. The bill will be twice what I expected. Shall he go ahead with the work?

Of course, I need the car and I haven't the time and energy to traipse around, taking it elsewhere to check the reliability or honesty of the dealer. So I give him my OK, annoyed that perhaps I'm being made a sucker of, but not knowing what to do about it and half-ashamed that my suspicions may be unfounded.

Now, none of these anxieties is at work in the village I spend my summers in — or in any other community where everyone knows everyone.

When I leave my car with Norm to be fixed, I am sure he is going to give it proper attention and not charge me a penny more than he should; he would no more send me a rigged bill than cut off his tire-changing arm.

Likewise, when I bring in a busted TV to Bruce, I know equally well that he's not going to replace tubes that are still operable or sock me for an expensive part it didn't need. Apart from their native honesty and decency, these men couldn't dare to operate a flagrant rip-off in such a tight, closed environment. Those who try it once don't get a second chance.

Size and density and complexity breed anonymity. And as our national population trends move relentlessly toward larger urban complexes, higher density, and greater complexity, more and more of us are forced to rely on strangers for our services and welfare. This provides them with an almost irresistible temptation to shaft us and leaves us with a chronic feeling of having been taken.

Little sense of community is possible under such conditions; only mutual suspicion, recrimination, accusation, and anxiety. The old-fashioned virtue called honor is possible only when people confront each other in their personhood and are forced to look each other in the eye for every long day of their lives.

Grouches, Sourpusses, and Louts

AN ELDERLY LADY I KNOW was terribly hurt by an act of raw rudeness, which was not directed at her so much as it was directed at the world. She just happened to be in the world's way at the time.

One of the hardest lessons to learn is that what seems to be "personal" may have little to do with us as persons. The driver who cuts across your lane in traffic doesn't even recognize you as a person.

Why are people dour and sullen and rude and unresponsive? Mostly because they are unhappy. They are miserable. They are having no fun.

It is pointless and counterproductive to snarl back at a sullen person. This will only confirm his or her bleak view of the human race. Rejection yearns to be justified by rejection.

By now we should be psychologically sophisticated enough to know that dourness is a kind of deficiency disease, a lack of emotional vitamins in the psychic bloodstream. Look upon glum and defensive people as ill people, and you will not get angry or upset, any more than you do at someone suffering from uncontrolled diabetes or pernicious anemia.

It is best to keep in mind that such persons are condemned to live with their miserable natures for a lifetime, whereas you have only a thirty-second contact with them. Consider yourself fortunate.

About one quarter of all the people in any given population are emotionally disturbed to a noticeable degree, so reconcile yourself to the fact that one person out of four you meet will act like a pill. Accept it calmly, and be grateful for the other three.

People who do not say "thank you," or do not hold a door open after them, or refuse to let you enter a line of cars, are not fit subjects for moral judgment. In most cases they are living half-lives, walking around in their sleep, oblivious to joy, filled with a pain they bitterly interpret as something else.

They lack nourishment of a certain sort. An essential area of their spirit is not being fed or fulfilled. They do not know what it is and may be only vaguely aware *that* it is, but they display the reactive irritability that pain always triggers. Imagine that they have chronic throbbing arthritis and can get no relief.

You cannot help them, but you can help yourself from being victimized by their condition. By being unhurtful, you become superior to everyone who is hurtful; by refusing to respond in kind, you keep the infection from spreading. Public health demands no less. And private tranquility depends on putting our pity in command of our punitive feelings. It is a strength, not a weakness.

The intellectual is uncomfortable socially because he wants both to be considered as an exception and to be accepted — and most societies are not willing to accept the exception.

*

The unfailing sign of a poor executive is that he reprimands his subordinates in public and commends them in private, when he should be doing exactly the opposite in order to elicit their best efforts.

There Are No "Pro-American" Dictators

THAT GREAT ALABAMA STATESMAN George Wallace, in London as part of the obligatory Grand Tour for U.S. presidential candidates, made a most revealing statement about his position on world affairs.

George opined as how he had nothing against dictatorships as such, provided that they were "pro-American." This tells us a lot about his firm grasp of American history, government, ideals, and origins.

Suppose for a moment that a medical man said, "I have nothing against the cancer cell, as long as it is pro-health." We would wonder if he had lost his mind, or had any to begin with. The cancer cell by definition is anti-health.

And so are all dictatorships, by definition, anti-American. The American nation was founded on a revolt from tyranny by one man or any group of men. Its founders proclaimed that men cannot give away their freedom — an inalienable right — even if they want to.

There is no such thing, and can never be, as a pro-American dictatorship. There may be dictators who cuddle up to us for temporary expediency, but they will always be our enemy: The cancer cell wants only to overrun and conquer what it joins with.

The most important thing we could do, as Americans, in the Bicentennial year was not to hold observances, celebrations, parades, historical tours, or pilgrimages. The most important thing was to read and study the papers, speeches, and other documents by the men who founded our nation, so that we truly understood what they were trying to do — not for their time, but for all time; not for our country, but for people everywhere.

They were proclaiming an utterly new doctrine: that legitimate government must rest on the consent of the governed, and moreover, that the governed can never consent to abdicate their own liberty. Once you allow yourself to be ruled by another, you are no longer a person.

Dictatorships deny this basic premise. They regard citizens as children, not as adults. They promise for the future what they withhold in the present. And they are by their very nature self-perpetuating and imperialistic. No dictatorship has ever been satisfied until its hegemony has been extended to the last possible outpost.

There are no "good" or "bad" dictatorships, any more than there are "healthy" or "sick" cancer cells. And none can be "pro-American" in any meaningful sense of the word. Before he runs for President, George ought to copy the Declaration of Independence five hundred times by hand, and then prove he understands what he is writing.

Bigotry Effectively Spurs Unity

THE FRIGHTENING AND TRAGIC THING about bigotry is that it creates, shapes, and solidifies the very element it dislikes. Without bigots regularly fanning the flames of prejudice, the objects of their dislike would fade into the background.

I was reading an editorial in the black magazine *Ebony* the other day which pointed out quite accurately that middle-class, educated blacks would under quite normal conditions identify with middle-class, educated whites more than they would with the uneducated blacks. But it is precisely the size and strength of the antiblack feeling in the United States that has solidified black feelings of allegiance to their color, crossing all social, economic, and educational lines.

Blacks want to be like all other Americans, sorted out according to their interests and abilities. By lumping them all together, the white population has succeeded in unifying them into a bloc in a way that they would never have been able to (or wanted to) accomplish by themselves.

Now there is truly a "black movement" in the country that places black interests first, because it is forced to. If blacks cannot take pride in being Americans, they will perforce take pride in being black. But this is purely a reactive formation to contempt, exploitation, and ostracism.

In much the same way, the state of Israel was created less by Jews and Zionists than by the powerful forces of anti-Semitism. Given a tolerant and accepting environment, Jews tended to take on the coloration of their habitat, and millions of them were hardly aware of their Judaic heritage until the rise of Hitlerism in the 1930s.

It was concerted anti-Semitism that heightened and hardened the sense of "Jewishness" around the world, and forced these people to look upon themselves as Jews first and citizens of their communities second. This was realistic on their part, and their passionate support of Israel represents less a dedication to Zionism than a desperate feeling that they must have some place to call their own in time of threat or peril.

The truly diabolic element in all bigotry is its power to bring forth what it seeks to subdue. Our own American Revolution, indeed, is a case in point: It was the arrogant attitude of the British toward the colonists that awoke feelings of independence; had the British treated us more as equals, we would gladly have remained loyal subjects. The new sentiment of "Americanism" was evoked, provoked, and promoted by British bigotry.

Learning to accept and live with human differences is the only way to diminish conflict. It is when differences are spurned and hated that they become hateful in turn (as we see in Ireland), and the cycle of conflict once again begins its weary round.

Stupid people define others by where they came from; intelligent people, by where they are going; wise people, by how they conduct themselves from point to point, no matter what the origin or the destination.

Know Thyself Before Criticizing Gays

YOU WOULDN'T THINK that some eighty years after the notorious Oscar Wilde case in London, the leader of Britain's Liberal Party would feel forced to resign because of homosexual allegations — but you would be wrong. Not as much has changed in the social order as we sometimes imagine.

Although my own chromosomes are as resolutely heterosexual as any man's, I can't for the life of me comprehend why a perfectly honorable and effective political leader should be blackmailed and hounded from office because his sexual preferences differ from those of the majority.

If we justify this persecution on the grounds of the Biblical injunction against sodomy and all it stands for, we are forced to recall that the Ten Commandments expressly forbid adultery and fornication as well. Who would deny that if we enforced these edicts equally, the vast majority of our politicians and public figures would be standing trial?

Recently, in fact, two psychiatrists who interviewed dozens of highly paid call girls and madams reported that "politicians and power brokers" composed some 60 percent of their clientele, in Miami, New York, Las Vegas, and California. Yet we shrug off this widespread flouting of the Mosaic law, reserving our indignation for the gay minority.

In point of realistic fact, homosexuality is far less a threat to our cherished institutions than the frenzied passions and deceptive practices of the "normals." It customarily does not involve rape; it does not contribute to the feckless growth of population; and in the few cases where it may wreck marriages and desolate children or become a breeding ground for crime and assault, this is because our censorious attitude compels it to remain relatively furtive and vulnerable to cruel social sanctions.

It does not appeal to my sexual sensibility, any more than eating raw oysters appeals to my gustatory sense; but I consider this a matter of taste more than of morals. If we do object on a moral basis, then we are arrant hypocrites for failing to enforce the current statutes against fornication and adultery — which, if carried out, would put half the population in prison overnight. We are not free to choose among commandments.

Many decades ago, when Reed Smoot's credentials as the new senator from Utah were being questioned for his religion's polygamous views, many of his colleagues were beating their breasts about keeping inviolate the "sanctity of the home." Senator Boise Penrose, aware of all the surreptitious philandering that went on, rose to defend Smoot, saying: "As for me, gentlemen, I would rather have seated beside me in this chamber a polygamist who doesn't 'poly' than a monogamist who doesn't 'monog.' "

Success Is Just a Little More Effort

WHAT MANY YOUNG PEOPLE fail to realize is the fact that you don't have to be much better than most others in order to do well. Only a slight superiority may be enough to make a vast difference.

Most of the people we call successful are not twice as smart, or twice as able, as the rest of the field. Indeed, if they are only 10 percent more proficient, this is generally more than enough to give them a consistent edge.

In sports, for instance, the best batting or passing records are not a great deal higher than the average. In field or track the differences are even smaller: a fraction of an inch or a fraction of a second may distinguish the winner from the also-rans.

Everyone is acquainted with the famous "law of diminishing returns." But hardly anyone is aware of the opposite law — that just a little extra effort can add up to a significant difference. One more ounce of energy in a push-off at a ski jump may give an extra foot of distance.

If you can average 5 to 10 percent better — no more — than others in your field, the rewards can be 100 percent greater; this is the compounding effect of achievement over a period of time.

Gambling is a singular example of small, steady increments making the ultimate difference. A gambling house does not have to be dishonest, or even to set the odds for a large percentage payoff. An edge of 5 percent, or even 3 percent, is enough to assure that the house will always win in the long run.

In chess, where there is no luck, the advantage of a single pawn between matched players is often decisive; in bridge, holding just one more trump card than the opponents may give the declarer or defender a lock on the hand. Experts win because they make slightly fewer mistakes, not because they perform brilliantly.

Young people are often overwhelmed by the spectacle of superiority, and wrongly imagine that leaders are endowed with vastly greater capacities than the rest — when the plain truth is that the similarities among men (and women, too, of course) are much closer than seem to be the case.

You only have to be a little bit better than most in what you do. Just a little smarter, just a little steadier, just a little more energetic, or whatever other prime quality is demanded in your field. If successes admitted this, they would not have cause to feel so conceited; and if the aspirants recognized this, they would not have cause to feel so left behind at the starting line.

Economics: A Field of Ethics

SUPPOSE THAT, in succeeding years, two astronomers had been awarded the Nobel Prize in their field. And suppose further that one of the astronomers held that the moon was composed largely of helium, while the other held that it was made of green cheese.

You would wonder, would you not, how two men with such disparate views could both be given the prize for outstanding contributions to astronomy? It would seem absurd, if not outrageous.

Yet this is precisely the case in the field of economics, where in the last few years the Nobels have been awarded to economists who hold totally differing views of how the economic machinery works and what might be done to improve its operation.

The prizes have been given, no doubt, for these men's technical expertise in what is known as microeconomics or econometrics. But what is important in that field is not technique but approach, attitude, and, ultimately, philosophy. What we need desperately to know is the best way to act economically for our private, civic, and world welfare.

And this is precisely what we do not know — nor do the economists any more than we. At least, they disagree among themselves as much as we do, when they move from micro- to macroeconomics.

Actually, it is worth recalling that the discipline of economics began as a branch of moral philosophy. Adam Smith was a moral philosopher. The purpose of his *Wealth of Nations* was to show us not how to get rich or stay rich, but how to promote just and decent relations among people.

Economics is *au fond* a branch of ethics. It must start with what you believe about the human spirit, about rights and responsibilities. If your sense of ethics is warped (as everyone's is, to varying degrees), it will inevitably warp your view of the economic and political process.

This is why debates and arguments on the economic level rarely get anywhere, and almost always fail to convince the other party. Behind the barrage of economic facts and theories lie the hidden assumptions about the nature of the human animal and the kind of society we want. These views are rarely expressed, but they color the arguments of everyone, from Professor Milton Friedman to a longshoreman.

The study of ethics is possibly the most neglected discipline in modern education, and perhaps the most desperately needed. This is not to suggest that moral philosophers will agree any more than economists do — but it is to suggest that as long as we argue economics in a moral void, we will not even be able to agree on what we are disagreeing about.

The Rub Is Finding the Niche

A YOUNG MAN I KNOW who was graduated from college this winter got a job on Monday and was fired on Thursday. His parents, with whom I had dinner the following night, were quite distressed at this fiasco.

From what I know of the young man, it seems to me he was fired for being too good for the job, rather than for not being good enough. A bright person often has a harder time holding down an elementary job than a duller, less imaginative person does.

Thomas Edison recalled being fired from two of his earliest jobs. The first was as a telegraph operator. He became so interested in the machine and its workings that he tried to figure out how to improve it.

"But I forgot all about the messages that were coming over the wire," he later said, "and I left a lot of messages unsent or undelivered."

Then he took a job in an office where there were a lot of rats running around, and he dreamed up a contraption that killed them by the scores — and also killed cockroaches. After a few days, the floor was covered with dead roaches, and they fired him for that.

Sometimes it may take years after leaving school for a person to find his or her proper niche in the world; and if there is undue pressure from parents or a premature marriage, the right niche may never be found.

The world is filled with disgruntled employees laboring in uncongenial or spiritually unrewarding jobs — the unrolling stone often deeply resents the moss it gathers. Robert Benchley once remarked, only half jokingly: "It was twenty years before I realized I wasn't a writer — but by that time I was so successful that I couldn't afford to give it up."

I am an optimist about people and firmly believe that every single person has one thing that he can do a little better than most people around him, and he has a sacred obligation to himself to find out what that thing is and to do it. (Most saints, after all, have been men and women not who soared to heights of achievement, but who sank to depths of service we would not dream of.)

Of course, to be realistic, it is equally true that many chronic job-losers are simply lazy or incompetent, like the butter-fingered lad who, after long unemployment, finally found a job in a chinaware house. The second day at work, he smashed a large, expensive vase and was summoned to the manager's office. He was told that the cost of the vase would be deducted from his wages each week until it was totally paid for, in the sum of $6000. "Oh, that's wonderful," the boy exclaimed. "I'm so happy. At last I've got a steady job!"

Fiction No Stranger Than Truth

ON THE PLANET Gryphth, in the solar system B24X, about one fourth of the inhabitants are born Red Headed. This is looked upon as a terrible thing on Gryphth, where everybody else is totally bald.

It is ancient knowledge on Gryphth that Red Heads can contaminate you if you get too close. So the Red Heads are kept at arm's length — or farther, whenever possible. (But oddly enough, dogs with red hair are quite popular pets on that planet.)

Because of their biological handicap, the Red Heads get the short end of everything. The worst jobs, if any. The worst housing and schools. When times are bad, they are even worse for Red Heads; when times are good, they are barely tolerable for Red Heads.

Now the Red Heads don't think anything is different about them, except their red hair, which they can't help. And when they are treated differently they get mad and act up. They drink more than is good for them. They attack each other, and sometimes even have the boldness to attack a Baldie.

Some of them refuse to take the rotten jobs offered them, and it begins to look as if they might have to be kept in a police garrison to prevent them from running amok. Gryphth has a terrible problem with its Red Heads.

Lately, a few of the Baldies have ventured to fraternize with the Red Heads and have come to the realization that they didn't get contaminated. They have tried to take this message back to the Loyal Order of Bald Eagles, which runs the planet, but have been laughed at, disbelieved, and even assaulted for their pains.

They have also tried to tell the Baldies that when you fraternize with the Red Heads on equal terms, Gryphth to Gryphth, as it were, they are as nice people as you would want to meet any day. But when you treat them like scum, they react like scum. How long can they be expected to turn the other scalp?

But few listen. Almost everybody who is anybody on Gryphth knows that the Red Heads are the cause of most of what is wrong, and the only way to keep them harmless is to keep them down. If they weren't meant to be treated this way, why did the Great God Epiderm give them red hair when everybody else is bald? It stands to reason.

And so the worse the Red Heads are treated, the worse they respond. And the worse they respond, the more the Baldies can say, "See, we told you — the only good Red Head is a dead, or at least a docile, Red Head." And the Baldies have no idea that it is they themselves who are contaminating the whole planet of Gryphth.

Thank the Great God Endoderm we live in a more advanced solar system.

"Elitism" is the slur directed at merit by mediocrity.

On Treating Others as Equals

CONSIDER THE TWO PHRASES "treated as an equal" and "equal treatment." Do they mean the same thing? Most people would say so, and most people would be wrong.

Consider now a horse race. Each of the horses must be treated as an equal — that is, each must go to the post carrying 116 pounds. Fair enough, isn't it?

But in order for each horse to be treated as an equal, there cannot be "equal treatment" in this case. Those horses with lighter jockeys must have leaden weight added to their saddles, to bring them up to 116 pounds.

Are those horses getting equal treatment? No. Are they being treated as equals? Yes. Each horse breaks from the starting gate with the same handicap. The horses with lead in their saddles have not lost anything they were entitled to.

I use the example of horses instead of people because nobody will get excited about it. It is not an emotional issue. If you want a good, fair race, the first and most important thing is to handicap it properly. Then, and only then, each horse has an equal chance to win. What could be simpler, more obvious, and more just?

Now, all passion and prejudice aside, isn't this precisely what is at issue in the case of so-called reverse discrimination at schools and colleges?

In order for all applicants to be treated as equals, they cannot be given equal treatment. Otherwise, some would be carrying 134-pound loads while others ran with only 116 pounds. The lighter jockeys (in this case, the less disadvantaged) are required to put lead in their saddles to make up the weight.

Thus, the candidates for admission to these schools and colleges start out roughly equal. The handicap given to the advantaged only balances out the earlier advantages they benefited from. It does not take away a right. It simply cancels out a privilege.

The U.S. Constitution guarantees each citizen the right to be treated as an equal under the law. Sometimes, in order to assure this right, we must apply unequal treatment, exactly as we do in honest horse races. Of course, it is much harder to do with people, and the results will not always be fair. But this does not mean that it should not be tried.

No owner would complain that his horse was suffering from "reverse discrimination" if it were compelled to add ten pounds to equalize the weight. There is a built-in semantic trap in this controversy, and we cannot resolve it by petitioning dumbly for "equal treatment."

The Paradox of "Know Thyself"

SURELY THE OLDEST and perhaps the most familiar of all sayings in any language is the ancient injunction of Socrates: *"Know thyself."* Almost everyone agrees on its importance, and many have tried to follow it — but with results that are more often disappointing than satisfying.

The failures come from a profound misunderstanding of the way to go about this process. For there is a paradox at the heart of the human situation, and it is this: *We can only know ourselves through knowing others, and we can only know others through knowing ourselves.*

In order to know oneself, no amount of introspection or self-examination will suffice. You can analyze yourself for weeks or meditate for months, and you will not get an inch further — any more than you can smell your own breath or laugh when you tickle yourself.

You must first be open to the other person before you catch a glimpse of yourself. Our self-reflection in a mirror does not tell us what we are like, only our reflection in other people does. We are essentially social creatures, and our personality resides in *association,* not in isolation.

As Buber insists, *meeting* is the ground of our humanity, and a sense of the other must precede any real sense of the self. People who feel isolated and alienated and at odds with themselves have somehow not learned to meet the other on even ground, to engage in dialogue, to accept the other as being as real as oneself.

It is a remarkable fact of psychology that the people who are most sensitive about themselves are generally the most insensitive about other people. Those whose feelings are most easily hurt are usually unaware of the feelings they evoke in others.

The second half of the paradox is that, conversely, the only way we can truly understand others is by self-recognition. We cannot decipher them from the outside, as it were, but only by being able to identify with their passions and responses, by recognizing our own defects and deceptions and distortions of reality. (This helps make us, at the same time, more perceptive about their motives and more sympathetic toward their needs.)

Nothing is really personal that is not first *interpersonal,* beginning with the infant's shock of separation from the umbilical cord. What we know about ourselves comes only from the outside and is interpreted by the kind of experiences we have had, and what we know about others comes only from analogy with our own network of feelings.

"Know thyself" has done as much harm as good down the ages, and possibly more, as long as people construed it in a narrow, individualistic sense. It is worth recalling that Socrates spent his days in the *agora,* discussing life with all manner of men, rather than retreating to a cave to scratch his psychic sores.

Each of us has a sense of justice, and each of us wants to live securely; what finally is the determinant of our character is how much of the latter we are willing to relinquish in order to satisfy the legitimate demands of the former.

School vs. Gang: No Contest

IT CAN BE ARGUED that, given the conditions and needs in urban slums, the gang offers a better educational bet than the school does. In addition, the gang "protects and serves" its members — which, curiously enough, is the motto of the Chicago Police Department.

A well-run slum gang will take in an ignorant boy of thirteen and teach him just about everything he needs to know for survival and sometimes supremacy in the world he inhabits.

It sends him out to rob and steal, and it is amazing how fast even the dullest school pupil acquires proficiency in these street arts. If he gets caught and sent away, he is likely to find an active chapter of his gang — or one much like it — in the detention home, where he learns even more.

And should he make it into his majority and suddenly find himself in an adult prison, his gang connection offers as solid an entry to the prison elite as a *Social Register* listing does at Bar Harbor.

What can school possibly do for a lad like this, if he lacks extraordinary powers of mentation or physical prowess? The school he sullenly goes to can at most ill prepare him for either a vocation he despises and will be mediocre at or one he cannot possibly attain.

It teaches him about the past, which he is content to remain oblivious of, and steers him toward a future that is highly problematic by the terms of his inheritance, environment, and peer pressures. Almost nothing in the school curriculum appears as even vaguely realistic to him.

Meanwhile, the gang is often mother, father, and big brother; the only focus for his latent feelings of loyalty and belonging; a buffer against the chill winds of indifference and downright hostility; and, perhaps most of all, a social institution that is practical in its functions and pragmatic about its goals.

How can the school in such areas compete with the gang? It

is patently a lopsided contest, and the gang is winning more year after year, because it provides what is needed and wanted. Pouring more money, equipment, and teaching staff into such schools is like trying to irrigate the Sahara with a sprinkling can.

Nobody wants to recognize this truth. We fatuously expect our schools to be able to do what parents cannot do, police cannot do, churches and public agencies cannot do. They have lost their moral force, if they ever had any there, and without moral force no other force can prevail.

There is only one moral force in the urban slum, and that is the gang. It demands, and gets, trustworthiness, loyalty, helpfulness, obedience, and all the other Scout virtues — but for itself alone. And why not?

Next Time, Send Older Men to War

THE ADVENT OF MODERN WEAPONRY presents a danger, but it also offers us a chance we have never had before. Now, for the first time in history, it no longer makes any military sense to take the youngest men first.

In all past wars, from the dawn of history down to the atomic age, the success of an army depended largely upon the health and strength of the ordinary fighting man, whether bearing spear, bayonet, or bazooka.

But the next world conflagration, everyone agrees, will depend upon hardware — and hardware that can be manipulated just as easily by an asthmatic man of sixty as by a healthy youth of twenty.

This being the case, those nations that prate about desiring peace and protest that they would only fight a "defensive" war, as a matter of survival, should each pass a law stipulating that in the event of overt hostilities on a global scale, the first men to be drafted for combat duty would be those in the forty-five-to-sixty-five age bracket.

And the first among these first should be the lawmakers and officeholders who support war as a legitimate means of conflict resolution, who urge larger and larger military budgets without allocating one cent or one erg of energy in a search for alternative means of preventing planetary catastrophe and the irrevocable loss of our best seed.

Of course, it is an absurd pipe-dream to imagine for a moment that any legislature might even glancingly contemplate such a threat to its political dominance. These older men, who so gallantly send off youngsters to their death, would have a dozen rationalizations for their own deferral. For one thing, who would then be left to guide the nation's destiny?

From my reading of history, it seems evident that the rising generation in nearly every epoch might have done a better job of leading their nation than the proud, querulous, suspicious, competitive, and infinitely self-serving statesmen who blundered from one war into the next. (Indeed, many reputable historians agree that World War II might have been averted had the cream of both British and German youth not been slaughtered in World War I, leaving only the defective residue to rise to positions of influence and decision-making.)

It is utopian to hope that today's youth could unite in some effective antiwar movement transcending national boundaries, desire it though they might. But it is not entirely hopeless that within their own nation they might attain enough strength to require the old ones to go first.

Until now, fathers have "defended" their sons by sacrificing them: a strange sort of nobility. Now, in the atomic age, let the old go forth to do battle, so that the survivors, if there are any, may represent the future and not repeat the sullen past.

The most obsolete phrase of the late twentieth century is "national sovereignty," for we live singularly in an era when an atomic war can be concluded before it is even declared.

Extremism a Vice, Not a Virtue

EXTREMISM IS A WORD we hear a lot this election year, and one of my children wanted to know why extremism is necessarily a bad thing. He pointed to the American revolutionists of 1776 as a possible example.

It is a terrible example. The American colonists were anything but extremists. They did everything in their power to prevent a break with the mother country. They pleaded, they petitioned, they promised undying loyalty to the crown if they were but treated as equal subjects.

It is precisely because the revolt of 1776 was a moderate revolution, a conservative revolution, that it became the only one in the history of the world that did not betray its own principles after it succeeded. The French Revolution culminated in a worse tyranny than before; the Russian Revolution is still in a totalitarian grip stronger than the czar's ever was.

What is wrong with extremism is not necessarily its *position,* but its *attitude.* Extremism really does not want, or believe in, opposition. It believes that it is so absolutely, so irrevocably right that any other position must be ruthlessly suppressed. It has no real tolerance for points of view that disagree with it, regarding them as agents of the devil as well as enemies of the state.

Yet opposition must be legally built into the structure of a government if it is going to survive, much less flourish. The institutionalization of opposition is one of the real advances in society, for before then it was only possible to kill or exile political opponents.

A government is not really strong, in the long run, when it is controlled by a monolithic party; it is weak. Rome fell largely because it was unable, or unwilling, to develop the institutions and processes necessary for a lawful and peaceful change in the government.

Politics is like architecture: It depends for its greatest strength upon opposing forces pressing and supporting each other. If one side or the other prevails completely, the structure collapses. This is what extremists, left and right alike, cannot seem to understand.

An extreme position may sometimes be necessary, in an emergency — but the extremist always sees an emergency, always is convinced that unless his viewpoint dominates, there is nothing but disaster ahead. His attitude is fundamentally antidemocratic, no matter what populist slogans he may chant or how he may pretend to represent "the people."

Conflict, dissent, opposition — these are the lifeblood of a civil society, and they must be built into the very foundation itself in a delicate balance between order and change. The extremist would upset this balance, in the fanatical delusion that his way is the only way.

War: The Revenge of Age on Youth

I DO NOT THINK WE CAN EXPLAIN the recurrence of war on a political or economic or social basis. These elements make war possible; they do not make it inevitable. But war has been as certain as death and taxes in human history.

It has long been my conviction that deep irrational impulses are at work in the promotion and perpetuation of war, in every century, in every society, in every part of the world. We can see it most clearly now, in the atomic age.

Atomic war has been proclaimed "unthinkable," but we are far from giving up thinking about it. Indeed, the atomic powers seem embarked on a collision course of building up such arms that nothing will avert a confrontation. But a war fought with nuclear weapons can end only in mutual destruction.

The main impulse I perceive, hidden well below the level of consciousness, is the envy of the fathers toward the sons. Nothing else fully explains why the fathers are willing to see their sons slaughtered in battle in nearly every generation.

In the past they might have justified it by victory — but there can be no victory now, as every leader on every side well knows.

I think that as men grow older and feel life and sexual vitality and power beginning to slip from their hands, they develop a death-wish for the young and vibrant who are about to seize the reins and control the future. They do not want a world to exist without them.

So they send to war the best, the healthiest, the youngest, the most capable, while they remain behind to pick up the pieces, if any. If war were rational and if men were rational about it, then the oldest, the weakest, the most dispensable for the future would go first. The freshest and strongest would be preserved for the ultimate need.

Can anyone explain why people everywhere, who profess to love their children so deeply, have at all times sent them forth to battle in wars that benefited only kings and chieftains and munitions makers? Why after each war was it seen to be "unnecessary" if only the right few steps had been taken — and they were never taken? All the historical interpretations fail, one by one, and we are left with the frightful suspicion that we do not love our sons as much as we fear and resent them; that perpetual wars are the revenge age takes against youth; that other "reasons" and "causes" are mere camouflage for a hate that dares not speak its name.

An atomic war, precisely because it threatens universal annihilation, is the perfect "final solution" for this demonic urge.

So long as most people continue to suffer from the delusion that the mere absence of war is peace, few efforts will be made to construct a dynamic and durable peacekeeping agency.

*

There is only one "ism" that can kill the soul, and that is the stubborn conviction that any particular "ism" can save it.

Responsibility Requires Knowledge

HARRY EMERSON FOSDICK, the preacher, used to tell a story about being awakened at 2:00 A.M. one winter night by a tipsy young collegian banging on the door. When Dr. Fosdick let him in, the young man said, "I'd like you to explain to me the difference between modernism and fundamentalism."

"Go home and sober up," the clergyman told him. "Come back later in the morning, and I'll be glad to give you the answer."

The collegian began to sob. "The trouble is, doctor, that when I'm sober, I won't give a damn!"

This little story encapsulates the intellectual history of the human race. When we are sober — that is to say, in our normal state of inertia — we aren't interested in the differences or distinctions between competing creeds and practices.

But when we are drunk — that is to say, ill or upset or shaken by crisis out of our usual apathy — we not only want to know about such things, but we want to know in a hurry. And as soon as we are "sober" again, when the crisis has subsided, we couldn't care less.

The turmoil in the Middle East suddenly jolted us into the realization that this is still a world of startling differences, not only in religious beliefs, but in customs, attitudes, morals, and the willingness to die rather than relinquish some of these tenets.

We have been dabbling, and more than dabbling, in international politics around the globe, but, as recently as 1979, about 90 percent of Americans could not distinguish Iran from Iraq or tell a Moslem from a Monza. In the early days of the hostage crisis we were indiscriminately stoning the shops of Albanians, Yemenites, and, for all I know, Lower Slobovians.

We still have a hard time distinguishing between Arabs and Moslems. We barely recognize that Sunnis are not Shi'ites, and we tend to lump together Lebanon, Syria, and Jordan, despite their multiplicity of differences, national, religious, and ethnic. From our reserved seats, they all look alike to us.

But we cannot at the same time be a force in world affairs and remain so provincially ignorant of the peoples whose lives we are interfering with. For a quarter-century our government sustained a despotic Iranian regime it had helped put in power (while toppling its democratically elected predecessor), and we neither knew nor cared.

If we want to be effective, we must be responsible; and responsibility implies knowing and caring — in the morning when we are sober as well as at night when we are drunk. Neither God nor Allah will save us as long as we worship at the altar of smug ignorance, suffering from the fatal fallacy that what we don't know can't hurt us.

War Is Not Eternal . . .

"YOU'LL ALWAYS HAVE WAR" is one of the most stupid and thoughtless statements a person could make. Because such a person has no idea what war means, historically and actually.

What such a person really is saying is that you'll always have aggression and hostility and conflict among people. There is no question of that; no utopia we can even dimly conceive would remove these unlovely traits from the human animal.

But war is a very different matter. War is a social institution, and like any institution it can be abolished — as cannibalism was abolished, as slavery was abolished — if enough of us want to.

We cannot stop people from disagreeing or from fighting over their disagreements. This is one reason every state has a police force and a judiciary: to nip conflicts in the bud and to bring the adversaries before a court with the power to resolve the issue.

The people of Milwaukee do not go to war against the people of Chicago when the latter protest that their water supply is being contaminated by the other city. The argument is taken to the courts, and the cities agree to abide by the courts' decision.

The countries of the world, however, are unwilling to give up their sovereignty in this respect. They do not want an international police force to arrest such conflicts or a world court with the power to enforce decisions. Every country wants to be the prosecutor, judge, and jury in its own case — and to decide favorably for itself.

This is the root cause of war — not man's instinctual aggressiveness or greed or any other emotional component. If we can settle our hostilities domestically by going to law, there is no reason we cannot settle our international hostilities by going to law.

Actually, while the notion of sovereignty might have made some sense three centuries ago when the modern nation-state was emerging, the new tools of war have turned it into a dangerously obsolete concept. The only sovereignty now possessed by even the strongest nation is the power to kill the enemy twenty times over while it is being killed only ten times over.

Nuclear warfare has made effective defense impossible; only retaliation remains as a threat. And even that is dubious: Enemy submarines can lob nuclear bombs upon our coastal cities and run away. Who can identify the enemy in such a covert and undeclared war? One that could be over, for all practical purposes, in twenty minutes.

Our most perilous cultural lag is equating modern warfare with wars of the past, when today it is not only quantitatively but qualitatively a different paradigm. We are confronting an entirely unique situation in the history of mankind, and either warfare must be abolished or we will be. "You'll always have war" could be mankind's ironic epitaph, when the very last war is staring us in the face.

In the final analysis there is no final analysis.

. . . or Holy

I WISH SOME ISLAMIC SCHOLAR could explain to me what is meant by a "holy war." I have never understood the phrase in any religious terms, and I wonder if it represents a true projection or a perversion of the Koran.

Buried in the news on the very same day the U.S. hostages were released was a dispatch from Lebanon, setting the stage for a conference of thirty-five foreign ministers from Islamic countries, in which Crown Prince Fahd of Saudi Arabia called for a *jihad,* or holy war, as the only course for resolving the Arab-Israeli conflict.

In what way can a war be "holy"? By definition, a war is a conflict in which innocent people are killed. They are killed because they represent "the other," and for no personal act of guilt or responsibility. Most soldiers have no idea why they are fighting, and do so only because they happen to have been born on a particular tract of land.

In every war, the just and the unjust are equally mixed on both sides — good, bad, and indifferent, regardless of what language they speak, what religion they profess, or what uniform they wear. Most wars have been pointless or fruitless; the most they do is plant the seeds of a future war.

It seems to me that if anything at all were repugnant to a just God it would be human beings shooting and killing one another because they have been ordered to by ambitious leaders or whipped into a frenzy of hate by demagogues. And most repugnant would be the "religious" banner under which this slaughter is justified and even sanctified.

A war is declared for many different reasons, some more or less worthy than others. At best, it should be engaged in with regret, as a last stand, an admission that nothing else will do, that we have failed in reason and brotherliness. To enter a war with gusto, proclaiming it a "holy war," is to me the ultimate depth of blasphemy.

Whatever the legal and human rights in the Arab-Israeli conflict (and I hold neither side guiltless), the notion of a "holy war" is so primitive, so exclusivist, and so fanatical that it forfeits whatever good will we might extend to its proponents. Three centuries ago, Roman Catholics and Protestants fought each other under such banners, but Christianity has long acknowledged the basic impiety of such claims.

If religion is to be respected — especially among the young who will fight and die — it cannot be misused for worldly conquest; if Jehovah, or God, or Allah, is to be worshiped, we cannot do so for sectarian ends. All war is unholy, desecrating what it seeks to defend.

Peace: More Feeling Than Field

THERE IS A COLUMN to be found in everything, as I have long since learned. Even in a typographical mistake. Some time ago, a word was inadvertently dropped from a sentence I wrote about Madame Curie's having been the only person to have received Nobel Prizes in two different fields. It should have read "two different *scientific* fields," and I received many letters pointing out that Linus Pauling had won Nobels for chemistry and for peace. "Aren't those different fields?" some readers asked mockingly.

Actually not. Chemistry is a field. So are the other Nobel categories. But peace is not. Peace is a feeling, an attitude, a relationship, a state, a condition. But it is not a field.

Nobody studies peace. There are no courses in peace, no examinations, no discoveries, and, alas, no advances. We are no farther on the road to peace than were the ancient Greek city-states, and perhaps we're farther away.

Nobody who has ever won a Nobel Peace Prize has moved us an inch closer to peace, and some have definitely moved us backward — like Woodrow Wilson, who won the prize in 1919 for having planted the seeds of World War II that sprouted in 1939. This is the richest irony in modern history.

Peace *could* become a field, and *should* become a field, if we were prepared to take it seriously. If we began to define it as something positive, not as something negative, a mere absence of war or a long truce. If we understood that peace without law is impossible, and that real law is impossible among sovereign states. If we recognized that a relatively new study called conflict resolution has already provided some valuable insights and strategies for achieving the first faltering steps toward peace. If we spent a fraction of public funds for disseminating the preconditions and procedures of peace that we do for arming ourselves against the almost inevitable nuclear conflict in which, this time, there will be no winners, only losers. If we grasped the fact that modern war has now become too lethal to be considered as merely "an extension of politics," in the classic phrase.

Peace ought to be a field — the most important field in the world for the survival of the human race — but in the eighty-one years since the inauguration of the Nobel Prizes, it has remained only a sentiment, like "love thy neighbor" and "do unto others." But sentimentality will not save us; only the realistic willingness to transform peace from a feeling to a field can even start us on the way to a human solution.

The three hardest tasks in the world are neither physical feats nor intellectual achievements, but moral acts: to return love for hate, to include the excluded, and to say, "I was wrong."

*

While it is necessary to see men's weaknesses as well as their strengths, it is essential to admire them for their strengths more than despising them for their weaknesses.

Nuclear Showdown "Inevitable"

THE LATE GREAT ROBERT HUTCHINS was importantly wrong only once in his life, in my opinion. When he supervised the development of the atomic bomb at the University of Chicago in 1942, he called it "the good news of damnation," contending that it would frighten people into banding together to avoid world suicide and achieve world peace.

Now, forty years later, we can see he was as wrong as Alfred Nobel, a half-century earlier, who predicted that his invention of dynamite would make war so horrible that men would voluntarily give it up.

A few years ago, the International Peace Research Institute in Stockholm — an independent organization with an international governing body, set up by the Swedish parliament to commemorate 150 years of unbroken peace in Sweden — issued a forecast to mark its tenth anniversary of existence. What was striking about the forecast was the institute's doubt that it might still be around ten years from that anniversary.

Within nine years, the forecast said, some thirty-five countries around the world will be able to make atomic weapons, and nuclear war will become inevitable. Not conceivable. Not possible. Not probable. Inevitable.

The institute has no vested interest in catastrophe or doom. It speaks for no nuclear power, nor for power at all. It addresses itself simply to the question of global stability and human survival.

As the Reuters dispatch put it, the forecast "painted a gloomy picture of far-reaching technical advances in nuclear, chemical, bacteriological, and conventional weaponry. It said the spread of nuclear capability to about thirty-five countries by 1985 would be a by-product of peaceful nuclear programs."

But this "good news of damnation," instead of scaring us, as Hutchins hoped it would, has only stunned us into apathy, resignation, or the equally futile resolve to retaliate in kind for any atomic attack. We still fail to understand the implications of the atomic age. We have not grasped the overriding fact — clear to every scientist who has studied the matter — that war is now qualitatively different from anything known in the past. It is no longer a zero-sum game, where one side "wins" what the other "loses." It is mutual suicide, beyond rational calculation.

The "near-nuclear" countries feel themselves threatened by those already in possession of the bomb. The pressure to compete will become — is becoming — irresistible. Like a bar fight, if one man has a broken bottle in his hand, the other is going to find a similarly lethal weapon.

It is an old-fashioned Western showdown we are heading for — the difference being that in this case, not only will the combatants kill each other off, but the saloon will go, the town will go, and the whole West will go. To say nothing of the East, North, and South as well.

The Rip-Off Society

THE CHAP WHO OCCUPIES the cell next to me — a struggling young cartoonist named Bill Mauldin — happened to be staying overnight at a hotel just across the street. He had two early-morning visitors, and called down to room service for three small orange juices, three bowls of Special K cereal, and three cups of coffee. The waiter arrived with the order and the bill — $14.97, not even counting the tip.

Nobody can tell me that this is "inflation" or "cost of living." It is pure and simple rip-off. It happens every day, every place. If a restaurateur's cost goes up a penny, he slaps on another dime charge to the customer. What's to stop him? Everyone's doing the same.

I can sympathize with the laissez-faire people, who would like to see far less government intervention and control in business affairs. But they are naive if they imagine that business will then automatically regulate itself, through free competition, to give the consumer the best quality and service at the lowest cost.

Both extremes, the Marxists and the laissez-faire people, are utopian in their view of the human animal. The Marxists suppose that socialism will get rid of greed, venality, and conspiracy, and the laissez-fairists suppose that individualism will do the same.

But there is no reason to suppose that the "invisible hand" of Adam Smith will change the processes of power any more than the heavy hand of collectivism has done in Russia and China and elsewhere. I have not noticed that people in business are generally any more decent or honest or restrained than people in government. Or even more rational.

We are living in a rip-off society. There is virtually no sense of community left. Surely this cannot all be blamed on government, any more than it can all be blamed on business. There is no single scapegoat for our predicament; it is a pandemic erosion of ethical standards and feelings.

The problem is not economic but moral. Almost any economic system will work if there is a basic sense of decency in the populace; and none will work if there isn't. As Churchill once said, capitalism is ruthlessly unequal in its share of blessings, and communism is ruthlessly equal in its share of miseries.

Of course, anybody in his right mind would choose to live in our society rather than in theirs, because with all its faults it still retains a self-correcting process without bloodshed or brutality. But this superiority is no excuse for turning the competitive system into a corral where the elephants trumpet "Every man for himself" as they dance among the chickens.

Repressed Anger Explodes

MOST OF US will agree that repression is morally wrong and that the people have a right freely to express their resentments and discontents as much as their preferences.

What the repressors throughout history have been singularly blind to is the fact that repression is also psychologically stupid and self-defeating. It is essential that people be permitted to find fault openly with those who rule them or represent them.

The repressed society is like a boiler without a safety valve; when the steam builds up, if it is provided with no outlet, it will blow up the whole boiler. This is largely what happened in Russia in the dozen years between the abortive revolution of 1905 and the Bolshevik takeover.

No rulers, or even leaders, really want criticism, although they may publicly pretend to be receptive to it. They want praise for their accomplishments and silence for their errors or failures. This is as true of any city alderman as it is for a king, a President, or a dictator.

Yet the one thing they do not want — protest, complaint, and criticism — is the one thing that can preserve them in office longer than a policy of censorship, repression, and retaliation. Leaders, just as often as the led, fail to recognize where their best interest lies.

Strangely enough, military leaders, who are supposed to be insensitive to human values, have always been shrewder than politicians in this respect: The best generals have permitted grumbling and verbal irreverence for authority among the enlisted men. They have known that this is the way psychic poisons are drained out and that discipline does not necessarily include a ban on bitching.

(Shakespeare, as usual, recognizes this psychological need in *Henry V,* when the king wanders unrecognized through his camp at Agincourt and runs across a discontentented common soldier,

Williams. They exchange gloves and later, instead of reprimanding the soldier, Henry returns his glove filled with money.)

It is not words that threaten a government, it is thoughts. As Nietzsche warned, "All unexpressed truths become poisonous." If thoughts are not permitted to take verbal form, they become a hundred times more subversive than when allowed free ventilation. The same atmosphere that disseminates them also dilutes their concentrated power.

But it is words that the repressors are afraid of, foolishly imagining that by damming up the flow of communication they can somehow inhibit the thoughts, when by so doing they are only adding to the pressure. It is not the complaining wife who finally takes the kitchen knife to her husband, but the one who never before uttered a single word of protest.

Bigger Isn't Always Better

THE WISCONSIN VILLAGE where I spend my summers has a permanent population of around two hundred. As a popular resort center, it can now hardly cope with the flood of visitors and tourists in its peak season.

People come there because it is quiet and friendly and bucolic and still not too congested. Its sparseness of population has been one of its chief attractions.

Now a high-powered big-city developer is wangling to buy a sixteen-acre tract in town, on the waterfront, and proposes to build a condominium of one hundred housing units on the grounds where only one house now stands. These will be winterized apartments for year-round use, available for rental by their owners.

Suddenly the home ownership population of the village would be more than doubled, for one hundred units implies at least two hundred persons. Can you contemplate the population of your town doubled overnight — double the people, the cars, the boats, the demand for heating, lighting, phone service, and garbage pickups?

But the village board and the county authorities have gone along with this proposal, because to many it spells prosperity and growth and development. But does it really?

John Maynard Keynes, the economist, became famous for, among other things, his "paradox of the aggregate." This states, briefly, that what may be a privilege when only a few have it turns into a drag when too many acquire it. This pursuit, as he puts it, brings everyone into collision in "communities of disappointment."

If you can live on the top floor of a high-rise with a commanding view of the lake, you have an advantage. But as soon as your high-rise is surrounded by a ring of the same, you have a view of nothing but other windows, and everyone has lost the privilege.

If you can go to a state park and camp in relative seclusion, you can get back to nature at little cost. But as soon as thousands go to the same place, nature is transformed into a rural ghetto, and you might as well stay home for the privacy you find there.

When there were relatively few autos on the road, it was a delight to tool around in a car. Then, as almost everybody could afford one, the pleasure turned into aggravation, congestion, and a frightful death rate.

Growth is not inherently good; in fact, growth is what a cancer cell is all about. It multiplies so much and so fast that it kills the body it feeds upon, and then must die itself. Our communities, like our citizens, ought to think less about getting bigger and more about getting better.

It is true that the first book of the Bible commands us to "be fruitful and multiply" — but that was depicting a time when the total human population of the Earth was two.

Finance Capitalism: The Manipulation of Wealth

MOST PEOPLE REALLY DON'T KNOW what they are talking about when they use the word *capitalism*. The conservative uses the word as an invocation of the deity, while the left-winger employs it as a curse against the devil. The ordinary citizen is merely confused.

This confusion arises, I think, because there are three different and distinctive forms of capitalism, but we generally use the same word to designate a ma-and-pa grocery, Standard Oil, and Lazard Frères. This is somewhat on the order of calling a drinking fountain, a fishing stream, and the Mississippi "bodies of water."

The early capitalism that Adam Smith knew and wrote about was commercial capitalism in its historic and primitive phase, and a vast improvement over the mercantilism whose place it took. Even Marx later admitted that this represented a progressive jump from the feudal and monarchial system it replaced.

But a hundred years later, this commercial capitalism became subjected and subordinated to industrial capitalism with all its strengths and weaknesses, bringing the highest standard of living the world had ever known, along with the bleak factory towns, the slums, the pollution, and the diseases.

This phase in turn was followed by the stage we have now been in for about a century — the era of finance capitalism. It is what has been called a paper economy, and its domination bears only an oblique relation to the actual, "real" world of production and distribution. (This was Henry Ford's early, and embittering, discovery.)

In finance capitalism — which is as far removed from Adam Smith's idea as the drinking fountain from the Mississippi — the dominant companies may be pure financial intermediaries, one or more removes of ownership away from the operating units that own factories and make products. They are interested in paper wealth rather than in real wealth.

The object of finance capitalism is not necessarily to make and sell more products and thus create more jobs and spending power, but to manipulate wealth in money and stocks and shares so as to maximize the profit regardless of the productive resources. The interest of finance capitalism does not necessarily coincide with the interest of the nation in producing real things for more people.

Wealth at this level is symbolic — a matter of state of mind, of controlling expectations and influencing climates of opinion. Since this is the case, little wonder that our practical solutions do not seem to work, that old formulas break down and common sense does not apply. Could Newton find his bearings in an Einsteinian universe?

Being Gay Is More Than a Preference

PENMANSHIP IS THE ONLY skill I can perform with my right hand. For everything else — cutting, throwing a ball, dealing cards, swinging a tennis racquet — I use my left hand. That is just the way I am.

It is not a preference of mine. In fact, this anomaly is often uncomfortable in a right-handed world. But there is nothing I can do about it, and I must conform to the world more than it caters to me.

I mention these dull facts by way of drawing an analogy with the current controversy about homosexual rights. There has lately been, as we know, an intense backlash in many cities relating to the rights of homosexuals to teach and engage in other public activities.

What has happened, I think, is that the gay liberation movement and its affiliates have begun to claim too much for their anomaly. They are right in insisting that their condition is neither a vice nor an illness. But they are wrong, in my opinion, in designating it as merely a "sexual preference."

Homosexuality, in almost all cases, is no more a matter of sexual preference than my left-handedness is a matter of manual preference. I have little choice in the matter, and they have little choice. Ours is a *condition* or a *state,* not a preference.

People who would punish or penalize them for this condition have no more justification than to punish me for left-handedness. Society has a high and severe obligation to assure all minorities — whether they be racial, religious, sexual, manual, or what have you — all their rights as human beings.

Beyond this, there is little we can do to eliminate the disadvantages of "lefts" in a largely right-handed world. I have as much right to play the violin as the next man, but on the other hand (to make a bad pun), a symphony orchestra would scarcely hire me to play in the violin section. My handedness is a disability in a manually dexterous society, and I must live with it.

Certainly, in my view, gays are no more "immoral" nor "sicker" than anyone else simply by virtue of their condition; but just as certainly, their condition is bound to have specific disadvantages in a heterosexual society. They should demand, and receive, equal treatment; but equal treatment, after all, does not mean identical treatment.

If we opt to be different, or even if we can't help it, we have to pay the price of that difference; and part of that price is to be looked upon slightly askance by the others. Since it costs a premium to declare and live by a difference, it becomes even more important that moralities of any kind be protected from added discrimination.

Neither Michelangelo nor Da Vinci would be permitted to teach art in the California public schools these days because of their "sexual preferences." (Even the medieval church didn't try to legislate such nonsense.)

Prisons Breed Crime

THE AVERAGE LAW-ABIDING citizen is well-meaning, but abominably ignorant and incredibly insensitive about crime and punishment.

A typical letter from such a reader attacks my assertion that punishment does not deter crime. It points out that a person serving a long sentence commits less crime than the same person given a short sentence, concluding that "at least the criminal is deterred from crime while in prison."

Not true, any of it. Criminals commit crimes in prison, and such crime is growing all the time. Most offenders get worse in prison, and the longer they are locked up, the worse they get.

They learn more about crime in prison. They make connections. They become determined to be more successful the next time. They are more bitter, more resentful, more vengeful, more vicious when they get out than when they went in.

Society may be protected for a few years, but this security is false. Prisons breed crime, as dirt breeds disease. Few leave the cell uncontaminated. Most leave with a greater contempt for law and criminal justice than when they entered. Their determination is not to reform but to get even.

In H. E. Barnes's and N. K. Teeters's classic textbook on criminology, *New Horizons in Criminology,* the authors say: "It is plain that social revenge is the only honest, straightforward and logical justification for punishing criminals. The claim for deterrence is belied both by history and by logic. History shows that severe punishments have never reduced criminality to any marked degree."

At one time or another, society has tried flogging, mutilation, branding, stocks and the pillory, confinement in irons, the ducking stool, and the branks and gag. Hands were cut off and tongues cut out. All these punishments were abolished, not because society became more compassionate or sentimental, but because experience demonstrated that they were ineffectual.

It is *swiftness* and *certainty* of conviction that deter crime, not harshness or length of punishment. It we kept all offenders in for a lifetime and gave up parole or probation, we would go broke building new prisons and housing the inmates, without diminishing the flood of crime.

Social conditions and the culture of poverty produce the bulk of lawlessness. We cannot rehabilitate the "mass of criminals," as this letter calls them, because after they have served their sentences, long or short, they are thrown back into the same environment that produced them, with little incentive for changing their ways.

Lengthy punishment does not deter but only postpones the criminal act. And heightens it: makes the criminal more skilled, more dedicated, more desperate to avoid prison again, even by killing. Some kind of deterrence, that turns out monsters where we sent in men!

"It's Not What You Know . . ."

OUTSIDE OF THE SCIENTIST and the mathematician, few laymen really understand the difference between "correlation" and "cause and effect." Most people take the one for the other, and commit a huge blunder in doing so.

There is a clear and steady correlation between the amount of formal education you have and the level of income you achieve. This correlation has led many people into the fallacy that education is the "cause" and income is the "effect" in this common equation.

It is not so. Young people with more formal education win better jobs and higher income not so much because they know more and can do more as because they know more people who can do more for them.

I have long observed numerous young men who finish college with few aptitudes or skills and even less learning. Most of them have little difficulty in finding a white-collar job — through family, friends, college connections, or the general social milieu in which they have grown up and live.

The unemployment rate among young blacks, for instance, is more than twice that among young whites, not because these youths are more ignorant or more shiftless or more unskilled, but largely because they lack ease of entry into the ranks of the employed.

I am not speaking here, of course, about the college-educated black, who is courted by many companies in need of fulfilling their minority quotas, but of the average high-school graduate or dropout, who can find only menial jobs, if he can find any at all.

One might say that a menial job is all he is equipped for, but one must make the embarrassing admission that many middle-class college graduates are not equipped for much beyond this, either. Yet because they know people on the ladder who are willing to give them a leg up, they usually start in a white-collar job, however lowly at first.

It is not education per se that raises the quality of the job or the level of income, but the whole social fabric and pattern of the community. Despite our protestations of democracy, we remain largely what we always were, a class-structured society — far more open than the European, but a lot more closed than most of us find it comfortable to believe.

Education is supposed to be the great economic panacea of our time, just as political enfranchisement was in the past, but it has not thus far worked out that way. The old cynical slogan "It's not what you know, but who you know" still operates to decide which youngster shuffles off to the car wash and which walks briskly into the anteroom marked "Executive Trainee."

If you are proud of never having contradicted yourself, you should be ashamed of failing to have grasped some of the fundamental paradoxes of the human condition.

The Arrogance of Riches

IT NEVER CEASES to amaze me how people don't like it when the shoe is on the other foot, or, as Mother used to put it, when they get a taste of their own medicine. Like our current indignation about Arabs buying up so many American properties.

During this whole century the United States has been the principal purchaser of enterprises abroad. We have sold our products indefatigably, set up factories, opened merchandising outlets, and settled hundreds of thousands of American employees in foreign lands on every single continent.

Now that the Arabs, glutted with oil money, are buying a few dozen mansions and banks and shopping centers and farms, we have the sudden feeling that the country is being sold out from under our feet, and some legislators even want to make it illegal for the sheiks and their shebas to own extensive property in America.

Europe and Asia and Africa and South America — not to mention Canada — have been concerned for decades about the "Americanization" of their industry and commerce. For a long time we have been a financial Gulliver striding (sometimes insolently) among the Lilliputians, buying what we wanted and selling where we could. Weren't we just "stimulating business" in those benighted countries?

But the Arabs, bringing large sums into the United States, are not viewed as stimulating business: They are seen by many as predators, or even expropriators, of our native land. The English, too, have become visibly alarmed by the acquisition of some elegant Mayfair hotels by the burnoosed band.

Yet beginning more than a century ago, Great Britain was the dominant financial invader, wherever it could pry open a privilege. It is no accident that most of the great hotels in Switzerland have English names, like the Albert or Victoria. And in our time it has been the Hiltons and the Sheratons that have commanded an international network of hostelries, with the natives employed mostly as flunkies.

Ours has been the arrogance of riches for so long that we are shocked when strange and swarthy multimillionaires begin doing to us — even on a relatively small scale — what we have been doing to others for so much longer. It reminds me somewhat of the philandering husband who turns into a self-righteous prig when he learns that his wife has been cutting a caper on her own.

I hold no special affection for the Arabs — you may believe it — but it is a question of turnabout being fair play. Money is the language we have spoken in international relations since we made our pile, and it is the same language the Arabs are now speaking so volubly, for the first time since the fall of Constantinople.

It is not agreeable to us, but then it is never agreeable to anybody to be addressed as "Hey, boy!" What is different is that we are feeling it for the first time.

Equality Is Not Identity

WILL EVERYBODY PLEASE write on the blackboard one hundred times the sentence: *Equality and identity are not the same thing*. You have to learn this if you are going to understand what the Declaration of Independence means and also if you want to understand what "equality between the sexes" means, or ought to mean.

Equality and identity are not the same thing. "All men [that is, mankind] are created equal." Obviously, this does not mean identical: All people are not the same size, the same shape, do not have the same brains and the same talent and the same anything. Only identical twins are identical.

We are created equal in that our differences must be treated the same under the law. In that everyone is entitled to life, liberty, and the pursuit of happiness. In that everyone possesses the same rights, regardless of birth, wealth, health, wisdom, or shoe size.

This is what the framers of the Declaration meant — this and nothing more. We insult their memory by assuming that they supposed all people to be alike, or identical, so that differences did not count. But differences must not count in respect to the basic worth of each individual.

Now, two hundred years later, we face the same confusion and misunderstanding about equality for women. Women are equal to men, but they are not identical: Their anatomy is different, their physiology is different, and these differences create differences in temperament and attitude.

Women cannot do everything as well as men do, nor can men do all that women can. It is simple justice to give women equal rights under the law; it is absurd to suggest, as some ardent feminists do, that women are identical to men in all capacities. The differences are real and cannot be obliterated; but the rights and responsibilities of each must be fairly apportioned, as they demonstrably are not today.

Some of the more strident feminists seem to want to turn women into men *manqué* — to ignore the inborn biological differences. But this, in my view, is an insult to women, because it takes the male as a model and insists that women can live up to this model. But woman is her own model, with her own particular resources and aptitudes, and not just a slightly weaker or slower male.

"As good as" does not mean "the same as." The goodness in women is complementary to the goodness in men, not an imitation or a rival. Each kind of goodness deserves equal treatment in all respects, legally, economically, and socially. *E pluribus unum* is as sensible a motto for the sexes as for the states.

Seeing Forests and Seeing Trees

Question: Who is better off, the person who can't see the forest for the trees or the one who can't see the trees for the forest?

Answer: Each is better off with the help of the other, but neither is willing to believe this.

THIS RIDDLE IS INSPIRED by years of experience in writing columns on subjects about which I know less than the people involved in them. If the columns are critical, those involved in the subject write in to complain that I don't know what I'm talking about, as an outsider, etc.

What they fail to take into consideration is that there is an inside view and an outside view to everything. Rarely do these two views coincide, and never does one view provide us with the whole truth. The outside view is often a necessary corrective to the inside one.

Professional groups, particularly, seem incapable of viewing their collective activity with any degree of impartiality. They always look better to themselves than they do to other people. They can see the trees — the many fine individuals who adorn their profession — but they are not able to step back and look at the forest as a whole.

The outsider, of course, sees the forest in its total profile, and recognizes that in many cases the whole adds up to *less* than the sum of its parts. Few doctors are as rabid or rigid as the American Medical Association.

Even the largest and most successful enterprise will from time to time call in consultants from the outside to obtain a more balanced perspective on its functions and directions. Certainly these consultants know less, in a sense, about the enterprise than the officers and employees do, but their very distance gives them an advantage in vision.

All organizations take a defensive stance against criticism from the outside; they are as protective of themselves as hedgehogs, and it makes no difference what they profess publicly or as a matter of principle. For years I was on the board of trustees of a private school that prided itself on its openness, its democracy, its encouragement of dissent — yet if even a board member dared attack some sacred shibboleth, the ranks would close and the others would bristle with official defensiveness.

"It all depends whose ox is gored" was one of the wisest things Martin Luther ever said. Doctors will excoriate lawyers, savings-and-loan people will go after bankers, the dairy interests jeer at their substitutes; but all adamantly reject criticism aimed at their own official bodies, insisting that outsiders have a distorted picture.

We cannot grow this way, we cannot learn, we cannot change, except painfully and by pressure. We need to recognize that the window is distorted from both sides, and peering out provides a no more complete picture of total reality than peering in does.

Eliciting Human Potential

SPEAKING AT A COMMENCEMENT of graduating teachers, I said that my whole message could be summed up in fewer than fifty words uttered by Goethe nearly two centuries ago: "If you treat a person as he is, he will stay as he is; but if you treat him as if he were what he ought to be and could be, he will become what he ought to be and could be."

This applies to most pupils everywhere; and the best teacher is not one who crams the most *into* a pupil, but who gets the most *out* of one. Education is a process not of stuffing people, like sausage into a casing, but of eliciting from people the potentialities hidden even from themselves.

And Goethe's sage comment applies to far more than teachers and pupils. I am constantly surprised at how many parents stereotype their own children at a certain age and persist in regarding them in the same light year after year, so that the child loses its motivation and incentive to change.

Actually, children themselves do the same with their peers Once a child receives a certain reputation among his classmates, their conditioned responses almost force him to maintain the same role, and it is devilishly difficult, if not impossible, to reverse the early image.

This is why, by the way, so many children in the later grades want to change schools and cannot give their parents any "sensible" reason. They are ashamed to admit or only half-conscious of the fact that they would like to break out of the mold in which they were cast at an early age and seek a new personal identity for themselves.

In marriage as well, the mates often regard and treat one another only as the persons they were when first wed, so that efforts to develop and grow and change are met with puzzlement, scorn, or resentment. We feel most comfortable, even with those we presumably care for, when we can put people into pigeonholes and keep them there.

There is something valuable to be learned here from a good coach or trainer, who regards his charge not as the person he is but as if he were about to become the person he ought to be and could be, in Goethe's words. The coach works with the potentialities, not only with the actualities, and recognizes that the desire to develop and improve is as vital a part of the person as his physical or mental makeup.

But this capacity, except in unusual cases, is as easily discouraged as encouraged; people sink back into themselves when they perceive that their teachers, their parents, or their mates persist in ignoring or rejecting an effort to shed the old skin and become what William James called twice-born.

Most people, I am convinced, have a residual capacity to rise to the level of expectations, to meet standards and goals, and to become more than they were. Only the most aggressive and determined can accomplish this against odds; the rest need help, but they usually find that more people than pigeons are put in pigeonholes.

The ACLU Fights for What It Hates

WHAT I LOVE MOST about the American Civil Liberties Union is that it is unique, in the pure and original sense of the word. It does what nobody else does.

What it does is fight *for* what it hates, while the rest of us fight (if we do at all) *against* what we hate. We defend only what we believe; the ACLU defends what it detests.

In New Jersey not long ago, a parochial high school refused to issue a diploma to a student because he was a leader of the Ku Klux Klan in the town, and he refused to renounce his membership in this rancid organization.

Nobody respectable rushed to his defense except the ACLU, which branded the school's action "a clear-cut violation of constitutional rights." It will take the case to court if it has to, and I have no doubt it will win. It usually does, in matters of civil rights.

Sometimes I think it is almost the only group in America that really understands, respects, and upholds our Constitution. Other groups are interested mostly in the rights they think will help them; the ACLU alone seems to realize that you have no protection unless you protect those you violently disagree with.

The organization was nearly wrecked a few years ago, when it also defended the right of the Nazi Party in Chicago to march through a suburb heavily populated with Jews. It lost a lot of Jewish members (who had been among its most stalwart supporters until then), but it stuck to its guns and was vindicated by the courts.

What has surprised and saddened me over the years is that its membership has been recruited largely from those who are called liberals in the political spectrum. Relatively few conservatives have ever joined it — but it seems clear to me that a genuine conservative has a deep and irrevocable stake in civil liberties.

If we really believe in our Constitution and in the freedoms it guarantees to those opinions we find most hateful, we have a moral and patriotic obligation to see that such freedoms are not curtailed for anyone. Otherwise we are phonies, invoking a liberty for ourselves that we are not willing to grant or defend for others.

When conservatives generally show as much alacrity in defending free expression — no matter how far left or right — as they do in invoking free enterprise, then I will begin to believe that they are something more than self-serving. And the best way they can demonstrate their sincerity and devotion to the Constitution is by signing up with the only group in the country that puts it on the line.

The Paradox of Parenthood

AFTER THIRTY YEARS OF parenthood, I have come to the conclusion that rearing children is so difficult because it calls for two opposite attitudes on the part of both parents.

On the one hand, a parent must do everything possible to make the child like himself or herself. On the other hand, the parents must instill in the child an active sense of self-criticism.

Getting a child to like himself and accept himself while striving to do better is nowhere as easy as it may sound. By far, most of the unattractive people we see around us every day were children with a low self-esteem who are now trying to build it up in illegitimate and ineffectual ways.

Instilling an active sense of self-criticism in the child is even harder, because the method most parents use is criticizing the child themselves — which only evokes resistance and resentment. The child then becomes defensive about his or her defects and erects psychological barricades against any criticism, from within or without.

We speak of "self-love" in a negative mood, but genuine self-love is far from vanity or conceit or egocentricity. In fact, it is a truism that you cannot love others until and unless you love yourself in the proper way.

And "in the proper way" means respecting yourself, accepting your inherent limitations, recognizing that what is precious to you is also precious to others and that we achieve our full humanhood only in *transaction,* not in isolation, as Buber never tires of reminding us.

The average child does not learn to like himself much in the six years before he enters school, because he is small and weak and ignorant and subject to continual correction, instruction, and chastisement. When he gets to school, he finds more of the same — and in addition is competing with many other children for attention and approval.

The implanting of guilt in a child before he has reason enough to know what he should and should not feel guilty about is responsible for more adult unhappiness than almost any other treatment. A child learns right from wrong far more by being encouraged when he is right than by being reproved when he is wrong, as he so often is.

It is not the balance between discipline and permissiveness that is so important as introjecting the child with the balance between a feeling of self-love and a sense of self-criticism. Then the parent has no need to smother with love or nag with anxiety. Most of this we learn, unfortunately, after the children are grown up.

What we loosely call happiness is more a disposition than an attainment; for some can be happy with very little, while others remain dissatisfied the more they are gratified.

*

Most parents learn too late that if they castigate, they should castigate the fault and not the child; if you reproach a fault, it can be reformed, but if you attack a personality, it can only defend itself.

What's in a Name?

NO PIECE I'VE WRITTEN in years — decades, maybe — aroused so much disputation straight down the middle as my column on Negroes' designating themselves as blacks. Naturally, almost all the letters came from Negro/black readers.

The way the "antis" lambasted me, you would have thought I was a charter member of the KKK instead of an immensely sympathetic fellow American who was born color-blind and intends to stay that way. They cussed me out six ways from Sunday for trying to "rob" them of their right to call themselves blacks instead of the detested "Negroes."

But an equal amount of mail poured in from the "pros," most of whom felt they had been intimidated by a militant minority into changing their designation from Negro to black and who resented this institutionalization of color as a way of characterizing themselves.

First off, let me say that I don't care what Afro-Americans call themselves; anything they prefer is fine with me, if it makes them feel comfortable and fits the image they care to carry around with themselves. I was not advising them what to name themselves; I was suggesting that "black," apart from being inaccurate to the point of meaninglessness, plays right into the hands of bigots and racists.

As to the argument that "Negro" is the name white people foisted on them and was not self-chosen, I pointed out that this is a universal tendency and has nothing to do with race. Few Christians know, for instance, that the early followers of Jesus called themselves simply Brethren, and that "Christian" was a jeering and sneering name applied by Romans and other pagans.

The Brethren shrugged and smiled and adopted it for themselves — and eventually "Christian" became the name that conquered the Roman Empire, the finest appellation you could have. The same is true, in a minor key, with "Quakers," "Mormons," and "Methodists" — all at first were derogatory nicknames hurled by outsiders, but then proudly worn and turned into a badge of merit and respect.

Besides, "black" is a parochial name, used here only. Natives of Africa do not call themselves that, nor do dark-skinned peoples living in Europe or Asia or elsewhere in the world. True, "Negro" originally meant "black" in the Latin tongues, but it has come to be an ethnic rather than a color designation.

Black is the color of my true love's hair, and that's where it belongs — in the palette, not on the passport or the I.D. card, as they insist in South Africa. Call yourselves what you like, you cannot force me to call you anything but God's children, now and forever.

Pregnancy or Abortion: A Wrenching Choice

MY DINNER PARTNER was a lady who for many years has been a guidance counselor at a small Eastern college that has gone coeducational. The subject of sex came up, and she mentioned that about a dozen or fifteen students become pregnant at the school each year. "At least those are the ones I know about," she said.

"How many decide to drop out of school and have their babies?" I asked.

"None," she answered, "or practically none. Virtually all of them opt for an abortion — and, of course, they can get them legally here."

"Does this bother some of them?"

She nodded. "Terribly. In one case recently, a pregnant girl brought along her best friend, who was so upset at seeing the fetus that she had an emotional breakdown and had to enter the infirmary for a couple of days."

"After so many years, what is your opinion on this?" I inquired.

"My opinion is that anyone who takes a black-or-white position on the subject of abortion is either a fool or a fanatic. It is the grayest moral area I can imagine, and I myself am torn in two each time it happens. Having the baby would be a disaster for most of these children — that's what they still are — and having an abortion is the most traumatic experience they can go through."

"Why don't these presumably educated girls employ birth control methods?" I wondered.

"That's the psychologically interesting part," she reflected. "You see, the ones who get pregnant are not the tramps, as some might call them, but girls with good moral standards. They won't use birth control methods because they feel that by doing so they are tacitly encouraging sex. To be prepared for it is in a way, they feel, to invite it. This way, if sex occurs, it is spontaneous or unexpected, and not calculated on their part."

"So in a sense," I ventured, "it's their moral posture itself that prevents them from being prudent. It seems rather ironic that a high moral code can lead to more downfalls than frank promiscuity."

"That's what is so heartbreaking in my job." She sighed. "It's really the 'nicer' girls who have to come to me with this problem — the more innocent ones, the more naive ones, the girls who denied their vulnerability. The hardened cases are too shrewd and systematic to get pregnant."

"It's a muddied picture, isn't it?" I said. "There seems to be no good answer anywhere between total abstinence and marriage — and sometimes marriage is the worst possible answer."

"There are only bad answers" — she shrugged — "and I've come to the view that the best a guidance counselor can do is offer a choice of evils."

If it is wrong to take a life in the womb, why is taking a life almost always justified later on the battlefield? Does the state have a claim superior to the mother's?

The Shabby Treatment of Veterans

I AM OLD ENOUGH to remember the veterans' Bonus March on Washington, which was dispersed by President Hoover with the gallant field leadership of General Douglas MacArthur. It was not exactly our country's proudest hour.

One of the strange discrepancies that has struck me over the years is the way a nation — our nation, at least — blows hot and cold on servicemen (and women now, too, one supposes).

Veterans have always been treated shabbily, promised and then disappointed, wooed with ardor and then shunned or neglected when the need for them is ended.

On the other hand, professionals who enter the armed services and may never have seen a single day of combat are retired on terms and with benefits that seem positively princely by comparison.

As an example, in 1977 the government spent more on pensions for healthy retired military men and women under the age of sixty-five than on all new Air Force planes or Navy ships.

Nearly $7 billion went to some 800,000 "retirees" who were under sixty-five and retired with no disability whatsoever. More than 90 percent of these were healthy and still of working age, while nearly half of them were still under fifty.

This is an enormous sum to disburse for such early retirement of still productive men and women — many of whom promptly take jobs in the private sector that may double their retirement pay or more.

Possibly no one would begrudge them these emoluments, were it not that the average enlisted man during wartime, who may be injured in combat, finds so little provision for training and subsequent employment when his spell of service is over.

Apart from a sporadic program like the G.I. educational bill, which did send many thousands of enlisted men back to school at government cost, there has always been a dreadful pall of negligence hanging over returned veterans after a war's end.

Years have been yanked out of their lives, at a most formative time, and there is little or no provision for reabsorbing them into the mainstream of society. Indeed, it was not until after World War II that much thought was even given to their predicament; World War I veterans were generally treated with the disdain MacArthur showed them.

If you want to spend the years between eighteen and fifty in the military, you are assured of a guaranteed income and splendid pension benefits under the third largest socialist organization in the world; if you go in to fight for a couple of rotten, dangerous years, the rest of your life (if any) may be pulled awry. Somehow the odds don't seem equitable.

On Terrorism

OUR SERMONETTE TODAY is on terrorism, and our text is taken from Exodus 20:5: "The sins of the fathers shall be visited upon the children." This means, of course, the sins of the founding fathers as well as the physical fathers.

If you look around the world today — if you can bear to — you will see that everything we describe as terrorism comes from one source and one source only, no matter the geographical or political differences.

In Ireland, in Palestine, in Holland, in South Africa — it matters not where — the frightful acts of terrorism are all the result of the same thing: aggression, exploitation, and colonization of one people by another.

The English had no business in Ireland, and especially not the dirty business they engaged in for centuries. The Dutch had no business taking over the Spice Islands in the Pacific. The British and the Boers, like the French and the Portuguese and others, had no business taking over and carving up large sections of the African continent.

As for Palestine, now Israel, it has had the most tragic history of all — overrun by a dozen different powers and religions, from the Romans and the Turks to the Egyptians, the Mamelukes, and the British.

All these accumulated sins of the centuries — and all, basically, the same sin of greed for other people's property — are finally being visited upon the children and the children's children. For if you examine the roots of each of the current conflicts and terrorist activities, you find that they are deeply entangled in the same historical injustice.

And the compounded tragedy today is that there is no simple black-and-white answer. Only zealots see right against wrong. The rest of us see it as two rights in collision, with no possibility of justice being done to both. This is the price the children pay for their fathers' sins. Nothing we can do will wash out the past, make it clean again.

Terrorism is barbarous and frightful and unfair and most often counterproductive. But so is aggression, so is exploitation, so is colonization. We in the United States will continue to suffer for a long time for slavery, a short-run "benefit" that has turned into a long-run nightmare. We are paying a high price for our seizure of Puerto Rico, just as England is now suffering from its past colonial policies.

Terrorists are made, not born, and are heroes to themselves, willing to die to vindicate their cause. They can be killed, but there is no way to extinguish the past. All of us, innocent though we may feel, must suffer for the sins of our fathers, and the best we can do is to make sure we do not pass a similar dread inheritance to our own children.

If a young person like Patty Hearst hadn't been brought up exclusively to believe that this is the best of all possible worlds, she wouldn't have been so shocked to have forcibly learned otherwise, and thus might not have recoiled so excessively into the opposite error of assuming it is the worst of all possible worlds.

The Problem of Diversity

ORGANISMS TRY to overcome obstacles by developing and growing; and then the very growth itself becomes an obstacle. This is a problem in magnitude our society has just begun to face squarely.

To take two examples, consider our recent efforts to achieve some degree of gun control and to impose a speed limit on highways. Neither has been successful, for reasons that go beyond politics and pressure groups, though both are involved.

To be effective, real gun control has to be nationwide; if it is only a local or state matter, thousands of illicit guns will be smuggled across state borders and into city limits. There is no way that "local option" can work.

At the same time, gun control does not mean in a small western town what it means in a crowded eastern city. In the former, the gun is a friend and a protector; in the latter, it is a menacing weapon that kills almost indiscriminately. How are you going to work out a federal law that satisfies both the rancher and the slum dweller?

Much the same is true in the case of the fifty-five-mile-an-hour speed limit. It is ineffectual on a piecemeal basis and demands national uniformity if it is going to save enough fuel and lives to justify its enforcement.

But we face the same rub here: Fifty-five miles an hour on a crowded New Jersey turnpike is not fifty-five miles an hour on a barren Montana highway. Distances are so much more vast in the West, traffic so much lighter, roads so much straighter and flatter, that there is no fair comparison.

In fact, the legislatures of nearly a dozen western and southwestern states are working on bills to set higher speed limits. The only thing holding back other states is fear of losing federal highway funds if they flout the present limit.

We are in a crisis of magnitude in which we are too interconnected to live together in little patches of local difference, and yet too big and various to be able to apply one mode or rule that works with equal fairness in all areas.

We have not tackled the problem of size, although as far back as Aristotle it was recognized that there is a definite optimum size for running a city efficiently, or for democratically administering a state. The United States is more than a country; it is a continent, and its differences are as real and as important as its similarities.

The question is: How do we integrate the similarities, while respecting the differences? I know of no easy, or even plausible, answer to this one.

Fascism: The Ultimate Degradation

IT IS GOOD, I SUPPOSE, that as many people as possible learn as much as possible about current history, and especially that bitter lesson that has come to be known as the Holocaust.

But sometimes a thing can be learned too well — so well that it serves to obscure or minimize something else equally important. This may be happening in the world, starting in West Germany, right now.

According to some U.S. foreign correspondents stationed there, the German people are beginning to use the Holocaust idea as a subtle expiation of Hitler's crimes. They are saying something like this: "It was a terrible thing he did to the Jews, and cannot be excused. But apart from that he wasn't so bad. If he had let the Jews alone and concentrated on giving us jobs and lifting the economy, he could have been a good leader of the German people."

No, no, a thousand times no! If he had never heard of the Jews, if he had never harmed a single one, if he had drunk with them and danced with them and decorated them, he still would have been an incarnation of evil. The Holocaust was not his sin; it was the sign of his sin. It was only the most visible mark of the Antichrist.

What Hitler and his party stood for, quite apart from their treatment of Jewry, was the most sophisticated barbarism, which went far deeper than primitive barbarism. It was violently anti-Christian, anti-intellectual, antiscience (while using its most diabolic devices), antihumanistic, antirational. It celebrated the most pagan passions: blood lust and race pride and militarism for its own sake. This was the core and crown of its ideology.

The Jews happened to be there and offered a marvelous target and opportunity. In another time it would have been Guelphs or Albigensians or Moravians or Anabaptists or witches or sorcerers or demons. Without some "devil" to challenge, such movements inevitably fall apart.

As for the jobs and the economy, they were based on war and aggression. The worst part of fascism seized on the worse part of socialism and yoked the two together to drive the nation into a frenzy of war production. (Remember, our country didn't come out of the Depression until Roosevelt inaugurated a tremendous rearmament program.)

The Holocaust is important and memorable, but it is not a blot on Hitler's escutcheon: The whole escutcheon is a blot. Root, trunk, and branch, fascism is the essence of evil, the bankruptcy of ideas, the ultimate degradation of man. What it did to the Jews will pass in time; what it did to the Germans is still stirring sullenly around the world.

The most damaging effect of communism, as practiced in Russia and China, is that its obvious deficiencies lead us to become smug about our own defects — like a delinquent kid who can point to the boy across the street as an example of worse behavior.

*

The perpetual irony of government is that rule by the majority is fairest, but minorities are almost always in the right.

Aristocracy and Democracy

I WAS DEBATING at a college not long ago on the subject of "Aristocracy vs. Democracy," and one of the questions put to me was, "Don't you agree that at any time in the history of a country, only a few hundred people at most make any difference?"

The question came from an advocate of aristocracy, and I was defending the democratic idea. He expected me to disagree with him, but I disappointed him by agreeing. In fact, this is the strongest reason for the democratic process.

Most people make little difference one way or the other; they are born, live, and die, and their effect beyond their immediate circle is nil. Whatever their personal worth as individuals, they play little part in determining change or development, except as followers.

A few hundred people in each generation are decisive for any country or culture. It is therefore imperative that these leaders be genuinely "aristocratic" in the original sense of the word — the *best* people, not the richest or the most aggressive or the most powerful or even necessarily the smartest.

It is, or should be, the obligation of every country to find and encourage and reward such people, no matter where they come from. Decent and humane leadership is always a rarity in the body politic.

Aristocracy and democracy, properly understood, are not opposites at all but dovetail into one another. And it is only through the freest and fullest exercise of democracy that we can attain aristocracy — that is, leadership by the best, with the consent of the governed.

Who are the best? I think an educated society would easily come to a consensus on this. The best are those whose personal qualities we most admire, those we would trust to make wise and fair decisions, those who keep their word, hold to their principles, and yet are flexible enough to appreciate the other side of any public question.

How do we get these people? Only by the broadest extension of democracy, by the promotion and encouragement and education of all citizens, so that leaders are not recruited from one particular class or ruling elite but may be found anywhere — just as musical talent or mathematical gifts may be discovered in the most unlikely surroundings. Otherwise, only the advantaged or the aggressive will lead us.

History has shown that no class is fit to rule, whether they be patricians by birth or proletarians by revolution. We must dig and drill for good people to lead us, as we dig and drill for gold and oil. Democracy is the process for digging in the most places, and therefore offers the greatest chance of finding the metal we are looking for and not the fool's gold we have quarried in the past.

Patriotism: A Two-Edged Sword

WHEN DR. JOHNSON, more than two centuries ago, asserted, "Patriotism is the last refuge of the scoundrel," he was not putting down patriotism as much as he was needling politicians who employ this sentiment for their own selfish purposes.

Nations, however differing their political philosophies, are alike in that any leader who waves the flag, brandishes his fist, and vows to defend the homeland to the death against foreign aggression arouses the passion and plaudits of his countrymen. It is a sure-fire way to get into office and to stay there.

If there is no aggressor, political leaders sometimes contrive one, in order to be able to oppose him and to fan the military spirit. A country without an "enemy," real or assumed, might begin to examine its own leaders more critically.

This nearly universal attitude among nations is what often

carries them to the brink of war, and sometimes beyond it. Our Mexican War (which Lincoln opposed), our Spanish-American War (for no reason but greed), and our disastrous venture in Vietnam were possible only because an ignorant and uninformed citizenry was duped into "defending our interest" by self-serving and short-sighted politicians.

It is not an easy problem to solve. On the one hand, patriotism can be a noble sentiment when it truly includes a defense of the values a people cherish, such as liberty, justice, and self-determination.

On the other hand, patriotism becomes a bestial mockery of itself when it is used to inflame the masses, to distort the real facts of the case, to keep a shaky regime from toppling or a venal regime from going broke. Far more wars, of course, have been fought for such ignoble reasons than for independence or survival.

Patriotism is a double-edged sword, wreaking at least as much harm as good in the world. We cannot abolish it, and should not if we could, or society would disintegrate into tiny atoms of cold selfishness. But if we do not control it, the human race will continue to kill its people off for the basest of motives.

Looking back on World War I, we can now see it was the cause of most of our twentieth-century tragedies: It bred fascism, Nazism, Stalinism, the Depression, and the inevitability of World War II. Yet not a historian today can provide a valid, legitimate, rational explanation for that massive conflict, in which millions died for "patriotic" reasons.

If patriotism flags, we become easy prey to subversive forces; if patriotism stiffens, we become vulnerable to the lies, deceits, and machinations of our leaders, who are no better or worse than other men in power. Is humanity perpetually to suffer at the hands of those who exploit its highest gift for the sake of its meanest goals?

Why Men Should March for Women's Rights

I DON'T HAPPEN TO THINK there is any virtue in agitating liberties on your own behalf, as necessary as it may sometimes be. After all, everybody is for himself; everybody wants as much for himself as he can get, whether it is justice, freedom, security, or Green Stamps.

And I don't think that such agitation will mean much — or have a solid moral base — until each group begins doing it on behalf of other groups, even more than for itself. This is what carries weight in the ultimate scale of democratic values.

Women should march for women's rights, but men belong there even more, if rights mean anything as a principle. Gays should march against the orange-heads of the world, but straights like me belong shoulder to shoulder with them, and there should be more of us than of them because there are more of us in the population.

Blacks and Jews and Latinos and all minority groups are little more than vociferous special interests as long as they devote all their public efforts to demanding justice and equality for themselves, badly as they may need it.

What they need to demonstrate — what would really be impressive — is their devotion to the same principles for everybody.

What do we have otherwise? Fragmented groups, each appealing to the same sense of fairness on the part of the general public, but each showing little sensitivity to or appreciation of the just needs and demands of other fragmented groups. This is more like lobbying than crusading.

What would grip the imagination of the public at large, what would drive home the democratic message, would be for each minority group — whether sexual, racial, religious, or what have you — to give its time and energy and passion toward the rectification of another group's legitimate grievances.

This is genuine morality, in the deepest and oldest Judaic and Christian tradition. I am quite aware that Hillel said, "If I am not for myself, who will be for me?" But the best way to be authentically for yourself is to ally yourself with all those others who face the same problem on a different front.

Liberty and justice are indivisible, no matter what one's gonads, genes, or genuflections proclaim to the world. If you assure the good treatment of others, you are assuring your own; but if you ask for yourself only, you are doing no more than any scoundrel might. Only by each putting the other first can all achieve parity.

Masculine Miss-Perceptions

I SUSPECT THAT THE FUEL that has fanned the flames of feminism in America has been less the social and economic inequities suffered by woman, real and prevalent as they have been, than the simple, pervasive, and infuriating fact that the bulk of men are insufferably clumsy in their confrontations with the other sex.

It is an easy assumption made by most men that, while they may not understand women, women do not understand them either — and thus that there is a mutually unexplored terrain that separates the sexes.

I do not believe this. If we have learned anything from the new field of social psychology, it is that minority groups of any kind have a greater awareness of the strengths and weaknesses of their masters than their masters have of them. Dominance makes a ruling group stupid.

It does not matter where you look. Servants have a shrewder perception about their employers than vice versa; blacks have been forced to grasp the inner dynamics of whites, purely as a matter of survival, more than whites have ever bothered to do the same; and homosexuals, I have no doubt, see more clearly into the ambiguities of the straight world than they are perceived by it.

Women, being also a minority group — socially if not numerically — have had to develop a "survival sense" about their male masters. I don't believe in something called woman's intuition (as George Jean Nathan said long ago, "Woman's famous intuition is only man's transparency"), but she does possess an insight into men's motives and moods that he utterly fails to reciprocate, being content to label her an enigma.

Because of this disparity in perception, men drive women up the wall with a repertoire of behavior and responses that corresponds only to what men imagine women are like and not what they really are. The male has set up an image of the female (much as the antebellum southern white did of the "darky"), and women by now are simply refusing to live up, or live down, to this uncomfortable distortion of reality.

What the whole spate of recent feminist books has been saying is that women will no longer put up with the traditional masculine attitudes — which are, to name but a few of the most prominent, condescending, patronizing, whimsical, heavily jocular, stereotypical, sexually demeaning, and grossly insensitive to real generic similarities.

It is less, I believe, an economic and social revolt than an erupting psychological one. Just as the black will no longer tolerate being called "Boy," the woman will no longer tolerate being dismissed as "Girl." It is her personhood she is proclaiming, not her independence.

Perhaps as much as 90 percent of what we call feminine or masculine traits have been culturally conditioned, not biologically determined; and these social fabrications obscure both the basic differences and the more pervasive similarities.

To Understand Politics . . .

WE HAVE NO RIGHT to discuss what we call politics unless we can clearly distinguish, in our own minds and to others, these common terms:

• The difference in meaning among *government, state,* and *society.*

• The three levels of *freedom* as a personal act, an interpersonal relationship, and a political condition.

• The three aspects of *peace* as an internal state, a civil condition, and an international relationship.

• The meaning of *equality under the law,* as distinguished from physical, mental, social, genetic, or any other kind of equality; and the important distinction between *equality* and *identity.*

• The notion of *law* as an instrument for civil conduct, and its relationship to ethics, conscience, and the concept of community.

• The implications of the doctrine of *individualism* and the implications of the doctrine of *collectivism,* and whether their relationship is necessarily antipodal, polar, or complementary.

• The relationship between political forms and their economic and social infrastructure — e.g., between capitalism and democracy, and communism and totalitarianism.

• The difference in meaning among *free competition, private enterprise,* and that popular modern hybrid *free enterprise.*

• The unconservative inconsistencies in conservatism, the illiberal inconsistencies in liberalism, and the orthodox inconsistencies in radicalism.

• The status of economics as a freestanding discipline, or its necessary subordination to the field of ethical philosophy (keeping in mind that Adam Smith, the father of classical economics, was primarily a moral philosopher).

• The distinctions among a *democracy,* a *representative democracy,* and a *republic.*

• The question of *rights* as inherent in the individual, or as delegated by the specific social and political order.
• The optimum relationship between the private good and the public interest; whether they are mutually convertible, contradictory, or isolate.

Now, note carefully, I am not suggesting that we must be "right" about such matters — merely that we must be clear in our own minds, free from self-contradiction; that each idea must be carefully joined to another to form a coherent whole, whatever our political philosophy may be. Now do you have a glimmering of why nearly all discussions about politics begin in confusion and end in futility?

Doctors Should Learn ABCs of Nutrition

One of the great persistent fictions of the medical profession is the myth of the well-balanced diet. The modern medicine men insist — and in a theoretical way, it's true — that a well-balanced diet is all that the average person needs in the way of nutrition.

But the fact of the matter is that the so-called average person doesn't have a well-balanced diet, and probably hasn't had one since childhood. Our national eating habits are deplorable, based partly on ignorance, partly on haste, and partly on seduction by the food manufacturers, processors, and sellers.

It is true that many food freaks and diet quacks conspire to extract millions from the public, but this is only because of our ignorance, which is connived in by such presumably respectable outfits as the A.M.A. and the F.D.A.

I am convinced that the average doctor in America gets less of an education in nutrition than the average person gets of a well-balanced diet. Only a handful of medical schools teach it more than cursorily, and even those few have a supercilious attitude toward the subject. Nutrition, after all, is a form of preventive medicine; and under our present system there is little money to be made in preventive medicine.

My own doctor, as straight and shrewd a bird as they come, when I asked him once, "Does vitamin B do any good?" retorted swiftly, "Yes — to the makers." I'm glad he knows more about everything else in medicine than he does about nutrition.

Indeed, I wouldn't be surprised if my own children know more; they have studied the subject seriously, know the available literature (both pro and con), and have ingested vitamins, minerals, and supplements for years. The empirical results are a glowing testimony to their health, strength, and endurance.

It is odd that a nation spending billions of dollars a year on drugs of all sorts is reluctant to learn about dietary deficiencies and to rectify them by regular dosages of supplementary vitamins and minerals. But then, we get absolutely no encouragement from the medical profession, which is happily writing out millions of prescriptions a month, many for conditions that would not have existed if proper nutrition had been attended to in the first place.

In ancient China, patients paid their doctors weekly when they were well and stopped paying while they were ill, to resume only when the doctor had made them better. That's the fastest way I know to make American doctors delve a little more deeply into the vitamin bottle, from A to Z and back again.

The angle at which you throw the ball against the wall is the angle at which it returns; this is why dishonest and oblique people perceive the world as composed of dishonest and oblique people.

*

A general practitioner is a doctor who treats what you've got; a specialist is a doctor who finds you've got what he treats.

II.
Of the Life of the Spirit

The New Pharisees

ONE OF THE RICH IRONIES of the so-called fundamentalist movement is that while it preaches Christ, it forgets Jesus. For the fact is that the living Jesus would not be an appealing figure to the members of the Moral Majority. For the fact further is that he was a thorn in the side of the fundamentalists of his own time.

Jesus wanted to reform and humanize the religion of his time and his church. He saw it as falling into the hands of the legalists and the narrow moralists. He saw it as becoming proud and priggish and punitive, when it should be humble and compassionate and forgiving.

The fundamentalists of his church reviled and condemned him for his actions, his attitudes, and his sayings. He associated with prostitutes and tavern-keepers and tax collectors. He mingled with the riffraff, not with the respectable members of the clergy.

He was a revolutionary in a moral, not in a political, sense. He reminded us that the Sabbath was made for man, not man for the Sabbath — which means that what is right or wrong to do depends upon the human end, not on the legal code or the ecclesiastical edict.

He was strict about the way we ought to behave toward one another, but lenient toward our personal weaknesses. He warned the self-righteous to "judge not, that ye be not judged." He preferred the poor, the outcast, the struggling, often the sinner, to the pious, respectable, hypocritical upholders of the law and trustees of the temple.

This is why they hated him and hounded him: because he saw that religion had hardened into ritual, that the early faith of the fathers had turned cold and formal and self-righteous, that the zeal of the prophets had been replaced by the dogmas of the priests.

You cannot read the New Testament without realizing that Jesus was irrevocably opposed to the Moral Majority of his time. His mission was to revitalize and rehumanize the Jewish church, to reawaken its early passion against injustice and oppression.

His idea of morality had nothing to do with gambling or dancing or drinking wine or such frailties. His idea was truly "fundamental" in that it went right to the bottom of men's relations with one another, in terms of brotherliness, tolerance, help, mercy.

His parable of the Good Samaritan was shocking and revolting to the Moral Majority of his day, for he showed how the priests and the pious passed by a fallen man, while the despised Samaritan (the outcast of Palestine) was the only one who tried to work God's will.

Whatever the modern fundamentalist claims in the name of Christ to be, he is taking the name of Jesus in vain. For Jesus was not setting up a church, or establishing rules, or condemning his brothers. He was showing us how God wants us to act toward one another, by his own example. It is a lesson the fundamentalists still have to learn.

Fundamentalists who take the Bible literally seem to have no idea that this attitude is precisely what Jesus was railing against in his attacks upon the Pharisees of his time.

Carter Confessed to Trivial Sin

I DIDN'T WANT TO COMMENT until after his election, because it really isn't a political matter one way or the other, but Jimmy Carter seems peculiarly innocent of theology for a Sunday-school teacher and a "twice-born" Christian.

In his now notorious interview in *Playboy* magazine, he totally misinterpreted and misunderstood the New Testament injunction about "lust in the heart." He used it as an example of "silent sinning," to show that he was not self-righteous or better than any other man.

But this is not even a venial sin; it is simply a natural weakness, which some saints have had. Looking at suggestive ads, or attending X-rated movies, or even "having immoral thoughts," deals only with relative occasions of sin: These actions are not necessarily sinful themselves.

It is probable even that virtue was practiced in managing these occasions. If your will is able to curb and control your natural appetite, you have won a moral victory; far from sinning, you have overcome an evil impulse. St. Augustine struggled for years against his lust, with ultimate success; until then, he confesses, his favorite prayer was: "O Lord, give me chastity and self-restraint, but not just yet."

In any sound Christian or Judaic theology, the virtue of justice is far more fundamental than that of chastity. Justice is the hinge from which many moral virtues swing, while temperance is the virtue from which chastity swings. Millions of people are able to be temperate — as much out of disposition or apathy or fear as out of virtue — while only a few are able or willing to practice justice.

In America especially, the sixth and ninth commandments seem to loom so large, while the seventh, eighth, and tenth are ignored. But these latter are more basic to the good life, since they regulate justice and curb avarice. One effective way of obscuring our major sins of injustice is by belaboring our minor sins of the flesh.

If Carter had confessed to greed, or a power drive, or failing to pay a just wage to people working for him, he would have given a proper, and important, example of violating his Christian creed. But people scarcely think of these sins as being religious at all, so obsessed are we with the comparatively trivial subject of sexuality.

Personal tragedies may ensue from unbridled lust, but not the great social catastrophes that follow from flouting the commandments to treat one another fairly and compassionately. Here is where most of the churches and their communicants betray the basic teachings of both Testaments.

Atheists, Like Fundamentalists, Are Dogmatic

I TELL YOU, one of the subjects it just doesn't pay to write about is religion. No matter what you say, vituperative letters pour in from the people who disagree with you. And the atheists are just as vocal in their denunciations as the believers are.

One spring I referred in a parenthetical remark to atheism as a false and shallow doctrine. Well, sir, you would have thought I attacked the Trinity, the Incarnation, and the Torah the way those letters gushed in from devout atheists who felt their creed had been maligned.

After all, I was merely stating my opinion, which is the most one can do on such a complex and recondite subject; but when you go after someone's basic belief (or basic disbelief, in this case), you rouse the furies to their fiercest pitch.

Some of my best friends — as the smarmy saying goes — and closest relatives have been dedicated atheists. My father, one of the loveliest men who ever lived, had no use for religion in any of its credal forms. As I have said before, he didn't believe in God, but God believed in him, which is more important; what you believe counts for less than how you feel and act toward your fellow man.

To be a convinced atheist strikes me as dumb — shallow, if not demonstrably false. This is why, about a hundred years ago, the great scientist Thomas Huxley coined the word *agnostic*. He felt the need for a word to describe and define those who neither affirmed nor denied a deity and felt it was a matter beyond human knowledge.

Now, agnosticism is a perfectly respectable and tenable philosophical position; it is not dogmatic, and makes no pronouncements about the ultimate truths of the universe. It remains open to evidence and persuasion; lacking faith, it nevertheless does not deride faith.

Atheism, on the other hand, is as unyielding and dogmatic about religious belief as true believers are about heathens. It tries to use reason to demolish a structure that is not built upon reason; because, though rational argument may take us to the edge of belief, we require a "leap of faith" to jump the chasm.

I personally find little difference between the rigid fundamentalist who insists that everyone is going to hell who does not share his notion of salvation and the obdurate atheist who insists with equal fervor that everyone who believes in God is deluded or demented.

Indeed, I find the atheist more culpable (if more attractive than the other) because the reason he venerates should lead him to respect the limitations of reason and turn him at least into an agnostic.

It's hard to know which are the greater number, those who disdain to read the Bible and thus miss a whole dimension of profundity, or those who read it assiduously and distort, simplify, or vulgarize its symbolism.

Bob Hutchins's Elusive Emperor

I'VE NEVER THOUGHT that the story "The Emperor's New Clothes" was such great shakes as a salutary moral fable. Even the dumbest little kid in town could tell the emperor was wearing no clothes; all it took was a touch of innocent honesty to blurt it out.

It is much harder when it is the other way around, when you can't see the emperor for the clothes. That is so hard that practically no one ever finds it out.

This was the singular accomplishment of Robert Hutchins, my old friend and teacher, who died in 1977. For nearly fifty years he cried out, "I see the clothes, but where is the emperor?" while most others were so taken by the elaborate costumes that they failed to note the total absence of the monarch himself.

Education was Bob Hutchins's emperor, his ruler and his ruling principle. The development of the mind as a reasoning tool, so that men and women could freely make sound judgments about values in important matters, was his single and continual goal in life.

He never confused education with any of its adornments, embellishments, or diversions. He never confused it with job training, numbers of buildings, sizes of student bodies, or aggregates of endowments. He knew that education is a process between minds, and if the process is missing, whatever else you have is not education.

Wherever he looked he saw costumes; he rarely saw the emperor himself. Often the trappings were most impressive, like Harvard thirty years ago; sometimes they were ludicrous, like Notre Dame thirty years ago. But whatever the disguise, Hutchins perceived and proclaimed that what was being offered was not education in any real sense of the word.

Education, to him, was what equips people to distinguish the better from the worse, to learn what is proper for a human being to be and to do, and to anticipate the possible or probable consequences of all the genuine options that are open to us. This will not ensure us against making mistakes; it will assure that they will be the best mistakes we can make, with the least disastrous consequences and the most chance for recovery.

During his long reign at the University of Chicago, hardly anyone else was educating, or even trying to, in his high and severe definition of the word. The emperor had abdicated, or died, and in his place was a procession of straw men, all wearing different regalia labeled "Education."

Hutchins was never fooled, as most people were. He knew that whatever we were turning out, it was not a generation of educated citizens who could cope intelligently with the problems of a free society. The proof that he was right can be seen on all hands today — even by the dumbest little kid in town.

If We Accept Black Holes, Why Not Pearly Gates?

SUPPOSE IN OLDEN DAYS you said to a medieval monk, "I will tell you what the universe is like. It is made up of millions of galaxies of incredible size. Each galaxy is traveling a million miles an hour in space." You would continue: "Not only that, but each galaxy is rushing away from all the others, faster and faster. And the farther they get, the faster they go. We can see no end to this process."

The monk would think you were mad if you seriously believed that. And if you told him that you had telescopes and other instruments to verify this hypothesis, he would think you were even madder. For the picture of the universe you have drawn is fantastically beyond imagination.

Now, there may be good reasons for a modern man not to believe in traditional religion, or the portrait of the cosmos as depicted in the Bible. But the very worst reason is that it is "unbelievable," that it "makes no sense," that it calls for "an act of faith."

Does the version of the new astronomers make any sense? Can we grasp it by reason? Is it not so inconceivable as to be almost an act of faith in our fallible human instruments and observations?

Indeed, the further we delve into such matters, the more they begin to sound like Lewis Carroll — with black holes collapsing in on themselves, with objects called quarks that may or may not have "charm," with pulsating energy perceived as the source of all creation, and matter only a gross illusion of our sense organs.

I am not suggesting either of two things here: that the traditional religious viewpoint is correct, or that the dominant scientific viewpoint is incorrect. But it seems clear to me that *reason* and *faith* are two words that have been wrenched out of their conventional meaning and no longer apply to speculation about the origins of life and the cosmos.

Vulgar scientism of the materialistic and mechanistic kind is as outmoded as simple-minded religiosity with its three-tiered universe and a bearded old man atop the layer cake. Today, it takes as much faith, of a different kind, to believe in the paradoxical cosmos of the astronomers as it did in the past to accept the naive version of the pious.

What astrophysics seems to offer at this time is strange, wild, contradictory, and ultimately unimaginable. If you can accept a black hole, you can believe in a pearly gate. The battleground is no longer between the rational and the supernatural; neither model makes any more or less sense these days than the other.

Astronomically speaking, man may be completely negligible – except for the overriding fact that man happens to be the astronomer.

Better Tolerance for Ambiguity Than Blind Faith in Dogma

ARE THERE PROBLEMS without any good answers? Certainly, although many politicians and most technocrats like to pretend otherwise. And gambling is one of them.

I could make out an excellent case for the legalization of gambling. There are three or four good reasons it should be administered and controlled by the state. Reasons of crime, reasons of finance, reasons of common sense.

The only trouble is that I could make out an equally plausible case *against* the legalization of gambling. Reasons of crime, reasons of finance, reasons of common sense.

Prostitution is another problem without any real answers, or even any mildly constructive ones. Here again, there are convincing arguments for legalizing and medically supervising this oldest of professions — and equally persuasive arguments for not doing so.

I bring up these ambiguous subjects because quite often readers will ask me to comment in print on one or the other — usually readers who already have their minds implacably made up and want me to ratify their views. They are invariably disappointed when I fail to come through, and blame me for being wishy-washy on such grave matters.

But just as it is morally culpable to be wishy-washy about problems that have clear-cut solutions, so is it morally culpable to be dogmatic or doctrinaire about problems that slip right through your fingers. Only people with tunnel vision, whose prejudices rule their minds, are certain that their views on gambling or prostitution are correct ones.

To be civilized demands, in large part, that we develop a tolerance for ambiguity. This entails the modest recognition that not all human problems have solutions, that some cures are worse than the ailments they purport to treat, and that doing nothing may be far preferable to doing the wrong thing for the right reasons.

Gambling on any meaningful scale does not exist in some countries, nor prostitution in others, although both have been prevalent since the beginning of human history. Their prevalence, or their popularity, depends upon the general ethos of the particular culture and not upon whether they are licensed, regulated, repressed, or criminalized.

When we find other, and better, things to occupy our minds and spirits, we will cease to gamble. When sex becomes seen as a relationship and not as an activity, the only customers for whores will be that small minority of the sexually and emotionally crippled. Until such times, if ever, it makes little difference what public stance we take. Prohibition didn't prohibit, and Repeal didn't repeal.

Yes, Virginia, There Is a Free Lunch

PEOPLE WHO LIKE to call themselves realists are fond of telling us that "there is no such thing as a free lunch" and of reminding us that "you can't get something for nothing." These statements are true only if your time span is foreshortened to the present. But if one takes a longer view, if one adopts a historical perspective, they do not hold water at all.

Virtually all we have has been handed to us free. As James Harvey Robinson noted long ago, can anyone living today flatter himself that he invented the art of writing or the printing press?

Has anyone discovered his religious, political, economic, and moral convictions? Has anyone devised the operations of feeding us and clothing us and making us safe and comfortable? Has anyone created the pleasures we derive from literature and the fine arts?

What is civilization but the continual process of getting something for nothing? What we have today is a free inheritance from the past, handed down to us by people who labored not only for their own profit but also for the accumulated "capital" we use so freely and casually. The wheel, the alphabet, tillage of the soil — all these are gifts we take for granted.

When I see a young man tooling his car down the highway as though it were his by right, I know he has never given a thought to the men who sweated in garages and laboratories and persisted through the bitterness of failure to develop his magnificent machine. He could not have done it himself.

Nor was it the thought of profit alone — if at all — that animated these creators and developers of devices they themselves might never live to see. It was a hope, a dream, a vision they lived on — and often died for. The man who invented the first lighthouse perished in his own primitive model.

What we call civilization is nothing but "free lunch," handed down the generations by men and women who labored for something more than glory and riches in their own day. Such as Madame Curie, who died from the X-rays she discovered; such as astronomers who went to the stake; such as theologians who courted excommunication and death for their liberating ideas.

Economic man is only a part of man — necessary, but not the most important or noble part. Those we owe the most to — including many individuals buried in the mists of time — have provided us with a perpetual "free lunch," and breakfast and dinner too.

History gives us almost everything for nothing, but we squander or misuse these assets as a wastrel dissipates the inherited fortune he never worked for.

Work and play are an artificial pair of opposites, because the best kind of play contains an element of work, and the most productive kind of work must include something of the spirit of play.

"Character Is Destiny"

ONE OF MY SONS is taking a course in dramatic literature, starting with the Greeks as it should, and he asked me the other day to explain the saying that "character is destiny."

The idea of Fate, or the Fates, is a recurrent one in early drama — which began as a religious ritual — but it has little to do with the concept of fatalism in Eastern cultures. To the ancient Greeks, your destiny was not written in the stars for all time but sprang out of the kind of person you were.

As an example, petty but to the point, I referred to my recent accident. Was it really an accident, like being struck by lightning or hit by a cornice falling from a building? Not a bit of it.

It happened because I was the kind of person I am — quick, active, and often impatient about little things. While my companion was opening the gate to our driveway, I decided not to wait in the car and dashed out to open the door to the house and get the lights and heat turned on. There was absolutely no reason for this hurry, since the rest of the family was not arriving for a couple of hours.

Twenty seconds later I was on my back with a broken right arm, like a poled ox on a block of ice. It happened before I knew it.

But was it an "accident" in the truly adventitious sense of the word? Of course not. I knew the driveway was slippery, knew that a few moments made no difference, and anyone with a more placid temperament would have been content to sit in the warm car until the chains were down and we could glide safely to the front steps.

It is in this trivial but symbolic illustration that we begin to perceive the truth of the Greek saying that "character is destiny." The kinds of things that happen to us, in the main, are *like* us. Sometimes a blow comes out of the blue, but in far more cases we go to meet the blow halfway.

As the Greeks would have put it, the ice was the *efficient* cause of the accident, but my impulsiveness was the true cause. Just as, on a vastly grander scale, the bitter Russian winter was the material cause of Napoleon's defeat; his vanity and megalomania were the real causes. Another kind of general would never have braved the Russian winter.

Twenty years before it happened, I and many others knew that Nixon would have his Watergate, just as Napoleon had his Waterloo. It had nothing to do with break-ins, tapes, buggings, or bribery — his character had already clearly prefigured his destiny. The ice was there, implacably waiting for him to get out of the car, just as Euripides said it would be.

Must We Worship Mammon?

ONE CANNOT HELP WONDERING, around Christmastime, what Jesus meant when he warned, "Ye cannot serve God and Mammon," and what he would have thought of the way we observe his birthday season.

Each year around this time, we grumble about the commercialization of Christmas. We say it is getting worse every year, and it seems to be; the Thanksgiving turkey has hardly settled in our stomachs before we are bombarded with the commercial barrage of Christmas propaganda.

But if it is bad, or cheap, or vulgar, to be commercial during the Christmas celebration, what makes it good to be commercial any other time of the year? If it is wrong to serve Mammon in December, why is it right in April or September?

This is an uncomfortable question, because the only honest answer must be that we feel obscurely guilty about commercialism, and our guilt shows up vividly when the propaganda of buying is tied in with the Gospel. We feel somehow that the two do not belong together.

And of course they do not. There was one thing that Jesus opposed all during his ministry, and this was the dominance of *materialism*. He saw it as the enemy of religion, the enemy of peace, the enemy of love. He warned us not to lay up treasures upon Earth.

One reason we reject Marxist communism, and properly so, is because it is a creed based on materialism, notwithstanding its idealistic goals. But the ironic part is that we hope to defeat it by becoming more successfully materialistic than they, by showing the world that our materialism can obtain more material goods than theirs can.

This is a curious argument. If materialism is ripping and twisting the fabric of the human community, as I think it is, we can effectively oppose it only by moral and spiritual values, by heeding the words of the Old Testament prophets and the new gospel of Christ. We cannot oppose it simply by becoming bigger, fatter, richer, and greedier materialists than our opponents.

Of course, material things are necessary to sustain life and to resist the brutalization of modern poverty (which is far from the kind of poverty depicted in the Bible). Materialism is a *base* on which to build human institutions, not a creed to determine human relationships.

When it becomes a creed, it corrupts our nature and makes a mockery of our religious pretensions. If we are busily engaged in buying and selling dubious treasures upon Earth, let us frankly worship Mammon, and not profane the spirit of Christmas by invoking a once-a-week God or a once-a-year Messiah.

If the sermons that ought to be preached were preached, half the congregations of half the churches would get up and leave in indignation before half the sermons were over.

*

As successful men grow older, they begin to recognize that many possessions do not make them happier; but they continue to cling to the pathetic delusion that their passing on such commodities may make their children happier.

No, Man Can't Live by Bread Alone

WHENEVER THERE IS A DISCUSSION of what people actually need, someone in the company is bound to exclaim that mankind really *needs* nothing but a loincloth, a fire, a cave, and a hunk of meat to exist on.

This is supposed to be a realistic and down-to-earth statement, proving that everything else is superfluous, or a luxury we have become used to.

In my opinion, that is one of the dumbest viewpoints anyone can have. It totally misperceives the character and nature of our species; it is historically erroneous, and it is psychologically obtuse.

As far back as we can go, what is known as *Homo sapiens* has exhibited basic needs no other species has even been aware of. The most primitive men we can trace drew figures on the walls of caves; the earliest tribes worshiped at least some rude form of deity; aboriginals everywhere engaged in some sort of barter or transaction.

Thus art, religion, and business (taking the latter in its widest possible sense) seem as congenital to the human species as flying to the birds and swimming to the fishes. Not to mention, of course, human speech — which both sprang from and generated distinctively human needs.

When the Bible tells us, "Man lives not by bread alone," this is far more than a spiritual exhortation. It is a sound anthropological statement. Man *qua* animal may need only a loincloth, a fire, a cave, and a hunk of meat; but man *qua* man has always required much more than these.

Man lives as much by abstractions as he does by necessities. Cave drawings are an abstraction of his esthetic sense. Sun worship is a crude abstraction of his religious sense. Ideas such as freedom, dignity, security, reciprocity — all of which culminated in that uniquely human abstraction known as law — are as inherent to man as hunger and sex.

Some men, indeed, have been willing to forgo food in order to satisfy their esthetic impulse; others have voluntarily denied themselves sex in order to comply with their conception of the religious impulse — men we have prized throughout history as the highest among us.

True, there are many things we imagine we need that we do not, or that we would even be better off without; but this does not mean that man can be stripped down to a primate squatting on his haunches in a cave.

It may be hard to devise an accurate calculus of human needs, but limiting the equation to physical necessities is as foolish as filling an auto tank with gasoline and ignoring the electrical spark that turns a static piece of machinery into a moving vehicle.

Hate Is Simple, Love Complex

WE THINK OF OUR EMOTIONS as being either positive or negative — love, on the one hand, or hate, on the other. But there is another important way in which emotions divide: They are also simple or complex. And this is what creates much of the trouble in the world.

Love, for example, is difficult to sustain not because it is a positive emotion, but because it is a complex one. Hate is easy to maintain for a lifetime, because it is a simple one.

That is, love requires the addition of other elements in order to play its proper role; it needs understanding, patience, tact, the willingness to be hurt or disappointed from time to time. Love alone, in its simplicity, is not enough to carry the burden of relationship.

Hate is a totally different matter; it is not the opposite of love. (As St. Augustine pointed out long ago, indifference is the opposite of love.) Hate is a supremely simple emotion that makes it enormously attractive to a certain type of mind and personality.

First, hate makes no demand on our mental processes, and

doesn't call on us to expand or change our views. In fact, it tends to remove doubt, and gives us a sense of decision and a feeling of righteous well-being.

It doesn't call on any of the other emotions for support; indeed, it puts them quite out of court. It rejects understanding, despises tact, condemns patience, and will endure no hurt or disappointment without quick revenge.

Besides being the simplest of emotions, hate can also be the most fulfilling for a certain kind of person, because it provides him or her with a meaning to life, something to oppose, to blame, to relieve the sense of frustration or failure.

Most of all, because of its seductive simplicity, hate seems to remove the need for reasoning (an intolerable burden to many people) and for any of its auxiliary efforts, such as reading, analyzing, estimating, and judging. Hate has only one function and only one object.

Love might be compared to the building of a tall and elaborate sandcastle, taking many hours of painstaking effort, cooperation, balance, and persistence; and hate might be compared to the foot that comes along and with one vicious or thoughtless kick destroys in a moment what has been built up.

There is so little love in the world compared with the amount of hate — both expressed and latent — not because it is harder for us to be positive than negative, but because it is harder to combine and coordinate a complex emotion in a creative act than to live blindly by blaming and attacking some "enemy" for our dissatisfactions and disappointments. It takes a dedicated genius years to build a great cathedral; any desperado can bomb it to obliteration in a second. Why shouldn't hate, being so much easier, be so much more popular?

Blaming and reforming never go together, because the blamer gets too much secret pleasure out of having things go wrong.

"Right to Life" Only for Some

I HAVE A LETTER from an organization calling itself Foundation for Life, in Toledo, Ohio. The letter commends a recent piece of mine in which I referred to the human race as our "most endangered species."

Foundation for Life is an antiabortion group. The poster accompanying the letter says: "We are dedicated to a very basic principle. That human life is sacred. Period. No qualifications or exceptions or conditions."

The poster points out that "in the United States today, a woman has the legal right to take the life of her unborn child. For any reason." Then goes on to say: "Is there some magic line that makes the life of an unborn child any less important than the life of a day-old child? Or a week-old child? Or a year-old child?"

Suppose we agree. Then what about an eighteen-year-old child? But the state has the legal right to send an eighteen-year-old boy to his death in any war it cares to declare, or even not to declare.

If human life is sacred, period, why do the antiabortion people speak out so forcefully on the right of the fetus, but remain mute when a lad who has been loved and cared for and educated is shipped away to face unnatural death on some foreign battlefield?

What about capital punishment? Does the state possess the right to take human life any more than the mother does? If human life is truly sacred, then it should be left to God to decide who shall die, just as he decides who is to be born.

The Foundation for Life says, quite correctly, "We believe we all have a responsibility to oppose what we think is wrong." But how can you think that abortion is wrong if you condone capital punishment and the evil institution of war? If you permit the state to kill "legally," why does not the mother have the same right?

The abortion issue is more complex and difficult to resolve than either its opponents or its proponents are willing to admit. But this apart, it has always puzzled me that people can be so passionately against killing a baby in the womb and so indifferent to murder by the state after the child reaches the threshold of maturity.

If life is sacred, then the state has no moral authority to take it. If there are "no qualifications or exceptions or conditions," then the right-to-life organizations must speak out as forcefully against war and capital punishment as they do against abortion. Otherwise, the concept of sacredness becomes a mockery at the age of eighteen.

We are not free to pick and choose among our modes of morality. If we do, we become special pleaders and not true believers.

"Unnatural" Creature, Man Struggles in Two Worlds

UNLIKE ALL OTHER ANIMALS, we live in two worlds, not in one. We live in a world we made, and in a world we never made. And we are fully at home in neither — this is the eternal human predicament.

All other species live in a world made for them. When it changes, they adapt or perish. But we change our own world, as well as the one given us.

We are not wholly at home in the world of nature. Since the earliest Promethean legend, we have labored to tame it and exploit it, to make it give us more for less. From cave to tent to hut to skyscraper, we have so reshaped the Earth that our forefathers would not recognize it.

At the same time, we are not really at home in the world we have so arduously fabricated. It is too dense, too noisy, too complex, too competitive, too anxiety-provoking. This is why we feel the pressing need to escape it from time to time — a "vacation" means vacating the premises we have constructed for ourselves.

Where, then, is man's place? What is his world, as the earth is the mole's world and the sky is the bird's world and the sea is the fish's world? Where do we belong, and how do we belong to it?

Is ours the world of sunset and birdsong and morning dew? But we have never been content with these — we have continuously and relentlessly urbanized the planet everywhere we could. The city is as old as the country; it is pre-Biblical and prehistorical.

Is ours the world of skyscraper and expressway and supermart? But we cannot rest and restore and rediscover ourselves in this world, with its fierce angularities and its perpetual abrasiveness. This is why "getting away from it all" is a compulsive tic of civilization among those who can afford it, and even many who cannot.

Can we have both these worlds together? Can we combine the world given us by nature and the world we have contrived?

It seems not — slowly but inexorably, the world of man obscures and then eclipses the world of nature. The sunset is blocked out, the birdsong is muted, the morning dew does not form on asphalt and concrete.

Man is the only "unnatural" creature in nature, for he has no habitat that satisfies all his needs. He is indeed Pascal's gigantic paradox, his monstrous bundle of contradictions. He cannot rest until he has changed the face of the Earth — and then he cannot rest. With the first fruit plucked from the first forbidden tree, he made his bed of thorns. It is the only home he knows.

Perhaps 10 percent of a successful person's achievements may be attributed to his positive qualities; the other 90 percent are merely the natural consequences of the ineptitude of the others.

The Blindness of Revenge

IF YOU'VE HEARD IT ONCE, you've heard it a hundred times: "An eye for an eye, and a tooth for a tooth." People invariably quote this saying when they want to justify an act of revenge.

What annoys me most is not their stupidity in parroting this phrase, but their ignorant assumption that they are following a Biblical injunction. They actually believe that something in the Bible sanctions such behavior — even though they cannot tell you exactly where to find the passage, or what it really means historically.

In point of fact, this *lex talionis,* as it was known in ancient times, represented a great reform over the previous law. What it meant was that the punishment should at most *equal* the offense, never exceed it. Until then, people would commonly take a life for an eye or even a tooth.

The Old Testament cites this saying as the extreme of retaliation; it is far better, we are told, to exercise mercy and not demand the equivalence in retribution for a violent act. Justice tempered by mercy is not, as many imagine, the product of New Testament teaching only. The Golden Rule, in various forms, far antedates the ministry of Jesus.

Scripture has been, and can be, the most dangerous weapon in the world unless it is carefully read and understood in full context. Taking any sentence in isolation represents a gross distortion — but it is done all the time, by persons or factions who are desperate to make a doctrinal point and are too lazy or too angry to peruse the full passage with calmness and common sense.

"Revenge is mine, saith the Lord" tells us plainly that we are not to take revenge into our own hands. Shakespeare understood this when he had Claudius remind Hamlet not to harm his mother for her transgression: "Leave her to heaven," where God alone will judge her.

But most of us hear only the first three words, "Revenge is mine," and proceed to act as though we have been given the right to imitate the Lord in this respect. And since every king and ruler has felt free to do this, why should not a private individual assume the same privilege? Regimes use the Bible — and the Koran, and the works of Marx — to extract whatever they feel lends substance to their cause, no matter how ingeniously they are forced to twist the original meaning.

Far from being commanded, or permitted, to exact an eye for an eye, we are instructed never to transgress this limit, and wherever possible to show more compassion to the evil-doer than he has shown to us. Otherwise, wherein lies our moral superiority? Of what practical use is our religion if we do no better than the pagans and barbarians do?

I suppose anyone has a right, of sorts, to demand tit for tat; what we have no right to do is to cite Scripture as the basis for such retribution when, in that wryly comical phrase, "the Devil made me do it."

Heard the One about the Angel . . . ?

HUMOR IS LACKING in almost every religion known to man, from the most primitive to the most sophisticated; yet man, presumably cast in the image of God, is the only creature capable of genuine laughter. How can we account for this?

There are a few strained instances of irony that may be construed as humor in the Old Testament, and absolutely none in the New. The apostles record that Jesus wept; nowhere are we informed that he laughed. And the sacred books of Islam and the East, except for a few Zen paradoxes and riddles, are equally devoid of humor.

How can laughter and merriment form so large a portion of man's nature and comfort, and yet be so absent in his worship?

I ask in honest perplexity, not in any spirit of contention or derogation. Humor is an immense solace in this world of woe; it preserves sanity, restores perspective, provides the spice and savor in personal and social relationships.

Besides, the cosmos is as comical as it is awesome, the product of a fantastic imagination. Whatever else the creator may be, he/she is not dull or drab or ponderous: Consider the hippo, the orchid, the volcano, the purple-bottomed baboon, the shooting star, and the duck-billed platypus. Noah's ark alone is a comic opera of incredible inventiveness.

Our minds are shaped to make, accept, and appreciate humor. A humorless person is considered to be deficient in humanhood, not fully developed; and every normal baby is born to chuckle as easily as to cry. Hardly anyone is more repellent to most of us than a pious person who is dour and humorless and takes no joy in living.

If we are truly formed in the image of our creator — and who am I to doubt it? — where do we find the prototype of this omnipresent human faculty? Why, in every chapel, is solemnity viewed as the mark of piety, and laughter branded as the sign of irreverence? Why are religious observances invariably grave, ponderous, hushed, and even joy muted within the sacred precincts?

St. Thomas tells us that we cannot know the attributes of God because he is not an "object" among other objects and does not take predicates; and I believe him. Yet all the predicates we attach to divinity are those of might, power, glory, dignity, domination, judgment. A divine sense of humor sounds sacrilegious to us, as though it would detract from perfection, while in a person it adds to perfection.

It confuses and perplexes me. Either there must be more to it than the sacred texts have given us, or humor is not the blessing I take it to be. Some day, somewhere else, I hope to learn the truth.

Ms. Bryant Is Better When She's Not Being "Good"

I NEVER WROTE A LINE about Anita Bryant when she was peddling orange juice and petitioning against homosexual rights, because when such people are in the public eye, they consider every knock a boost.

Now that her world has come unstuck and she is beginning to reglue it, I feel free to point out that she is a better person than when she was so busy being a "good person." Sometimes we have to fall from grace to know what grace really is.

In a recent interview with a women's magazine, she admitted that she had acquired the Valium habit, had become dependent on sleeping pills combined with wine, and had even contemplated suicide as her marriage was breaking up. Responding to her husband's charges of unfaithfulness, she confessed, "I can't say that I'm totally innocent."

Instead of being the smug, self-righteous crusader for the home and family, she can now say, "Having experienced a form of male chauvinism among Christians that was devastating, I can now see how women are controlled in a very un-Christ-like way . . . the problem is that most men are insensitive to women's needs."

As for gays, she now feels that "the church needs to be more loving, unconditionally, and willing to see these people as human beings." Her eyes have also been opened to "valid reasons" for militant feminism.

Finally she sounds like a person who has lived and loved and suffered, not a radiantly smiling face on a candy box, encased in velvet and wreathed with roses and totally insulated from the realities of life.

A bad marriage ("It was never much good to begin with") almost wrecked her — but it also saved her, because she grew rather than shrank, expanded her range of sympathies rather than shriveling into self-pity.

The Lord, we are told, works in mysterious ways, and I believe it. Sometimes being dragged to the depths is the only way we glimpse the heights; being desperate and disconsolate and defeated is the only way we redeem ourselves from pride and self-satisfaction.

In pain, Bryant is starting to be a Christian now, which she only thought she was before. "Live and let live" has become her creed, which is approaching St. Augustine's "Love, and do what you will." She is no longer passing judgments on who is "moral" and who is not.

The visible church may have lost a militant member, but the invisible church has gained a soul. The Moral Majority may be frowning, but the Eternal Majority must be rejoicing that she has put down the frosty glass of orange juice and picked up the warm chalice of charity. As Santayana once wisely said, "It is easier to make a saint out of a sinner than out of a prig."

Survival of the Fittest

WHEN PEOPLE USE THE PHRASE "survival of the fittest," do they know what they are talking about? In most cases, no. The phrase has become perverted into a slogan to justify the use of force or cunning or greed in the competition for material goods.

What is the fittest? It is not the largest, the strongest, or the smartest. The two species that have lived longest on Earth and have survived every change and catastrophe are the cockroach and the rat.

Size did not save the dinosaur, as fleetness or agility did not save many other species. In many cases, weakness and stupidity have survived, while the strong and the cunning have gone under. As Charles Fort has pointed out, "There is no way of determining 'fitness' except in that a thing does survive."

So *fitness,* then, is only another name for *survival;* and Darwinism is the theory that survivors survive. This is about as useful as knowing that older people are those who live longer and beautiful people are those we find most attractive.

In any event, survival of the fittest cannot legitimately be transferred from the species to the individual. The aim of every organism is to reproduce itself as much as possible, and not merely to live as well as it can. Bees and ants sacrifice themselves for the community; they do not plunder or exploit it for individual well-being.

As social animals, we have been designed more like bees or ants than like cockroaches or rats. Individually we can do little; collectively, we can accomplish a great deal — enough to allow us to determine our own fate, to change the course of biological evolution itself. Other creatures have natures; only man has a history.

Life on Earth is by no means a simple matter of dominance and submission; if it were, the strongest species would now be in control, while the weakest would be enslaved or exterminated. Survival instead has been largely based on the ability to adapt to changing conditions — and such adaptation has little to do with strength, force, or guile.

Different species demonstrate their fitness by surviving for different reasons; there is no one particular trait that assures perpetuation of a species. Each must learn, by trial and error, the best way to adapt to an ice age or a dwindling food supply or a new kind of predator. Extinction is certain only when the creature persists in the same old habits.

We are just beginning to learn that our same old habits, like the exploitation of nonrenewable resources, may make us at one with the auk and the dodo; and we have scarcely begun to learn that if we change our environment too drastically — through hydrogen bombs or their equivalent — there will be no fit, fitter, or fittest among us to survive. Our force, our cunning, and our greed may leave only the rat and the roach to inherit the Earth.

Life's Unfairness Doesn't Excuse Passivity

"I'M TIRED OF HEARING that life is unfair," said my daughter at breakfast the other morning. "I wish President Carter had never picked up that phrase. Why don't you write something about it?"

I knew just what she meant, because I have felt the same way. Life is unfair enough in accidents and tragedies so that people don't have to add to its unfairness by their actions, or to excuse what they do or don't do by tossing off that easy phrase.

Life is unfair in that a plane crash may kill innocent people or spare some worthless ones and maim the useful. Anything can happen to anybody at any time, regardless of merit or worth to society.

But precisely because of this we have a special obligation to see that fairness works wherever we have the power to make it work. People aren't mired in poverty because of "life," but because society doesn't really care enough to get rid of slums and rotten environments.

The best young people die in wars not because life is unfair, but because the old men who run countries are more interested in their power and their glory than they are in working out some plan to outlaw war as a way of settling national differences.

There are many things we can't control in nature, so there will always be a kind of built-in unfairness in the universe. But we don't have to add to it by being selfish and indifferent and narrow-minded and by simply shrugging off problems we *could* control, just by pointing out that life is unfair.

The whole idea of fairness is a human one, anyway. Animals don't have it; nature is beyond good and evil. And I suppose we developed the idea when the first men realized that life itself was so hard and unpredictable to begin with that we have a responsibility to try to make it easier for one another.

Isn't that actually the moral basis of religion? President Carter called himself a born-again Christian, but the old Hebrew prophets and the newer Christian disciples didn't feel that we should tolerate the same injustices over and over again on the grounds that life is unfair and anybody might die at any time.

If science and medicine felt that way, people would still be perishing by the millions from plagues — which some people once accepted as "the will of God." That's why we've promoted laws and reforms and ethical codes: They can't make life fair, but they can make it a lot *fairer*. And that's all anybody really asks.

The Bridge Lesson

SOPHISTICATED PEOPLE laugh at fortunetellers, but I feel sorry for the clients who patronize them. Not just because fortunetelling is fraudulent, but because it is a pathetic delusion to want to know the future.

All that mankind can do is to hope for the best and to prepare for the worst; beyond that, any attempt to peer through the curtain of time is not only futile but self-defeating. Nothing could be worse than to be able to anticipate our personal future.

Fifteen hundred years ago, St. Augustine wrote: "God will not permit man to have a knowledge of things to come; for if man had a foresight of his prosperity, he would become arrogant and careless; and if he had an understanding of his adversity, he would become listless and despairing."

Whether or not you agree with Augustine's theology, in a psychological sense he was right on target. We are far better off, in every way, not knowing what is going to happen to us. It is the very contingencies of life that keep us alert and active, building and planning, just as though we were going to live forever. Our ignorance is our impetus.

In point of fact, even with our nescience about the future, most people fail to understand the proper way to approach tomorrow — they think and act in precisely the opposite way that they should.

I have mentioned elsewhere the difference between the expert bridge player and the duffer. It is axiomatic among good players that when you hold a hand that looks absurdly easy to make, you search for every possible danger that might wreck the contract and play to avoid that contingency.

Contrariwise, when a hand seems nearly impossible to make, you hope for a miracle of distribution that will succeed. You are bleakly pessimistic when fortune seems to be smiling and wildly optimistic when your chances seem slight.

The average player — and the average person in life — adopts exactly the opposite view. He who seems to hold a winning hand becomes, in Augustine's words, "arrogant and careless," and he who has been dealt rotten cards turns "listless and despairing." (This is one reason, by the way, that 5 percent of tournament players win 95 percent of all tournaments.)

King Midas foolishly imagined that if he could turn everything he touched to gold, life would be beautiful — and instead, his blessing turned to a curse. Likewise, those who yearn to gaze into their futures suppose that foreknowledge would serve to their advantage, when actually it would stultify their minds or paralyze their will. We learn more about our probable fates from looking back than by peering forward.

You are not finally grown up until you cease thinking of life as a matter of good or bad choices and begin regarding each alternative as a trade-off in which some plus must be given up and some minus tolerated.

*

It is the very core of the human predicament that the most important things in life we need to learn are precisely those things that cannot be taught.

Sins of the Spirit

"WHENEVER I SEE OR HEAR the word *spiritual,* it makes me grit my teeth," said a friend of mine who teaches philosophy in a nearby college. "It's become the favorite word of people who don't even understand what it means."

I quite agreed with him. The word *spiritual,* used in its popular sense, has come to mean the opposite of *physical.* Anything that is "spiritual" is good, is positive, is virtuous, is desirable, is loftier than the merely physical.

This is not only nonsense: It is dangerous nonsense. Just as physical things can be either good or bad, so spiritual things can be either good or bad. The word itself is quite neutral and has no intrinsic value.

Indeed, as C. S. Lewis pointed out in his book *Christian Behavior* some years ago, "The sins of the flesh are bad, but they are the least bad of all sins. All the worst pleasures are purely spiritual: the pleasure of putting other people in the wrong, of bossing and patronizing and spoiling sport and backbiting; the pleasures of power, of hatred."

Most of the evil in the world has been generated on the spiritual level. A power-driven and hate-obsessed man such as Hitler had no interest in physical pursuits; he was as abstemious as a monk, and as dedicated to the diabolic (which is a spiritual thing) as the monk is to the divine.

The people who create the mischief and the sorrow in the world are not the libertines and the drinkers and the wastrels; these are pathetic people who create, at the most, private tragedy. The vast public tragedies are created by the people who are dominated by some perverse spiritual drive — by pride, by anger, by hostility, by envy.

True spirituality is as rare as true bestiality in human beings. And those few who achieve it are those who are terribly aware of the perils of spirituality — who know, as the Romans warned us, that a corruption of the best becomes the worst. Which is why, to quote Lewis again, "Of all bad men, the bad religious man is the worst."

Unlike most other religions, both Judaism and Christianity accept the goodness of physical things and do not dismiss them as delusions or devices of the Devil. And those who despise the physical too often use their "spirituality" as a bludgeon for punishing the weak, while they themselves revel in the pleasures of pride, of power, of exactly those spiritual qualities that define the nature of their enemy, the Devil.

Sex and Morality

QUITE A LOT OF READERS were incensed, to say the least, by a column of mine in which I concluded that "there are certain absolutes for the human race . . . but sexual customs and practices and attitudes are not among them."

The fact of the matter is that different societies at different times have had varying sexual customs and practices and attitudes, and while some may be more just or practical or socially harmonious than others, we cannot condemn such differences out of hand, as we condemn lying and stealing and cruelty and hypocrisy.

The patriarchs of the Old Testament had many wives and concubines, yet their way was not barred to heaven, if I read the book correctly. St. Paul found all sexuality distasteful, and reluctantly conceded that "it is better to marry than to burn," though he obviously felt it was better to do neither.

It is notable that Jesus was upbraided for living among sinners and wine-bibbers, but it is plain from everything he said that he preferred those who sinned against the flesh to those who sinned against the spirit. Sensual transgressions are a weakness more than a vice; it is hardness of heart that he railed against.

One does not have to like, or approve of, polygamy or homosexuality or cohabitation outside of marriage, any more than one has to like, or approve of, the subordinate position given to women in the Judaic, Christian, and Islamic faiths. But these are mostly social and cultural patterns, which change with time and conditions, whereas the absolutes for mankind do not.

Monogamy has prevailed because it is a more sensible and fair arrangement, corresponding more closely to human needs, and not because it is necessarily more "moral" than polygamy — the Mormons are an exceedingly moral folk. And women are assuming equality among all the Western religions for the same reasons, because the previous churchly attitudes were based on ignorance, superstition, and male chauvinism.

Sex is only a minor part of morality, but for most people today the two words are nearly equated. Thus, if people follow orthodox prescriptions in the area of sex, they cannot imagine how they are being immoral in their personal and social relations. But *injustice* is the basic immorality, as the great prophets all testified, and one cold-hearted and selfish man does more to rupture the fabric of society than a thousand bigamists or other deviates from conventionality.

I do not think all sexual attitudes are as productive and humanizing as all others, but I do firmly believe that in judging morality, we should raise our eyes from the loins to the heart.

Does God Believe in You?

A LAWRENCE COLLEGE student writes to ask, "Is there any evidence that Bertrand Russell recanted his agnosticism on his deathbed and said it would be anomalous if life was created without the aid of a God?"

I have no idea, but I doubt it. Besides, a deathbed recantation may mean no more than the glib slogan that "there are no atheists in foxholes." It is how you behave the rest of your life after you leave the foxhole that is decisive, not what you feel under fear of dying.

It has long seemed to me that the question of believing in

God is a nearly meaningless one. Almost anyone can persuade himself that he believes in God, if he wants to, without this belief's having the slightest effect on the way he treats people around him or conducts his life outside the established ambit of religion.

What is important, if I may put it this way, is whether God believes in you. By this I mean whether you are a person worthy of having a God to believe in. It is the existential worthiness of a person, not his abstract belief, that alone has any value, both here and in the problematic future. A saintly atheist is surely preferable to a pious bigot; Bruno was a better man than those who burned him.

What happens to religions — to all of them, unfortunately, in one degree or another — is that they eventually obscure the message of their founders more than illuminate it. They make subsidiary beliefs more central than the core — and their communicants are happy to accept these, because it is far easier to celebrate a cult than to live a creed, easier to kneel before an altar than to "pick up your cross and follow me."

Religion is fragmented into a thousand bits, each bit imagining it carries the seed of the truth. But the truth, as Aristotle said, is like a barn door: Nobody who throws at it can miss it, but nobody can hit all of it. All religions have a bit of truth by the tail, but no more than that. What would Jesus "be" if he returned today?

If there is a comprehensible God, and I believe so, he is better served by our trying to determine what he would like us to be to one another in our daily intercourse, and by our trying to live up to that. Bertrand Russell tried to, as much as he could, as much of the time, though he was a wicked man like the rest of us.

I wouldn't want a God who judged me on whether I thought I was an atheist or not. My father thought he was, but if that lovely man is not now in Abraham's bosom, we need a new idea of heaven.

"Thou Shalt Not" Allows More Freedom Than "Thou Shalt"

ONE OF THE THINGS that puzzles young people when they read or study the Decalogue is its negative form. They cannot understand why the Ten Commandments are couched in prohibitions, in "Thou shalt nots" rather than in "Thou shalts."

This negative form does repel many moderns, who would prefer to be pointed positively toward some goal rather than prohibited from some forms of action. But if one gives the matter a little thought, it becomes clear that the negative actually gives us far more freedom than the positive.

It is relatively easy to know the things we should *not* do, for these encompass large categories of behavior — stealing, lying, coveting, and so forth. It is much harder to know the things we *should* do, for these are singular and specific acts, depending upon changing circumstances and calling for individual judgment.

The Old Testament sages recognized that it is impossible to draw up a code of positive behavior that would cover all situations, all contingencies, all relationships. There is simply no way to determine beforehand, and so, in a sense, the patriarchs anticipated the modern theological notion of "situation ethics."

The most a moral code can do, realistically, is to delineate the broad areas in which we harm others and ourselves and to proscribe such conduct in general form. But even these areas have exceptions — St. Thomas condoned stealing if it became essential to keep one's family from starving.

In fact, the flaw in what has become known as the Golden Rule is its positive form: "Do unto others as you would have them do unto you." It was better and earlier expressed in the negative: "Do not do unto others what you would not have them do unto you." This makes much more psychological sense in terms of respecting the integrity of other people and not forcing our views or ways upon them.

Prohibitions are guidelines on a moral map: They mark out precipices and swamplands and other dangers that we traverse at our peril. They do not tell us which routes to take, for there are many, but which to avoid. A so-called positive code would be far more repressive and restrictive, forcing us to take one approved route only.

What we call the Ten Commandments have been poorly translated; their original name is the Ten Words or Ten Sayings. They do not command as much as they warn, with the same negative brevity as a sign next to a gas tank saying "No Smoking."

As Humanity Grows, So Grows God

ALL THIS ARGUMENT and controversy about the evolution of man, and no thought about the evolution of God. Fundamentalists and modernists disputing the origin of species, and no consideration of how our species has changed its view of God since the earliest times.

In the beginning, in the first books of the Old Testament, we find a vengeful as well as a gracious god, a tribal god exacting duty and devotion by ritual and sacrifice.

Then, as the Bible progresses, we find a strange thing happening. God himself changes, in the eyes of the Israelites. He becomes less fearsome and more compassionate; he expands from a tribal to a universal deity. As men grew in understanding, God grew in stature.

At first, he rejoiced in the slaying of Israel's enemies. But by the time of the Babylonian Exile, he was already depicted as a god who wept that the Egyptians were drowning in the Red Sea after the Israelites had safely crossed over. He cries, "Are the Egyptians not my children too?"

(This may be found in *Midrash,* the earliest commentary on the Hebrew scriptures.)

And by the time we reach the great prophets, such as Deutero-Isaiah, man has discovered a god who is far closer to the precepts and parables of Rabbi Jesus than most of us realize. Many of Jesus' sayings are direct quotations or paraphrases of the Old Testament, for he never considered himself anything but a pious Jew.

The evolution of God continued during his ministry, for he set about to reform and expand and deepen the vision of a loving and redemptive deity, placing the spirit above the laws that had come to cramp and rigidify the Old Guard fundamentalist Jews of his day.

The ministry of Jesus was a further liberation from ritual for its own sake. ("It is not what goes into a man's mouth that defiles him, but what comes out of it.") It was an evolutionary breakthrough in men's conception of the creator and his relation to us.

Alas, the church founded in his name (which I think would have shocked and scandalized him) retrogressed, as all establishments do, and became in its own way as repressive and ritualistic and rigid as the synagogue he rebelled against, again placing law above spirit.

God grows, as we grow, for he reflects what we become; and when we grow to the fullest, we will have the fullest god — not a god of the fundamentalists, but a god of fundamentals, a light, not a lash.

The only "true church" is that which admits there is no way of knowing which denomination God belongs to.

*

An idealist believes that the short run doesn't count; a cynic believes that the long run doesn't matter; a realist believes that what is done or left undone in the short run determines the long run. (Historically speaking, Rabbi Jesus was the supreme realist.)

Why Get a Liberal Education?

ONE OF THE BEST testimonials I have ever heard for a liberal arts education came from a seventy-year-old man released from twenty years of imprisonment in Germany.

The man is Albert Speer, the architect and Nazi politician who became minister of munitions and armaments under Hitler and head of the group that controlled much of the slave labor used by Germany during the war.

Speer said that the thing he regretted most was that he grew up with a technical education only, in architecture and engineering. He learned little of the liberal arts and humanities, and nothing of philosophy at all.

"It was this lopsided education" (I am paraphrasing him as best I remember) "that made it so easy for many of us to fall under the spell of Nazism," he said. "We were technical barbarians, who did a fine job but never inquired about the purpose, or the ultimate results, of the job."

Speer did not seem to be copping a plea when he said this. He admitted his guilt, but felt he had paid for it with twenty years in prison. And now he was simply an old man reflecting on what might have been.

"If we had been given a proper education as to the probable moral and social consequences of Nazism," he said (and again I paraphrase), "many of us might have taken steps to abort the movement before it took full power. But like your Watergate people, we thought we were being 'loyal' — we had never learned what real loyalty ought to mean."

People who ask what practical purpose there is in studying such subjects as history and philosophy need to be reminded that these are the only subjects that ask fundamental questions — what is the nature of man, what is the good society, what are the proper ends of civilization, and so on.

Some of these questions are not answerable in a positive sense, but we can collect "nonanswers": We can learn the things that are wrong for man to be and do, the dead ends, the delusions, the fantasies and hysterias that have driven peoples and cultures to self-defeating policies. Any genuinely educated person could see where Hitlerism was going from its inception, as a philosophy of death, not of life.

The Germans were the most educated nation in the world, in the narrow sense of scholarship and technical skills, but this was not translated by their academic system into ethical or philosophic terms. Too many talented men like Speer grew up innocent of the moral truths and social options it took him twenty years in prison to recognize.

Padlocking the Pulpit

THE EMBARRASSED MINISTER of a church in a western city wrote to cancel a forthcoming lecture I was scheduled to give there one spring. It seems that the board decided it wanted no speakers who were not "inside" the church.

To paraphrase Groucho Marx, I would not care to belong to a church that would not want an outside speaker, and I was just as glad to get the cancellation. As the minister put it, "Apparently the people in this church are lacking the first word of the sign . . ."

What a church, any church of any denomination, needs most of all is an occasional, or even frequent, outside speaker to let in some fresh air. Because the fact is that you don't know what you think until you hear someone who thinks differently from you.

The only way we clarify and revise and strengthen our own beliefs is by testing them and weighing them against other beliefs. A group that cuts itself off from such dialogue becomes smug and stupid and incapable of defending its own beliefs except by dogma.

Ideas must compete in the public arena, just as athletes must, if they are to remain vital instead of inert, flexible and not rigid. This is what St. Paul meant when he enjoined us to "test all things; hold fast to that which is good."

You really don't know your own religion until you can grasp both the similarities and the differences between it and other creeds, just as you do not know your own language fully until you at least have the rudiments of a foreign tongue.

Every church should have a half-dozen outside speakers a year, and as outside as it can get, from Adventists to Zen Buddhists and back again. This is not only a splendid way to wake up the congregation and promote some of the ecumenism we talk about, but you can also learn something at the same time. At the very least you learn a new set of pious platitudes; at best, you get a deeper dimension of the religious impulse and a broader sense of what ties us together.

I think that even humanists, agnostics, and atheists, if they have something pertinent to say, should be encouraged to address congregations and then to engage in dialogue. Often they know more about religion and Biblical history than the docile devout and can serve an astringent function in sprinkling icy water on sleepy faces.

The church that bars its pulpit to an outsider is closing its heart as well as its mind. Freedom to speak means little without the comparable willingness to listen; and freedom of religion should mean more than the right to close your ears to a different drummer.

An exchange of useful information is more valuable than an exchange of goods, because in the former case each has more than he had before, whereas in the latter case he has only the equivalent. (This is why knowledge is augmented, while commodities are only circulated.)

The Proper Study of Mankind

"WHY DON'T YOU WRITE something about the energy crisis?" asks a reader in Colorado. "We'd really like to know what you think about it, and what would be best to do."

I don't know what I think about it, because I don't feel that I have enough solid facts to make a judgment. It is hard to know whom to believe, and a column merely expressing my feelings would be a waste of energy on my part to write and on yours to read.

There is, however, another and deeper reason that I normally don't deal with such subjects — I don't think they are important enough, which may strike you as ridiculous.

Mankind has always solved its technical problems, in one way or another. We are an amazingly resourceful species, and our inventive capacities have scarcely yet been tapped. If something is physically possible, we will find a way to do it.

Our real problem, as we all know, is moral, not technical. Moral in the broadest, most basic sense of finding out *the right relations among people*. We know what these relations ought to be in the abstract, but we have had little luck putting them into practice throughout most of human history.

Martin Buber, my own intellectual mentor, suggested that the most important study we could venture into is "philosophical anthropology." This is a long academic phrase for learning more about the true nature of man and how we can direct it toward its proper goals.

We study everything but ourselves. We pour billions into research of every kind, but in the six thousand years of recorded history we have not learned to live together any better than the ancient Babylonians. All our sociology, our psychology, and our philosophy have penetrated hardly an inch into the inner dynamics of the human organism.

Mankind can adapt to almost any conditions, on Earth and even on the moon if we have to. We know an immense amount about a dozen different sciences, from the nucleus of the atom to the solar system. But we remain largely strangers to ourselves, ignorant of our deepest needs, unable to control our destructive drives, unwilling to change our primitive notions for a rational design to secure our survival.

If we fail as a species, it will have nothing to do with energy or any other technological obstacle; it will have to do with the way we regard ourselves and others as threats, rivals, and enemies rather than as members of the same family. Until we know who we are and what we are supposed to do, all our other knowledge cannot save us.

The Awesomeness of Reality

THE STRANGE THING about science is that if you have only a slight and superficial acquaintance with it, you are likely to lose your religious beliefs; but if you bother to delve somewhat more deeply, you are just as likely to renew and confirm your reverence for creation.

I do not happen to believe in the so-called miracles described in the Bible, not because I think they are impossible, but because I consider them to be trivial. Not because they are beyond the creative will, but because they are beneath it. They are mostly primitive folk tales, unworthy of a cosmic deity.

Today we have a long list of modern "miracles" that are even harder to believe — and yet each one of them can be, and has been, verified. They disclose a creative power and imagination of infinitely greater domain and sophistication and magnificence than ever dreamed of in ancient Palestine or anywhere else in the world.

As only one example, who in the past could have believed that as physical objects increase their speed and approach the speed of light, their mass increases indefinitely and they shrink toward zero thickness in the direction of motion? And that time for them would come near to stopping altogether?

Nothing that Yahweh is supposed to have done in Biblical tales equals making a cube of one inch that weighs eighty tons, but modern astrophysics assures us that we find such an inconceivability in the neutron stars throughout the universe. No medieval doctor of the church would have believed it, but every contemporary scientist accepts it as a fact.

We may balk at the Old Testament tale of the Lord creating a cosmos out of a chaos, or out of nothing, but now we are aware of something inexplicable called quasars — explosions of unimaginable violence that destroy millions of worlds in one second.

Even less likely, but true, is our present cosmological picture of innumerable galaxies receding from one another — and the farther they go, the faster they recede. The mind boggles at this in a way that no Bible story can even remotely approach.

And, as a fitting culmination to all this, we now have fields of force that science tells us are "universal, virtually infinite, presumably eternal; they display internal consistency and are therefore intelligible; they come as near to being ultimate causes as the mind can grasp. They cannot be directly experienced by sense perception, but their presence is now beyond challenge."

Who needs miracles when reality is so much more awesome, so much more persuasive of a power, a purpose, and a plan beyond our petty comprehension?

Scientists like to imagine that they are "hard" and philosophers are "soft," but the more deeply science delves into the basic stuff of the universe, the softer it seems to be, until matter is dissolved in energy — and energy is . . . what?

*

The better we know a person, the less a portrait of him seems to capture the whole personality; for even the best portrait is static, while the essence of a personality is its dynamism.

Of Loving and Liking

MY PIECE ON WHAT the word *equal* really means and how it is commonly misunderstood reminded me of the most prevalent word in our language that is even more misunderstood. It is the little word *love*.

A large part of the confusion springs from the fact that English, unlike some other languages, does not distinguish among different types of love. Ancient Greek, as we know, had three forms: *eros* for sexual or emotional love, *philia* for brotherly love, and *agape* for love of God.

When we are commanded, in all the Bibles of the world, to "love our neighbor," it is the latter two forms of the word *love* that are being enjoined, not the first. For we cannot be commanded to love emotionally, since this kind of love is a feeling and not an act of the will.

We commonly suppose that love of this sort is an intensive of *like,* just as *hot* is an intensive of *warm*. This is true only of romantic or sexual love, where the affection we feel for one person is of a much higher degree than our feelings toward other people.

But *philia* is the kind of love that has nothing to do with liking. Perhaps the difference can be clarified by quoting Samuel Johnson's aphorism, "It is not in our power to like, but it is in our power to be kind."

Emotionally, we cannot control our reactions to different personalities, and the great prophets and religious leaders were not so stupid as to suppose we can. Whom we like or dislike is not a matter in our command, or hardly so.

But *philia,* as distinct from *eros,* is a matter of commanding our will, not redirecting our emotions. It is possible to love someone you do not like; in fact, that is the highest virtue. Even the lowest and basest among us find it easy to care for those who attract them, but only the best among us can love those they do not like.

It is hard, very hard, but everything worthwhile is hard, and there will be nothing resembling brotherhood on Earth until most of us learn this lesson. I cannot do it: I keep trying and failing and trying and failing; but at least I know it is what I am called to do.

Before we can even begin, however, we must comprehend the kind of love the Good Books mean and not confuse it with sexual love, or parental love, or love of country, or a taste for Bach and oysters. These are natural loves that come out of liking; *philia* is what some would term an unnatural love, because it goes against the grain. It is, indeed, the sublime foolishness that confounds the wisdom of this world.

Sinners, Saints, and Single-mindedness

I AM NEVER SURPRISED at the people who start out with nothing and end up with a great deal of money. They may or may not have much brains or talent or anything else; what they do have, in abundance, is *single-mindedness*. They are totally goal-directed and will not deviate a hair.

If you want something hard enough and are willing to devote yourself exclusively to it and will sacrifice everything else for it, then unless you are conspicuously defective, you will reach your goal. It may turn out to be a goal not worth reaching at such cost, but this is another matter — and a matter that never concerns the single-minded.

The man who makes a career out of amassing knowledge is little different in this respect from those who amass fortunes, however different he may be (or pretend to be) in his personal value system. Again, it is more often than not single-mindedness that distinguishes him from his colleagues or collaborators or competitors.

Einstein once told an assistant at Princeton that he considered the following incident to be the most characteristic anecdote that could be related about him:

They had finished the preparation of a paper and were looking for a paper clip. After opening many drawers they finally found one which turned out to be too badly bent for use, and so they began looking for a tool to straighten it.

Opening many more drawers, they came upon a whole box of unused paper clips. Einstein immediately started to shape one of them into a tool to straighten the bent one. When the puzzled assistant asked why he was doing this when he had a whole box of new clips, Einstein replied, "Once I am set on a goal, it becomes difficult to deflect me."

What we have here is more than mere persistence or perseverance or stubbornness, if you will; it is, in its own way, a kind of tunnel vision that can be perilous or profitable, depending upon the context of the situation. Napoleon's refusal to abandon the prolonged Russian invasion was a fatal mistake; Ehrlich's six hundred fruitless experiments in bacteriology were eventually a dogged success.

The cost of such single-mindedness is too much for most people to be willing, or able, to pay. In most cases it involves neglect of family, the slighting of social responsibilities, a kind of solitariness at the core of one's being, and a ruthless sacrifice of everything and everyone that seems to stand in the way of the goal.

Much of the good and most of the bad that accrued to human society have been the consequence of single-minded endeavors. Both Hitler and Gandhi had only one goal — in the former case, conquest and enslavement; in the latter, freedom and dignity — but in the unswerving pursuit of their antipodal aims, sadist and saint were more alike than different.

Self-discipline without talent can often achieve astounding results, whereas talent without self-discipline inevitably dooms itself to failure.

A Good Man Is Easy to Recognize

SKEPTICS AND CYNICS and very young philosophers are fond of saying that "everything is relative." Drawing a wrong inference from Einstein's theory of space and time, they suppose that all codes of ethics and behavior and human relationship depend upon the time and place and conventions of any given society.

But they mistake customs and traditions and taboos for a genuine code of morality. While it is true that different societies may vary in their social habits and practices, it is equally true that all societies respect and honor much the same traits in their members. Morality is, at bottom, *a right relationship* between *persons* — and this relationship is perceived as much the same everywhere.

I have been reading a biography of Sir John Frederick William Herschel, the eminent astronomer and son of the same. After surveying his notable contributions, the author gives a concluding tribute:

> In private life, Sir John was a firm and most active friend; he had no jealousies; he avoided all scientific feuds; he gladly lent a helping hand to those who consulted him in scientific difficulties; he was pleased by appreciation of his work without being solicitous of applause. It was truthfully said of him that his life was full of the serenity of a sage and the docile innocence of the child.

It can be submitted that hardly any society known to man, past or present, would not have loved and honored such a person — one free from pettiness, from vanity, from contentiousness, honest and open and helpful, respectful of the feelings of others, and dedicated to some purpose outside and greater than himself.

This is what we instinctively feel a person is meant to be and do. It is what most of us lamentably cannot live up to, but we know it is as admirable as it is rare, and we use these traits and virtues as a touchstone for judging the conduct of ourselves and those around us.

Of course, different societies have evolved rituals and customs that seem bizarre or perverted to us — but we cannot find one in which hostility is preferred to friendship, deceit preferred to honesty, treachery preferred to loyalty, cruelty preferred to kindness within the group itself. And for great men, the group becomes the human race.

Essential morality is and has always been the same everywhere at all times, though its form and dimensions may differ. Our real task is to try to separate the basic code of right conduct from all the cultural convolutions and encrustations that come with time. Gleaming through these, a character like Sir John Herschel's makes us realize that while a good man is always hard to find, he is easy to recognize, no matter what his costume, his color, or his century.

Drugs That Help Also Hurt

MOST PEOPLE SEEM to believe that the words *problem* and *solution* are antonyms, like *hot* and *cold* or *high* and *low*. Just as you can't have hot without cold or high without low, they imagine, you can't have a problem without a solution.

But they are making a philosophical as well as a grammatical mistake. Some problems — some of the most essential human problems, in fact — have no real solutions. They have, at best, uneasy compromises.

As one important and persistent modern problem, take the matter of drugs for medication. How long should a new drug be tested? How safe must it be found to be allowed on the market? When are the side effects serious enough to ban it? How do we measure its possible abuse against its probable effectiveness?

There are no clear-cut answers to any of these questions. There is no solution to the problem of drug manufacture and distribution. There is only compromise, made on the basis of experience, common sense, and a kind of rough calculus of public good and private danger.

It has been widely remarked that if aspirin were discovered now, it might take five or ten years before it was permitted on the market, if ever, because we really don't know how or why it works. Also, it can have serious side effects on some patients. Yet as an overall pain reliever, it is unparalleled in medical history.

England and many European countries adopt a different approach toward drugs from ours. They permit new concoctions to come on the market much sooner and faster than we do, but they monitor their effects much more carefully than we do. The United States, on the other hand, inhibits the development of new drugs by interminable regulations, but when a drug is approved, the government seems to feel its responsibility is ended. This is demonstrably unfair both to the drug manufacturers and to the public. The former are discouraged in their competitive search for new compounds, and the latter are often denied the benefits of a drug for years after its relative safety has been demonstrated in other countries. We seem to be too tough in the laboratory and too casual in the marketplace.

For one thing, Americans have been conditioned to be prescription-happy. No visit to a doctor is complete until he hands a prescription to the patient, whether that patient requires it or not. Doctors are partly to blame for this situation, but even more so is our prevailing national myth that there is a drug for every affliction.

This completes the circle of problem and solution. If every problem has a solution, every ailment must have its appropriate drug. It is a childish attitude that, unfortunately, neither the pharmaceutical houses nor the medical profession has done anything to discourage. Most drugs that are strong enough to help you are also strong enough to hurt you, and there is no way out of that dilemma.

Why Sex Is Not Easy to Discuss

SEX IS PERHAPS the most difficult subject in the world to write about — and therefore to discuss — because we cannot agree on what we mean by it. That is to say, we cannot even agree on what we may be disagreeing about.

What is proper and improper in the area of sex? What is natural? What is moral and what is merely conventional? What is relative to our time and culture, and what is permanently and universally right or wrong?

No one yet knows the answers to these questions, though many pretend they do — and would enforce their own answers upon the whole of the community, the country, or the world, if possible. There is far more authoritarianism in the realm of sex than in the field of politics.

I was leafing through Tennessee Williams's *Memoirs* the other evening, brushing up on the background of one of his plays I was about to review. In one chapter he lingers lovingly and long on his homoerotic experiences with male hustlers, which I found tedious and tawdry and totally purposeless.

Then he breaks off and mentions that someone had phoned him about seeing the film *Last Tango in Paris*. "I was reluctant to go," Williams tells us, "because I had heard that it was pornographic."

He is apparently unconscious of the vast irony here, because nine readers out of ten would have deemed the whole previous chapter to be pornographic. Yet in his eyes it was merely "amatory adventure." Obscenity or pornography seems to be best defined as "whatever goes beyond the perimeters I have set for myself." Or that my background has set for me.

You can be an absolutist about sex, or you can be a relativist. Whichever you choose, you end up in absurdity or self-contradiction. Hardly anyone would want to go back to the primness and hysterical repression of the Victorian age, yet how far can we drift from it? And hardly anyone would want to go all the way with the child-seducers, yet where is the place we can intelligently and conscientiously draw the line?

If you pretend to know, you are fooling yourself. Sex is still largely *terra incognita* to the human race. Each culture and epoch gropes its own way, has its own totems and taboos, and turns them into absolutes. I happen to believe there *are* absolutes in sexual relations, but I cannot say with any certainty what they may be.

The root of the trouble seems to be that we have not yet adequately defined what a person is or ought to be — if he ought to be anything. When we get our generic identity right, we may get our sexual roles right.

Are We Slaves to Technology?

ONE OF THE LESSONS we should have learned in the last few winters — and I wonder if we did — is that in many ways we are far less equipped to deal with crippling cold and snowstorms than our grandparents were.

The really odd, and ominous, thing about much technology is that the better it gets, the more vulnerable we become. In our electronic and mechanized society, an old-fashioned act of nature like a blizzard is apt to do more damage than was possible in Grandpa's time. We are simply not set up to handle it.

We can begin with something as trivial as our clothing, and work our way up from there. Grandpa took to long johns or red flannels, because his house was cold much of the time. Our underwear, if any, is a joke when the wind whistles through the windowpanes. Especially those new synthetic materials, which are clammy-cold to the touch at any time.

We don't have an extra load of coal in the basement, as he did, or a couple of cords of hardwood under the house. We don't have a horse and buggy or, better still, a sleigh. We don't have an old-fashioned wood-burning parlor stove that can heat up a house far better and faster than most duct systems.

If drifts block us off from the grocery store for a few days, we are in trouble. But Grandma did her own preserving and canning, and there was usually enough in the basement pantry to keep a family well nourished for a couple of weeks if need be. (In the smaller communities, you made bread at home and got your eggs from the chickens.)

On a larger scale, we are totally dependent upon the utility companies. If they go out, we go out. We have sacrificed our former autonomy for a great deal of comfort and convenience — but those are centralized now, and out of our individual hands. Our plumbing is connected to the city sewer system, our heating and cooking facilities may be piped in for thousands of miles, and we are impotent to jury-rig substitutes.

So far, we have observed mostly the benefits of our mushrooming technology; but there is a dark side to that moon, as cruel winters give us an ugly glimpse of.

Conservatives are fond of saying about government, "Any government big enough to give you what you want is big enough to take away what you've got," and the same homely axiom applies to our technology: Any system big enough to provide our comforts is big enough to forfeit them if it breaks down.

This is the part we haven't understood yet — just as, in a grimmer context, we fail to understand that the growth of nuclear weapons may make us "stronger," but at the same time far more vulnerable to global extinction.

If we could find a way of relieving boredom for the human race, it would reduce mischief and crime far more than a hundred schemes to promote morality and punish evil-doing.

*

Economists need to be reminded regularly that the idea of growth for its own sake is precisely the philosophy of the cancer cell.

Being Fruitful Beats Being Right

SOME YEARS AGO, I recall, a poll of more than one thousand scientists and educators in fifty countries voted for Isaac Newton as "the greatest scientist" of all time. He won easily over Aristotle, Euclid, Archimedes, Copernicus, Galileo, and a score of other celebrated innovators in every realm of scientific exploration.

What was most interesting about this selection was that Newton, who formulated the laws of gravity and motion, ultimately turned out to be only partly right. Newtonian physics has been left behind in the twentieth century, his concepts of "masses" and "forces" and "inertia" superseded by the discoveries of Einstein and Maxwell, Rutherford and Planck.

Today's picture of the cosmos is sharply different from the one presented by Newton. Our whole idea of space, of matter and movement, is in startling contrast to the mechanical universe he explicated. Yet most modern scientists elected him as the greatest — even greater than the men who subsequently proved him to be wrong.

It seems to me there is a lesson here for all laymen. What makes an innovator "great" is not the ultimate truth, or even the ultimate workability, of his theories. It is the new light he throws into dark corners, the originality and profundity with which he attacks ancient problems. And most of all, it is the kind of questions he asks, which bear fruit long after his death.

What makes a man great, in any field of exploration, is his *fruitfulness;* that is, the incentives he provides for further research in the field. The universe of Newton has collapsed; his fruitfulness has carried us to undreamed-of limits.

Lately, some newer gods have begun to topple — Darwin and Freud among them. The neo-Darwinians and the neo-Freudians are reshaping and revising their founders' theories, discarding some parts, adding to others. There is a tendency, along with this, to discount the monumental work these men performed.

But Freud knew and wrote that his theories would be changed, developed, and improved by others. His greatness lay not so much in his permanent rightness of view as in his courage, his tenacity, his willingness to ask foolish and embarrassing questions.

So, too, did Darwin recognize that his evolutionary theory was opening a science, not closing it. He may very well have been wrong in some aspects (as Freud was), but eventual triumph in the realm of knowledge depends less on providing the right answers than on opening doors.

The More We Know, the More We Can Ask

IN UNIMPORTANT MATTERS, the more we get to know, the less there is left to find out. When you finally learn how an auto engine works, you have exhausted its possibilities for use.

In important matters, however, the more we get to know, the more we learn how little we know. This is true both of something as large as the universe and of something as small as the nervous system of a bird.

We know tremendously more about the cosmos than we did a century ago, or even twenty-five years ago. We have charted distances and detected movements at magnitudes believed impossible by our forebears.

Yet if you followed, as I did, the conferences on astrophysics in Munich a few years ago, it is evident that the more we get to know, the less we understand. Rather than simplifying our conceptions of the universe, new discoveries seem to make it more complex, more puzzling, more contradictory and confusing.

At the same time, biologists studying the migration and navigation of birds have lately found evidence that makes these functions even harder to explain. The homing pigeon, which can sense the position of the moon and changes in the Earth's magnetic field, is more of a mystery now than it was when we ignorantly assumed a simpler theory.

The greatest secret, of course, which we have scarcely begun to crack, is that entity we loosely call "human nature." We have as yet pierced only an inch or two beneath the surface, with Freud's delving into the unconscious structure of the mind and the feelings.

Despite the tons of books and papers on the subject, we still know as little about the core of human behavior as ancient geologists did about the center of the Earth. We still do not know what social or economic system is best fitted to us, what sexual and familial relationships are the most workable and beneficial, and what religion or code of belief will spur us to practice the principles we preach.

Both the "macro" of the cosmos and the "micro" of the creature continue to elude us. The scientists and positivists of the last century were sure that investigation and experiment would eventually make these matters clear to us, in a simple and mechanistic way. But the more we study, the more complicated, obscure, and paradoxical they seem.

This is not to say that such research is not important. It is to suggest, along with Hamlet, that there are more things in heaven and Earth than are to be found in our philosophy. If there is such a thing as ultimate truth and it is findable, I suspect that its discovery will strike us as more of a miracle than any myth or metaphor to be found from the first book of Genesis to the last of Apocalypse.

The most worthwhile form of education is the kind that puts the educator inside you, as it were, so that the appetite for learning persists long after the external pressure for grades and degrees has vanished. Otherwise you are not educated; you are merely trained.

The Lord's Prayer Updated

A LORD'S PRAYER FOR OUR TIME:

> Our parent who is everywhere in the cosmos, we honor you today and every day; may what you want for us come to pass on this tiny Earth, obeying the laws of the universe; give us now our daily food, and forgive us for forgetting you, as we will try to forgive those who forget us. We respect your power, as we remain ignorant of your nature, but confident that your plan is loving and inclusive. Amen.

What does this do, what does this mean, what does this lose, what does this gain for us?

It loses the *father,* who should go. It loses the *hallowed,* which hardly anyone understands and has become just a mumbled catchword. It loses the *kingdom,* which is only a historical metaphor, since Biblical times knew no other form of government.

It loses *heaven,* which is so distorted in modern minds that all it means is white robes and harps and pearly gates and something "up there" in space, which only impedes religious understanding.

It loses *trespasses,* which can mean anything from dancing and playing cards to the deepest social injustices, and blurs the whole point of our forgetfulness of what is demanded of us as persons.

It loses *glory,* which is a poor translation of the numinous quality of our creator, and is now even spoken of as "glory in war," which is surely not what Jesus had in mind.

It gains a parent who is not sexist. It gains *honor,* which we can comprehend better than the archaic *hallowed.* It gains *the laws of the universe,* rather than an outmoded form of government. It gains a reminder of our ultimate ignorance, so that none of us may become spiritually proud and particularist in our form of worship.

It means that our respect and reverence are not enshrouded in obsolete terms that contradict what little we now know of the cosmos. It means that the prayer cannot be used as a chant to shut out nonbelievers, but — as Jesus intended it — is broad enough to embrace everyone who feels the same impulse, regardless of dogma or doctrine.

And we must remember that it was basically a Hebrew prayer that Jesus intoned, not a Christian one; he knew nothing of Christianity. This alone should humble us in our separatist professions of faith. For if there is one thing that Jesus preached, it is that the things uniting us are far greater and deeper than whatever separates us.

If this is not your basic conviction, whichever words you use, you are praying to the wrong Lord.

The Collaborative Nature of Knowledge

THE GOSPEL OF INDIVIDUALISM may spur some people to heightened efforts, but it is a dangerously two-edged sword if it cuts them off from a sense of collaboration and debt toward those around them and those who came before.

If we study the history of inventions — which seem so individual a matter — we soon learn that the man credited with a particular device was only one in a line of originators and developers. Even the steamboat, the telegraph, and the sewing machine were not solely devised by the men whose names are associated with them, and much less the auto, radio, and television, where each of many contributed a little.

Goethe, long considered one of the most original thinkers and writers of his time, once confided to Eckermann: "People are always talking about originality, but what do they mean? As soon as we are born, the world begins to work on us, and keeps on to the end. What can we call ours, except energy, strength, will? If I could give an account of what I owe to great predecessors and contemporaries, there would be but a small remainder."

More than a century later, the pre-eminent scientific mind of our time, Albert Einstein, said much the same in a public speech: "Many times a day I realize how much my own outer and inner life is built upon the labors of my fellow men, both living and dead, and how earnestly I must exert myself in order to give as much as I have received. My peace of mind is often troubled by the depressing sense that I have borrowed too heavily from the work of other men."

There is hardly an important discovery that has not been made at much the same time in different countries, by men working independently in body but sharing a common stock of knowledge inherited from the past. And in the arts, the greatest geniuses have learned and borrowed from one another — for greatness lies in *transformation* as much as creation of an idea, a technique, a motif. Mozart did absolutely nothing new; he simply built on Haydn to perfection in height and depth of feeling.

Thoreau seems to have been the most independent and individualistic of Americans, yet as Lewis Mumford has pointed out, "The more self-sufficient an individual seems to be, the more sure it is that, like Thoreau at Walden Pond, he carries a whole society in his bosom."

Both in a physical and in a spiritual sense, we are, as the Book says, "members of one another." This is all we have ever been or can ever be. Nothing is done alone, as it may seem to be, and individualism is a snare and a delusion if it moves us from the goodness of self-motivation to the evil of self-assertion and self-importance.

The layman supposes that scientific problems are solved in laboratories, when they are solved in human heads; all the apparatus does is confirm or reject what was in the head to start with.

The Meaning of "All Men Are Created Equal"

IT REALLY RILES ME when somebody who should know better perpetrates (and perpetuates) a gross illiteracy. Like the political writer for a big-city newspaper, who recently opined that our troubles began when the framers of the Declaration of Independence wrote that "all men are created equal."

If everyone is equal, he went on to ask, how can any candidate be more qualified to sit in the Oval Office than the fellow who delivers the mail or changes spark plugs?

Does he really think that Jefferson and his compatriots were so stupid or so ignorant that they believed all men are equal in intelligence, in skills, in judgment, in experience, in character, any more than they are all equal in height or weight or hairiness?

What the phrase means, of course, is that in this new republic all men were to become equal before the law and would be treated equally as human beings. That it is the social system, not the Creator, that makes aristocrats and peasants, landowners and serfs, who in every other country were treated quite differently by their governments according to their rank and wealth and background.

All men are equally entitled to life, liberty, and the pursuit of happiness. In this sense, and in this sense only, are they equal. In all other respects they may be as unequal as chalk and cheese.

In the Old World it was almost impossible to change your born status. In the new nation, such distinctions went by the board; what was important were precisely intelligence, skills, judgment, experience, and character. For it is only when all men are treated equally that these natural differences have a chance to sort themselves out, with the real cream rising to the top.

The old way protected the incompetent from their sins and errors. The Declaration offered everyone an equal shake, so that genuine superiorities could manifest themselves. The proper end of democracy is not to rotate offices between the mailman and the mechanic, but to give all a voice in choosing the most qualified, no matter what his origin or occupation.

If democracy is a failure — which remains to be seen — it is not because we have gone too far in egalitarianism, but because we have not pushed it far enough, so that every person gets a fair start. This is what the political writer should know. If he has no notion of what "all men are created equal" really means, what can his readers learn from him?

Who Will Speak for Mankind?

"HUMANITY" IS AN abstraction. *Mankind* is a word. It is hard to feel passion or loyalty for words and abstractions. Hard, but necessary.

Everyone gives his loyalty to something larger than himself — the father to his family, the communicant to his church, the citizen to his country, even the juvenile delinquent to his gang.

But who is loyal to humanity? Humanity has no flag, no song, no colors, no troops, no salutes, no rituals, no face nor body. It is a word, like *justice* or *peace* — cold, perfect, and dead.

Yet all the crises of our time can be rolled up into one crisis — that nobody speaks for mankind, even though mankind today is threatened with annihilation as a whole species.

Watching the United Nations proceedings in 1980, I thought of how fluently and ardently the partisans of each nation spoke up for their sides. But nobody spoke up for everybody, for that faceless, stateless man called humanity.

Almost every other species of animal is loyal to its own kind, and not merely to its own pack or flock or den. Only man and the shark regularly attack their own kind and represent their own worst enemy.

The other species are loyal by instinct, and we must learn to be loyal by intellect. But the time is running out for us as we learn that it is not enough to be a good parent, a good communicant, a good citizen. It is time to be a good man.

This means that no loyalty must override the survival of mankind, that in any conflict of interest between this and lesser loyalties, the lesser loyalties must be curtailed or surrendered. If no one speaks for humanity alive, what is there to prevent humanity's death?

Space and time have shrunk with terrifying compression in our age. Ancient boundaries are meaningless, except for practical purposes; old divisions of clan and tribe are sentimental remnants of the preatomic age; neither creed nor color nor place of origin is relevant to the realities of modern power to utterly seek and destroy.

Yet we walk around as if nothing had changed, mouthing the same old platitudes, waving the same frayed flags, imagining somehow that we are invulnerable to the tremors that are shaking the whole of the Earth. It is hard, almost impossible, to cherish mankind beyond all else. But nothing less, in our century, will suffice. This crisis in loyalty may well be the watershed of the human race, leading to survival or extinction.

The only value of misfortunes is to correct our faults; but if we blame others or fate for them, we lose even that value.

*

Most people are mirrors, merely reflecting the mood and emotions of the times; few are windows, bringing light to bear on the dark corners, where troubles fester; and the whole purpose of education is to turn mirrors into windows.

*

The first step taken toward the civilization of mankind was the concept of law; the second step was learning to get around it, by force or fraud.

III.
Of the Mind and Passions

Virtue Is a Habit

WE BECOME what we do. One of the greatest mistakes we can make — and some of the smartest men who ever lived have made it — is to assume that we can do false or discreditable things and still "deep inside us" remain good people, or the same people.

We become what we do. If we do it long enough, or often enough, the act or the habit transforms the person. It is much like that old temperance saying: "First the man drinks the drink; then the drink drinks the drink; then the drink drinks the man."

We can see it plainly in the case of something like alcohol, but it is harder to see in the weaknesses of the spirit: in habitual envy, or greed, or duplicity, or faithlessness. This is part of what Aristotle meant when he said a long time ago, "Virtue is a habit." A habit of the mind, of the will, of the heart.

But the inescapable fact that we become what we do has its positive side also. It is renewing and renourishing as well as punishing. We can also become what we were not by what we do, in an upward and growing way. This is psychologically true, or it would not be morally true.

Max Beerbohm, who is generally not thought of as an "uplifting" writer, has a superb short story that is little known, called "The Happy Hypocrite," that makes this point touchingly.

Its central character is a cynical Regency rake named Lord George Hell, a debaucher and despoiler of women who inexplicably falls in love with a saintly young lady. To gain her trust and affection, he conceals his corrupt and ravaged features with the mask of a saint.

She, being naive and vulnerable, takes the appearance for reality and falls in love with him. They marry. All goes well until a jealous siren out of his past enters the scene and threatens to expose him for the vile hypocrite he is unless he takes off the mask and exposes his true nature.

Having no choice, he pulls it off in front of his bride — and astonishingly enough, beneath the saint's mask is the face of the saintly person he has become by wearing it in love.

This Dorian Gray story in reverse, as it were, exemplifies the maxim that we become what we habitually do and what we habitually feel. In a sense, there is no "deep inner self" that remains inviolate despite our actions and relations with the world.

Personality is more like an onion: Peel off layer after layer, and when the final layer is peeled, there is no onion left. The core of us resides within the layers of love or hate, straightness or crookedness, in our daily dealings and in the habits we form and are formed by. Alas, it often takes a lifetime to learn this.

Meliorism and Pejorism

I'D LIKE TO INTRODUCE you to a couple of words you may not know. Not for the sake of increasing your vocabulary, but in order to understand points of view a little better.

These words are *meliorism* and *pejorism*. They are familiar to students of ethics and philosophy, but to hardly anyone else. They belong with the words *pessimism* and *optimism*, and complete the gamut.

It has always seemed odd to me that when we discuss temperature, we have *hot* and *cold* on either end, then we have *warm* as a modifier of *hot* and *cool* as a modifier of *cold,* with *tepid* right in the middle.

But when we discuss human temperament, or basic attitude, we are stuck with only the extreme words *optimism* and *pessimism.* This is a severe limitation, because most people are neither cockeyed optimists nor bleak pessimists, but range somewhere in between.

Meliorism is the opinion, or attitude, or temperament, toward life of one who does not see this as the best of all possible worlds but does feel that things are generally improving or will improve in the long run. You might call it optimism tempered by resignation.

Pejorism is the feeling that things are getting worse, but not inevitably or cataclysmically. It is pessimism tempered by hope.

Most of our opinions are based not on fact or on a realistic extrapolation of the present, but on our inborn temperament. What we think about the future is partly a matter of training and prejudice, but is basically determined, I believe, by our genetic disposition.

This disposition, I also believe, follows the familiar bell-shaped curve of statistics, in which the great majority of people are heaped near the middle, with fewer and fewer extending to the extremes. A radiant optimist is as rare as a despairing pessimist; most of us flutter much closer to the middle ranges of the temperamental scale.

When people ask me whether I am a pessimist or an optimist, I usually have no intelligible answer, because the question is too narrow. Actually, I am neither. In most matters, I am a meliorist — I think things are bad, and probably getting worse, but as an article of personal faith I expect them ultimately to get better.

I am neither hot nor cold but on the warm side; others may be on the cool side. What is important is recognizing the temperature of your temperament, and adequately discounting it when you appraise a situation or a future possibility. And we need more gradations of feeling than *optimism* or *pessimism* to do justice to our views.

True Love Provides a Quiet Anchorage

PERHAPS THE ONE THING young people yearn to know more than any other is how they can tell when they are really in love. It is so easy to see the counterfeits when one looks back later, and so difficult to discriminate when the blood is running high and the moon is full.

Why do so many people seem to pick disappointing lovers and inadequate mates, so deliberately, so stubbornly, so obviously doomed to failure? I think it is largely because romance, like liquor, feeds on its own delusion: The more we consume, the more intoxicated and distorted our judgment becomes.

One of the best and truest tests of a real affinity — though one not congenial to the youthful passions — may have been provided by St. Bernard of Clairvaux when he said, "We find rest in those we love, and we provide a resting place in ourselves for those who love us."

When the infatuation has run its course, as it always does, the feeling that remains must include *repose* at its core — a quality much neglected and overlooked in most romantic literature and lore. If a relationship requires constant stimulation — spats and tears and reconciliations — then it is doubtful that when the fever subsides there will be enough contentment simply to be with each other.

Marriage, of course, does not change people; it merely unmasks them. It strips off the strangeness, the glamour, the appearance of strength, the fascination of novelty, the treacherous sense of uniqueness that every couple feels at first.

Faced then with the thousand annoyances and perplexities of everyday connubiality, two persons have to rest easily within each other, or the ordinary abrasions of family life will begin to wear away the relationship, leaving little but wistfulness and puzzlement and, eventually, resentment that the reality is nothing like the romance.

A resting place is what we need as we grow older. A place not to gaze at each other in mutual fascination, but to look out at the world together from much the same angle of vision. A harbor, a shelter, a refuge, a source of nourishment and support. This is not what creates a marriage, but this is what sustains it.

There is little rest, little refuge, in the world at large — perhaps less so today than ever before, in the bustle of business and the clash of interests and the change of life-styles. Two people must make a space for themselves and a clearing around them, for retreat as much as for sociability. Conjugal love is a resting place or an empty form. But by the time we learn this lesson, it is often too late.

On Coping with Ambiguity

THERE ARE TWO FAMOUS DRAWINGS that Gestalt psychologists like to show to their students. One is a picture of an old, witchlike woman; the other is a picture of a rabbit. But if you look at the old woman long enough, she turns into a pretty young woman wearing a boa; and if you look at the rabbit long enough, it turns into a duck. And if you look even longer, they reverse themselves again.

The point is that you cannot see the old woman and the young girl at the same time, nor the rabbit and the duck. Each picture is a composite of both, depending upon your shifting range of vision.

What is the "reality" in these drawings? There is no single reality, for the drawings have been cunningly composed to show that the same composition looks quite different to us at different times, and when we see one formation we cannot see the other.

There is a deep lesson in this piece of Gestalt trickery. It indicates that what we call our view of life is a shifting image, not a continuous reality. Our lives are ambiguous patterns made up of different strands, and at different times we choose one pattern to look at rather than another — but neither is more real than the other.

A great deal of people's anxiety is expended on trying to reconcile these two pictures, or trying to decide which one is real. Most of us are extremely uncomfortable with ambiguity, and want to resolve it one way or the other.

But maintaining one's sanity and sense of balance depends in large part upon the acceptance of ambiguity, in recognizing that this is part of the human condition. Except for a few extreme lucky or unlucky cases, no one's life situation is so good that he sees the pretty girl all the time or so bad that he views the witch all the time.

In the most common instance, that of marriage, many couples are perplexed and churned up when the picture turns into its opposite. On Monday, everything seems fine, or at least decently tolerable; on Friday, it seems bleak. Which is the true picture, the rabbit or the duck?

You can go crazy trying to decide, until you realize that (again, excepting the rare extremes) every marriage is part rabbit and part duck. So, with few exceptions, is every job. And parenthood, of course, is a perpetual oscillation between satisfaction and disappointment.

Life, in the main, is not either-or, but both. Reality is not one picture, but two. We cannot see them together, but they are both there. Accepting this fact, and holding them in equilibrium, is more than half the art of coping with ambiguity.

The stress in living comes from the fact that we have to conduct ourselves every day as if we were omnipotent and indestructible, and yet at the same time we must leave a margin for awareness and acceptance of our frailty and contingency.

Why Parents Aren't Rational about Kids

ARE PARENTS RATIONAL about their children? No. Parents aren't rational because love isn't rational. Young people can recognize this about romantic love, but they find it hard to accept the same fierce element in parental affection.

What brings this up was my eldest daughter's question the other day. "Let me ask you something, Dad," she began, in a tone of patiently controlled exasperation that every experienced parent is familiar with.

"I sailed around the Mediterranean in a schooner when I was seventeen," she recited slowly and carefully. "I hiked through the Pyrenees from Spain to Paris. I've done rock climbing and deep-sea diving and slept in rain forests in the jungle of Indonesia. Right?"

"Right," I said, shivering at this recital as a man would who gets hysterical while taking a shower if a bit of soap stings his eye. "So what?"

"So this," she went on. "When I'm home and I'm going to the corner drugstore to pick up some shampoo, why do you always tell me to be careful how I cross the street?"

There is no satisfactory answer a parent can give to this.

All I could mumble in response was that when I was a man of fifty, my mother would lean out of the window when I left and remind me not to drive too fast. If I were eighty and she were still alive, I would be getting the same admonition. No matter the age, a child is a child.

There is another factor, too, that children find it hard to understand. When they are far away, there is nothing we can do about their safety or welfare. They are in the hands of the gods. Parents try not to think about it, hoping that if they blot the children out, the fateful call or cable will never come.

But when the children are close by again, the old protective urge quickly reasserts itself, and it matters not how far they have been or how long gone, or what experiences they have endured, or even how well they have demonstrated their survival ability.

Most accidents, after all, happen around the corner, not in the rain forest. Man is a more dangerous foe to man than the elements of nature or animals in the wild. The most instinctive act of nearly every creature is to protect its young, and with humans this response persists for a lifetime.

In the parent's mind, a child grows but does not age. Rational? No. But if we were wholly rational, would we want children at all?

Defective Oysters Produce the Pearls

EVERYONE KNOWS that the pearl we find in the oyster is actually an ulcer — it is mostly calcium carbonate caused by irritation within that strange creature. Without the irritation, no pearl.

What is not as commonly known is the fact that pearls are far more likely to be found in those shells that are irregular in shape or stunted in growth, which bear excrescences or are honeycombed with boring parasites.

It is thus the oyster that is "defective" — both internally and externally — that provides the pearl. The normal oyster simply goes about its business of doing nothing in particular except surviving.

I do not want to press the analogy too far, but we should at least recognize that people are somewhat like oysters in this respect. It is the abnormal ones who make most of the contributions, as odd or unlovely as they may seem to us on the surface.

We are proud of our creators and innovators, but at the same time we generally expect them to be more or less like everyone else, and often resent it when they are not. Yet it is probably a kind of "irritation" within them that causes them to be different from the rest of us, and it may well be the irritation that produces the pearl.

We do know that most highly creative persons begin showing signs of "difference" at an early age, and that precocity in the arts and sciences is the rule more than the exception. Some are so detached from the world that they almost appear to be retarded, like young Thomas Aquinas or Einstein or, on a somewhat lower level, Edison the boy.

It may be no accident, for instance, that the founders of the three great religions were reported to "bear excrescences" like the pearl-producing oyster: Moses stuttered badly, and both St. Paul and Mohammed are reputed to have been victims of epileptic fits. Possibly without these impediments they would not have found their visionary leadership.

The two looming figures in science, Newton and Darwin, were strange ducks, indeed: The first was born posthumously and prematurely, left with his grandparents, taken out of school early to become an inept farm boy; the second suffered one mysterious ailment after another for much of his adult life and was always in pain, to his dying day.

The history of the arts, of course, is even more replete with such irregularities and abnormalities. Nobody knows why; even Freud was modest enough to halt at the threshold of creativity, admitting that its secret is beyond the bounds of psychoanalysis. If the creators and innovators and visionaries were more like the rest of us, there would have been no first man to open up the stunted oyster and find the first pearl.

A person's defect may also serve as a source of strength for the total personality, just as metallurgists deliberately build defects into their crystals to improve their strength. (Indeed, by sticking defects into perfect crystals, solid-state physics has given us the semiconductor, which revolutionized modern technology.)

Whatever Your Job, Love It or Leave It

I HAD JUST RETURNED HOME from a lecture tour, tired and not feeling very well, and here I was tapping away at my typewriter, sipping a cup of hot tea and humming to myself.

The lady I live with said, "If you don't feel so good, why don't you go up to bed?" and I replied, quite truthfully, "It makes me feel better to sit here working."

This is the beauty of doing work you enjoy, so that while it is a chore in one respect, it is a pleasure in another. And I earnestly urge all young people contemplating their careers to keep in mind that nothing in work is finally rewarding unless it is work you would be willing to do for nothing if you could afford to.

This is the ultimate test for lifelong congeniality in a career, of no matter what sort. Money is not the most important thing; fame is fleeting and uncertain; even status is irksome and uncomforting after a time. All that remains at the end is satisfaction — and occasionally delight — in the performance itself.

Do not do what does not please you; it does not pay, no matter how beguiling the material rewards may seem to be. The pot of gold that appears to be gleaming at the end of the rainbow is less gratifying than the rainbow itself.

The best recipe for a long and happy life is to be able to approach each new morning with anticipation and zest for the job, whatever it may be. This does not mean, of course, that we are not sometimes disgruntled or frustrated or even bored; but over the long haul these disaffecting moments are washed away by the tide of contentment, the swell of gratification at doing well what one does best.

If you are engaged in work you like, even the drudgery and tedium involved in it seem worthwhile. The talented wood-carver who works patiently for hours and whistles at his work is getting more out of life — and of himself — than the affluent stockbroker who needs three martinis to get through the afternoon.

The people I have known who seem to rest most easily within themselves are those who have found, by design or lucky accident, the niche made just for them, in whatever field it may be, lofty or humble, so long as it gives them a sense of being needed, of being purposeful, and of doing it a little better than most others can.

And those who seemed most unhappy, whatever their degree of external success, were the ones to whom the job was a *means*, not an end, a way of earning a living rather than a way of living. All they can look forward to is retirement, as boring, in a different way, as their jobs are. When the heart goes, the hands should still be tapping away happily.

On the Uses of Intellect

ORDINARY PEOPLE underestimate the importance of the mind; extraordinary people, on the other hand, overestimate the importance of the mind. Few are able to put intelligence in its proper perspective.

I thought of this while browsing through the current issue of the *Mensa Bulletin,* a monthly put out by the Mensa Society, composed of high-IQ people; one has to pass a rigorous test for admission. The society is devoted to "extolling the human mind and fostering human intelligence" by research and activity around the world.

What is interesting to me is the ordinariness of the thinking revealed in the society's magazine. Apart from the obvious fact that the contributors score well on IQ tests, there is little in the contents to indicate exceptional powers of mind or thought.

I say this not to put down the Mensa members, but simply to point out that while intelligence may be a *necessary* condition, it is by no means a *sufficient* one to help unravel the perennial problems that afflict the human species.

Something more than mind is needed, and that something more has little to do with the intellectual level. It is how the mind is *used,* in conjunction with other parts of the personality, that makes the difference.

Most people use their minds, no matter how good, to confirm and reinforce their emotional defenses and their social prejudices. Rather than a probe to reach out to the unknown, the mind is used as a pike to repel the strange or the threatening or even the uncomfortable. The so-called best minds in any profession have generally rejected and condemned the innovators in their own field.

Thus the letters and articles and other contributions in the *Mensa Bulletin,* while perhaps more literate than most, betray the same emotional biases and cultural conditioning one might find in any magazine of general circulation, and no more originality of thought or evidence of creativity in conception.

"Extolling the human mind" is as futile and as fatuous as extolling the human body; both are simply tools and may be used gloriously or perverted to any purpose. The smartest people are not the best people, by any means, nor even the wisest, in many important respects.

I do not mean to feed the flames of anti-intellectualism, which already leap too high in this country. But while the intellect is a thing to be respected and cultivated, it is not a shrine to worship at. The research we most need is to find out why so many rich minds employ these assets in the service of their emotional defects.

Freud's prescription for personal happiness as consisting of work and love must be taken with the proviso that the work has to be loved, and the love has to be worked at.

Sexual Freedom and Personal Development

EVERY GENERATION, more or less, draws its own line in matters of morals and sexuality. Most of us will agree that the Victorians drew theirs too close to repression for a healthy release of the animal spirit. But have we today drawn our own too far from the human spirit?

Not all repression is bad; Freud himself would be the last to deny this, as a highly moral man by contemporary standards. He was by no means a "pansexualist," believing that anything goes in private. Sexuality has a wider range than the Victorians admitted, but not an unlimited one, as so many moderns seem to think.

The prevailing school of thought, at least among young people and older ones who seek to recapture their youth, holds that sex is an adventure, an experience, an activity, an expression, a part of the full personality — and therefore whatever we care to do, with no rights or wrongs, is simply "our thing."

This may be a normal and expected reaction to the puritan and Pecksniffian past; but, as in most cases, it is an overreaction, with the pendulum now swinging too far to the other extreme. The Victorians denied the legitimate needs of the body; the moderns deny or ignore the legitimate claims of the mind, the spirit, and the social self.

Parts of the personality have to be suppressed: All of us, within ourselves, have the potentialities for murder, for theft, for lying, for betrayal and exploitation of others. It is good to know this, for it keeps us from self-righteousness; but we learn it by reflecting upon these matters, not by exercising them, by experience or expression.

Sex is a relationship and not merely an activity; if we mature, it becomes less satisfying as an activity in itself and more gratifying as a relationship. It teaches us more about ourselves and our partners than we knew before and helps to integrate the whole personality. It is, at best, healing as much as vivifying.

It has an essential and important place in the hierarchy of human values; but it does not transcend all values, as hedonists seem to think. Like all our appetites — for food, or learning, or honor — its proper end is the development of the total person. Thus it is a discipline as much as a recreation — a joyous discipline, but not a riotous one.

Sexuality remains one of the aspects of the human creature we still do not fully understand in all its complexity, and it is foolish to pretend otherwise. All we can know with some certainty is that, just as our forebears erred in marking it off as an area of shameful darkness, we err in celebrating it as the apex of freedom.

Sexual Equality Begins in the Nursery

MOST OF WESTERN SOCIETY is so arranged that men — or parts of men — can stay little boys for a lifetime, while women have to stop being little girls at one time or another. Certainly nothing in women remains as girlish as men's love of sports and games remains boyish.

Our society provides ongoing outlets for men to indulge in their boyhood fantasies of superior strength and cunning and dexterity, so that oldsters in their seventies are still puttering around the gold courses, cackling at their puny victories and resolving to avenge their defeats the next time out.

Women, on the other hand, are tacitly discouraged from following similar enterprises and are expected to settle down to the realistic and maturing business of breeding and rearing children and taking care of the needs of their menfolk. A man who enjoys the sportive scene is convivial; a woman is merely flighty.

I suspect that the damming up of girlhood fantasies and the expectations of greater sobriety and stability may be responsible for what we call the more romantic attitude of women as they slope into middle age. Certainly the books men and women read and the films they are attracted to differ widely in their appeal.

Men, obviously, prefer external action; women concentrate on inner feelings.

What may turn out to be most important in the long run about women's emancipation is not so much the social and economic opportunities as the early recognition that the female needs to be as active and physical and competitive as the male does. In the past, girls were given dolls and boys baseballs; I think that both need both — the young male needs to be permitted more tenderness, and the young female more toughness.

Much of the wistful romanticism to be found in older women is a displacement of the competitive instinct that society has denied them in other areas. "Accomplishment" for a woman has meant largely a victory in the area of sex relations, whatever her other pluses or minuses as a person. The one thing she can do better is get a better man; and if she cannot get him, she will fantasize him in film and novel and daydream.

Men, because their lives remain challenging and competitive, both at work and in play, shed their early romanticism toward their wives and then in middle age try to revive it — but with a younger woman, because they begin to resent the very maternalism they depend on in their own wives.

History has painfully emphasized the differences between the sexes; it is more than time for the basic similarities to be expressed and encouraged. An enduring marriage is based on emotional equality in the same way that a stable government is based on political equality. And equality begins in the nursery, or it never takes root.

One wonders how many marriages dissolve just because one of the parties belatedly discovers that the other isn't a "nice person" simply on human terms, which has little to do with the marital relationship as such.

Intelligence Is No Guarantee of Compassion

EVEN IF THE SOCIOBIOLOGY experts are right and genetics is the basis of human intelligence, I have never understood what compelling reason would prompt us to breed people for the quality of intelligence as such. There seems to be no persuasive evidence that intelligence is the most important or the most beneficial attribute of mankind.

In fact, the more intelligent a person is, the more harm he can do, if his character and feelings are not commensurate with his mental powers. Fools may do private harm to themselves and a few around them, but it is the clever men with crooked principles who create most of the mischief in the big world.

Intelligence is a tool, not a product; in itself it is neutral in character. Good and bad men have it in equal amounts, but most bad men have power drives, while good men do not, and so the former tend to dominate in the field of action. A Lincoln is thus a rarity among Presidents, and a Lee among generals.

Even in the academic area, where intelligence plays such a preponderant part, the men who become deans and administrators and heads of colleges have used their brains for ambitious purposes more than for the acquisition of objective knowledge; they become politicians of a sort, and like all politicians soon begin to place their reputation and influence above that of the community they are supposed to serve. Not all, of course, but many, if not most.

Unfortunately for the human race, the most intelligent people are not necessarily the best people in any field. Character seems to be a quality that is independent of mind, and geniuses have not been notable for their generosity, their sweetness, their self-sacrifice, or their public leadership. Nor is there any record that smart men make better husbands or fathers or friends than their duller brethren.

I have no wish to disvalue intelligence; obviously it is, in itself, as much a virtue as physical skill or moral probity, and as much to be desired. But to bend genetics to the purpose of creating a race of more intelligent beings is as one-sided as trying to produce people with large muscles. A muscular man can be a hero or a bully; nothing in the build predisposes him to the one any more than to the other.

What we want in people, to make a better world, is more compassion, a keener sense of justice, a willingness to subordinate one's ego to the common good, a lively sense of humor, and vitality. These are moral and temperamental qualities, and there is no known way to produce such a felicitous combination in the test tube or through the DNA chain. We can, by selective breeding, raise intelligence, but we have no idea how to use biological processes to make people who are kinder to one another.

When the sociobiologists find a sure-fire formula for this, I will sit up and take notice. Until then, we can't do very well until our brains catch up with the decency to be found even in the dumb.

The Danger of Positive Thinking

A READER IN VANCOUVER wants to know why I have from time to time derided or made fun of the "inspirational" approach to life, as exemplified by Norman Vincent Peale and Clement Stone, that apostle of the positive mental attitude.

"What is wrong with being positive and optimistic?" he asks. "Isn't it better than being negative and pessimistic? Aren't the people who get things done the ones who believe that they *can* be done?"

There are at least two fallacies in his assumptions. Let me deal with the second one first — namely, that "getting things done" is the most important thing.

What is important is the thing being done. Caesar got things done; Napoleon got things done; Hitler got things done. But they were mostly things that should not have been done, and the world would have been far better off if such men had been less positive, less confident, less aggressive, less single-minded in their pursuit.

If an object is bad, the more enthusiastically you go after it, the worse you become and the more harm you do. Positiveness is a virtue only if your *goal* is positive; unfortunately, most people who are unstoppable in their drives toward power, money, fame, success, or glory are running in the wrong direction.

Second, it is by no means always better to be optimistic than pessimistic; best of all is to be realistic, which means that you know when optimism is the better policy and when pessimism is. I have mentioned before the finest example I know, which is playing a hand of bridge.

The most important psychological factor separating the champions from the also-rans in bridge (or any comparable game, for that matter) is that the champions know exactly which attitude pays off when. The duffers do not — which helps keep them duffers.

In bridge, you are optimistic, wildly optimistic, when things look bad. You hope and pray for luck, for a specific distribution of cards that alone will help you bring home your contract, and you play for the cards to be placed that way even if the odds are a hundred to one against you.

On the other hand, when things look good, when you seem to be in an ironclad contract, then you take the gloomiest view and try to anticipate the worst possible breaks in distribution. The optimist will usually go down in such a hand; the pessimist will not.

Most players, of course, are exactly the opposite: despairing when a hand looks bad and carelessly jubilant when it looks good. Optimism and pessimism are neutral qualities; each is necessary in its proper place. Wisdom consists in learning that place, not in repeating the stale slogans and magic incantations of the Happiness Boys.

Mining for Ideas

YOU HAVE TO DRILL through mud and water to get oil; you have to sift through sand and silt to get gold; you have to chop and hack through stone to get diamonds. So why do so many people feel that the treasure of ideas should come to them with little or no effort?

We recognize that in the physical world you get nothing for nothing: no labor, no fruits; no sawing, no woodpile. Even the simplest crop calls for coping with bugs and mold. Yet in the world of ideas we expect it all to be laid out on a platter, cut up, prechewed, and even predigested if that were possible.

The common notion, particularly in our country, that education ought to be painless does not apply to any other area. The athlete sweats and strains, exercises and conditions himself to obtain mastery over his chosen field; the auto mechanic goes back to technical school to acquaint himself with the new electronic gadgetry; the business executive toils amid the increasing complexity of global competition.

Only when it comes to the great thinkers and writers, the theorists of ideas, the scholars and sages, do we complain of difficulty, as though the hardest thoughts should be the simplest and clearest to express, while everything else in the world is getting more complicated.

As a random example, Nietzsche was and remains one of the most rewarding writers and thinkers who ever lived — but you have to learn how to read him, just as you have to learn to drill for oil or pan for gold or dig for diamonds. And like these, there is much silt and mud and rock in his works that must be discarded in the process.

No man has all the truth by the tail. No thinker is free of error, bias, contradiction, or even absurdity. When you have great depth, as he has, there is also murkiness; you cannot descend a mine and find sunlight. You have to come equipped with a lamp you have brought yourself and be prepared to sweat a little for your reward.

Whatever else educating ourselves may be, it cannot be easy. It cannot be painless. It cannot be spoonfeeding. But it can be a delight, as any difficult challenge can be a delight if we look upon it as an adventure, not an inconvenience or a burden.

This is no doubt why Whitehead, one of the seminal thinkers of our time, entitled an early book *Adventures in Ideas*. An adventure without travail and exertion is as empty as a romance by mail, and as profitless. Why is education the only activity we are willing to spend so much on and resigned to getting so little in return from? No rigger, no miner, no farmer would be stupid enough to make such a bad bargain.

A Great Teacher Has Many Descendants

A RECENT OBITUARY of a University of Chicago professor ended with the bleak sentence: "He left no survivors." A former student of his called me sometime afterward to protest that this was not the case.

The professor, a lifelong bachelor, died without next of kin. But, as his student pointed out, he left dozens and perhaps hundreds of "survivors" all over the country and the world.

His survivors were his former students, whose thoughts, feelings, and sometimes characters were shaped by this man's influence. A great teacher, even if he writes not a word, may be survived by generations, even centuries. This is his ultimate reward, and his glory.

Dr. Arnold, the headmaster who made Rugby the model of an English public school, exercised an influence that persists down to this day. In our own time, Robert Hutchins, who died in 1977, has survivors in every college and university in the country. His educational ideas, never a success in his own institution, flourish as much among the living legions as they lie within his books and papers.

Socrates, like Jesus, wrote not a word during his lifetime. Yet his disciples, Plato and Xenophon, keep his nobility of thought eternally fresh. He acquires new students every year.

In some ways, however, the power of a teacher's personality is even more decisive and permanent than the ideas he inseminates in his pupils. In the fundamental task of living, we learn far more by example than by abstract mental processes. It is the "presentation of self" in a good teacher that makes the lasting impression.

This may have been in part what Einstein meant when he defined education as "what is left after you have forgotten everything you learned in school." What is left is the indelible memory of the teacher's moral courage, his respect for reason, his desire to share, his eagerness to learn from his pupils as much as he is teaching.

There are not many teachers of this sort, not enough by any means; but excellence is rare in every field, which is why it must be so cherished and encouraged and paid honor to long after its temporal life.

Of course that professor had survivors, not in the narrow legal sense, but in the broader sense of those who drew and still draw nourishment from remembrance. Perhaps these are the only true and meaningful survivors — not the widow or the children or the relatives, but those passing strangers who, for a crucial time in their lives, learned how to transcend themselves and partake of the sweet strength of character that still makes Socrates more alive than most of us.

Classes ought to be graded on the performances of their weakest members, so that learning would become a cooperative rather than a competitive process, as it is in schools today. (Cheating, for one thing, would be automatically eliminated by this system.)

Desired Differences Foster a Relationship

I WAS LUNCHING with a friend and the name of a mutual acquaintance came up. My friend shook his head and said, "I don't know how he puts up with her — if I had a wife that aggressive, I'd shoot her."

What my friend ignored is the obvious fact that this man adores his wife. And one reason he adores her is precisely her aggressiveness. He finds it a desirable trait and is inordinately proud of her for it.

Attractions between two persons may be chemical or whatever, but *lasting* attractions, I think, depend upon a particular combination of reciprocal feelings that are not as common as we generally suppose.

Persons who are much the same may have a narcissistic relationship, in that each sees himself or herself reflected in the other; but these eventually become boring, and one or the other starts seeking variety.

Persons who seem to be quite different may also be initially attracted to each other, but in most cases the differences become more abrasive and the pair grow further apart in their sympathies.

The right formula, it seems to me, is one that combines *difference* with *desirability*. That is, where the different traits are admired, not resented, and where each partner gets support and grows by learning from the other's differences.

One solid fact that stands out in a marriage, or any similar relationship, is that you cannot change the "undesirable" traits of a partner. In most marriages, a sensible mate ignores them where he or she can and tries to live with them.

In easy or lasting relationships, however, these differences between temperaments and personalities are viewed by each partner as virtues. The husband who admires his aggressive wife finds that she expresses something that is repressed in his own personality; she is acting out for him a role he finds difficult, supplying a deficiency in himself.

It has been often noted that couples get to be more like each other as time goes by; this is because each has grown and changed and learned something from the other's differences. In poor marriages, they will continue bickering about their differences to their grave, if they stay together that long.

The ancient adage that "opposites attract" is, like so many ancient adages, only an important half-truth. To make the attraction permanent, the opposite trait or temperament must be an element we find missing in ourselves, and one we would like to acquire. Our mutual acquaintance doesn't see his wife as aggressive, but as admirably independent.

On Growing Older Gracefully

SOME PEOPLE NEVER grow up, and some people never grow old. But they are not the same people, though it may sound like it.

Never to grow up is childish; it is to remain boyish or girlish throughout life, not to know maturity or mellowness. Never to grow old is the whole point of growing up — to keep the senses alert and the spirit alive as long as the biological machinery holds out.

The paradox is that you cannot remain young until you have matured. It is a process from simplicity through complexity and back to simplicity again — but the simplicity of age is far different from the simplicity of childhood. It knows what is not worth having or doing.

The world is full of aging boys and girls who turn rotten before they turn ripe. They may pride themselves on looking and acting "young," but their looks and their acts are merely a simulacrum of youth. They may dress young and talk young, but it is all mimicry and fools no one except themselves.

Those who never grow old may dress like Granny and carry a cane — such things don't matter — but they retain a spirit of wonder and delight, they remain open to the world, they can accept what is new and different without repudiating what is old and dear.

Young people have a keen nose for this distinction. They laugh at older people who try to imitate youthful dress and speech and attitudes, but they enjoy the company of older people who remain young inside, where it counts — who combine a solid respect for the values of the past with a zestful appreciation of the way the world has changed.

Socrates said that life is an exercise in learning how to die. He meant this not in any morbid or fateful sense, but simply in the sense that we must bloom before we wither, and to remain a bud is to thwart the whole purpose of living. The acorn that never becomes an oak tree has failed to fulfill its mission.

No one can capture and hold youth by refusing to acknowledge the fact of aging, by using artifice and agitated mimicry, by grasping for the *dernier cri* — the latest thing or the newest craze. A sixty-year-old man with a shirt unbuttoned to his navel and a medallion dangling on the chest still looks like exactly what he is: a desperate man.

This is a sign of not growing up rather than of not growing old. It is reaching back rather than reaching out. It is trying to become what you are not rather than trying to become what you should be — an aging person who is ageless within, who has conquered time not by resisting it but by subduing it to the spirit of acceptance without surrender.

The whole point of the Socratic injunction to "know thyself" is then to be able to forget yourself and get on with the business of living; it is not so much a prescription for finding oneself as a recipe for losing oneself in something larger.

What Human Quality Do You Admire Even If You Lack It Yourself?

COLLEGE STUDENTS ASK all kinds of questions, pertinent and impertinent, when they get a visiting speaker in a bull session. Most of the questions are predictable and banal. Once in a while you are hit with a real zinger that you have never answered before, or even thought about much.

Recently a student pierced my professional armor with this query: "What quality in other people do you admire most that you lack in yourself?" I had to ponder that one to come up with a deep and honest answer, which is the only kind that youngsters recognize and accept.

"There are many qualities I admire that I lack," I said reflectively, "but I think the one that I most lack and would like to possess is the art of lending dignity to people's shortcomings."

The men and women I have most admired seem able to do this naturally. They are protective and supportive of other people's weaknesses, whereas I tend to be critical and impatient with them. They make people feel better about themselves, and when you feel better, you do better.

I am aware of this, intellectually and philosophically. Yet it has been an uphill battle all my life to put this knowledge into practice. People who diddle and dawdle, who are vague or dilatory or indecisive or befuddled or in any way less competent than I, usually get short shrift at my hands.

More than that, I have secretly felt that such people should be reprimanded, if not punished, for these deficiencies, stripping away whatever dignity they still possess. Of course, this is the most counterproductive thing you can do, as silly as bawling out your partner at the bridge table, which only succeeds in making him or her play worse.

This tendency to expose or deprecate the weak and limited goes against everything I believe — my politics, my ethics, and my psychological understanding. Yet so strong is one's inborn temperament plus conditioning that I have had to resist it as resolutely as an ex-boozer shuns the bottle.

And I look up enviously at those more gracious personalities who seem so easily able to accept shortcomings they do not possess. For they do even more — by conferring dignity, they raise the other person's self-esteem, which is always the fulcrum for improved conduct, as the best teachers have quickly found out.

Persons who consider themselves strong and competent must learn that real strength embraces a spirit of generosity in making judgments about others. When this is lacking, possibly the weaknesses in others are too threatening to the spurious strength that is devoid of charity and must precariously maintain itself only by a show of superiority.

It's Not So Much What You've Got as What You Do with It

A VERY RICH YOUNG MAN I was lunching with in Detroit not long ago said to me, "I'd never confess this publicly, but I don't mind telling you that the money I've inherited has proved as much a burden as a blessing — and maybe more of a burden."

"You mean all the legal and financial problems it entails?" I asked.

"No, not that," he replied. "I am speaking psychologically. You see, like the beautiful girl who never knows if men want her for her looks alone or if she is valued as a person, I don't know what I would be or do if I didn't have all this money."

"What do you think?" I inquired. "How do you view yourself?"

"Well," he answered, "sometimes I think I would have done

well on my own, and sometimes I feel that without this fortune behind me I would just be another person struggling to get along. It seems simply a matter of luck, which I don't deserve more than anyone else."

"Everything starts with luck," I said. "Yours just happens to be a certain kind. The beautiful girl is lucky in her looks. The bright man is lucky in his brains. The star athlete is lucky in his body. And all of us are lucky to have been born where we were and to be living here, instead of in a rice paddy in China or a hut in Africa."

Warming to my subject, I went on: "Nobody has a right to take credit for what he or she was born with — only for what they have done with it. That's why the person who is proud of his ancestry seems so ridiculous: He did nothing to earn it, and in fact must justify it by his own efforts.

"Some people are born with minimal talents and make absolutely the most of them. Others are born with large native endowments and just fritter them away. It is what you *do* with the gifts at your disposal that makes all the difference. The most perfectly coordinated athlete in the world would be a bust without courage, determination, and patience.

"What will determine your own sense of worth is how you *use* your money. To what purpose you put it will decide if you deserve your luck. You can use it to amass more, to indulge your fancies, to exercise power; or you can use it creatively and imaginatively, so that it becomes a tool for enhancing not only your life but many lives to come.

"It's foolish to be ashamed or embarrassed at any gift life has handed you — the only shame is to make the least of it, to turn a lucky chance into a source of disappointment or sorrow. The only woman buried in Westminster Abbey, after all, is one who used her money for the ultimate benefit of everyone around her."

I let my young friend pick up the check, just as a start.

On Celebrities: One Eye Pays Tribute, the Other Seeks Flaws

"WHAT IS HE REALLY LIKE?" is the first question someone asks you after you have met a celebrity or a famous personality. What they want to know, of course, is whether the private person conforms to the public image.

As a newspaperman who has met many such people over the years, I have been asked this question often, not least of all by members of my own family. And whatever answer I give is less important, psychologically, than their own expectations — for at the same time they want to believe and not to believe.

That is, when we observe someone who seems larger than life — more heroic, more gifted, more beautiful, more virtuous, or what have you — a part of us would like to be assured that he or she is really this way in person; yet another part of us wants to be informed that he or she is nothing at all like the public personality.

We cannot understand why heroes so easily fall out of favor, or why stars so quickly lose their luminosity, until we recognize that the public is always ambivalent toward leaders of any kind. It has a childlike yearning to believe that they are what they seem to be, but it also would like to find out that they have feet of clay.

It is much like the attitude of an audience watching a tightrope performer. Consciously and audibly, they are cheering him on to make it to the other side; unconsciously and silently, they are anticipating the fall, which will prove to them that he is really no better than they are. What we loosely call the thrill in such an event consists of the psychological tension between our opposite desires.

All performers are only too aware of this fierce contradiction; this is why Oscar Hammerstein, the producer, referred to an opening-night audience as "the two-headed monster." They have come to applaud a success, but, equally, to trample upon a failure. To a performer, the audience is an enemy — an enemy that must be won over at all costs. An actor's expression of triumph is, "I murdered them tonight."

So, in the same way, the public regards its current luminaries with a double vision: one eye paying tribute, the other seeking flaws and deficiencies. Hardly anything exemplifies the Biblical notion of original sin more than the homage we pay to superiority or greatness, while at the same time regarding it with suspicion and resentment.

When I have answered the question, "What is he really like?" in the affirmative, assuring the questioner that the celebrity is at one with his public image, there is relief — but there is also disappointment. We are such disjointed creatures ourselves that we feel undone by the vision of greatness and betrayed by the knowledge of frailty.

Children Are People, Not Parental Ornaments

I'M GOING TO DO A LITTLE BRAGGING today, but only by way of example, out of gratitude and not out of pride.

Many, if not most, parents, as their children go through high school and into college, become terribly competitive on their children's behalf. By this I mean that they get so keenly concerned about how well their children are *doing*.

They will tell you at dinner parties that this child got into such-and-such a college, that this one is working on a master's, that another is making a certain team or winning a scholarship.

Some of these, of course, are legitimate things for parents to be proud of. But there is all this emphasis on *doing*, and so little said about *being*.

What is the child who is getting into these schools and making these grades and receiving these honors like? As a person, as a family member, as a human being? — not as an achievement machine reflecting on the parents' greater glory.

I more than suspect that children (especially of upwardly mobile middle-class families) feel these parental pressures intensely, and in time many come to resent them. A child should not be a surrogate for a parent's own frustrated wishes or a substitute for worldly disappointments and vexations.

Let me tell you what pleased me most recently, and perhaps it will give a clearer idea of what I mean. Not long ago, my eighteen-year-old daughter, away at college, telephoned home and learned that her younger brother and sister were about to start a ten-day school vacation and had made no plans.

She urged us to send them to visit with her for a week, promising to take them skiing and backpacking to see the sights generally near her campus. They were both thrilled, of course, and we sent them off in a fine tizzy of anticipation.

Now, how many eighteen-year-old girls, involved in their own affairs at a new school, would volunteer to take a fifteen-year-old kid brother and a thirteen-year-old kid sister for a week of frolicking and sightseeing? And that is what I am bragging about — not the grades or the honors or the medals, but the reaching-outwardness, the family feeling, the warmth and openness and acceptance so often missing between one age bracket and another in the same family.

What a youngster *achieves* may or may not be important, now or for the future; but what a youngster *is,* how he or she relates to family and friends and the world at large, is a permanent index of character and worth. And this is what we should be grateful for when we see it in our children — more than all the outward marks of "success" in the classroom or the stadium. And this is the way they want us to regard them, as people, not as producers, promoters, performers, or parental ornaments.

The most "deprived" children are those who have to do nothing in order to get what they want.

We Are Bundles of Paradoxes

ONE OF THE PARADOXES of human intimacy is that the better you know a person, the less accurately you can describe him or her, and the harder it becomes to delineate a full, fair, and three-dimensional portrait.

Invariably, when I lecture at a college or university a group of English teachers will cluster around me to ask about a famous literary figure with whom I grew up. "What is he really like as a person?" is the one question they have in common. And they think I am being evasive, or at best discreet, when I reply that I don't know what he is like.

It is easy to describe in a few pithy phrases someone we know only casually or superficially — and especially his obviously unattractive traits or peculiarities. But as we get to know someone better over the years, we find that such easy categorization does not do justice to anything as complex as a human personality.

Of course, we all have surface traits that can be drawn in broad strokes — this person is outgoing, another is reticent, a third is melancholy or vain or rude. But these things are matters of *personality,* not of *character,* and it is the basic character of a person that determines his ultimate value and meaning in human relationships. (Some of the pleasantest personalities I have ever known have had the rottenest characters, and vice versa.)

As we get to know another person better, and longer, and deeper, we more and more perceive the complexities, the contradictions, the levels of being that operate in different spheres of activity, and we learn, or we should, that only an absolute saint or an absolute sinner (each as rare as the other) demonstrates an inner consistency of character.

For the rest of us, we are bundles of paradoxes, like a many-faceted stone, reflecting a different surface sheen to each angle of light. And the better we know someone, the more prismatic he or she becomes, so that the totality never adds up to the sum of the parts. (Prince Hamlet is so perplexing a character precisely because he is the most "real" of Shakespeare's fictional creations and thus defies our full understanding.)

Paradoxically, therefore, it is only great fiction, never fact, that can penetrate into the deepest recesses of the human heart. It is the vision of the seer and the poet that reveals most about ourselves; this, no doubt, is what prompted Aristotle to proclaim that the truths of poetry (by which he meant all genuine works of imagination) are superior to the truths of history.

I haven't the faintest idea of what my friend is "really like." If I did, he would become an object of my interest and no longer a subject — or, as Buber put it, an It rather than a Thou. To pluck out the heart of Hamlet's mystery is to reduce humanhood to taxonomy.

Success, Failure, and Adaptation

WHAT ALL THOSE "SUCCESS" BOOKS don't seem to emphasize, or even to mention, is that very often the same qualities that take you to the top also drop you to the bottom. Qualities don't exist in a vacuum: What may be a virtue in one situation may become a detriment in another.

The same man who builds up a big organization from scratch may also wreck it if he does not modify his drive and change his attitude after he has made it. Determination may get you to the top, but it is flexibility that keeps you there — and the two don't often go together.

Leaders who last a long time seem to be those who are able to combine opposite qualities — knowing when to be firm and when flexible, when to assume responsibility and when to delegate authority. If they cannot do this, they rise and sink as quickly as a Jimmy Carter.

It is an old axiom in show business that it is easier to get to the top than to stay there, and I suspect it is just as true in any other business or endeavor. And the main reason is that if you persist in the attitudes that got you there, you are ill equipped to cope with the problem of survival.

We know that a species derives its survival value not from strength or size or even numbers, but from its ability to adapt to changing conditions. It is a truism that the dinosaurs died out because they could not adapt, while many smaller, weaker species did. Man's chief asset is his nearly infinite capacity for adaptation to new conditions.

The Caesars and Napoleons and Hitlers are really self-defeating personalities, because the very same traits that drove them to power were the ones that sealed their fate. Such men are one-geared creatures: They cannot shift gears when the terrain of history calls for it.

As a popular example, the mammoth Hollywood studios were built up by a certain type of man, perhaps the only kind who could have done this; but, as the country's tastes and social patterns changed, these pioneers were unable to modify their creeds or conduct, and one by one the studios passed from their hands to a different sort of corporate and creative control.

Concentration of purpose and a certain ruthlessness seem to be among the requisites for gaining the topmost rung; but a keen sense of equilibrium is the determinant for maintaining this precarious posture. Even a man as principled as Abe Lincoln altered his posture after grappling with the problems of the presidency.

In the end, all of us are betrayed by our dominant trait if we do not learn to temper it with other elements in our personality so that the tool with which we forged our success does not turn into a weapon threatening self-destruction. Rigidity gives us strength; but it also inclines us to crack when we should bend.

Real intelligence consists not so much in knowing how to do what you have learned to do, but in knowing how to behave in circumstances for which no prior experience has prepared you.

It's How You Ask It . . .

WHAT A LOT OF PEOPLE fail to learn, even as they grow older, is that the way you ask a question can determine the kind of answer you get. The professional pollsters are keenly aware of this and can elicit seemingly contradictory answers by asking the same question in somewhat different ways.

As an example, I recall the story of the two priests arguing about whether it was proper to smoke and pray at the same time. One said it was, and the other said it wasn't. To settle the matter, they agreed that both should write to the Pope for his opinion.

A few weeks later they met and compared notes. Each claimed that the Pope had supported his view and suspected the other of falsifying the reply he got from the Holy Office.

Finally, one asked, "How did you phrase your question?" The other replied, "I asked whether it was proper to smoke while one is praying, and the Pope answered, 'Certainly not, praying is a serious business and permits of no distractions.' And how did you phrase your question?"

"Well," said the other, "I asked if it was proper to pray while smoking, and the Pope said, 'Certainly, prayer is always in order.' "

Some years ago, two large auto companies made expensive public surveys at much the same time to try to find out what kind of car the American motorist might buy in the future.

One company's pollster asked the direct question, "What kind of car would you like to have?" The majority of auto owners replied that they wanted a car that was compact, economical, functional, and subdued in looks.

The other company's pollster was far shrewder and more sensitive to the self-deception most of us unconsciously practice. He asked: "What kind of car do you think your neighbor would like to have?" And there the majority replied that their neighbors coveted large, ostentatious, gimmicky models that looked more like boats or airplanes.

The first auto maker nearly went broke putting out sedate little cars long before the public was ready for them, while the second enjoyed a banner year with its rakish, gaudy, rear-finned models. In fact, the first company was forced to retool to meet the competition.

It is far harder to devise fair and "unweighted" questions than it is to find the answers. Indeed, the most significant advances in science have come not from finding answers, but from beginning to ask the right questions in the right way. Like that simplest one of all, which no one asked until Newton, "Why do apples fall down instead of up?"

On Growing Up

GROWING UP MEANS:

• Doing what you have to do first, and then doing what you like to do. (Fortunate are those who find these tasks to be the same.)
• Knowing where you want to go before you start out to go there (with a willingness to change destinations if need be).
• Learning to get the most out of the least, like kids who build their own toys, and not the least out of the most, like kids who are handed everything without effort.
• Accepting the wise old saw that "the first step is half the distance."
• Proportioning the means to the end, so that you don't fire off a cannon to kill a caterpillar or wave a rod to repel a wild bull.
• Adjusting your goals to fit your talents and your limitations, so that reduced goals do not make you frustrated, angry, or bitter.
• Discriminating between pleasure, which is a state of having, and joy, which is a state of being. (Pleasure palls, joy refreshes.)

• Giving up blaming others, and then giving up blaming yourself. (Blame is the most unproductive reaction of all.)
• Discovering the similarity between things that seem different and the differences between things that seem similar. (Otherwise, one's judgment remains childish.)
• Recognizing that others can see you more truly than you can see yourself, and learning more from your critics than from your friends.
• Knowing when common sense must be applied and when it should be flouted in particular cases, in favor of uncommon sense.
• Accepting the fact that if you do not know how to take orders, you are not competent to give them. (They are opposite sides of the same coin.)
• Moving from the passive voice to the active voice: that is, to cease saying, "It got lost," and to say, "I lost it."
• Retaining a part of each past age as you pass into another; not forgetting what it was like to be a little child, an adolescent, or a young adult and thereby condemning what you have repressed or rejected within yourself.
• Being serious without being solemn, and funny without being foolish, and wise enough never to utter the fatal words, "When I was your age . . ."
• Finally, finding more satisfaction in what you have given than in what you have gotten for it.

Perhaps the whole art of maturity consists of achieving a delicate equilibrium between the youthful axiom that pleasure is a reason and the aging conviction that reason is a pleasure.

*

Life is so rarely lived at its fullest stretch because so few are able to function at the same time as if they were going to live forever and as if they might die tomorrow.

An Early Goal, a Happy Life

AN OLD ACQUAINTANCE of mine died this winter, at a ripe age, after a good life. I always thought of him as one of the lucky people because, he was fond of saying, "I knew what I wanted to be when I was ten."

He knew it, he pursued it, and he became it. A splendid sports cartoonist, he was grateful for his small gift and accepting of his limitations. He was not an artist and did not yearn to be one.

There are many ways we might divide people into lucky and unlucky — by birth, by looks, by health or strength or money. I have always considered the possession of a specific talent at an early age one of the luckiest elements in life.

Most young people in school and college have little idea of what they want to do in later life; and the choices they make are often arbitrary, enforced, or counsels of desperation. But perhaps 10 percent have a definite goal and never waver from it, whether it is to write, to make music, to paint, to teach, to invent, or to repair machinery.

The goal itself may be grand or mundane. What is important is that the young person does not feel the customary need to wrestle with his identity or fret about his future.

If he has a talent at all commensurate with his vision, he will sooner or later become what he wants to be — and if he has enough drive, sooner rather than later. When your compass is set in a straight direction, you arrive far faster than the others do.

I feel sorry for the majority of young people, who may be bright and energetic but have felt or displayed no particular attraction to a calling in life. They have to fabricate a career, as it were, while the possessor of a special talent is drawn to it as if by a magnet.

It is not merely the initial impulse that gives them an advantage; it is the fact that throughout their lives they are getting paid for work they would gladly do for nothing if they could afford it. The happiest men I know are animated not by money or power or position, but by a sense of mastery over their craft, by a deep pleasure in the operation itself, regardless of its ultimate outcome.

Given this lucky gift, the disabilities of birth or looks or even health may be surmounted — so many of the most creative and dedicated people in the arts and sciences have been of frail or uncertain health, but their spirit has been sustained by love of what they did.

My friend died with a feeling of fulfillment. He knew he was one of the lucky ones all his life long, and he would want no one to mourn his return to dust.

Sane or Insane?

THE TROUBLE with the word *insanity* is that it has never been a medical or scientific word, but purely a legal one. The way the law is worded in any particular state defines the condition, and up to now no unanimously satisfactory definition has been found.

Is a man who kills and buries a score of youths sane or insane? We might say that anyone who could bring himself to do this is per se insane; on the other hand, we might say that the cunning and deliberation indicated he was sane.

How do we resolve this? There is no way out of this true dilemma except by escaping through the horns. And that is by creating another category, a *tertium quid,* as the ancient philosophers put it, called "moral insanity." I have long advocated such a class of offenses.

For instance, was Hitler sane or insane? On one level, he suffered from paranoia and megalomania, accompanied by hysteria and melancholia. But should he have been acquitted of his crimes and adjudged "mentally incapable" because of these personality defects?

He was also a wicked man, by any standard you care to use — not merely in what he did to his professed enemies but in what he did to Germany, to his own people, deluded and mesmerized by him.

People like him suffer from moral insanity as well as whatever mental quirks they may possess. Others are not real to them; others exist only to be used, manipulated, or disposed of, in pursuit of some obscure egocentric goal.

Most heinous criminals, whether leaders of gangs or of nations, possess this enormous blind spot. They are not lunatics in any clinical sense of the word, in that they function well and often brilliantly; but they are cracked and disjointed in their area of sympathy for their fellow creatures, driven by the need to dominate and destroy.

A mass murderer is crazy to do what he does, but not crazy in the way he does it, or conceals it, or manages to live with it until he is discovered or deposed. Stalin, as well as Hitler, possessed this kind of moral insanity toward anyone he felt was in his way. Most despots are merely criminals in a larger theater of action.

As it now stands, the law will get absolutely nowhere trying to decide if the killer of a score of youths is insane or not. Mental health (or illness) is not a sharply defined science, and perhaps can never be. A moral lunatic is someone who is utterly mad and frightfully sane at the same time — and our present system of jurisprudence and criminology does not know what to do with him.

The reason that legal language states the same thing in six different ways is the quite rational fear that some lawyer will come along and find a seventh way of stating it, to his client's advantage. Law is more a struggle for semantic supremacy than a matter of justice or equity.

Mortality and the Human Condition

"WHAT IS THIS 'HUMAN CONDITION' you keep referring to?" asked a reader in Florida. "How is the human condition different from any other condition, simply because we are human and other creatures are not? I am puzzled."

Let me offer a concrete example. Not only does man love in a way no other creature does, but man alone knows about loss and death. We are so constituted that we must love and be loved to fulfill our natures. We must be needed, and we must feel that our needs are filled in return.

At the same time, we know what a precarious investment this is. Accident, catastrophe, and death come to all, at any time, in any way. The ones we love may perish in a twinkling, simply by some caprice of fate — in a turning of a corner, a twisting of a knob.

We are peculiarly designed to be aware that all life ends in loss — of a parent, a mate, and sometimes, most cruelly, of a child. The anguish of such a loss may be almost unbearable, but still we are driven to forge these bonds of affection, for without them we are incomplete.

This is the most dramatic example of the human condition: It is painfully problematic at its deepest level. The giving of love exposes us to irremediable suffering; but the withholding of love, the wish not to be hurt, cuts us off from the nourishment we need most to realize fully our human selves.

When we think of unity, we think of oneness, of individuality, the way a stone or a leaf forms an individual unit. But the person is not individual in the same way that a stone or a leaf is.

As George MacDonald once put it, "There can be no unity, no delight of love, no harmony, no good in being, where there is but one. Two at least are needed for oneness."

Two at least are needed for oneness. It can be husband and wife, friend and friend, parent and child — whatever the combination, unlike other creatures, we are not at one with ourselves as long as we are alone. The final end is oneness in duality, the ultimate paradox of humanhood.

This being so, we are compelled to face the peril of loss, one way or another. If the gamble is not taken, we do not become what we were meant to be; once taken, there is no return from the dreadful risk of loss. Because human life encompasses the knowledge of death, it takes on an added dimension of meaning no other creatures know.

Who else would make a child's heaven, where we join our loved ones again? Such a consoling myth serves to soothe the pang of mortality at the heart of the human condition.

How to Win from Losing

HOW CAN YOU WIN when you lose? This is a hard riddle, but it was propounded and answered well over two thousand years ago by Epicurus in little more than a dozen words: "In a philosophical dispute, he gains most who is defeated, since he learns most."

If you have taken a wrong position on a question and someone bests you in the argument, you are not a loser but a winner, for you are better off than you were before; you have gained more than your opponent has. You have learned something you did not know; he has not.

Obviously, this makes sense, but we do not commonly look at disputations in this way. We imagine that winning an argument means beating an opponent down, browbeating or deriding or manipulating half-truths until he is silenced. It does not matter who is objectively correct; we want to feel dominant and triumphant.

This kind of winning is really losing, if the facts are not on our side. This is a debating victory, an oratorical contest, not a mutual determination to seek for the truth together — which is what all honest and productive arguments must be.

Most disputations are fruitless at best because the contestants want to instruct, not to learn; to persuade, not to investigate; to feel justified, not corrected or reproached or convicted of error. And the more heated the controversy, the more both antagonists lose sight of reality, of reason, and of the common objective to discover where the good resides. What is worse, however, is that arguments tend to polarize; each side becomes more extreme; nothing of value is credited to the other side, not even decent motives, and disputants turn into bitter enemies. All one has to do is to read the history of religious disputation in the seventeenth and eighteenth centuries to see how people pledged to the same God and the same Savior persecuted and slew each other over points of theology no one today even comprehends. (What is infralapsarianism?)

Most of us are incapable of arguing about principles without soon involving personalities. When our opinions are refuted, we feel that we ourselves are rejected, demeaned, and discounted. We take a disagreement as a personal affront; an attack on our convictions is construed as a slap in the face. It is wounded vanity and not a zeal for truth that feeds the flames of most such controversies.

Differences of opinion are opportunities for learning, new footholds for change and growth, valuable exercises for minds grown sluggish and characters grown smug. But not one in a thousand uses them for such creative purposes; not I, not you — and I wonder about old Epicurus himself.

Children begin by honestly saying, "I don't know," until they are taught (*mistakenly*) *to be ashamed of ignorance; and this is why so many adults remain ashamed of saying, "I don't know" when they should say it. Ignorance is shameful only when we have had the opportunity to learn something and rejected it.*

Marital Compatibility Requires Self-Compatibility

WHAT WE LOOSELY CALL incompatibility in marriage is in itself one of the dumbest reasons for divorce, although it is perhaps the reason most commonly given. Men and women are by nature incompatible — it is the last successful integration we shall ever see — and practically the whole task in marriage is to learn how to compat.

While gross and irreconcilable differences do exist, of course, I should guess that for every one case of true incompatibility, there are twenty cases in which this word is used to disguise a deeper fact: that at least one of the marriage partners is not compatible with himself or herself.

It may be one of the hardest lessons in life for some persons to learn that getting along with someone else, at close quarters, for long and steady periods, first implies the ability to get along with oneself. A person who is disjointed is looking for opposite things in the same mate, like the woman who wants a strong husband whom she can nevertheless dominate. There ain't no such critter to be found.

The real pathos of so many divorces may be found in the subsequent quest, needless and ceaseless and usually futile, for a "right" mate. But nobody can be right for long if you are wrong with yourself.

We have all noticed how much-married persons keep repeating the same mistake or making the opposite one, which comes to the same thing. This is not to deny that second marriages may be more successful than the first, but they can be so only when a loser takes realistic stock of himself and recognizes that *being* the right person is more important than *finding* the right person.

Marriage does not make us better, any more than it makes us worse; it merely intensifies what is already there, both for good and for bad. And marriage cannot make anyone happier who does not bring the ingredients for happiness into it. With the ingredients, any number of the opposite sex can be "right"; lacking them, no one can make up the deficit.

The person (and there are relatively few of them in our unstable society) who is secure and easy within himself, who knows both his gifts and his limits, who is seeking a reality and not a fantasy, has little trouble with compatibility and can handle what trouble there is.

Those who are in conflict with themselves cannot find a complementary mate, for no human can satisfy opposite needs at the same time. It is not merely that too many couples become divorced prematurely; it is that far too many become married immaturely.

Fame and Fortune Aren't Enough

DOZENS OF REASONS have been given for writing books, ranging from the desire for money and fame to the itch for immortality. The most honest reason I have heard was expressed by B. F. Skinner at the last American Psychological Association convention.

Asked why he wrote his recent autobiography, the eminent behaviorist explained simply, "In order to make people love me." This laudably candid reply recalls Stephen Leacock's remark that the true title of every lecture is "How to Be More Like Me."

Everyone wants to be loved, deny it or reject it as some may. In fact, it is my suspicion that those who seem to prefer to be respected or feared have adopted this posture as a substitute for the love they do not feel they can win.

One of Freud's shrewdest early observations was that money, or fame, or even honor, do not really satisfy us as adults because they are not what a small child wants — and it is only the satisfaction of our earliest emotional needs that is capable of gratifying us over a period of time.

This would go a long way toward explaining one of the perennial puzzles in society — the misery of the so-called successful people.

It seems incredible to the average person that a rich, popular, and much-admired personality — and their names are legion, especially in the entertainment field — may commit suicide, or die more slowly from booze or drugs or depression, when he or she seems to have everything to live for.

But the child within us knows nothing of these things, for it remains encapsulated in its own timeless world. And if, within that world, the proper emotional currents have not been generated, if the capacity to give and accept love has not been stimulated and released, then no matter where else gratification may be sought, it will not be found.

Indeed, the reason so large a percentage of celebrities destroy themselves is that, while the rest of us may hope that success and fame and adulation will compensate for this lack, they have already been disillusioned, for it is only colder and lonelier at the top of that mountain. Personal contact is more remote, not more accessible.

What we need most is what we are supposed to get earliest; and when that emotional mechanism is jammed for one reason or another, whatever we fire off misses the mark and is ultimately a disappointment.

Even Professor Skinner's little black box has within it a wistful child's heart fluttering for love, more love, and still more.

Love is demonstrably superior to money, not only on a sentimental plane, but even on a computable basis: The more money you give away, the less you have, but the more love you give away, the more comes back to you.

What You Don't Know Can *Hurt You*

"WHAT YOU DON'T KNOW won't hurt you" is the most treacherous and misleading maxim of all. What you don't know can hurt you terribly if it is something you ought to know.

Most people before Columbus didn't know the Earth was round, and this ignorance didn't particularly hurt them. But they also didn't know that witchcraft was a malicious myth, and this ignorance perpetuated much unnecessary fear and rage and unjustified violence.

If you know that you don't know something, you are partly protected against the consequences of your nescience; but if you suppose that you know something you really don't know, then you are in deep trouble, and so are those around you.

The psychological trap for most of us is that we become anxious and uneasy in a state of suspended belief. It is like being on a tightrope: Our object is to reach the safety of the platform at one end or the other, to plump comfortably into a settled belief rather than stand in tension on the quivering rope.

In many cases, "I know where I stand" means "I know where I rest." We prefer resting in a dogma to standing on a doubt, even though the dogma may not correspond to the facts, the truth of the situation.

As a prime example, almost everyone has a firm conviction about our political, social, and economic structure. We are "liberals" or "conservatives" or "libertarians" or "single-taxers" or whatever. But the fact is that we have yet found no objective way to validate these positions, and it is very likely that all of them are as much false as they are true.

We simply do not know, at this point in human history, what is the optimum form of living, socially, politically, and economically. I have no doubt that Adam Smith had a piece of the truth by the tail, but so did Karl Marx. How do we separate their valuable detached insights from the errors and exaggerations and encrustations?

Nobody enjoys being tentative or indecisive; much as we protest being labeled by other people, we relish labeling ourselves as one thing or another, out of a deep need for identity and communality, even when we may not totally agree with everything the label stands for.

What we don't know, or want to know, leads us into wars and massacres and corporate cruelties that no individual would countenance on his own. We have an innate drive for certainty and the emotional security it seems to bring, but to be certain of what we should still be in doubt about is a form of ignorance that is not only foolish but too often fatal.

The Stone of Opposition Sharpens Ideas

PEOPLE TEND TO BUY the nonfictional books they think will agree with them; we may pretend we are looking for enlightenment, but most of us are looking for confirmation of our prior beliefs and prejudices. Most books of this kind are published for a preselected audience.

But this is precisely what we do not need. A book that agrees with our views may be gratifying to the ego, but it does nothing to develop flexibility of mind or independence of judgment. Moreover, it makes us narrow and rigid in the defense of our most warmly held opinions.

Lord Acton said a long time ago that one has no right to attack or oppose a contrary view until one can express that view not only as well as but better than its proponents can. In other words, not until we can make out a better case for the opposition than it has made out for itself can we be sure that we are knocking down a live enemy rather than a straw man.

And it is rare in any disputation that we do not distort the principles or premises of our opponents. We tend to make parodies or caricatures out of them — so much so that one might wonder how anyone could believe such things. And of course they do not: What they believe is generally far more coherent and subtle and complex than the gross cartoon we have turned it into.

A further irony resides in the fact that the advocates of a particular view even distort their own founts of belief; this is why Marx said that he was not a Marxist and Freud disclaimed being a Freudian, after hearing some of the perversions of their theories from the mouths of their own disciples and interpreters.

I am equally confident that Adam Smith, the father of capitalism, would likewise repudiate the ways in which his "system of natural liberty" has been perverted by modern apologists for laissez-faire. (If you doubt this, read "Adam Smith and Modern Political Economy," a symposium of Bicentennial essays published by Iowa State University Press.)

A small chain of bookstores in New York gave to anyone who bought a copy of Henry A. Kissinger's *White House Years* a free copy of *Sideshow* by William Shawcross, which takes the opposite view of our foreign policy — a practice to be highly commended in all such controversial matters. Indeed, publishers would do well to issue such contrary books bound together in debate form.

If you don't really understand your opponent's position fully, then you don't really understand your own. This is why most arguments end in either a bang or a whimper, but rarely in a real resolution.

Honesty consists of the unwillingness to lie to others; maturity, which is equally hard to attain, consists of the unwillingness to lie to oneself.

*

We do not grow as we get older unless we begin to find elements of truth in opinions contrary to our own which we can usefully assimilate to our own views.

On Growing More Able to Give with Joy

I RAN OUT OF SPACE before I ran out of gas the other day, talking about the ways in which we change in going from youth to age and how surprising it usually is to find ourselves so different in some respects.

One heartening change, however — and far more meaningful than the matters I mentioned earlier — is our attitude toward taking and receiving. That is, if we really mature as we grow older, which not everyone does, of course.

The Biblical injunction "It is more blessed to give than to receive" may strike us as a piece of moralizing or sentimentality or pure hypocrisy when we are young, because it is obviously so much more fun to get a birthday or Christmas present than to give one.

I have long felt that what we call a spiritual truth can be validated only if we can legitimately turn it into a psychological truth. The best way to test the Biblical saying is to translate it into "It is more *satisfying* to give than to receive" and to check it against one's deepest feelings.

And there is absolutely no question that as we become older, the pleasure diminishes in receiving presents, while the satisfaction grows in giving them to those you care for.

As a parent, I couldn't care less what my children may give me for birthdays or Christmas, in a material sense, if affection goes with it. But I get a tremendous charge out of giving them (besides my affection) what I think will genuinely please them.

Nor is this mere sentimentality, for nothing we get nourishes the psyche at its very core as much as pleasing another person. Indeed, it would not be going too far to say that a good working definition of that elusive word *maturity* consists in the expanding capacity to get more joy out of giving than out of taking. I feel sorriest for those who never know this.

Of course, a caveat is necessary here. As Cardinal Mercier warned us, "We must not only give what we *have,* we must also give what we *are*.'' It is easy to give a material object in lieu of oneself, rather than as a tangible symbol of our feelings. A child who is handed gifts as a substitute for attention knows and resents this as mere bribery.

So, along with its frailties and limitations, aging brings its own compensations. Youth is a tight little ego, all wrapped up in itself. The shell cracks as we get older, and the petty pleasure of grasping transforms itself into the more gracious posture of offering. Only after you come to that point in life do you know what it is we were always meant to be and to do.

What's in a Face?

THE ADAGE that you can't tell a book by its cover may very well be true, but I have never held with the corollary that you can't tell a person by his or her looks. After a certain age, you can.

As I recall, it was Somerset Maugham who said that after the age of forty, every man is responsible for his face. What he meant, of course, was that while we can't help the looks we were born with — Lincoln was acknowledged to be one of the homeliest men in the country — our character and conduct shape our expression as we ripen into maturity.

What made me think of this was a passage in Otto Friedrich's fascinating book about Berlin in the 1920s, *Before the Deluge*. Artur Schnabel, the great concert pianist, had come to study with Busoni, the legendary composer and pianist, and relates their last meeting, shortly before Busoni died: ''When I entered the room, he said, 'Schnabel, you are acquiring a face.' It impressed me deeply — a great compliment. It meant that I had none until then, of course. I was then forty years old.''

If we compare the faces of most of our leaders, both public and private, with those of creative people who have made a significant and permanent contribution, we can see a very real difference.

The shallow people, the hollow people, no matter how handsome or dashing, equally lack individuality or distinction. Their faces may differ in detail, but they are nearly indistinguishable from one another, like so many movie starlets, whatever their age.

But when you look at the face of an Einstein, a Frank Lloyd Wright, a Marc Chagall, a Bertrand Russell, it is there that one finds genuine individuality and an imprint of personality that has not been conformed or contrived like a product for public consumption.

Whatever their other faults of temperament, people who work and live for something beyond themselves acquire a look that is rarely found in the courthouse, the clubhouse, or the conference room.

"A man finds room in the few square inches of his face for the traits of all his ancestors," said Emerson, "for the expression of all his history, and his wants."

Nor is it merely a matter of accidental genius or talent. You can find great character in the face of a peasant, a priest, a potter of no special renown. What is decisive is the set of values he lives for, the strength and steadfastness he has drawn from his experiences, the reaching out for growth rather than the mere grasping of power and pleasure and possessions. Schnabel could not really play Beethoven until he acquired a face.

A person's faults and virtues usually go together, just as concavity and convexity go together — take away a fault, and his complementary virtue is likely to collapse.

*

Perhaps the most common, and most dangerous, self-delusion is to imagine that we are what we believe, when the deeper truth is that we are what we feel — especially when our feelings run counter to our professed beliefs.

As the Days Dwindle Down, Time Seems to Shrink

EVERYONE KNOWS that the older you get, the faster time seems to pass. It is a psychological truism that when we are young, each day leading to Christmas can drag like a year; then, as we round middle age, a whole summer seems compressed into a fleeting few days.

This summer seemed to go even faster than ever — just a bright blur between Memorial Day and Labor Day. Everyone I spoke with had the same impression; but, then, all of us were a year older than we had been.

I think that this telescopic quality of time can be explained as a matter of proportion, if we look at it arithmetically and not sentimentally. Time actually does move faster for us as we increase in age.

When we are young — say, eight years old — a year represents a full one eighth of our total experience, and even more than that, for few of us can remember back to our infancies. It is an enormous amount of time in proportion to the little we have known.

By the time we hit forty, a year is only one fortieth of our total experience. Objectively it is the same twelve-month segment, but subjectively it is only a small fraction of our remembrance of things past. It is like adding one thin sheet to a fat folio of thirty-nine other sheets.

A child has only a few sheets in his collection, so that adding one more represents a substantial addition to the memory bank. Time in this respect is much like money.

If you have $30 or $40 saved up and you add another $10, it seems and is a considerable chunk. But if you have a few thousand saved up and add another $10, it seems insignificant, even though it is the same amount. And the more we have, the less each increment counts.

Thus, when we are quite old and have seventy or more years

behind us, one more year flies by like a week, in comparison with the memories and impressions we have banked over the decades. And each year, of course, the amount of experience we add is decreasingly smaller in proportion to the grand total.

So it is not entirely an illusion, or the faulty mechanism of a failing mind, that year by year time seems to increase its pace. It is an arithmetical ratio, like the $10 that dwindles to nothing as we amass more and more capital.

"Time passes," we say; but, actually, *we* pass while time stays on. The hour, the day, the year maintain their steady pace; it is we who rush faster and faster through eternity. The young at first cannot wait for Wednesday to turn into Saturday; now old, they wonder on Saturday where Wednesday got to.

Is Something Foreign "Better"?

MOST PEOPLE SEEM to have a split personality about foreign manners and matters and materials. One part of them laughs or sneers at things foreign, while another part imitates and respects them.

I thought of this while I happened to examine a tie on the counter of a men's store. The label read: "Imported Polyester." What could be more ridiculous, since polyester is a synthetic and its country of manufacture is wholly irrelevant?

But the word *imported* gets us, or a part of us, every time. The rise in the popularity of Scotch whiskies (when earlier Americans would drink only bourbon) is at least as much a matter of social cachet as it is of taste. And vodka is vodka wherever it is made, but we willingly pay a premium for a Russian label on the bottle.

We are not alone in this, of course. Authentic Levi's, I am told, are currently selling on the Russian black market for more than $100 a pair. The Russian cognoscenti prefer Polish vodka to their own, while Germans who fancy themselves to be beer experts import a Czechoslovakian brand.

At the same time, people everywhere ridicule or deprecate the strange habits and tastes of "foreigners" — except in those areas where they can feel superior to their compatriots.

America is much looked down upon as a barbarous and tasteless nation by many upper-class Europeans. Yet the same people fall over themselves to acquire American conveniences, and even ordinary commodities by our standards. After the war you could get almost anything you wanted in any part of Europe for a carton of American cigarettes and a Hershey bar.

Every nation has the same odd ambivalence toward others: a feeling that it is the best and others are ludicrous or inferior, but at the same time a contrary feeling that whatever is imported somehow marks its purchaser and possessor as a knowledgeable and tasteful member of the elite.

It doesn't add up, but then few of our feelings are rational or consistent. It reminds me somehow of a marvelous cartoon strip I once saw, perhaps in the *New Yorker* magazine. A man was watering his front lawn. Along came a lovely, lissome lady and he put down the hose to gaze at her as she turned into a house down the block.

In the second panel, another, even lovelier lady comes along. He stares at her until she, too, turns in at a neighboring house. Then along comes a third, far lovelier than the other two. He doesn't even look at her, but busies himself with the hosing. She, of course, turns into his door. The other ladies were imported; she was domestic.

We desire equality only with those we consider to be better off than we are, never with those we consider worse off.

*

The "free world" consists largely of those nations that find it more expedient at this time to toady to us than to toady to our enemies.

What's Wrong with Being Proud?

WHAT A LOT OF DAMAGE a little word can do, if you don't understand what you are saying or what someone else is saying. Entire religious sects have been formed — and persecuted — because of disagreement about the meaning of a word.

A reader in Tequesta, Florida, asks me if I can resolve his puzzlement about the word *pride*. Is it a good thing to have or a bad thing? Pride, after all, is one of the seven deadly sins — and the worst, according to most theologians, because it elevates the self to the place of God.

On the other hand, my reader asks, "What is wrong with healthy pride — the pride of a craftsman in his work well performed?" Or the pride of someone who refuses to accept public charity? Or the pride a citizen takes in his country, a father in his children, an athlete in his prowess?

The trap here is that we are using the same word in two quite different senses, and we rarely bother to distinguish between them. Pride as a sin is an *attitude* toward oneself and others, while the other thing we call pride is a *feeling* about excellence. To take pride in one's work is not the same as taking pride in one's birth. The first is a form of self-respect; the second is a form of snobbery.

Pride is considered the root of other sins because while all the others attach themselves to vices and work their end, pride alone attaches itself to virtue and destroys it. The drunkard and the thief do not pretend they are doing what they are doing for any good reason, but people can actually be proud of their humility. The most insidious of sins, pride creeps in everywhere, before we are aware of it.

This is the real difference between genuine patriotism and an arrogant nationalism. Patriotism is proud of a country's virtues and eager to correct its deficiencies; it also acknowledges the legitimate patriotism of other countries, with their own specific virtues.

The pride of nationalism, however, trumpets its country's virtues and denies its deficiencies, while it is contemptuous toward the virtues of other countries. It wants to be, and proclaims itself to be, "the greatest," but greatness is not required of a country; only goodness is. Indeed, the pride of nationalism, in my view, is the single most destructive force in the world today, a monstrous perversion of the virtue of patriotism.

Obviously, we need two different words to describe and define the two aspects of pride. If you do not take pride in your work (if that work is worth doing), then you are less of a person than you should be. But if you are swaggering or smug and take personal credit for the gifts God gave you, as if they make you better than other men, you debase and corrupt the very excellence of your efforts and become more despicable than anything you despise.

We Learn from Our Mistakes

A FRIEND ASKED ME at lunch the other day about a certain doctor I know, who has had the finest training and is generally recognized as an expert in his field. I advised against going to see him, which surprised my friend.

"What's wrong?" he asked. "Isn't he capable? Isn't he honest? Doesn't he care about his patients?"

"None of those things," I said. "But he has one fault that overrides all his good points, in my opinion — he can't stand to be wrong."

Vanity is often the greatest enemy of competence. No matter how good you may be at something, whether it is playing the piano, analyzing the electron, or palpating the patient, if you have an imperative need to be right all the time, you are betraying your professionalism.

My own doctor, when recommending surgery some years ago, urged me to get a second opinion, even though he was sure that I needed the operation. Many doctors resent it when a patient indicates a desire to get a second opinion; they look upon it as an implicit reflection on their medical judgment.

Genuine self-confidence does not feel threatened by being questioned in this way. In the first place, even the greatest practitioner can make a mistake; and second, the best kind of insurance against a malpractice suit is confirmation by another expert with no vested interest in the treatment.

If you can't stand to be wrong, you have no business giving crucial advise to people on any subject. If your ego forces you to justify and defend all your decisions, you are temperamentally disqualified from giving such advice, no matter how eminent you may be in your chosen field. The need to be right can be more corruptive than any other influence.

The most grievous and costly mistakes, whether in medicine, the law, or business dealings, are not clinical or technical or fiscal but personal and emotional. They spring not from ignorance or incompetence, which are intellectual defects, but from stubbornness, vanity, self-esteem, and pride, which are moral and emotional defects.

I would rather consult a doctor who knew a little less and knew how little he knew than one who knew a great deal and thought he knew more. Ignorance per se is not nearly as dangerous as ignorance of ignorance, which is why the Delphic oracle told the wisest Greek that he alone recognized how little he knew, which placed him above the others.

Rightly, we ought to be grateful to learn we have been mistaken about something; this is the only way experience turns our bad judgment into good judgment. It is only the weak man who feels he cannot afford to utter those three words of supreme strength: "I was wrong."

If you feel you have all the answers, you may be sure you are asking yourself the wrong questions.

The Trap of Technology

"YOU CAN'T GO HOME AGAIN" is the rubric made popular by the late Thomas Wolfe, and it is true as far as it goes, for what we return to is never what we left. His observation, however, extends in time as well as in space. You also can't go back to an earlier era after you have known a later — in big or little things. The world of convenience particularly seems to be irreversible.

I thought of this driving a friend's car to the country while mine was in the shop. His car lacked power steering, and it irritated me almost beyond endurance in trying to get in and out of tight parking spaces. Yet for most of my driving life I did not have power steering, and the lack never bothered me.

Even more vividly, I recall going to movies in the summer on Saturday afternoons and staying there for six or seven hours (two features, a cowboy serial, and three cartoons), sweating profusely in the 100-degree-plus temperature of a non-air-conditioned theater. Yet it never occurred to me that I was suffering; there simply was no air conditioning at the time.

We miss only what we have had; we do not miss what we have never had. As Aristotle put it, no one regrets the lack of a third eye.

Today it would be hard to find an American of any age who would be willing to sit through even a single film in a sweltering house. Entire cities, such as Dallas, are air conditioned from portal to portal, and a broken machine is considered as much a hardship as lack of electricity or water in the Sun Belt.

This is the trap of technology: It begins as a comfort and ends as a crutch. If the refrigerator goes out, we are helpless; there is no alternate system available for keeping food cold. When I was a boy, the iceman came around every day or two, responding to a sign in our window. Now we may have to wait a week to get the fridge repaired.

What we call civilization, in a material sense, is largely a system of increasing dependence on factors over which we have little direct control. We can no longer make our own heat, obtain our own water, repair our own vehicles; more than this, when we are deprived, we cannot exercise options. There is only one phone company, one water supply, one specific part for one specific make of an appliance.

But more than this, emotionally and psychologically we have conditioned ourselves to experience conveniences as necessities, and we can't go home again to the hot movie house; not, in such cases, because home has changed, but because *we* have, for good and for bad.

Speaking Up and Piping Down

A NEW BOOK came across my desk the other day, all about the need to speak up, to assert yourself, and to say no when you feel like it instead of saying yes when you don't. I think this is fine advice for about half the people; for the other half, I'd suggest the opposite book: about the need to shut up, to go along, and to say yes even when you feel like saying no.

Sometimes the world seems divided between the people who won't speak up and those who speak up more than they should. Most of us are on one side or the other of this line; very few personalities are able to keep a delicate balance between self-assertiveness and complaisance.

My own besetting sin has been the former; it has taken me decades to learn that saying less can be more effective than saying more, and I still speak up before there is any occasion to. But at least I am able to ventilate my feelings, abrasive as the process may sometimes be to others and eventually to myself. I think the nonassertive people suffer more than we do; after all, we speaker-uppers impose the suffering on others. But of course there are compensations the other way: The nonassertives are far better liked than we are.

We like the people who go along, who don't complain or

object, who give in to us because it's less trouble that way; conversely, we resent the people who speak their own minds bluntly, even if we are the sort who do the same. Nonasserters appreciate each other far more than asserters do.

The fact of the matter is that some personalities need to be pulled out and others need to be pushed in. And it is no accident that they usually marry each other, with a more or less unconscious desire on both parts to achieve this mutual effect. This is why it is said that opposites attract.

They attract because the nonasserter is looking for someone to do his (or her) dirty work for him (or her). Someone who finds it hard to express complaints or resentments can obtain gratification from a mate who plays this role; and contrariwise, the bold speaker-outer equally feels a secret need for a companion to soften the impact of his ego.

Even two friends who are quite different can fulfill these urges for each other; in fact, persons of the same type rarely get along well together. Two nonassertives wallow in futility; and two assertives are continually at one another's throat.

Oddly, it is the differences between personalities that can make a harmonious balance, if the differences compensate for deficiencies more than they strike a discord.

Will Women Make Better Leaders?

EVERYBODY SAYS, "We need leaders." But what kind of leaders do we need? Everybody says, "We need strong leaders." But what exactly is a strong leader?

My own reading of history leads me to believe that we need leaders who are strong enough not to need to prove it. A man who is quietly sure of his strength and not secretly doubtful about his own masculinity cannot be forced to act more boldly than he should.

A couple of years ago, at a meeting of the American Foreign

Service Association, Barbara Tuchman, the perceptive historian, spoke about different leaders' ways of dealing with unpleasant truths and "the fear of not appearing masterful, or a ruler's sense that his manhood is at stake."

She suggested that "proving his manhood" was a factor pushing President Nasser of Egypt into provoking war with Israel in 1967 "so that he could not be accused of weakness or appear less militant than the Syrians." Then she moved on to the United States, illustrating: "One senses it was a factor in the personalities of Johnson and Nixon in regard to withdrawing from Vietnam; there was that horrible doubt, 'Shall I look soft?' It was clearly present in Kennedy too; on the other hand it does not seem to have bothered Eisenhower, Truman, or FDR . . ."

In the book *Power and the Corporate Mind,* the coauthors gloss Ms. Tuchman's view by observing: "Masculinity and potency are by-products of the demands of a grandiose self. Richard Nixon needed to feel he was masterful, in control, able to deal manfully with crises, rather than submissive, weak, and, by implication, castrated. He therefore accepted American withdrawal from Vietnam, but only after he ordered savage bombing and thereby asserted our awesome military power."

There is no reason to believe that women are more moral creatures than men; their common humanity makes the sexes more alike than their separate genders make them different. But women are devoid of the need for displaying *machismo* and thus of the drive to prove themselves as strong and potent.

Psychologically, one of the most important reasons for seeking more female leadership in national and world affairs is that a woman would not feel her womanhood was at stake if she dealt with crises in a sympathetic and conciliatory fashion. This is not to say she always will; but it is to suggest that the man's fear of appearing weak is not a built-in component of her nature.

It is just barely possible that what we so patronizingly designate as women's liberation may prove to be the liberation of men quite as much — even perhaps the liberation of humankind from crippling ancient fears.

Intelligence Isn't a Single Entity

MANY DECADES AGO, long before the current controversy about IQ tests and their doubtful validity, John Dewey, the trail-breaking educator, sardonically gave his impression of what he called "this intelligence-testing business." Dewey said it reminded him of the way they used to weigh hogs in Texas. "They would get a long plank, put it over a cross-bar, and somehow tie the hog on one end of the plank. They'd search all around until they found a stone that would balance the weight of the hog and they'd put that on the other end of the plank. Then they'd guess the weight of the stone."

I have been reading a book called *Human Intelligence,* by Jack Fincher, which more than bears out Dewey's irreverent analogy. What seems to be the heart of the problem is that intelligence very likely is not a single entity — that is, there are *intelligences,* but there is no one thing we can properly label *intelligence.*

What has been called intelligence in the past may be a relatively narrow, if important, ability to manipulate symbols and make abstractions. Since this is the essential element in the formal learning process, it has been taken for the whole of that complex response we loosely call intelligence. But as we know, academic geniuses can also be fools.

It seems to me that I can distinguish at least a half-dozen different modes of intelligence, none of them necessarily related to any of the others. I myself am proficient in one or two, and deficient in the same number. If you ever saw me try to put a tricycle together on Christmas Eve, you would (rightly) consider me the mental equivalent of early Cro-Magnon man, if that.

There are two hemispheres in the brain, and each seems to

be in charge of different cognitive faculties. It is the left hemisphere that regulates the kinds of skills and apperceptions so dear to the hearts of the psychological testers — which is mostly the manipulation of words and symbols. The right hemisphere seems to control other faculties, such as spatial arrangements or musical abilities or even athletic prowess.

Human Intelligence is not a seminal or a scholarly book; it adds little to our previous knowledge of the subject, but for the first time it brings together research from the diverse fields working on this complicated subject and arranges the material into a coherent picture of where we are now and where we are most likely to go.

It seems highly probable that the old IQ test is about as obsolete as the old Texas method of weighing a hog. It was never any more reliable, but it was the best we had, with the planks, cross-bars, and stones at our disposal. It is now more of a disservice than a help, and good riddance.

Human "Greatness" Is Often Measured by Raw Power

IT SHOCKED ME, but didn't surprise me, to learn that more than seven thousand readers indignantly canceled their subscriptions to *Time* magazine when it featured on its cover a portrait of Ayatollah Ruhollah Khomeini as "Man of the Year."

In fact, what surprised me was that more readers didn't make the mistake of confusing a factual statement with a value judgment. It is a fact that he was the most important man of the year — just as Hitler and Stalin were in previous years. Which of course has nothing to do with our opinion of their characters or conduct.

The word *greatness* is a curious one, for people can be great in different ways — like a Newton or a Pasteur on the one hand, or an Alexander or Caesar on the other. Conquerors and mass killers are called great because of the extent of their influence, just as an earthquake is called great if it exterminates many thousands, and not because it does any good.

Every schoolboy knows Lord Acton's dictum, "Power corrupts, and absolute power tends to corrupt absolutely." But hardly anyone recalls the sentence immediately following it: "Almost all great men are bad men."

It is hard to think of leaders we would designate as great who did not in the end commit more evil than good. Perhaps a handful would come to mind, whereas history is replete with leaders who became famous (or infamous) for their cruelty, their covetousness, and their corruption. The Caesars and Napoleons hurt their countries; we rarely hear of those who heal them.

Lincoln himself was suspicious of what we call political greatness. When he was only twenty-nine, he warned about a possible threat to American democracy by "some man possessed of the loftiest genius, coupled with ambition sufficient to push it to its utmost stretch."

If someone of that sort arose among us, he said, "it will require the people to be united with each other, attached to the government and laws, and generally intelligent, to successfully frustrate his design."

It was Socrates, long before that, who observed that the only men who can be trusted with power are those who do not crave it. But those who do not crave it do not get it, and those who crave it have an insatiable appetite to be not only Man of the Year but Man of a Lifetime, and beyond if this were possible by any means.

It is well to remember that in France all the kings had nicknames, but only one was called the Just.

Most revolutions soon become either corrupt or repressive because the qualities that make men successful revolutionaries drive them to other excesses after they have achieved power.

"Less Is More" Applies to Humans Too

MIES VAN DER ROHE, the modern architect, is famous for his gnomic saying, "Less is more." What he meant, of course, is that simplicity makes the best and most lasting impression, whereas the ornate and fussy defeats its own object.

He was speaking structurally, but his words apply with as much force psychologically and socially. Less is more when you are presenting yourself as a person, and more is less in a deep and permanent way.

One of the hardest lessons to learn for a certain type of person — and some never learn it at all — is that when you try to make yourself more, you are actually diminishing yourself.

Young people often think they can inflate their importance by pretending to skills or attributes or positions they do not possess; but sooner or later their pretensions are discovered and even their good points are disvalued.

More important, the insecure person who feels that he has to brag or even lie about these matters is really demeaning himself; he is confessing that in actuality he does not live up to the image he would like to project and desperately needs to keep up a false front.

You can fool other people for a while, but within your own unconscious you cannot fool yourself. Pretending to be more makes you feel less; feeling less forces you to strive harder to impress; and finally the imposture becomes so gross and so grotesque that it collapses in self-contempt and public shame.

Even when we are "somebody," it is diminishing to trumpet the fact. I recall the story Leonard Lyons told many years ago about Gregory Peck entering a crowded restaurant with a friend and finding no table available.

"Tell them who you are," the friend urged Peck, who simply shrugged and said, "If you have to tell them who you are, you aren't anybody."

One of the admirable traits of the Englishman, more than most people, is letting others find out for themselves who he is and what he is and what he has done and what he can do. (It is no mere accident of language that Britons "stand" for Parliament, whereas we "run" for Congress and other offices.)

"Less is more" applies to people as much as to buildings. Some know it instinctively, from youth; others have to find out the hard way. Perhaps these cautionary paragraphs may help them shorten the painful span from self-assertion to self-respect.

Do You Come On Too Strong to Be Lastingly Appealing?

ALL OF US HAVE FRIENDS who have friends we wouldn't want to be friends with. For each of us has only a partial view of another personality — like astral bodies, we react only in relation to the gravitational field of our own orbit, not in relation to someone else's.

"What do you see in him — he's such a stick!" exclaimed a lady of my acquaintance, when I mentioned I was off to lunch with a man we both know. But he's not a stick at all to me, no matter how woodenly he may behave in her company; he has many virtues she cannot perceive.

Some people put all their merchandise in the window at once, while others just display a single piece, as it were. The first kind seem immediately attractive, interesting, and vital. But by the second or third encounter they have lost their appeal, like a stage comedian who repeats his little act time after time, rapidly growing tiresome.

Then there are others who on first or second meeting seem dull or rigid or conventional, polite or proper, but in no way appealing. Yet if one bothers to take the time with them, one is often in for a pleasant surprise. They are harder to know, but more rewarding in the end.

These are the one-piece-in-the-window people. Like most of

the better shops, they do not try to beguile you with a dazzling variety of trinkets, but are cool and slow and deliberate in disclosing any more of themselves until they are sure who and what you are. And the longer you know them, the more layers you find beneath the understated surface.

One of the reasons the English suffer a universal reputation for being reserved, or standoffish, is that they are brought up to present only a formal version of themselves in public, withholding their private selves for the time when acquaintance ripens into real friendship.

When the shell cracks, the stuffiness is suddenly transformed into conviviality, informality, and sly, whimsical humor. No other nation I know of is so thoroughly capable of laughing at itself as the English, which is one of the truest tests of a genuine civilization. (While the Germans, who are so publicly radiant with *gemütlichkeit,* have virtually no sense of humor about themselves, as their dark history testifies.)

I had a splendid time at lunch with the "stick." But the next time he confronts that lady of my acquaintance, she will again wonder what I saw in him — never imagining for a moment that it is her own limited angle of vision that distorts the profile of his personality.

I Wish I Had Known at Eighteen . . .

• That the most fatiguing activity in the world is the drive to *seem* other than you are; it is finally less exhausting to become what you want to be than to maintain a façade.
• That the familiar phrase "the pursuit of happiness" should be reversed to read "the happiness of pursuit," for there is more pleasure to be found in the quest than in the goal.
• That you can sometimes change the mind of a person who possesses an idea, but never the mind of a person who is possessed by an idea.
• That those people will not believe we are acting decently and

honestly if they know they would not be acting decently and honestly in our place.

• That although everyone holds up justice as a model, what we really want is something less than justice for those we dislike and something more than justice for ourselves.

• That careful observation of others can teach us to avoid their mistakes, but no observation can prevent us from making our own mistakes.

• That only shallow people imagine they really know themselves; and perhaps they do, if there is little to know.

• That youth finds no value in the views it disagrees with, but maturity includes discovering that even an opinion contrary to ours may contain a vein of truth we could profitably assimilate to our own views.

• That no one can achieve a character by adopting a set of mannerisms, for eventually the mannerisms become a substitute for character.

• That it is absolutely impossible for others to respect you if you lack basic self-respect.

• That much of what looks to us like sophistication when we are young and far removed from it looks more like feverish desperation when we are older and closer to it.

• That the trouble with cleverness is that understanding a thing too soon often prevents one from ever understanding it thoroughly enough.

• That when we tell ourselves we are choosing the lesser evil, we are invariably choosing only the more comfortable one.

• That those who marry mostly to escape an unhappy home soon find that they have just added one more to the total number.

• That ambiguity has its own uses, and it is better to be vaguely right than precisely wrong.

A real friend is not so much someone you feel free to be serious with as someone you feel free to be silly with.

Obvious Flaws Often Have Hidden Reasons

MARSHALL MCLUHAN'S sudden death at the end of 1980 reminded me of an important lesson I learned some dozen or so years ago. It was probably a lesson I should have learned long before then, but really didn't.

He and I were scheduled to debate before a large audience in Windsor, Canada — so large, in fact, that the site had to be changed to Detroit to accommodate the overflow demand. McLuhan, then at the crest of his popularity, was of course the drawing card; I was only his foil, something like a prelim boxer signed up just to give the champ a chance to show his stuff.

We were debating about education, but it turned out to be no contest at all. The issue was never joined; instead of sticking to the subject, McLuhan wandered all over the map, talked about what he wanted to, and totally ignored the points I made. It was obvious that he was unprepared and indifferent to the topic assigned us.

I was not only disappointed but disgusted. His performance was insolent to the sponsors and insulting to the audience, who had come to hear a clash of opinions and got just a rehash of his well-known views on messages and media. "The man's a palpable fraud," I told my family.

A few weeks later I read in the papers that McLuhan was in the hospital in Boston. It seems that for a long time, unknown to anyone, including himself, a tumor had been growing in his brain, affecting his behavior and control. He was sane and rational in most ways, but the ailment derailed his concentration to the vanishing point.

The chastising lesson I took from that was, first, not to make private assumptions from public conduct, and second, if we have to judge, let our judgments be provisional, not ultimate. We do not really know why people do what they do, even when we are close to them — and sometimes especially *because* we are close to them.

Of course, not many people who behave erratically have an organic illness at the root. But there are other unknown causes equally hidden — emotional disturbances generated by a bad marriage, an unsatisfactory career, disappointing children, some deep sense of personal failure. People kill themselves every day, often surprising their dearest friends.

Whenever I am tempted — as I often am, being by temperament a judgmental person — to pass a hasty verdict on unattractive or bizarre behavior, I think back to that afternoon in Detroit and the nervous figure pacing the stage with that ugly thing growing minute by minute inside the delicate brain.

Debate? It's a marvel the man could stand up at all.

Strong-willed Not the Same as Self-willed

TWO WORDS THAT SOUND much alike are *strong-willed* and *self-willed*. Yet there is a whole world of difference between them. I thought of this when I heard the mother of a teen-age boy describe him as strong-willed.

He does pretty much as he pleases, comes and goes when he wants to, spends his allowance on the first bauble that catches his fancy, and cannot wait to be gratified when he desires something. This is an almost complete definition of *self-willed*.

A self-willed person has a weak will, not a strong one. In a sense, he has no will at all: He is driven, willy-nilly, by his appetites and needs of the moment. In terms of the old "association" psychology, his appetites control his will and his will dictates to his reason.

A truly strong-willed person operates exactly the other way around. His reason directs his will and his will regulates his appetites. A strong-willed person can postpone the satisfaction of a present need in order to gain a higher and more permanent satisfaction at a later date.

A strong will can withstand frustration, and cope with it; a self will is spurred by frustration into premature action or reaction. A strong will can accept the limitations of reality and live within them; a self will is always manipulating and distorting reality to conform to some wish-fantasy.

George Washington was a strong-willed man; Benedict Arnold was a self-willed man; and their respective public careers accurately reflect the profound difference between the two. Washington worked for what was best for the country and thus ultimately best for himself. Arnold worked for what he imagined was best for himself, ultimately betraying both country and self.

Washington's strong will enabled him to surmount both the privations of war and the slings and arrows of the presidency; Arnold's self will led him to desert the colonial militia in the French and Indian Wars, to invade Quebec vainly, to be court-martialed because of quarrels with the civil authorities, and finally to betray his country and die in exile.

A strong will *does not what it wants to do, but what it perceives must be done;* a self will does not possess the inner freedom to make this choice, but is forced by its own neediness to satisfy an immediate hunger. A strong will possesses a measure of distance and independence from itself; a self will is totally enslaved to its own fatal gratification, like gamblers and alcoholics and compulsive libertines.

That mother's son has the weakest will in the world. He is simply a palpitating bundle of wants and needs, none of which will achieve a tranquil satisfaction until he can strengthen his will to rein in the wild horses that race always toward the precipice.

If some people seem to have more good luck than others, it is mostly because a lot of what we call bad luck is determined by the contour of the personality rather than a mere accident or chance.

Now, a Reverse Pride for Parents

PARENTS OF NEWLY GROWN CHILDREN today are fond of shrugging and saying, "It's a new ball game," but that is an understatement. It's a new ball park, too, with dimensions nine times as large, and all the positions have been changed.

It used to be that parents were proud of what their children accomplished; now they are compelled to be content with what their children *don't* do. If they don't wind up in jail, on dope, or prematurely pregnant, the parents consider this a notable victory.

Many a father who years ago told himself he would turn his daughter out of the house if she openly had an affair has now resigned himself to the fact that his twenty-year-old (or younger) is living with a Bulgarian shepherd on a cranberry farm in Manitoba. "At least he makes an honest living," the father is reduced to muttering to himself.

And the same parents who in the past bragged about their son's college record and grades now tell you, with a sigh of relief, that he is a carpenter's assistant in the Colorado mountains, "but working hard and keeping out of trouble." The fact that he was registered as an applicant for Yale at the age of two has receded in their minds to the dim outlines of the early Ice Age.

We used to expect, and even demand, positive things from our children; now we are privately relieved at the mere absence of negative things. We rapidly tick off a list of the vices and troubles they have managed to avoid, and feel obscurely grateful for this minor blessing.

On the whole, we have been forced to become a hell of a lot more modest about what our kids are doing, and this alone must be a good thing, for them as well as for us. Those dreadful parental pressures to "achieve" at any cost have been relaxed to the point of limpness, and this must represent an improvement in the natural relations between parents and children.

But still, it is a rude shock to the parental ego, gazing out at this new ball park into the receding distance and scarcely recognizing the dimensions or the strange positionings of the players. We can't keep score any longer, either: The teams seem to change uniforms and batting orders every inning or so.

All this is terribly confusing and upsetting to us, but most of us find that our emotional ties are stronger than our moral preconceptions, and we accept what we never thought we would, with good grace, or a pretense of it. Those who don't quickly find that the ball park is utterly closed to them, and there is nowhere else to go.

Before Your Eyes Turn Green

ENVY IS NOT ONLY the most unrewarding of emotions, it is also the most stupid and thoughtless. For what it invariably forgets is that you have to make a full trade, not a partial one.

Envy of another person — his or her looks, brains, success, social position, money, or what you will — abstracts a few desirable attributes of that person whom it covets. But you have to take the whole person.

You can't just swap attributes; if you would like to be that person in some respects, you must be prepared to become that person in all respects. And if you knew all respects, the odds are high that you would be unwilling to make the exchange. For the fates customarily rake away with one hand what they give with the other.

I have just finished reading the book *Haywire,* a brilliantly moving chronicle of her family by Brooke Hayward. She was the eldest daughter of Leland Hayward and Margaret Sullavan. Her parents were rich, influential, famous, handsome, charming. She herself was bright and beautiful, featured on the cover of *Life* magazine when she was sixteen.

Who would not envy a girl like this, born with everything?

Only those who experienced her life from the inside, as she did, and so poignantly depicts it.

Her father was married five times, her mother four. Her mother killed herself — and so did her father, less obviously, by compulsive overwork. Her only sister spent time in a mental institution and then committed suicide. Her only brother served most of his adolescence in another mental institution. She herself was married and divorced twice before the age of forty.

She grew up without permanent roots, permanent friends, or permanent schooling. The family lived everywhere and nowhere. As the old man said in the Saroyan play, there was no foundation, all the way down. There was love, of its own kind, but as another old man has told us, "love is not enough." It needs continuity, understanding, consistency, patience.

Anyone would have envied Brooke Hayward, traded with her, as a cover story in *Life*. No one would be willing to make the exchange after reading a few chapters of *Haywire*. Not that there is the slightest trace of self-pity; she is too smart and strong for that. But she makes us see that having "the best of everything" can be a bitter and hollow illusion.

Socrates once remarked that if all the world's troubles were piled up in one heap and each of us was asked to take an equal share, we would gladly settle for what we already had. You may envy the face, the figure, the bankroll, or the brain — but you have to take whatever else goes with them, and it is not a good bargain in nearly every case.

"Living for pleasure" is either the worst or the best of philosophies, depending upon how narrowly or broadly one defines pleasure, *or whether one equates it with joy.*

*

Our opinion of others depends far more than we like to think on what we believe their opinion of us is.

"Keeping Busy" Works Two Ways

THERE ARE FAMILIAR SAYINGS that cut both ways, and most people who use them don't understand how they cut the other way. Like the man I heard today, remarking to a friend at lunch, "I just love to keep busy."

He was a stranger, so I don't know anything about the implications of his remark. But there are two opposite ways we can love to keep busy, and they are totally different in motive and consequence.

The healthy way to keep busy is to project yourself, as a person, into the life of your work or your family or your community, so that you are looking forward to tomorrow. Without this sort of involvement, we tire easily, age rapidly, and turn crabby and self-involved.

But there is also an unhealthy way to keep busy. This is to engage in activity for its own sake, to use busyness as a device for warding off reality. Activity can be a narcotic, just as alcohol can, for deadening the senses to personal relations, family obligations, and community responsibility. And for keeping tomorrow at bay.

Work and love, said Freud, are the two elements that combine for a satisfactory life. But many people who seem to love their work use it as a substitute for working at their love. They let their families go to pot (emotionally, if not materially) while focusing all their libido on a company, a merger, a stock issue, or any commercial enterprise.

Not to be involved in work of some kind is stultifying to the human spirit; and obviously, the best kind of work is that which you would be willing to do for nothing if you could afford it. But not many are lucky enough, or talented enough, to find so creative an outlet for their energies.

Women too, of course, are not exempt from this syndrome. The "busy, busy" woman who is always attending club meetings, working for causes, or performing civic duties may be doing so because she has an abundance of vitality and concern — or because she is escaping from a genuine relationship with her husband and her children. Which takes work, too.

It is the inner dynamics of the situation, not the raw facts themselves, that determines whether our busyness is a heightening of our powers or a lowering of them, an advance into more givingness or a retreat to some compulsive fugue that will not let us rest and reflect and re-examine our reasons for loving to keep busy.

Most of us require a balanced life in order to reach the optimum satisfaction for our diverse needs; too much industry can be as crippling as too much indolence. But people tend to be proud of their industry, while secretly ashamed of their indolence. If many of them examined its emotional roots, however, they might begin to recognize that, just as all that glitters is not gold, all movement is not necessarily getting anywhere.

The Lure of Physical Labor

MEN SEEM to remain boys far longer than women remain girls, and maybe forever. I thought of this on my way out to lunch the other day, passing a huge construction site where a new high-rise is going up.

There were several dozen men lounging on the railing, just looking at the operations, and not a single woman. The men included the usual number of loafers, truants, unemployed, and retired, but also more than a scattering of business and professional men on their lunch break.

Although the work was slow and an observer could scarcely calibrate the progress, the men were fascinated with the mere mechanism of digging and removing huge piles of dirt from one place to another. And they gave the power-shovel operators their most respectful scrutiny.

Whether it is biological or culturally conditioned, there is something in most men that wants to keep doing what they did as boys — that is, sheer physical effort that culminates in a tangible product or that somehow changes the course or shape or size of their environment.

And those who mature into occupations that are deskbound seem to feel that they have relinquished a part of their masculinity in opting for a career that does not call upon their body and their hands as much as upon their minds and their mouths.

These business and professional men would not in reality change places with the power-shovel operator or the other workmen. Yet a part of them is wistful and nostalgic about the loss of their physical prowess, and possibly a little ashamed that the work they are so well paid for is so undemanding of their masculine powers, of their proclivity to construct.

In our paper society, sedentary work seems parasitical, or at best tangential. It lives off what is elsewhere cultivated or produced, and is often more highly rewarded than the efforts of the cultivators and producers. We can perhaps rationalize this discrepancy, but there lingers a remnant feeling that body and soul together should be involved in worthwhile projects.

This is possibly why professional and business men play so hard on their weekends and during vacations, engaging not only in taxing sports but in strenuous hobbies of building fences or repairing boats or renovating sheds or any activity that serves to remind them of the kinetic pleasures of boyhood, when the project (and not status, money, or power) was its own reward.

It is a paradox in our society that no one wants to do "menial" work, yet the further away we get from it, the more attractive it seems. But perhaps it is attractive only when, as in boyhood, it is not done under economic compulsion.

When we are young, the world is full of mystery and magic; as we mature, we see it sensibly and straightforwardly; but as we get older, it is borne upon us that the mystery and magic were not wholly an illusion of childhood.

Talent Is Rarely Across the Board

PEOPLE TEND TO BE terribly confused about talents and abilities; perhaps that is why so many people are chosen for the wrong jobs, with consequent surprise that things didn't turn out better.

Some friends the other day were disbelieving when I mentioned that my thirteen-year-old daughter beats me at Scrabble more often than I beat her. "How is this possible," they wanted to know, "when you know at least ten times as many words as she does?"

But a game like Scrabble does not depend primarily upon the number of words you know; it depends upon how quickly and keenly you are able to make words out of separate letters. It calls mainly for powers of *perception* — and children are extremely good at this, as anyone knows who has been humiliatingly beaten at Concentration by a small child.

In somewhat the same way, the game of chess does not require a massive intellect, as most nonplayers suspect; it takes merely a special kind of mind that can visualize three-dimensionally. Some of the greatest intellects in the world have been *patzers* as chess players, while conversely, a Bobby Fischer displays about as much nonchess intellect as an itinerant shoe-lace peddler.

Talents that seem to be allied are often at deceptive cross purposes: General Grant was a first-rate military leader but a disastrous President. There is an enormous difference between leadership qualities in a civil democracy and in an authoritarian group. The general must inspire, but the politician must conciliate.

It is the ability to deal with people, I think, that bears the least relation to other specific talents. A man can be a marvelous administrator in a technical sense, but if he is deficient in handling people, all his technical efficiency goes down the drain —

in fact, it operates against him, for efficiency only brutalizes when it ignores the human element.

England's two great heroes, Wellington and Nelson, offer a classical study in contrasts. Wellington became known as the Iron Duke because of his harsh discipline; Nelson, though just as strict, was revered by his men because he took them into his confidence and made them partners rather than mere subordinates. His genius as a tactician was equaled by his genuine charisma as a naval leader.

But Nelsons are extremely rare, in any field. Most of us are good at only one thing, if at that. Trouble begins when we imagine that our ability in this area gives us expertise in some cognate field; but chess and checker players, using the same board, are wholly different breeds.

Parents Set Woeful Marriage Model

A HALF-DOZEN PUPILS from my children's high school were briefly interviewed on TV recently on the subject of marriage, where they displayed a remarkable unanimity of opinion. All agreed that they would prefer to marry later rather than earlier — which on the whole I think is a healthy and mature attitude — but it was their reasons for this decision that disturbed me.

They uniformly regarded marriage as a closing, an ending, a tying down, a restrictive and repressive pattern of living. But this is a dangerously distorted half-truth, for while marriage is in one sense confining, it can also be in another sense creative and liberating.

It made me wonder what models of marriage these young people saw at home, for doubtless most of what they profess to believe about the marriage state is based, consciously or unconsciously, on their own limited experience in their own households.

And it seemed as if, in their experience, marriage marks the end of self-expression, self-exploration, and self-development. Most of them wanted two separate lives: first a career and openness, then marriage and closedness. In their minds, these two modes of existence are immutably opposed to one another.

Yet it need not be so, and should not be so. Granted that most marriages do not reach the ideal, neither do most jobs or careers. In fact, more jobs than marriages are dead ends, where further development is impossible and only a grinding routine represents the foreseeable future.

Marriage should be a growing and a sharing and a creating as well as a responsibility. It should not preclude being onself; rather, it should make it more possible, and more gratifying.

But as these children seem to view their parents' marriages, this is evidently not what they see, and so they are turned off on the institution until they have had a "full life" after schooling and are ready to "settle down." Marriage as a dynamic and productive joint enterprise has hardly entered their minds — possibly because they have not seen one in operation.

This is a dreadful indictment of what we as parents have modeled for our children. It is also testimony to the fact that too many marriages are regarded as endings and tying-downs by the partners themselves. Their failure or unwillingness to explore its creative possibilities have given their children no incentive to seek a sharing and mutually supportive marriage.

One of the strongest reasons for accelerating women's most recent bid for equality is that it can provide the liberating momentum to turn dead-end marriages into participatory democracies, and demonstrate that the marriage union can make both parties free as much as it binds them together.

If more young people would stop looking *for the "right one" and spend more time trying to* become *the "right one," pairings would be simpler and far happier.*

The Deadliest Sins Are Ones We Can't See in Ourselves

KNOWING YOUR OWN STRENGTH is a fine thing. Recognizing your own weakness is even better. What is really bad, what hurts and finally defeats us, is mistaking a weakness for a strength.

The reason that the seven sins are so deadly is that they are mostly unknown to their possessors — and they are unknown because they are called by different names. The stubborn man imagines he is resolute. The vacillating man supposes he is flexible. The envious man, the lustful man, the cold man — each translates his defect into positive terms. (Obviously, I use the word *man* generically, including women, too.)

John Calvin, for whose general views I do not have much admiration, was a great and purposeful man because he knew the best thing in the world to know about himself. "I have not so great a struggle with my vices, numerous as they are," he wrote, "as I have with my impatience. My efforts are not absolutely useless; yet I have never been able to conquer this wild beast."

A lesser man than Calvin would have persuaded himself that his "impatience" was really the virtue of energy, efficiency, or zeal. Calvin, as a realist about human nature, did not attempt to fool himself.

It is too often the trait we are proudest of and feel the strongest in possessing that is a greater defect than any vice we might admit to. I feel sorry for Bobby Kennedy, so proud of his ambition, so ready to cut down anyone in his way, who might still be alive today if he had restrained himself a little in his precipitous leap toward the presidential primary.

I think of Ernest Hemingway, swaggering in his false sense of manliness and finally blowing out his brains when the façade collapsed, as it was bound to do in time. What he wrongly imagined to be a strength turned into megalomania and proved to be his fatal defect. How much more of his talent he might have given us — and how much more honestly — had he been able to accept a little more softness at the core of himself.

All around us, we see people misinterpreting and misusing their weaknesses: the pleasure-bound think they have a lust for life; the power-driven delude themselves that they are natural leaders; the hard of heart call themselves pragmatists; and the smugly intolerant fancy that they are high-principled.

Jesus is recorded as preferring the company of the disreputable, the avowed sinners, the failures, because they at least did not fool themselves that their weaknesses were strengths. The only person in the New Testament ever promised eternal life was a self-confessed thief.

The longer students live together in mixed dorms, the less important a part sex will play in their personal relationships; enforced segregation of the sexes intensifies the sexual role far more than proximity does, especially in a society that constantly stimulates the erotic appetite.

*

Many people think enough of their mates to love them, but not enough to trust them; yet trusting is a greater compliment than loving. (As Job trusted in God even through pain, anger, and resentment.)

*

We have to overestimate ourselves in order to achieve our highest level of success and underestimate ourselves in order to make that success palatable to others.

*

Great philanthropy is a silent confession that more was taken in the first place than should have been.

IV.
Of the Fine and Vulgar Arts

You Can't Write Writing

GERTRUDE STEIN is most famous among the ignorant for her incantation "Rose is a rose is a rose," but she knew what she was saying, and she knew what she meant. She would never have said, for instance, "A writer is a writer is a writer."

This is the mistake being made by the public television channel in New York, which is using a grant to commission original plays for television, to be written by distinguished novelists and short-story writers.

A writer of stories is not necessarily, or usually, a writer of plays. A writer of plays is not usually a novelist. A novelist is not usually a poet. A poet is not an essayist. An essayist is not a fiction writer.

The differences in writing are far different from the differences within the other arts. A composer composes, a painter paints, a sculptor sculpts, using the medium of tone and color and line. But while you compose music and paint a picture and sculpt a figure, you cannot write writing.

There has never been an author, including Shakespeare, who could write equally well in every form.The use of words is far more limiting and circumscribed than the use of tone and color and line.

If these novelists and short-story writers could have written plays, they would have written them long before. If a poet could say something in prose, he would not have to say it in poetry. If an essayist or critic had the imaginative capacity and talent, he would be writing masterpieces instead of writing *about* them.

George Bernard Shaw published five novels, all of them failures, before he abandoned the form and learned that he was really a playwright. Henry James tried time and again to write plays, which were dismal flops on the stage, although his short stories and novels are superb.

Dozens and scores of writers, many of the first rank, have toyed, and more than toyed, with other forms, but in almost every case they have given up and returned to the form they handled best and most naturally. Some of the finest writers, indeed, have not been "writers" at all — like Freud, a medical man, who wrote the purest German of his time.

A great composer may show equal facility in writing a symphony, an opera, a sonata, and a piece of ballet music. But writers are more specialized creatures, because words do not have the *plasticity* of music or painting or sculpture — so little so, that even a splendid playwright may not be able to adapt his own drama to the films.

It is a noble and generous thought to offer novelists and short-story writers a shot at TV plays, but Gertie would have known better.

The virtue of knowing one subject thoroughly is twofold: It not merely gives us mastery over the subject, but it should also provide us with a grounding for what knowing really consists of, and thus humility in the face of other subjects we only have opinions on.

*

Our merits may impress others, but it is our flaws that make us congenial; and those who try too rigorously to conceal their defects may be buying respect at the cost of friendship.

Blasting Music to Drown Out Reality

THE CONTRACTOR sent around two sullen, slack-jawed young assistants to do some repair work on the tennis court across the road. They brought with them, inevitably, as standard equipment for the job, a powerful portable radio which kept blasting away for a full afternoon.

Call me any ugly word you will, such as snobbish or elitist, it remains my firm and unshakeable opinion that such people are as close to the moronic line as it is possible to get and still function in a social order. The tolerance for a high decibel rate, masquerading as "music," is in my opinion inversely proportional to the level of intelligence.

I can understand the need for what my children call elevator music in some factories or even restaurants, to keep the help from falling asleep or brooding on the essential monotony of their jobs. It less pardonable in dentists' offices and such, but there it is at least relatively soft and easily ignored.

But these young men were working in August among grass and flowers and birds and birch trees, with a lovely view of the water and the cliffs and everything you might want to feast your senses on; instead, they anesthetized themselves with the junkiest of junk music throughout this God-given afternoon in a serenely sylvan setting.

My own theory is that people such as that turn on the radio not to bring something in, but to shut something out. It is not in order to hear the music, but in order that the vacuum in their minds may be soothed by sound, so that silence does not force them into thinking about themselves or experiencing the real world of perception and sensation.

And basically, what they want to shut out is the reality of their existence. This urge, almost a compulsion, to keep reality at arm's length is nearly pandemic in our society. It accounts not only for the incessant, frenetic music, but also for the drugs, the booze, the sports mania, the television addiction, the intense preoccupation with trivia — all of which act as opiates, dulling any sense of reality.

Marx's harsh dictum of the last century can almost be turned upside down today to read: "Opium is the religion of the people." And nowhere — not even in drugs or booze — can this be more clearly seen than in the kind of music spewing forth from portables and automobile radios and most hi-fi sets.

Music began as a celebration of nature and an exploration of the human spirit. Bach elevates us, Mozart delights us, Beethoven deepens us; all bring us closer to the wellsprings of life. Now this great gift has been turned against itself, blasting forth a cacophony to dull and deaden and dehumanize the soul.

Is It Too Late to Save the Theater?

One wonders how many barn doors have been locked after how many horses have been stolen. What calls this ancient saw to mind is word that the League of New York Theater Owners and Producers voted to impose a levy on all Broadway and touring shows under its jurisdiction, in order to "promote the legitimate theater and clean up Times Square."

Payments were expected to produce more than a half-million dollars by the end of 1976, as a cooperative effort to "develop and hold a wider theatergoing public than exists now." But it may be many years too late for that.

Years, and even decades, ago, it was time to save the American theater from vulpine landlords, mushrooming production costs, outrageous union demands, astronomical salaries, and the resultant tripling and quadrupling of theater ticket prices.

Then everyone was at the trough, lapping up as much as possible and giving as little as possible in return. Meanwhile, the whole neighborhood centering on "Broadway" began degenerating into a sexual slum, with peepshows, massage parlors, prostitutes and pimps, muggers and scammers, topless bars, bottomless bistros, and anything you might perversely desire in the way of carnal excitation.

Worst of all, from the economic, if not moral, point of view, was the growing fact that only one Broadway production out of ten won financial success; that the hit shows reaped millions in returns, while even moderate successes could not operate in the cost crunch of that exploitative environment.

But theater, as a business or a profession, cannot exist with only a few multimillion-dollar hits; it needs, as in London and other capital cities, a few dozen theaters operating at the same time, so that all esthetic tastes may be satisfied, actors employed, and houses kept open on a regular basis.

A couple of decades ago the League should have levied a tax on the big hits in order to support the lesser productions and to keep the Times Square area at least minimally decent. As in a social poker game, the winners should have "kittied out" a certain percentage for the losers — not out of sentiment or generosity, but in simple recognition that the industry could not survive without the broadest base.

If the performing arts are to flourish without governmental subsidy (which they get nearly everywhere else in the world), then all their diverse producing units must begin to collaborate on the same basis, with the strong supporting the weak. In the arts, unlike other businesses, when the weak go to the wall, the victors soon fall victim themselves.

Every life makes a difference: The most insignificant creature can spawn a criminal, and the most unlikely influence can transform him into a Beethoven.

*

It is the single-purposed man who reaches the goal most surely and swiftly — and then has the most time to find out that having a single purpose is not a satisfactory goal in life.

If You Can, Don't Give That Advice

ONE OF THE THINGS acquaintances are fond of doing is giving me a ring to say that someone they know is going into New York for a few days or a week, and would I please recommend some new plays for them to see, since I happen to be the drama maven for my local paper.

In my early days I was always glad to oblige and swell the coffers of what I considered to be worthy plays. But then it gradually dawned on me that it is difficult, if not impossible, to recommend a good play to someone you do not know.

If their taste is drastically different from mine, they will curse the day I got them to invest $40 or more for a pair of tickets to a "dog," and my reputation (such as it is) for dramatic perspicuity will go down the drain with them. And who needs it, after going to the trouble to compile an up-to-date list for someone you have never seen?

For much the same reason I reluctantly recommend out-of-town restaurants; one man's Escoffier is another man's Automat. And the man, instead of shrugging philosophically and murmuring "De gustibus" to himself, will only bear a grudge for having squandered his money on your rotten recommendation.

Actually most people do not want advice; what they want is a confirmation of their own prior tastes and fancies.

"When someone comes to me for advice," said the late George Nye, "I find out what kind of advice he wants, and I give it to him." This cynical appraisal hits closer to the truth than we care to admit. Most of us are not looking for new experiences, either in food or entertainment; we are looking for something novel that is at the same time close to what we have already enjoyed or experienced.

Most of our foreign travel is conducted along the same lines — we like to hear about strange and exotic places and intriguing customs, but when we visit such places, we expect all the comfort of home, all the familiar amenities of hot water, cold martinis, air conditioning, and a swimming pool in every piazza. This is the whole explanation of the Hiltons' success throughout the world.

But . . . I still keep making recommendations; few of us have the strength of character to refrain when asked. One such man, a president of Amherst, was lovingly recalled by John Erskine in his memoirs, *The Memory of Certain Persons*.

One autumn he rose in chapel to address the students at the first assembly of the year. After a few welcoming sentences, he broke off and smiled. "I intended to give you some advice, but now I remember how much is left over from last year unused." With which he took his hat and walked out.

Writing about Children

A READER IN FLORIDA wants to know, as others have also inquired, "Why don't you write about your children anymore?" Simply because my children are now grown-up people — my "baby" is a sophomore in college — and you insult their dignity if you keep on writing about them beyond a certain age.

Indeed, when they reach that certain age, they are probably more competent to write about their parents than the other way around. Our vision is blurred by nostalgia; we have a hard time separating what they have become from what they were as little children.

In fact, our view of them will be colored forever by those early years. They, however, begin to see their parents in a somewhat different light. Just as lovingly, we may hope, but more realistically; more critically, but also more compassionately.

They see that we are not as great as they thought, but not as awful and unreasonable either; they begin to understand our excesses, our deficiencies, and, most of all, the fact that our standards and attitudes were shaped by our times, as much as theirs have been.

Parents who want their children to love them as uncritically as when they were little are really, whether they know it or not, yearning to retard their children's development as independent adults.

It is easy to love someone in whom you are too blind to see faults; the merit consists in loving, faults and all. Not denying or excusing, but accepting, as we want ourselves to be accepted as we are.

Last fall, my younger daughter selected and edited five years of my columns for this book. She was objective about them as I could never be — rejecting some, questioning others, suggesting changes in a few. And almost always right.

She could detect the flaws an author rarely recognizes in his own work, not errors of grammar or even of fact, but, more important, the tones and undertones we cannot hear in ourselves — vanity, and arrogance, and forced jocularity, and anger that is more self-righteous than righteous.

With the passionate honesty of youth (which unfortunately tends to desert us as we get older), she can see far more clearly into me than I into her. She is still growing and changing into the person she will eventually become; her father has become nearly everything he is going to be, stuck with himself in most essentials.

It is instructive to write about our children when they are young; it is an impertinence when they reach the time of departure. We may know more about the world, but they know more about us, and if we are unwilling to listen, it is our loss as much as theirs.

What we call compassion when we feel it is labeled sentimentality when we don't.

Critics: Use the Darts on Yourselves

IF YOU ARE LIKE most people, as I assuredly am, then you may have noticed how we change roles as we change functions, and are hardly ever aware of the discrepancy.

Driving a car puts us into the motoring function, where the pedestrian is regarded as a dangerous idiot and an obstruction to vehicular speed, safety, and sanity.

But the moment we become a pedestrian for an hour, the function of walking shifts our psychological role — and then the motorist turns into a homicidal beast and a wildly inconsiderate menace to life and limb.

At another level, I think of this every time a new book of mine comes out. One of my professional functions is that of drama critic; and when the critics are assailed (as they customarily are), I bristle with resentment at the unfairness and obtuseness of these attacks.

Yet when my own books are reviewed by the literary critics, I unconsciously shift gears and find their comments intolerably short-sighted, prejudicial, and arrogantly opinionated.

It is then, and only then, that I can clearly see how each critic filters a work through his own personality, and reads into or out of it whatever is most congenial to his own value system, while supposing that he is really being "objective."

While most of the reviews have been favorable, for which I give grateful thanks, even the laudatory ones tend to disagree on what they find in the book.

One sees me having too optimistic a faith in the possibilities of human nature; another views me as far too cynical. One finds me not engaged enough in political discussion; another finds the pieces too politically slanted. Again, I am too simple, and too complex.

And so it goes. These are all contradictory views, which cannot be true at the same time, yet it rarely occurs to critics that they are revealing as much (and perhaps more) about themselves as about the work being criticized.

One of the few ironic geniuses of our time, Anatole France, understood this quite well when he once prefaced an essay with the remark, "I am about to review myself by way of this book." He realized that the profound skepticism of his temperament would inevitably tincture everything he wrote in praise or dispraise of another person's work.

Scientists have learned to subtract what is called the personal equation from their observations, for they recognize that they are not merely passive registers of the phenomena they are inquiring into. This is harder, perhaps impossible, to do in the arts — but every critic should regularly expose himself to the vulnerability he finds in others.

Why Is Something Good or Bad?

I HAVE BEEN BROWSING through an amusing book that was sent to me, called *Best, Worst and Most Unusual,* by a pair of chaps named Felton and Fowler, whose chief qualification for writing the book seems to be that they felt like it.

Although it is meant to be fun and not taken seriously, I think the authors might have performed a useful service in a book such as this by distinguishing between subjective and objective judgments.

For instance, whether chocolate ice cream is a "better" flavor than vanilla ice cream is a wholly subjective judgment, and can be nothing else: It depends on taste and temperament, and there are no criteria for evaluating ice-cream flavors.

But in much the same realm, whether a Château Rothschild wine of a given year is "better" than some Sicilian blend of no pedigree whatever is not subjective at all, and every oenologist will select the former.

In the book, the authors choose Beethoven as the best composer of all time, which is a purely subjective judgment. I would have chosen Mozart, and somebody else might have picked Bach, and there is no rational way of deciding who is right in this rarefied realm.

(Which reminds me of the lovely distinction made by some musicologist whose name I forget: "When the angels play for God, they play Bach; when they play for themselves, they play Mozart.")

However, if the authors had chosen Grieg or Sibelius or Ravel, then it would no longer have been merely a matter of taste — for no one who understands music could for a moment rank any of these near the same level as Beethoven, Bach, or Mozart.

Where many people go wrong is in assuming that because *better* and *best* are meaningless in some areas, they are meaningless in all; that therefore there is really no hierarchy of values, and one person's judgment or taste is as good as another's along the whole spectrum.

Of course, one cannot objectively judge degrees of greatness — Tilden or Budge, Dempsey or Louis, Citation or Secretariat? — but one can calibrate the degrees leading up to greatness, if one possesses enough expertise, in wine, in music, in tennis or boxing or horses (not a highbrow pursuit, but followed by the devotees of racing, who handicap steeds on precisely this basis).

It is, to be sure, an error of snobbishness to venerate the expert, who, being mortal, can always be wrong; but more often in our times, we commit the opposite excess of deifying ignorance with the slogan "It's all a matter of taste," in matters where taste must be trained.

A moralist who is not also in some way a humorist is soon ignored, while a humorist who is not also in some way a moralist is just as quickly forgotten.

Another Kind of Movie "Projection" Stirs a Ruckus

IN THE DISPUTE between the gay community and the producers of the film *Cruising,* I can sympathize with both sides. There is really no fair and rational way of resolving such differences, and it has nothing to do with the feelings of the gays or the profits of the producers.

What we are dealing with here — as always — is that peculiar convolution of the human mind we might term *projection.* That is, people tend to generalize from specifics: Most of us are incapable of judging a character or situation in itself, but regard it as a model, a pattern, or a typical representation of the whole environment from which it sprang.

The gays are no doubt right that the film reviles and distorts homosexual life; the producers are equally right in that the story line is admittedly based on real-life occurrences. The gays insist that the film will intensify the straight public's hostility toward them; the producers rebut that all drama is by its very nature a heightened slice of life and might well offend the sensibilities of any group it depicted. (You can hardly have ethnic bad guys anymore.)

We find much the same problem, and the same arguments, going as far back as Shakespeare's *The Merchant of Venice,* with its scathing portrait of Shylock, the Jewish usurer. Jewish groups object to this play because many viewers, rather than accepting Shylock as a character in himself, regard him as a paradigm of Jewish cupidity and use this dramatic portrait to justify or solidify their anti-Semitic feelings.

(Shakespeare, by the way, was aware of this tendency and tried to soften the impeachment by including the "good" Jew, Tubal, whom nobody pays attention to in the play, as a balancing factor.)

On the one hand, *The Merchant of Venice* is a valuable drama, deserving to be seen and studied; at the same time, it indubitably does create or strengthen animosity against the Jewish people. Should it be shown or boycotted, especially among impressionable youths in school?

The fault in such matters is squarely ours, not the dramatist's, or the producer's, or the protesters'. As long as we continue to take the part for the whole, no one is safe from calumny or contempt. If we suppose that *The Godfather* reflects the Italian community, or *Cruising* reflects the gay community, or Shylock stands for the Jewish community, we are guilty of the crime of projection; and until we straighten out our crooked thinking, we are straights in name only.

A Wry Twist from a Pompous Fool

SHAKESPEARE, WHO WAS a waggish fellow as much as a great poet, was fond of playing jokes on posterity. The good ones have gone on forever. Like the speech by Polonius in *Hamlet,* containing the famous line "to thine own self be true."

Many people, today as then, proclaim this speech of Polonius, in which he gives advice to his son, as their "philosophy of life." But if they would bother to read the whole play (which they rarely do), it would become painfully evident that Shakespeare's joke is on them.

In the first place, Polonius is intolerably long-winded — which is why Shakespeare has him say that "brevity is the soul of wit." In this terse aside, the playwright shows us the glaring discrepancy between Polonius's advice and his personal conduct.

Moreover, Polonius is plainly a yes-man who is *never* true to himself but is always what young people today call a suck-up — he sucks up to everyone in authority, even Hamlet, whom he considers crazy. He is a toady, a time-server, a hypocrite, a fuss-budget, and a fool.

Shakespeare shows some mercy to his villains; he shows nothing but contempt for Polonius, who does not even have the strength for wickedness, and therefore imagines he is above it.

The playwright knew perfectly well that all the Poloniuses of his time and the future would seize upon this platitudinous speech as their "philosophy of life," just as in another context they use the Golden Rule as a grand abstraction to mask their amoral behavior, or as politicians use the flag and motherhood to camouflage the hollowness of their views.

"Neither a borrower nor a lender be" — and all the petty, prudent people seize upon this mocking remark to justify their selfishness or prissiness. Yet anyone who knows Shakespeare knows that he admired, above all, the "magnanimous man," who gave as freely as he took. The safe bourgeois virtues enunciated by Polonius are a large part of what prompted Hamlet to exclaim, "Denmark's a prison."

It has been said that of all the characters in all the Shakespearean plays, Hamlet is the only one who could have written them. It is certain that the playwright identified with him more intensely than with his noble friend, Horatio, who was not "passion's slave."

There are levels in Shakespeare that the ordinary reader never reaches, because he does not want to. He prefers the "sane" Polonius to the "mad" Hamlet, not recognizing that until more of us become as fiercely conscious of our own moral weakness as Hamlet was, the world will continue to be run by men as blandly unconscious of their failings as Polonius was.

When we are tempted to begin a statement with "If people would only . . . ," it is good to keep in mind that "people" is an abstraction standing for "I and thou," and that at least half the responsibility for human conduct rests upon the "I."

*

At times one could almost divide the world into those who are insane and don't know it, and those who are sane and doubt it.

Greasepaint — Where the Actors Hide

THERE IS A LESSON some people never learn — that the obvious answer is almost always the wrong answer. And, unless they learn this lesson, they can never understand the people around them.

As an example, the average person believes that actors and actresses are attracted to the stage because they want to show off their personalities. Quite the contrary happens to be true.

The actor is interested not in exhibiting his personality, but in *disguising* it. He is not showing himself to the audience; he is rather concealing himself.

As a drama critic for a dozen years, I have seen countless evidence of this. Only recently, a famous Broadway actress, who is soon going on tour in her new play, wrote to me declining an invitation to lecture to my club while she is in town.

"I am simply terrified at standing up and talking in front of an audience," she confided. "I tried it once, years ago, and almost died. The only time I feel confident is when I have a script in my head and am playing a character. Then I feel I am simply the instrument of the playwright."

Offstage, most actors and actresses are not at all the vivid and colorful figures they seem to be. Only a few are distinct individuals; the others are bland and neutral personalities with little to say, and that little is generally dull.

They are transformed into different persons, however, the minute the curtain rises. The actor takes on stature and dimension, becomes impressive and articulate; the actress assumes glamour and depth and exudes an appeal that is noticeably lacking in the dressing room.

A first-rate stock actor confessed to me this summer: "I feel like a nobody until I'm on the stage in a part. I don't feel I have any identity or substance in my personal life, and it's only when I lose myself in some stage character that I am able to find my meaning and my strength."

What is true of performers is often true of other kinds of people: The trends and traits they seem to show in their professions or occupations may be the exact opposites of what they really are.

And so-called common sense cannot give us the correct answers about human drives and motivations. No expert is as arrogant or dogmatic in his views as the average man who smugly believes that "common sense" provides him with an X-ray into the mind and heart of his fellows.

Experience and Writing

A WOMAN I KNOW on the West Coast has written a humorous children's book, and a mutual friend was deprecating her efforts to find a publisher. "Why, she's never had children," the friend remarked, "so how can she write a book that will appeal to their comic sense?"

This is in the same category of thoughtless criticism that would suggest Victor Hugo had to be a hunchback to write about Notre Dame, that Shakespeare had to be Jewish to portray Shylock effectively, or that Dickens had to be insufferably mean to give us Scrooge.

In point of fact, it is singular that the greatest fantasists and humorists of the nineteenth century — Edward Lear, W. S. Gilbert, Lewis Carroll, and G. K. Chesterton — were all childless. Imagine a publisher turning down *Alice in Wonderland* because the author was a lifelong bachelor.

In our own time and country, perhaps the most consistently successful author of children's books is the man known as Dr. Seuss — who is not only not a doctor, in any medical sense, but is not a father either. Yet millions upon millions of youngsters have hugely appreciated his vast sense of the comic, while most of his would-be imitators have fallen by the wayside.

It is true only in a limited sense that an author needs personal experience in order to write persuasively on a given subject. Even a genius such as Dickens, we may reasonably believe, could not have portrayed Oliver Twist and David Copperfield so convincingly had he not spent part of his youth in the grinding toil of the blacking factory.

But in another and deeper sense, the creative imagination can grasp characters and conditions not directly experienced, because the creator *has access to all parts of his personality*. To use the fashionable word, he has empathy with characters unlike him, because he knows that deep down he shares some of their unlovely traits.

There is something of Scrooge in all of us, but we hide it from ourselves and refuse to admit its existence, however latent. The author is in touch with the Scrooge in himself and uses it for literary purposes. Hugo knew how to feel like a hunchback, Shakespeare knew how to feel like a Jew, because all of us are crippled in some way, all of us are at some time a rejected minority.

After all, the woman on the West Coast has once been a child herself; that is all (plus the talent, of course) that is necessary to write a children's book — so long as you keep in touch with your past, remember what it was like, and summon forth the feelings and responses you once had. What others among us bury or distort, the artist revives, refurbishes, and rejoices in.

We Need Courses in Criticism

I WAS SPEAKING down at a southern university not long ago, where the journalism department has expanded fourfold in the last few years, with a staggering budget for all sorts of new communications technology. But in all the courses, there was not one devoted to the craft of criticism — a subject generally ignored in journalism schools, although the media have always had a shocking shortage of qualified critics.

In all the arts — books, music, painting, drama, the dance — a critic is considered a second-class citizen by most editors and news directors; they assume that almost anyone who is competent in general news reporting can take on a critical post at a moment's notice.

This is largely because they themselves are news-oriented and don't think anything is truly important unless it emanates from the corridors of power. Art and culture and all that is just so much fluff to them, stuck in to pacify the minority who bother themselves about such piffling matters.

As a result, of course, most of the critics they pick are grossly unqualified for the jobs, and nobody knows or cares, except the few performers who come to town, or a handful of cognoscenti who get their cultural information from more elevated sources.

I have been to good-sized towns where the same person on the newspaper staff covered movies, plays, operas, and art shows, knowing equally little about all of them, and in many cases simply rewriting the puff sheets handed him over lunch by the publicity agent for the project.

Even on the larger organs, the standard of criticism is appallingly low, as any author, musician, painter, or stage director is more than willing to tell you. And this is not because they are castigated by the critics; they are more often praised, but ignorantly so. There is little judicious evaluation of their work, or of what they are trying to do.

One of the crying needs in our journalism schools is a severe course in criticism, not as an abstract theory but as a living craft. A music critic should be able to read a score; a drama critic should at least know how a play is blocked out; an art critic should have some conception of visual esthetics. All of them should be trained in the practical aspects of the discipline, by working on real projects in a live setting.

A critic is a necessary catalyst between a creator and his audience; his comment should be helpful to the former and informative to the latter. His function is to act as a bridge, not a barrier. It is only the ability to transmit that justifies the critic's function, providing an eager and perceptive audience for the visions of the creator.

Narrow "Realism" Misses the Point of Real Vision

ONE OF THE HALF-DOZEN most difficult words in the world to define or to understand is *realism;* and yet people use it all the time to make judgments about many things, including the arts.

What does a man really mean when he says he likes realistic painting? He means, in most cases, that he likes a picture to represent objects the way the eye sees them. But the eye does not see reality.

When we look at a chair, we do not see the real chair, but an optical illusion. The real chair is a mass of particles moving at incredible speeds with ceaseless energy.

When we look at a person, we see the face, the limbs, the clothes. Are these the real person? Nobody would deny that it is the character, the spirit, the emotional structure beneath the bone that makes the real person.

A telescope sees big things more "realistically" than the eye; a microscope sees little things more "realistically" than the eye. If we do not expect the scientist to look at the world with our naive realism, why should we expect the artist to do so?

What we call reality is merely the surface of things, the appearance of objects. There is no truth to be found in this, and both the scientist and the artist seek a truth not visible to the naked eye.

Actually, we do not even believe in our own realism; we do not believe that the Earth is flat, as it seems to be; we do not believe that the man who looks kind is kind, as he seems to be. We ourselves apply more critical, more sophisticated, and (to use a dirty word) more intellectual yardsticks to everyday things around us.

The artist goes us one further. He accepts *nothing* as it seems to be, for it is his task to throw a searchlight on the caverns and labyrinths of life. Now, his searchlight may be weak, or soiled, or focused in the wrong way, and the art he gives us will then be dim or defective.

But whether he is a good or bad artist, we cannot ask him to look at the world the way we do, for then he would see nothing more than we do. If anything, history shows that the mass of mankind spend their todays in trying to catch up to the artists of yesteryear. We have just barely begun to come to an appreciation of Blake's visions.

There is an amusing story about realism and Picasso. A sailor once complained to him that his paintings were not realistic, and then took out a tiny snapshot of his child for the painter to see. Picasso squinted seriously at the snapshot and handed it back to the father, merely saying, "Small, isn't she?"

Only a Few Are Creative

NOT LONG AGO, while lecturing at the drama school of a university, I referred to acting as an interpretive art rather than as a creative one. Quite a few in the audience resented this; they preferred to think of what they did on the stage as being creative.

I purposely made the distinction, because it seems to me that the word *creative* is terribly abused these days. At any moment we might expect to see an ad offering a course in "Creative Mortuary Management," if there isn't one already.

Actually, nature has defined *creativity* for us by the relative rarity with which it produces genuinely creative personalities. For every thousand excellent actors or actresses, there may be only one or two excellent playwrights. For every thousand talented pianists or violinists, there may be only one composer of real merit.

Indeed, one of the perennial problems in the theater (in all countries everywhere) is the high ratio of first-rate performers to third-rate scripts. We almost never see a play where the writing is better than the acting: In almost every case, the interpretations are better than the play deserves. And for every choice role there are a hundred qualified candidates.

In a loose sense, of course, everyone may be more or less creative, from the little child devising a variation of an old game to an Escoffier preparing ingredients differently to produce a new dish. But strictly speaking, real creativity is rare even in the highest disciplines: There is only one Einstein in a century of gifted scientists, only one Tolstoy in a century of talented novelists.

Nothing is gained by debasing the currency of language so that interpretive talents may regard themselves as creative. And a great deal is lost — for if every activity is creative, from cooking and flower arranging to mortuary management, then the word loses its singular impact when applied to genuinely creative efforts and accomplishments.

If every private in the Army were called a general, what would there be left to call a general? If everybody is somebody, then nobody is anybody (as Gilbert so neatly satirized in *The Gondoliers*). Our modern tendency to reduce everything to its lowest common denominator so that nobody will feel inferior is a false and dangerous egalitarianism.

Nobody is inferior as a *person,* but miming Rhett Butler on the screen is scarcely comparable to penning the *Divine Comedy*. As old Confucius warned long ago, corruption in society begins when things are not called by their right names.

To execute a murderer is simply to adopt his point of view.

The World as a Never-Ending Subject

IN WELL OVER three decades of writing a daily column I have heard almost everything, but there is one recurrent question that never fails to puzzle and astound me. It is the first question I am asked most often by most people.

"How do you find material to write a column every day?" they invariably want to know as soon as we meet. To me, this is the equivalent of asking a skywriter how he finds enough space for his messages.

Robert Louis Stevenson versified that the world was so full of a number of things that he thought we should all be as happy as kings; and while I cannot share his optimism (nor his sanguine view of royalty), I heartily agree about the multiplicity of objects in the world.

Indeed, there are not enough hours in any day, or enough days in any year, or enough years in a lifetime, to express one's thoughts and feelings about the whirligig of creation and recreation, production and reproduction, constancy and change, and the sheer wonder of it all.

Find material? Nobody has to find material — it is here all about us, in almost infinite abundance. One could spend a lifetime writing about a single subject — psychology alone, or history, or, more delightfully, music — and not nearly exhaust the wonder and the strangeness and the novelty and the discovery.

The "material," as they call it, is as available as the air in the sky or the sand on the beach or the leaves in a forest. All I do is squint at it from my own angle of vision, trying to understand it a little better and to pass on my personal vision to others who may see it differently, or not at all.

The really difficult task in writing is not mine, but is carried by the imaginative creators — by the poets and the playwrights and the novelists. They form their material not from the world we share, but in the private world of their own which they create and people like an act of God.

Since I cannot do what they do, I am just as thunderstruck by their uncanny ability to produce truth and beauty and meaning out of nothing, as it were, as my readers seem to be by my own renditions and translations of reality.

Our age does not — perhaps no age ever did — pay enough tribute and respect to these masters of imagination. The poet cannot make a living, the novelist fares best as a peeping Tom, and the playwright as a Simple Simon. But the mere commentator, who does little but rearrange the obvious, who invents nothing and ennobles nothing, is considered something of a marvel.

Of all the objects in the world I wonder at, I wonder most about the people who include what I happen to do as one of the objects of their wonder.

On the New and the Known in Art

A HUNDRED YEARS AGO, in 1880, a painting submitted to the Royal Academy in London was condemned by the judges' committee to the dark cellar of the rejected and the despised. The judges contemptuously dismissed it as a "thing," "a confounded arrangement," and "an insult to the art of painting."

It was the last picture the artist ever painted that was to be seen at the academy during his lifetime. No individual or institution anywhere would then pay even a thousand dollars for a painting that is now deemed priceless.

It seems inconceivable to us, a century later, that this familiar picture was ever attacked as revolutionary, half-baked, incompetent, and demeaning to the classic tradition of painting. Even its modest title, *Arrangement in Gray and Black,* was ridiculed by curators and staff.

Looking at it today — where it is one of the most precious possessions of the Louvre — we see only an elderly woman in a dark dress and a white shawl, sitting calmly in a chair. To our eyes, it is a quiet and conventional portrait, almost quaintly old-fashioned. If anything, we find it a little trite, somewhat too pictorial for our taste, a museum piece we may remotely admire but cannot get excited about.

What in this sedate and peaceful arrangement could have stirred the critics, the public, and so many fellow artists of 1880 to such wild outbursts of indignation, scorn, and derision? We might understand why Van Gogh's strange suns and fantastic flowers could and did provoke laughter or revulsion — but this tame, almost too "realistic" old lady in a chair?

Well, the next time you happen to visit an art gallery or are otherwise exposed to what is known as modern art, try to keep this little story in mind. For it is well worth remembering that each generation is too close to the work of its contemporaries to judge it fairly and rationally. Only a few eyes are open to the genuinely innovative.

I do not suggest that we automatically have to appreciate whatever is new and startling; that is mere trendy snobbism. But neither should we feel that we have a right to dismiss or despise whatever is new or different; that is mere philistine stuffiness. We need to learn to suspend our ultimate judgment until we have developed a new way of looking at a new object. "I know what I like" only means "I like what I'm used to."

The picture, of course, is now commonly, if inaccurately, known as *Whistler's Mother*. And it strikes us now as a rather outmoded birthday card.

What we really want is to evaluate those around us with a divine justice, while we want them to evaluate us with a divine compassion.

*

It is impossible to take with full seriousness someone who displays no sense of humor, for it is only humor that redeems profundity from pretentiousness.

It's a Lot More Loverly When the Fair Lady Is British

A NEW YORK REVIVAL of *My Fair Lady* nearly foundered when the "alien committee" of the Actors' Equity union refused to permit a British actress to be hired for the Cockney role of Eliza Doolittle. This kind of foolishness has been going on for some thirty years.

The union will not accept a foreign actor in an American production unless he is either an international star or performing a role that cannot be done successfully by an American. This second stipulation has proved a real stumbling block, for who is to define what *successfully* means in terms of stage performance? (Happily, the union lost its case.)

It should be obvious to anyone who has seen *My Fair Lady* that no American actress is capable of reproducing the accurate accent or cadence of a poor London Cockney girl as well as the genuine article could. In nine productions, both on Broadway and on tour, the only ones that thrived were those that had cast an English actress as Eliza.

I once saw a production of *Guys and Dolls* on the London stage, in which half the actors were British and making absurd efforts to ape the Damon Runyon lingo. It was pure disaster — something like casting *Oklahoma!* with an all-Korean company. Some plays translate well into other cultures; but some lose everything of their original flavor.

Narrow nationalism and protectionism of the sort promulgated by Actors' Equity has no place in the arts, most of all. Indeed, it is "imports" of talents across national borders that raise the level of performance and stimulate the public demand for the best that can be found, regardless of national origin.

The success of the Ballet Russe in its prime years, and later of the Sadler's Wells company, gave tremendous impetus to such American groups as Ballet Theater, the New York City Center Ballet, and others. When the Old Vic visited New York, it raised our own dramatic standards and heightened audiences' interest in the theater generally.

Like science, art is transnational and must have a free exchange among diverse cultures to grow to its fullest dimensions. In nations like Soviet Russia, where the arts are intensely nationalistic by official policy, few creative developments are possible. Art is in the service of the state, and nothing worthwhile has ever come of this.

Free trade in creators and performers is as necessary and beneficial as free trade in products. In seeking to protect the employment of its native members, Actors' Equity unwittingly betrays the whole raison d'être of the theater and its allied arts, which is to offer the public the highest skills and talents available, regardless of the artificial boundaries imposed by politics, prejudice, or provincialism.

"Quincy" Is a Poor Rx for Medical Grads

PLEASE BELIEVE IT'S NOT jealousy or sour grapes on my part — I have more commencement addresses than I can handle each June — but it faintly disgusts me that the 1980 graduating class at the Mount Sinai School of Medicine in New York voted overwhelmingly for an actor named Jack Klugman to deliver its commencement address.

Not because of his capabilities as an actor, mind you, but because he portrays "Quincy," a crusading forensic pathologist in a television series. It tells you something about the educational and intelligence level of these medical graduates that they prefer fantasy and fiction to fact.

Klugman knows no more about pathology, or any area of medicine, than a hog knows about Sunday. I remember many years ago when William Bendix was cast in the title role of *The Babe Ruth Story,* he had to be taught how to hold a bat, and the Babe himself walked out of one rehearsal session in disgust.

Actors customarily know nothing except acting; they will make a plausible doctor, lawyer, or Indian chief if you hand them a script, and at the end of the performance they are as ignorant as when they started. My old friend Basil Rathbone, who was the essence of Sherlock Holmes on the screen, could barely find the dial in a phone booth.

One cannot fault Klugman for accepting — it is a nice publicity ploy, and some flack will compose an amusingly relevant talk for him — but I personally would not care to be tended or treated by a member of the 1980 graduating class at Mount Sinai, if they suppose that "Quincy" has any words of wisdom to impart as they embark on their medical careers.

You would think, or hope, that young doctors in New York were at least a cut above the primitives who actually believe that actors write their own lines or are really anything like the characters they portray. We really haven't progressed that far in public sophistication from the frontier days when males in a western audience would leap on the stage and try to assault the villain who was torturing the heroine.

Sometimes, actually, the more weak-minded among performers begin to take their parts seriously. When Raymond Massey was playing Abe Lincoln on Broadway, he was so infatuated with the role that he wore his makeup, beard, top hat and all, around town after each performance. He was pontificating one night at the bar of the Lambs Club when Oscar Levant, standing next to him, whispered loudly to the bartender, "That guy really won't be happy until he's assassinated!"

And if he were still doing the part, no doubt Mount Sinai would invite him to give the commencement address on "The Presidency as I See It."

It is only a sentimental half-truth that the best things in life are free; while they may be, it is equally true that we need the money to buy the time to enjoy them.

Writing Schlock with Socko Sales Is No Mean Feat

I REMEMBER one of the children asking me, years ago, why I didn't write a junky novel that would be a best seller and make a lot of money for the family. I replied at the time that I wouldn't do it as a matter of integrity — and I wouldn't — but I failed to add that I *couldn't* do it, either.

Actually, writing a junky best seller is just as rare a gift as writing a serious and profound novel. Beginning writers imagine that anyone with a little talent can turn out a popular work of fiction, but that is a gross misconception.

There is a special knack to writing bad novels that appeal to millions of readers, and only a handful of authors can do it. Most of them seem to be named Harold or Irving, for reasons that elude me. They are hacks and have no literary merit or meaning beyond their own brief day, but nevertheless what they do is both difficult and rare.

It is not worth doing, of course, except as a cold commercial enterprise, but they reap such rich returns precisely because so few can do it. Hundreds of rotten, overblown novels are published each year, but only two or three have that indefinable *je ne sais quoi* that makes a sensational hit in the market.

A serious novelist, even though he might want to for mercenary reasons, could not duplicate this dubious feat, any more than an operatic prima donna could sing a popular repertoire with great effect. Anyone who has heard an opera singer warbling musical comedy tunes knows that she is vastly inferior in this medium to an untrained singer.

Perhaps the most successful writer in the world in our time was the late Agatha Christie, whose mysteries sell in the tens of millions. Yet if you read her autobiography, you will learn that she didn't consider herself a writer in any serious sense of the word; she merely accepted with gratitude the knack she had been given for turning out highly popular fluff of a sort no one could copy.

What made her work so much more appealing to so many more readers than the mysteries of Sayers, Allingham, Marsh, Tey, and other far better writers than she remains a mystery more impenetrable than any that Hercule Poirot or Miss Marple ever disentangled. I doubt that Irving Wallace or Harold Robbins themselves could tell us.

It is more than luck or an accident that only one or two badly written books out of a thousand make it to the top. They are badly written in a special way that no good novelist could imitate, and these geniuses of perversity are every bit as rare as real masters. The only difference is, thank God, they don't last nearly as long.

The Inner Clocks of Creativity Tick at Any Pace They Please

IN HIS VALEDICTORY ARTICLE, Max Beerbohm confessed that for him Thursdays were the least pleasant day of the week. Explaining why, he said that Thursday was the latest possible day he set aside each week to get his writing done.

It is indeed strange how temperaments and habits differ in terms of getting necessary work done. I don't think there is any rule I have ever read that someone has not successfully broken. I am convinced that the best way to work at anything is the way that happens to be best for you.

There are people who are absolutely immobilized until the very last moment and then throw themselves into a frenzy and do well in an hour or two what they could not have half so well done in a week.

There are those who swoon at the thought of such procrastination; they do what has to be done each day, at the right and proper time, and finish comfortably ahead of schedule. They would panic and collapse if faced with a sudden deadline.

Every one has his own inner clock and even calendar that may bear only a remote resemblance to public time. Why do I get to an airport in time to take an earlier plane, while my friend arrives just as they are pulling up the gangplank?

I remember being in Hollywood one summer, in a hotel bungalow next door to a famous comic-strip artist who locked himself in his room for two weeks at a stretch, turning out a six-week supply of cartoons. Then he would loll at the poolside for a month, until the time came to immure himself again. He was in effect his own prison warden.

This would drive other artists utterly mad; they work day by day, one day at a time, on a rigid schedule, which is the only way they can meet their professional obligations. Their inner clocks are set at a far different beat, or alarm system, than the others.

Some people are so prolific, of course, that it makes little difference how or when they work. It is said that Rossini composed his operas while lying abed in the mornings; if a sheet of paper slipped to the floor, he didn't even bother to retrieve it, but simply wrote out another melody.

There are no regulations or prescriptions for creativity, whether it be scientific, intellectual, or artistic. Beerbohm could not have written on Monday to save his soul, as long as he knew he had until Thursday as a deadline. The only rule I have found useful is not to wait for inspiration — for work doesn't come from inspiration, but inspiration comes from work.

It is only people of small talent who profit by being "in the swim"; for if you want to be in the swim, you have to go with the current, and nothing of permanent value has ever been accomplished in the current — only against it, or at least away from it.

On Storytellers and Actors

WHY CAN SOME PEOPLE write a story that you believe, and others cannot? I haven't the vaguest answer to this question, but I am certain that the storytelling ability has nothing whatever to do with any kind of literary skill or merit.

By now I can pick up a new mystery or spy novel and read one page to know if I want to take it home and dip into it. Just a few lines of dialogue or a paragraph of description, and the author reveals himself as a storyteller or not.

At an early age I knew I was a writer, and not much later than that I knew I would never write a short story, much less a novel, because I totally lack the ability to create convincing characters who walk and talk on their own power and carry their own authenticity with them.

Some of the finest writers are natural storytellers, while others are not. And some of the most deplorably deficient stylists have the natural gift of fiction, and little else. It is almost like being double-jointed, or being able to whistle through your teeth — a knack that is irrelevant to anything else.

The fictional talent, it occurs to me, is more like being an actor than a writer per se. You are either an actor or you are hopeless; you can either throw yourself into another character and become that characte, or you remain a dumb stiff clod mouthing lines no one believes.

The actor has the imaginative power to *project* himself out of his skin and into another's; likewise, the born storyteller can make other people come alive under his pen. It may be no accident that the greatest master of creating characters, Dickens, was also an immensely successful public reader of his novels, changing voice and personality as he read.

Most of the popular best sellers have this knack; and no matter how shallow or contrived or even meretricious the books may be, the public responds to their imaginative universe. This is one reason that so many bad novels make exceptionally good films: A film is dialogue and action, without much thought. (A "serious" film is usually a disaster.)

The will cannot be made to do the job of the imagination; no skill or artifice can compensate for a lack of the storytelling ability. In fiction, it is what Sir James Barrie said about charm: "If you have it, you don't need anything else; if you don't have it, nothing else helps." So many fledgling novelists would save themselves years of grief and disappointment if they honestly tested themselves for the absolute pitch that is required to make the fictional scale ring true.

Serious Art Needn't Be Solemn

SITTING IN THE REVERENTIAL HUSH of the concert hall listening to the Fine Arts Quartet playing Mozart, I inadvertently chuckled out loud — and from the angry looks darted my way by the people sitting near me, you would think I had committed a nuisance in the aisle.

Yet Mozart obviously wrote the passage in a humorous, whimsical vein, intending to amuse us. His work is filled with impish surprises that invite a smile, and sometimes a chortle.

Because it was "serious" music these people were listening to, they felt it almost impious to relax and enjoy it as it was meant to be taken. They make the common mistake of confusing the serious with the solemn, and omitting humor and high spirits from the airtight compartment of culture.

No less a critic than Matthew Arnold made the same error when he denied to Chaucer a place among the greatest writers because Chaucer was not sufficiently serious in the same way that Virgil, Dante, and Milton were.

To Arnold, and to other esthetic prigs, if something is comical it cannot be serious and therefore cannot, by definition, be "great."

This nonsense syllogism — which the culture-intimidated

public tamely accepts — would exile from the realm of great art nearly the complete works of Balzac, Rabelais, Boccaccio, Petrarch, Horace, Catullus, and Aristophanes.

It would exclude huge hunks of Shakespeare, including *Hamlet,* which contains some of his lewdest and funniest lines. It would ignore the best piece of narrative fiction ever written, *Don Quixote,* which is just one huge joke raised to perfection.

Chaucer is no less serious an artist because his vision of the world is humorous; indeed, in my opinion he is considerably greater an artist than Milton, whose lofty genius is sometimes windy and pretentious. *The Canterbury Tales* are ribald, but they are also true, in a different but just as deep poetical sense as *Paradise Lost.*

In the same way, Mozart, Beethoven, and other master composers wrote a great deal of playful music; the scherzo movement is specifically meant to be amusing. But we have become so overimpressed with seriousness in classical music that we sit like mummies, breathing dumb adoration instead of taking a joke in the spirit it is offered. We forget there is as much of his greatness in Beethoven's gusts of laughter as in his funeral march — and that the fool in *King Lear* expresses more wisdom than the tragic king does.

The Play Is No Longer the Thing

THE WORDS *play-goer* and *concert-goer* have the same formation, which may fool us into thinking that they apply in the same way. But they are vastly different.

I have never heard a concert-goer say, "I went to an Isaac Stern concert last night. He played 'Three Blind Mice.' Of course, it isn't much of a composition, but that man certainly knows how to get the most out of the violin."

Absurd, isn't it? What concert-goer, of any level, wouldn't walk out of the auditorium in disgust and indignation if a Stern strutted onto the stage and began fingering "Three Blind Mice" on his Stradivarius?

But this is precisely what so-called play-goers say time and again. They went to see this celebrated actress or that distinguished actor, and though the play was junk, they certainly enjoyed the way the performer got the most out of it. But isn't it basically as demeaning and insulting to watch a fine actor declaiming the equivalent of "Three Blind Mice" as it would be to listen to a great musician playing it on the violin or piano? If a piece isn't worth doing, is it worth doing well? And the better it is done, the more wasteful is that talent. *Nicht wahr?*

This is one of the main reasons that our level of dramatic culture is so inferior to our level of concert culture. No concert-goer would tolerate a Stein or a Horowitz debasing his gifts on a baby exercise; but time and again we applaud, say, the Lunts, cavorting in some infantile charade.

We attend concerts to hear good musicians performing worthwhile compositions. We attend the theater largely to see stage personalities exhibit their tricks and mannerisms, regardless of the quality of the material they regale us with.

As long as this public attitude persists, there is little incentive for those stage performers to offer us anything more than amiable nonsense or pretentious folderol. If we are as eager to see them in *Sorry, Wrong Room* as in Chekhov or Ibsen (and maybe more eager), then why should they bother to work hard for a *succès d'estime* when it scarcely pays?

The play is very much *not* the thing in contemporary society; the player is. We worship personality beyond mere prowess; we lay out cash to see Names, and eventually the Name becomes a substitute for the Thing, the Package for the Product. In this commercial shell game, the pea has totally disappeared.

Play-goers today are mostly star-gazers. Concert-goers are music-listeners. And each get precisely what they want, and ask for.

Society Is Two-Faced Toward Education

WE SEEM TO BE a totally schizophrenic nation when it comes to the subject of education. Let me offer a few of the more glaring contradictions in our attitudes and our practices.

On the one hand, we sanctify education; we warn our children that they can get nowhere without it, and the more the better.

On the other hand, thousands upon thousands of young people who have taken this admonition seriously and earned their Ph.D., the highest degree possible, now find that there are no jobs available for them, and are working as clerks, cooks, cab drivers, and carpenters — if they are lucky enough to have any job at all.

On the one hand, we complain that there aren't enough generalists entering the world of commerce, but only narrow specialists and technicians who can't grasp the relationships among specialities.

On the other hand, our education is more and more focused on the vocational and practical side, while the humanities and liberal arts languish; and we continue to turn out graduates with little sense of language, logic, history, or philosophy — everything that is needed to make a full person and a full citizen.

On the one hand, we spend hundreds of millions for buildings, books, laboratories, stadiums, gymnasiums, and equipment.

On the other hand, we spend virtually nothing on a program that could improve teacher selection and training, and would encourage the upper 10 percent of college graduates to enter the field, instead of the lowest 10 percent, as at present. We ignore the obvious fact that education can be no better than those who instill it, and we would hardly choose our doctors in the same negligent or capricious fashion.

On the one hand, we apportion the largest part of our property taxes for public education; in some towns and villages, the public schools are really private schools on the basis of hidden tuition paid by homeowners.

On the other hand, parents and taxpayers care little about the quality and extent of education their children are receiving, as long as marks are satisfactory and diplomas are awarded. Their concern about funds, coupled with their indifference to the quality of the actual product, perpetuates school budgets that are distorted to make the administration look good, while little of real value is being taught.

On the one hand, we pay abstract respect to the idea of education.

On the other hand, we suspect and resent persons who display perceptible signs of being educated, and place more reliance on experience than on academic training. Until we know that each without the other can be sadly deficient, we will not have an educational policy worth a nickel.

The Past Enriches the Present

As I go around lecturing at colleges, many English professors invite me to attend their classes, which I do if the hour is not obscenely early and the room is on the first floor.

What appalls me — as it does most of these teachers — is not only the students' innocence of our great literature, but also their reluctance to take any English courses that go back further than contemporary writing. To make matters worse, when they choose contemporary literature, most of them pick science-fiction or the mystery-adventure field.

I quite astonished one such group recently by jousting with them on their own field. One of their favorite modern works is the *Lord of the Rings* trilogy by Tolkien, who is perhaps the most popular author among young people today. I asked them what, in their opinion, made Tolkien's books so interesting and so superior to most of what is written in the field of fantasy these days.

They mumbled something about his storytelling ability, his imagination, his talent for creating characters, and so forth. But many trivial writers, from Zane Grey to Agatha Christie, possess those gifts in common.

As Robert Adams pointed out in a review of Tolkien, what is singular about his work is that it contains "a number of extremely good stories which many readers seem to be encountering for the first time."

For his *Ring,* Tolkien drew upon motifs from the books of Genesis and Revelation; parts of *Beowulf;* bits of Wagner; fragments of Malory and Macpherson's "Ossian"; dabs of the Norse sagas; the Gaelic legends; the Breton lays; the *Chanson de Roland;* the *Poema del Cid; Orlando Furioso, The Faerie Queen, Paradise Lost,* and a host of other ancient and medieval sources.

"Now," I said, "if Tolkien had known as little as you do about old literature, it would have been impossible for him to give you the pleasure and excitement he did in his trilogy. He was drawing upon the past, getting strength and inspiration from tradition in order to make a new work of imagination for modern readers." No one in class had been told this.

It takes an educated (or highly self-educated) person to write a superior book. We cannot write wholly out of our own internal resources; the past is an indispensable tool. If we want more Tolkiens, the schools have to encourage the backward look — even for writing about the future. When we break this continuity with the past, we lose the thread of humanity.

Unless you can transcend yourself — in Jesus' words, "throw yourself away" — you cannot find yourself; what we mistakenly call self-knowledge is not a burrowing in on oneself, but an arching out toward others, which is far more difficult.

Creating a Monster — In Ourselves

IN A LITTLE QUIZ not long ago, I dealt with a number of well-worn phrases and parables that are commonly misunderstood — which reminded me of that most popular creature in fiction, Frankenstein's monster.

Since Mary Shelley wrote the story in 1817, it has been reprinted, dramatized, filmed, televised, and recounted so many times that most people by now suppose that Frankenstein is the name of the monster (who was given no name) instead of its creator, a young medical student.

But the whole point of her story is generally missed in most of the adaptations. It was conceived as a horror story — but in the *moral,* not in the *supernatural,* sense.

In the first place, it was not a monster that the student created. A dedicated young scientist seeking knowledge to help mankind, Frankenstein did not make the creature for evil or malicious purposes. Nor was the creature evil when it first took on life: It yearned for human sympathy, affection, and understanding.

As it said when turning on its master, "Once my fancy was soothed with dreams of virtue, of fame, and of enjoyment. Once I falsely hoped to meet with beings who, pardoning my outward form, would love me for the excellent qualities I was capable of unfolding . . ."

But the creature was shunned by all who came into contact with it, because of its inhuman appearance. It was different; it was alien; and so it was scorned and feared as a revolting sight.

Faced with this treatment, the creature truly becomes a monster, with these words: "I cannot believe that I am the same creature whose thoughts were once filled with sublime and transcendent visions of the beauty and majesty of goodness. But it is even so; the fallen angel becomes a malignant devil."

He then proceeds to kill Frankenstein's brother, the creator's wife, and eventually the creator himself, who had refused to regard him as an equal. A close reading of the original story makes it impossible not to sympathize more with the monster than with his maker.

What does this tale tell us about the way we commonly regard people who are alien, whose outward form we will not pardon for being different from ours? Whatever their inner yearnings or aspirations, however they respect "the majesty of goodness," our revulsion drives them to the bitter edge of the demonic.

Who is the monster in the Frankenstein story — the man who contrived a servant and a slave, or the creature who hoped to be treated like another human? Perhaps it is no accident of illiteracy, but a deep Freudian slip, that the monster has become known by the name of its maker.

Harold Teen: A Buoy of Boyhood

I MENTIONED HAROLD TEEN at family dinner the other night, and even my eldest son, who is well into young manhood, wanted to know who that was. His question not only saddened me, but aged me a few more years, culturally if not chronologically.

The comic strips I grew up with were as much an integral part of my world as my mongrel dog, my Scout patrol, and my Junior Louisville Slugger bat. And Harold's hangout, the old Sugar Bowl, was as real to me as any soda fountain in my neighborhood — maybe more so.

I, along with all my friends, felt just as companionable with the Katzenjammer Kids, with Winnie and Perry Winkle, with Uncle Walt and Skeezix and Jiggs and Maggie and Mutt and Jeff and old Barney Google. We joined their clubs, wore their emblems, and shared their fond and foolish tribulations. They were the great mythic symbols of our age.

What I find lamentable today is that while many of the comic strips are far more cunningly drawn, wittier, and more whimsical and more sophisticated, their drawing power and staying power has shrunk ominously. They are modish: A few years, at the most, on top of the heap, and they are relegated to obscurity, as a new strip catches on. Very few, if any, possess the durability of my old pals.

What has happened has nothing to do with the quality or character of the strips themselves, but is simply a result of the accelerated rate of change in all our entertainment media. Nothing lasts as long as it used to — a popular song is now a "golden oldie" after a few brief years, whereas it used to dominate the gramophones and player pianos for a decade or more. "Stardust" alone spans several generations of Americans.

Today we are flooded with sensory inputs, so much so that no one thing has much of a chance to take hold, to become rooted in the popular folklore. An occasional "Peanuts" may resist this tide, but it too turns into a giant industry, becoming more of a trademark, a cosmic cliché, than the comforting little fantasy it started out as.

I happen to think that children, right through puberty, have a deep emotional need to identify with fictional characters over a long period of time; they nourish their roots on continuity and repetition and familiarity. The less the world changes, the less frightening, the more secure it is to them. Our dizzying rate of change has permeated the world of the comic strip as much as anything else, and young people have largely lost the sense of extended family the old cartoons provided.

We need outside markers as we are growing up, buoys that float on permanent moorings. It is not only Harold Teen that is gone; it is the soda fountain as well, and all it stood for in my youth.

One of the comforts of growing older lies in discarding the illusion of youth that other people are thinking about us, and recognizing that they, like us, are thinking about themselves.

Success Doesn't Guarantee Self-Acceptance

IT WAS YEARS AGO that I learned a valuable lesson about the vanity of human feelings. I was buying a pair of shoes, and a then-famous figure in early television walked out with a package under his arm.

"Isn't that so-and-so?" I asked the clerk. He nodded and then added indiscreetly, "He comes here about twice a year to buy elevator shoes we order especially for him."

What was surprising to me about this confidence was that the TV star was well over six feet tall in his bare feet. "You won't believe it," the clerk went on, "but we sell more of those shoes to tall men than to short ones."

I found out later that he was speaking the truth, and this was part of a larger truth: that people with gifts are often just as unsatisfied and insecure about them as people lacking in any distinction. Possession may be nine tenths of the law, but it is not even half of self-confidence.

The little world of chess, which I happen to know better than most, is I am sure a microcosm of the big world; and examples of this kind of self-doubt are rife even among the world masters. Most of them refused to give their prime challengers a chance to meet them in a head-on match, just as their predecessors tried to deny them the same chance.

The great Tarrasch, after losing two world championships to Lasker, filled his books with "proofs" that he should have won. Bogolyubov, losing calamitously to Alekhine, made the absurd charge that he had been hypnotized by the Russian master.

Alekhine himself, possibly the greatest player of the twentieth century, was the worst of all. Not content with his incredible record of victories, he actually falsified the annotated notes of his games to make himself look better in his published books!

Not long ago the international world of science was shocked by much the same thing, when a distinguished British psychologist was posthumously found to have fabricated statistics supporting some of his basic research on intelligence. He could not leave his eminence alone, but had to topple it by pretending to be even more impregnable in his findings and conclusions.

The ordinary person generally supposes that the talented and gifted are fortunately armored against the feelings of inadequacy that attack the rest of us, and cannot understand why a best-selling author or a famous actress would inexplicably commit suicide at the height of a career. But the internal measuring rod has little to do with that height, and self-achievement is no guarantee of self-acceptance.

Be Wary of a "Bad Success"

THEY WERE TALKING about this talented young TV actor who took his life and wondering what prompted someone with such a glowing present and limitless future to do away with himself.

I had never seen him, but I have known of authors in similar circumstances who did the same thing — Ross Lockridge, among many others — and it was just as puzzling to the people around them. But that may be because the people around them don't understand the different meanings of *success*. *Success* is not a univocal word, though it seems so to us; it does not mean one thing, and one thing only.

It is notable, in fact, that in two different plays Shakespeare uses the phrase "bad success," which sounds odd to our ears. We look upon success as something good by definition, but earlier usage distinguished between the kind of success that is good for us and the kind that more nearly resembles failure.

The kind that is good for us is creative and productive — and internally nourishing. It helps us grow, both in our professional skills and our personal relationships. It lifts us from one plateau to a higher, summoning more of our gifts and deepening and strengthening the sources of our success. This is the only kind worth having, or keeping.

The second, and far more common sort of success in our commercialized society, is bad for us. It does not help us grow, but keeps us as we were, frozen in the posture that brought initial popularity. It may make us famous and give us prestige, but at the same time it cuts us off from our roots and alienates us from our friends.

It replaces personal relationships with pecuniary ones — with managers, agents, lawyers, promoters, sycophants, and assorted hangers-on. It turns the person into a product, a package, a symbol. He becomes literally the slave of his success, and like the Red Queen in *Alice* has to keep running as fast as he can just to stay in the same place.

Obviously, this was the kind of success granted to the young TV performer. Too much money, too fast. Too much exploitation of his talent, and too little husbanding of his inner resources. Nothing to grow on, for everything around him was parasitical. No one really to talk to, except perhaps a paid psychiatrist, who can only shore up the damaged sea wall of the psyche, not restore it.

Never, in any society in any time, have so many celebrated and gifted persons as Ernest Hemingway and Marilyn Monroe and dozens of others killed themselves at the height of their "success." It should at least make us pause and wonder if the Shakespearean use of the word wasn't far more precise and perceptive than our careless label.

Man begins by generating a symbol to represent reality, and then clings (often fatally) to the symbol long after the reality has altered, become corrupted, or even vanished.

*

A smart person isn't really smart until he knows how to get along with fools — which is the chief reason so many intellectuals remain socially powerless and suspect.

Literary Creators Are Often Unlike Their Creations

SOMEONE AT LUNCH the other day remarked that he had met a distinguished novelist at a party and was "utterly disappointed" in the man. "A very off-putting chap," he said, "not at all warm and sympathetic, as you might expect from his novels." This is an old refrain. The creator and his creation are not necessarily the same, or even similar. What goes into an artist's work is the best part of him, what he aspires to; what comes out of him socially and personally may be the dregs left over after the vintage has been poured.

I have met too many creative people over the years to be disappointed in any of them. And the finest, most sensitive poets are perhaps the worst of all in some respects. So much distilled loveliness goes into their work that the residue is dark and bitter. Robert Frost was one such; Dylan Thomas, in quite a different way, was another.

For sheer disappointment, though, humorists probably take the booby prize. It is not that they are usually not funny in private; no reason they should be. It is that they are often crotchety and vain and mean, so that you cannot believe they have written such delightful piffle. As hard to believe, in fact, as Lewis Carroll's being the Reverend Dodgson.

Brendan Gill's book *Here at the New Yorker* displays James Thurber in some of his less attractive moods and moments as not the sort of fellow you'd want to ask in for a drink. Though he was a great humorist of our time, Thurber's testiness got worse as he got older. By the time I reviewed his last book for the *Saturday Review,* even his writing had curdled into petulance and acerbity. He resented not having won a Nobel Prize.

S. J. Perelman, my favorite humorist of this century (along with the vastly different Stephen Leacock), has never been described as a barrel of fun to be with. He left New York in a pet some years ago, to live in London, and returned not much later in a pet about London. Unlike Falstaff, he is witty in himself, but not the cause of merriment in others.

People are people, whatever else they may be. Louis Untermeyer, the poet and anthologist who died peacefully of old age a few months ago, was fond of telling a story on himself to illustrate this general point. He was attending a New Year's Eve costume party one evening and flinging himself into the spirit of the thing by wearing a ridiculous paper hat and raucously blowing a horn.

A college girl walked up to him, peered into his face, and then turned on her heel. "Hah!" she snorted as she walked away. "And he's Required Reading!"

Whatever the Era, Life Copies Itself

IT'S INTERESTING the different ways that different people will regard historical characters on the stage or screen. Some expect them to behave as if they knew they were historical, with period posturings and quaint mannerisms. Others, like myself, expect them to behave and sound much like us.

Watching a musical play about ancient Egypt not long ago, I was impressed with the fact that the author gave the characters a simple humanity that we could identify with, even though separated by several millennia. But one critic protested that the performers seemed too much like contemporary American youngsters thrown into an antique setting.

Yet every era to itself has seemed contemporary and even modern. The breeches and powdered wigs worn by the worthies of the eighteenth century were not historical or old-fashioned but as up to date as today's jeans and tank shirts. And the language they used, although sounding strange and stilted to us, was as demotic and idiomatic as our own speech.

People, and periods, do not change that much. One age may be a little more formal and another more casual, but old people in Shakespeare say much the same things old people say today, and youngsters have always taken liberties with costume, comportment, and conversation.

Not only do age distinctions remain pretty much the same over the centuries, but social distinctions do even more so. In *As You Like It,* written some four hundred years ago, one of the nobles complains that servants aren't what they were in the olden days, when they could be relied upon to be loyal and dutiful to their employers.

And of course Elizabethan drama is shot through with references to upstart merchants, cheating mechanics, insolent children, and wayward youth. Old people felt neglected then, just as now, while those rising in the world felt their way blocked by the old and entrenched.

Two of Lear's daughters are scarcely examples of filial piety; Juliet, at fourteen, is hardly a model of obedience and rectitude.

No, the people in Nefertiti's Egypt may have dressed oddly and worshiped beetles and cats, but to themselves they sounded just like we do to ourselves. Royal families squabbled in the same way, priests were just as minatory or unctuous, generals as blunt and belligerent, and lovers uttered much the same inanities in Thebes as in Brooklyn.

It was indeed in high antiquity that Terence, the Roman playwright, exclaimed, "Homo sum; humani nil a me alienum puto." ("I am a man, and hold that nothing human is alien to me.") Strange customs or costumes or turns of phrase are only the veneer of a culture; beneath these, Washington in a wig felt little different from Eisenhower in a field cap.

We tend conveniently to forget that there are exceptions to Aristotle's "golden mean" —for certain virtues cannot be held in moderation, or they fall, as a bicycle cannot be ridden below its proper speed. It is impossible, for instance, to be "moderately loyal" or "moderately truthful," as some would like to be.

It's ironic that the bookstore shelf labeled "Adult Books" is designed precisely for those readers who have not yet become adult.

*

When pornography is seen not as an offense against morals but as an offense against sexuality itself, then it will begin to lose its appeal; both the puritan and the pornographer have perverted views of sexuality, and each plays into the hands of the other. (Which is why the battle has no victories and never ends.)

*

There is no way to understand the general except through the particular; only by the act of loving one do we adequately grasp the nature of love itself.

*

Every community needs a newspaper that is better than it deserves; if the paper simply reflects the community, it is not doing a good enough job.

*

The fundamental kink in masculine nature is that no father of forty wants his daughter to do what he wanted other men's daughters to do when he was twenty.

*

A revolution customarily is initiated by righting wrongs and then is sustained by wronging rights.

*

A moralizer is someone for whom morality begins at the waist and goes downward; but in fact, most basic immorality exists above the neck, not in the loins.

Genuine love is a kind of surplus energy in living, and it imparts vitality to its object; spurious love, which comes from neediness more than from givingness, can always be discerned because it tries to suck vitality out of its object.

*

Nine times out of ten, when we say, "I'll think it over," we have already made up our minds.

*

Ecologists are that rare and necessary breed of people who are capable of regretting the future.

*

Female novelists, generally speaking, understand their male characters far better than even the finest male novelists understand their female characters. Men tend to idealize their heroines, whereas women tend to humanize their heroes.

*

If you find yourself habitually saying to some other, "Get off my back!" the odds are heavy that you put the saddle there yourself.

*

When we "get even" with someone, that is literally what we are doing — becoming even with them, that is, descending to their level in vengeance and losing whatever moral advantage we may have had.

*

Books on the art of acquiring and using power are as intellectually fraudulent as all those books on how to get rich — for those who have to read books on either subject lack the natural gifts that the powerful and the acquisitive instinctively utilize.

People are silly to have a "friendly divorce" — if you can be friends, you've already got more than most married couples have.

*

A miser makes a terrible contemporary but a marvelous ancestor.

*

There is in many areas an inverse ratio between quantity and quality: When I see someone who is "everybody's friend," I tend to doubt that he or she is anyone's friend very deeply.

*

Knowing when to say nothing is 50 percent of tact, and 90 percent of marriage.

*

Jealousy of the old for the young may explain recurrent wars as much as any political or economic theories.

*

A "consultant" is more often than not a person brought in to find out what has gone wrong, by the people who made it go wrong, in the comfortable expectation that he will not bite the hand that feeds him by placing the blame where it belongs.

*

Economics is a social science that keeps trying to turn itself into a natural science, and the harder it keeps trying, the further it departs from its innate character and disposition.

*

Can taxation without representation have been any worse than it is with it?

The most important element in marriage, bar none, is learning what to overlook.

*

The "mass" is that larger part of the citizenry I don't happen to agree with at the time. (When I agree, they are the "electorate.")

*

The most important psychological lesson we have not yet learned is that all cruelty is an expression of weakness, not of strength.

*

If moralizers genuinely believe that virtue is its own reward, they should also believe, as a corollary, that vice is its own retribution, and should not desire to add society's revenge to nature's punishment.

*

An avant-garde thinker is someone who is ready to repudiate his own ideas as soon as a sufficient number of the public begin to accept them.

*

The difference between a good person and a bad person (and each of us, naturally, is a little of both) is really very simple at bottom: The good person loves people and uses things, while the bad person loves things and uses people.

*

Nothing that is truly worth loving can be utterly possessed; at the heart of every loved object there must remain a core of inviolability. (This is why lovers and collectors are rarely the same persons.)

The act of rape is only technically a sex crime —psychologically, it is basically antisexual in its dynamics, an assault expressing hate and denigration of the female.

*

The paradox of punishment is that it works only with those who have retained a sense of justice; for the rest, it merely evokes resentment and a vow of retaliation.

*

It is not the presence of sorrow but the lack of joy that makes so many lives depressed and depressing — the absence of positive satisfactions, rather than the pressure of any negative force.

*

Young people seem so cynical precisely because they are so idealistic; when they learn that a god has clay feet, they do not merely demote him, they designate him as the Devil incarnate.

*

Contrary to wishful thinking, if the human lifespan were doubled, it would simply take us twice as long to recognize our follies, and time would still be too short to rectify them.

*

The most important tactic in an argument, next to being right, is to leave an escape hatch for your opponent, so that he can gracefully swing over to your side without an embarrassing loss of face.

*

The dilemma of the absolutist is this: If you are certain you possess the absolute truth, how can you be tolerant? And the dilemma of the relativist is this: If you believe all truths are relative, how can you be indignant?

The best reason for invoking equality under law is precisely the fact that people are born unequal; *if they were equal, there would be no need for it.*

*

The pessimist sees only the tunnel; the optimist sees the light at the end of the tunnel; the realist sees the tunnel and the light — and the next tunnel.

*

The great and crushing contradiction in tourism is that it ruins the very location and atmosphere it rushes to pay respects to.

*

Love that is not expressed in loving actions does not really exist, just as talent that does not express itself in creative works does not exist; neither of these is a state of mind or a feeling, but an activity, *or it is a myth.*

*

Religions tend to be hostile and divisive among themselves, while the sciences are necessarily allies — indicating there may be more of a religious core of unity in scientific investigation of the truth than in the religious exhortation of piety.

*

"If you're not part of the solution, you're part of the problem" is a smug and misleading maxim — for even the solvers are part of the problem at different times, and in different ways not noted by themselves.

*

The tragedy of the human race is not that we do things for self-interest, but that we so rarely see where our true self-interest lies.

Half the difficulty experienced by young people in trying to write is that they have nothing particular to say.

*

Man has taken on the task of mastering nature as an escape from the more difficult task of self-mastery, on the easy assumption that it is easier to build a dam or a skyscraper than to suppress envy or extend kindness. (And of course it is.)

*

Most of the so-called sexual incompatibility in marriage springs from the delusion that sex is an activity *when it is primarily a* relationship; *if the relationship is faulty, the activity cannot long be self-sustaining, or truly satisfactory.*

*

I should like to hear how the advocates of capital punishment explain the fact that Jehovah did not decree the death of the first murderer, but branded and exiled him — a far more meaningful punishment for him, and a persistent reminder to others.

*

There is more resentment among the middle class than among the working class, for while the workingman rents out only his labor, the white-collar worker leases his personality as well.

*

When a child loses, he blames luck; when he wins, he credits skill. Becoming an adult means learning to reverse these judgments.

*

A proverb is a statement we enthusiastically embrace when we are unwilling to examine the particulars in a general situation.

An author retains the singular distinction of being the only person who can remain a bore (and even more so) after he is dead.

*

The myth of romantic France in America is equaled by the myth of materialistic America in France; actually, the French are the most practical and realistic of people, and Americans the most idealistic.

*

The whole vexed question of nature versus nurture is a will-o'-the-wisp, for heredity shapes environment, and environment influences heredity, and the two are coordinates rather than entities.

*

Sons of famous or highly successful men tend to look much younger than their years far into middle age, for having such a father gives a son an expression of perpetual juniorship.

*

When someone says to me, "I'll level with you," I get the distinct impression that leveling is not that person's customary form of communicating.

*

A "highly advanced country" is one in which the cost of packaging, shipping, and advertising the product far exceeds the cost of the product.

*

Liberty and equality are not possible together, except as trade-offs, any more than smokers and nonsmokers can be equally free in the same room.